GEOFFREY ROBERTSON

Freedom, the Individual and the Law

SIXTH EDITION

PENGUIN BOOKS

PENGUIN BOOKS

Published by the Penguin Group
27 Wrights Lane, London w8 5tz, England
Viking Penguin Inc., 40 West 23rd Street, New York, New York 10010, USA
Penguin Books Australia Ltd, Ringwood, Victoria, Australia
Penguin Books Canada Ltd, 2801 John Street, Markham, Ontario, Canada L3R 1B4
Penguin Books (NZ) Ltd, 182–190 Wairau Road, Auckland 10, New Zealand

Penguin Books Ltd, Registered Offices: Harmondsworth, Middlesex, England

First published 1963
Reprinted 1964
Second edition 1967
Reprinted 1969
Third edition 1972
Reprinted 1973
Reprinted with revisions 1975
Fourth edition 1977
Reprinted 1979
Fifth edition 1982
Reprinted 1983, 1985, 1987
Sixth edition 1989

10 9 8 7 6 5 4 3 2 1

Made and printed in Great Britain by
Richard Clay Ltd, Bungay, Suffolk

Contents

Preface to the Sixth Edition

In the United States there are hundreds of books dealing with civil liberties. So far as is known, this is the first book which attempts to survey comprehensively the state of civil liberties in Britain. One reason for the striking difference is that it is easier to expound a written constitution than to grub in the law reports, Hansard, and newspaper files, to inquire in Whitehall and of the various 'fringe' bodies like the British Board of Film Censors and the Independent Broadcasting Authority, whose activities raise issues concerning our liberties. It is in the belief that our liberties will be the more firmly established the better their extent and limitations are appreciated, that the following survey is attempted.

> Harry Street, from the introduction
> to the first edition

Freedom, the Individual and the Law made its first appearance in the summer of 1963. Stephen Ward was standing trial at the Old Bailey and two reporters had just been gaoled for refusing to disclose their sources to the Vassall spy tribunal, while in Beirut MI5 was furtively offering an immunity from all prosecution to Mr Kim Philby OBE. Sheffield police had been caught beating suspects with rhino whips, in London Detective-Inspector Challoner had been framing political protesters, while throughout Britain consenting adults were facing criminal charges relating to abortion and homosexuality. The Lord Chamberlain had stopped the Royal Shakespeare Company from performing a play because it was 'anti-American, beastly and left-wing'. Penguin Books had good reason to commission a work on civil liberties: it had recently been accused at the Old Bailey of corrupting wives and servants by publishing *Lady Chatterley's Lover*.

Harry Street's achievement was not merely to be the first to attempt an authoritative modern account of the legal basis for various executive interferences with the liberties of British citizens. It was to do so in a style which was both comprehensible and comprehensive, simple without becoming simplistic. The reader did not have to be a lawyer to understand the book – a merit which produced a wide circulation amongst the general public, while at the same time providing inspiration to those beginning a career in law. This was no smug Dicey, abominating foreign law and lauding a constitution that did not in fact exist: it was the work of a street-wise academic who knew what was in the Emperor's wardrobe and was not afraid to point out to the crowd the need for new clothes.

Harry Street died in 1984, four years after completing the fifth edition of the book. Since 1980 there has been an avalanche of legislation affecting the liberty of the subject, making many of the original chapters of historical rather than practical interest. The *Police and Criminal Evidence Act* (1984) has placed the powers of the police on a comprehensive statutory footing, the *Public Order Act* (1986) has codified the law relating to meetings and demonstrations, the *Interception of Communications Act* (1985) purports to provide some legitimate basis for telephone tapping, the *Data Protection Act* (1984) is a first stab at regulating invasions of privacy, the *Contempt of Court Act* (1981) determines what may be published about forthcoming legal proceedings, while the *Indecent Displays Act* (1981), the *Video Recordings Act* (1984) and a plethora of 'sex shop' legislation has sought to keep pornography out of sight, if not out of mind. The courts of this and other countries have been kept in constant session as the Government has sought to staunch leaks from the security services, and to prevent the British public from reading *Spycatcher* – a book on open sale throughout the rest of the world. The European Court of Human Rights has found British law incapable of guaranteeing certain basic freedoms, and there has been increasing support at all levels for an Act to incorporate the European Convention in domestic law. The belief that people may be made good by Act of Parliament has once again become fashionable at Westminster, inspiring legislation against surrogate mothers, 'video nasties' and offensive scenes on television.

By 1989, major reforms had been announced in relation to broadcasting: the Broadcasting Standards Council was in place and 'extremist' political parties had ben banned from the air waves. The Government was pushing through Parliament two important pieces of legislation, the *Security Service Bill* and the *Official Secrets Bill*, together designed to revive the criminal law to punish any leak from the intelligence community, however important in the public interest. The old 'Section 2' had been discredited by the jury acquittal of Clive Ponting, and the Government responded by creating a host of new crimes to which there will be little or no defence. At the time of writing, both bills had virtually completed their Parliamentary passage. I have treated them in the text on the assumption that they will be enacted in accordance with the Government's intentions. A much more welcome legislative initiative in 1989 was the Children Bill, which draws on the lessons of the Cleveland crisis to give parents more effective legal rights to challenge decisions to take away their children.

These developments had dated much of the text of the fifth edition of *Freedom, the Individual and the Law*. Recent years have seen the appearance of weighty 'civil liberties casebooks', and detailed textbooks on single topics in the field, but these welcome tomes hold little attraction for the general reader. There are now so many bulky and intricately drafted laws on our statute-books that liberty can be lost in the small print. For this reason the scope of the book is confined to the law in force in England and Wales; there are differences, especially in regard to minor offences, in Scottish law, while civil liberties in Northern Ireland requires another book altogether. Although very little of Harry Street's original text remains, I have tried to maintain his focus on the practical consequences of legal rules and those areas which require reform.

The views in this book have been formed over many years of advising and representing individual clients, and to them I owe my greatest debt of thanks. Penguin Books and the Street Estate did me the honour of inviting me to pick up Harry Street's baton; Andrew Nicol and Keir Starmer provided valuable comments on individual chapters; Jonathan Riley, Claire Davis, Peter Philips, and Helen Bramford wrestled the manuscript into shape. The law is stated as of 1 May 1989.

Geoffrey Robertson

Introduction

> If liberty means anything at all, it means the right to tell people what they
> do not want to hear.
>
> George Orwell (from his unpublished
> introduction to *Animal Farm*)

Liberty in Britain is a state of mind rather than a set of legal
rules. Unlike most Western democracies, the United Kingdom does
not have a constitution embodying written guarantees of personal freedoms. Instead, it relies upon formal procedures and established institutions to protect the individual from oppressive behaviour by those Orwell
termed 'the striped-trousered ones who rule'. Since the institutions are
manned, and the procedures operated, by the self-same 'striped-trousered
ones', the rights which are allowed to citizens in practice are no more
than officialdom, at any particular time, will tolerate. That the extent of
that toleration has been considerable is a tribute to a civilization whose
history, literature and cultural values have conjoined to produce a presumption in favour of the liberty of the subject to speak freely, protest
openly and be judged fairly. Members of Parliament do not hesitate to
raise constituent grievances and to pressure Ministers; the civil service is
untainted by corruption; the judiciary is independent of Government
and philosophically committed to fair play. Such appearances are reassuring. Lord Hailsham, in his 1983 Hamlyn lectures, could boast:

> We can claim to live under a system inherently more agreeable than any
> other I can personally think of . . . I do not find anything in the essential
> structure of our institutions or our law, or our sense of continuity with our
> past, which I should wish to alter.

Lord Hailsham's agreeable system has some rather disagreeable features. For example:

— There is no right to *privacy*. The use of electronic eavesdropping devices and lie detectors is not subject to regulation, and nor is the burgeoning private security industry which operates them for espionage purposes. There is no legal limit to police use of surreptitious surveillance devices, or to the collection of information by the State about individuals. Newspapers are free to obtain and to publish details of private lives without any public-interest justification. There is no law against obtaining, by deception, information about bank and building-society accounts. There are few rights of access to files kept by private organizations on individuals, let alone to those built up within Government departments. The Data Protection Act of 1984 provides belated and limited rights of access to certain computerized files, but fails to impose satisfactory measures to protect against leakage and linkage of information. Most Western democracies now protect their citizens' privacy more effectively than Britain.

— There is no right to *public protest*. Demonstrations are held by police permission, or not at all. Processions may be 'blanket banned' by the authorities for periods of up to three months. Except at election time, there is no right to hold meetings in public halls or parks. Demonstrators who commit no criminal offence may none the less be sent to prison if they refuse to submit to 'bind-over' orders. Public servants who wish to speak out against waste, mismanagement or dangers to public health risk prosecution under the Official Secrets Act, or discipline through internal Whitehall procedures. Foreigners who demonstrate risk deportation if they commit minor public-order offences, or if their presence is deemed 'undesirable' on inscrutable 'national security' grounds.

— The right to *personal liberty* is subject to the discretion of police forces that are not answerable to Parliament or to local authorities. Suspects are not informed of their rights, and may be denied the opportunity to consult a solicitor prior to interrogation. Thousands of individuals each year are unnecessarily taken into police custody or placed under ' arrest' for minor offences instead of being proceeded against by summons. The rules governing arrest, detention and interrogation are not backed up by a satisfactory system for handling complaints against police misconduct. There is no legal inhibition on the use of *agents provocateurs*:

citizens may be convicted of crimes they would not have committed but for the instigation of a police agent. *Habeas corpus* is in practice suspended for persons held under the Prevention of Terrorism Act.

– The right to a *fair trial* is hedged about by rules which can produce miscarriages of justice. Many offences carrying prison sentences cannot be tried by juries. Justice in magistrates' courts is second-class justice: magistrates are selected upon unacceptable criteria, legal aid is often withheld on spurious grounds, and there is a wide variation in sentencing patterns. The value of trial by jury is undermined by excessive delays and by inequality of resources between prosecution and defence. There is no law against jury vetting. In cases where juries convict, there is no satisfactory mechanism for overturning the verdict when fresh evidence of innocence comes to light. There is no right to compensation for wrongful imprisonment.

– *Freedom of speech* is subject to numerous restraints: libel, contempt, breach of confidence and copyright, obscenity, blasphemy, official-secrecy legislation and the like. Some of these restrictions are justified, to some extent, but they can have the result of curbing and suppressing stories of public importance. In general, they impose more restrictions on the Press than are found in comparable legal regimes in North America and Europe. The most noticeable difference between the British and other Western governments is its persistent refusal to enact freedom-of-information legislation, which would give the public access to the facts and arguments behind major policy decisions. Official secrecy is bolstered by rules which unjustifiably require public records to be kept secret for thirty years and, in some cases, allow civil servants to suppress information for all time.

The picture which emerges when British liberty is measured against standards that have won international acceptance is not so reassuring. Although judicial institutions are impressive enough, the absence of any constitutional guarantees of freedom means that they often lack the legal power to protect individuals against agents of the State. The inventory of the current condition of civil liberties in England – our national intangible assets, so to speak – shows a poor growth rate, a lag in production compared with other Western democracies, and a failure to adapt to the challenges of modern technology.

What is required is a political resolve to make better provision for civil liberty. That resolve is notably lacking at a time of low budgets and rising crime. Liberty is, after all, an expensive and inconvenient idea, far removed in its common application from the romantic associations evoked in its rhetoric. The plain fact is that most accused persons are guilty of crime. 'Free speech' can be a euphemism for foul obscenities. Demonstrations drain public resources and clog the traffic. Anti-discrimination laws are bad for businesses which aim to give the public what it is thought to want. A data-bank society has the advantage of isolating those unworthy of credit or credibility. The lie-detector test may catch out the odd spy, just as the random 'stop and search' may pull up an incautious drug trafficker. Another day in the cells and the unconfessed criminal may crack – a prospect which might be jeopardized by a solicitor's visit or the presence of a mechanical recording device. There is a pragmatic case to be made against any civil liberty, on grounds of cost and of convenience.

The cost of liberty is already being used to justify its diminution, in unscientific and ill-judged ways. The Royal Commission on Criminal Procedure, for example, was instructed to produce recommendations 'taking into account the need for the efficient and commercial use of resources'. Whitehall opposes a Freedom of Information Act on the basis of the cost of photocopying and collating, conveniently ignoring the value of allowing public opinion to play on policy debates. The judiciary, too, have allowed cost-consciousness to motivate their decisions to curtail traditional rights: recent cases have limited the right to make bail applications, to have the full prosecution case presented at committal proceedings, and to cross-examine. The Home Office resisted demands for an independent tribunal to review dubious convictions by claiming that this reform would be too expensive at a time of financial stringency. It is a poor society indeed which finds justice too expensive, although it has taken an accountant, not a lawyer, to point out the omission in the costing:

> The costs resulting from the wrongful conviction of an innocent party are likely to depend upon two factors, namely the costs of the punishment imposed and in addition any general loss of confidence in the effectiveness of the system ... In addition to the resource costs entailed by mistakenly

imprisoning an innocent party are the more general costs which may result in the event that the mistake comes to light . . . If it becomes known that mistakes are frequent, public confidence in the criminal justice system will decline and some of the deterrent impact of punishment may be lost. Any increase in the sense of insecurity experienced by citizens as a result of their coming to fear that they run an increased risk of being imprisoned for crimes they have not committed will represent a loss of aggregate happiness or social welfare.[1]

We should apply the same accounting principles which so generously value the 'goodwill' of a business to the value of fairness in the business of justice. Not only in the cases where rights protect the innocent, but where they protect the guilty as well. For example, how do we begin to value the right of suspects to be fairly treated? If police break the rules in order to extract a confession, the trial judge will none the less be asked to admit that confession into evidence. The discretion is his, and by admitting the confession he will make it much more likely that a public nuisance will be put behind bars. But the value he will sacrifice is the value of due process, the value of living in a society in which the agencies of Government – in this case the police – work according to rules. If that case is thrown out because the police have broken the rules, it might mean that a lot of police time had been wasted. That would be expensive. But to convict on the basis of an unfairly obtained confession would also mean that a principle had been sacrificed: the principle that all suspects must be fairly treated. Is there not a value to be placed on a system which acquits a person, not because he or she is necessarily innocent, but because the rules of fair play were breached in the course of drumming up the evidence of guilt? Every time that evidence is rejected because of breach of a rule, it means that the police will be less likely to break that rule again. They will get their evidence properly, or not at all. A system which allows defendants to walk free when police break the rules is, more significantly, a system which is genuinely concerned to ensure that police do *not* break the rules.

Rights can be understood, and even appreciated, through such arguments without necessarily becoming popular. There will always be more votes for the party which promises to bring back the death penalty than for the party which promises to guarantee to suspects the right to silence. The traditional liberties are easy to erode when the times call for financial sacrifices or for action against terrorism. For politicians, the rhetoric of liberty sounds loudest in opposition. Conservative governments have been concerned to bolster police powers, heedless of consequent cut-backs in citizens' rights. Law officers in the most recent Labour Government launched oppressive prosecutions against pacifists and journalists. The Zircon affair, when police raided the offices of the BBC, and the *Spycatcher* débâcle, were both noticeably absent as election issues in 1987, confirming former Home Secretary Merlyn Rees's cynical reply, when confronted by his own back-benchers over the Labour Government's failure to deliver its manifesto promise on freedom-of-information legislation, that 'Only two or three of your constituents would be interested.'

Much of the impetus for liberalizing British law comes from the European Court of Human Rights in Strasbourg. In 1930 the Lord Chief Justice of England could slightingly refer to 'continental despotism': ironically, it has been only as a result of commercial and political arrangements with other European States that many advances in the protection of human rights in Britain have been secured. They have forced the United Kingdom Government to legislate for data protection, to reform the law of contempt, to make changes to the prison and immigration rules, to abandon 'in depth' interrogation in Northern Ireland, to end birching in the Isle of Man, to provide additional rights for mental patients – and much else besides. The irony is compounded by developments in Commonwealth countries, which share the same institutional framework as the United Kingdom. Australia and Canada have recently legislated to provide freedom of information. Barbados now has a law protecting privacy copied not from England but from a report by the Australian Law Reform Commission. Trinidad has a constitution which spells out the right of a suspect to have access to a solicitor when held in a police station. In 1981, the Privy Council said that this written guarantee was binding on the Trinidadian police. It was a rule of law, and no defendant could be convicted on the strength of a confession obtained when the rule was broken. But in Britain, without a constitution, it is just another provision in the massive Police and Criminal Evidence Act which is subject to a number of exceptions and which, if breached, will not necessarily result in the confession being excluded or the police being disciplined.

The British people have never entered into a written pact with their rulers defining the thresholds of power. Magna Carta was a squalid compromise between the King and his barons which set the seal on aristocratic privileges rather than citizens' rights. The Bill of Rights in 1688 was a political settlement designed to protect the position of what was, by modern standards, an undemocratic Parliament. The reform movements of subsequent centuries secured the fundamental rights to vote and to combine, but these advances decided *who* should exercise power rather than *how* it should be exercised. British history has bequeathed no statute of liberty, no Bill of Rights forged on the anvil of revolution, to serve either as a check on overweening authority or as a checklist against which to measure the standards of justice achieved by legislation and legal decisions. Remarkably, a language rich in the rhetoric of liberty has never been deployed to enumerate, in an authoritative and binding code, the content of the 'rights' which those who speak it shall possess.

Instead of a set of basic principles, which can be taught and understood and valued by all citizens, we have a vast array of disparate statutes and decided cases from which, as often as not, no satisfactory principle can be derived. The litigation in 1987 and 1988 over the Government's attempt to ban reports of *Spycatcher* provides a good example: nobody knew, from one day to the next, what 'law' the courts would declare to exist. Much of our policing is done not according to law, but by reference to 'Home Office guidelines', which make unenforceable suggestions about matters as basic as the criteria for secret surveillance and use of informers. Vast discretion is reposed in the 'Home Secretary' – not so much a person as a cipher for the decisions taken behind closed doors by Whitehall mandarins. The Official Secrets Act of 1989 casts a security blanket over decisions taken 'in the national interest'.

The following chapters examine the state of English law as it relates to the liberties that are recognized as most fundamental to the fulfilment of human aspirations. Law has a limited but crucial role in securing individual freedoms: criminal law must not, in terms or in operation, infringe basic rights; administrative law must offer a remedy against the unfair actions of officialdom; statute law may additionally establish avenues and institutions to combat discrimination and to discipline over-zealous or corrupt agents of the State. In each of these three areas, British law will prove defective, notwithstanding the reforms which have been made in recent years. That most progress in the protection of civil liberties over the past decade has been directly inspired by the EEC or the European Court of Human Rights in Strasbourg stands as a reproach to our own institutions, where slothfulness and secrecy, rather than any desire to oppress, have been the major obstacles to necessary reforms. Our preference for pragmatism rather than principle has been convenient in the short term; its cost may be measured in the gaps which still remain in the rights of British citizens to obtain speedy, effective or indeed any remedy against abuses of private and public power.

Personal Liberty
and Police Powers

There are 140,000 policemen and women in England and Wales, and each year they arrest over one and a half million citizens. Every arrest involves some deprivation of personal liberty, as the suspect is detained in the police station for hours – sometimes for days – before being set free or released on bail or brought before a court which may order a further stay in police custody. The act of arrest is a dramatic moment, pregnant with legal consequence, and what goes on in the police station in the period before the suspect is charged with an offence is often fateful. What goes on is interrogation, and what comes out, very often, is a claim that the suspect has confessed to a crime. Hence the decision to arrest and the treatment of suspects in police detention prior to charge are of central importance to civil liberties: the rules which govern police conduct at this point are our basic protections for personal freedom, and our most important safeguards against forced or fabricated confessions. We look to the law to ensure that no person is arrested without substantial cause, and that those suspects detained in police custody are treated fairly. Otherwise, there is a danger that justice will miscarry – either because the innocent are convicted on the strength of false confessions, or because the guilty are acquitted by juries who refuse to believe confessions extorted by police misbehaviour.

English law attempts to strike a balance between the public interest in ensuring that criminals are caught and the interest of members of the public in going about their business without interference. For the most part, this involves a common-sense political compromise: the detection of crime ceases to be the prime consideration at the point where detective methods upset law-abiding citizens or create social tension. The law governing arrest and detention was hammered out in detail during the parliamentary passage of the Police and Criminal Evidence Act in 1984, and it was influenced by the Government's basic trust in the police and willingness to tolerate increased powers for it in the interests of combating crime. None the less, the Act was inspired by the Report of a Royal Commission which was sensitive to the dangers of justice miscarrying, having itself been set up in response to the Confait Report on three youths wrongfully convicted of murder on the strength of false confessions.[1] The Act was additionally influenced by Lord Scarman's report on the Brixton riots of 1981, a wise and robust warning against heavy-handed policing of the impoverished inner city.[2]

This chapter focuses upon the police and their powers over the person up to the point at which they make a formal charge. It is convenient to consider, at the outset, the office of the constable and the merits of the controversial tradition which frees the police from political control. Police discretion, be it noted, is severely limited by the law: the citizen has inalienable rights of non-cooperation and even forcible resistance to the over-zealous bobby. There is an analysis of the power of arrest and the rights of the suspect in detention and under interrogation. A 'right' is empty rhetoric unless it can be enforced, and the remainder of the chapter examines in some detail how abuses of police power may be brought to book by civil actions, official complaints and rules about exclusion of evidence. Police powers to stop and to search, to mount covert surveillance and to break up protest meetings are dealt with in later chapters.

A POLICEMAN'S LOT

The modern police officer has evolved from the ancient office of the constable, a man hired by local magistrates to help keep the peace. As every citizen has a right to maintain order and arrest criminals, there is a romantic notion that the policeman remains a 'citizen in uniform' – 'a person paid to perform, as a matter of duty, acts which if he were so minded he might have done voluntarily'.[3] Today, this principle has little basis in reality: Parliament has armed police officers with a battery of powers unavailable to ordinary citizens, who would risk heavy damages if they dared to exercise them. The principle does serve one useful purpose, however, in reminding us that any and every power exercised by the police must be based on a law: however sensible or meritorious a police action may be, if it is not justified by some specific law it is an abuse of power which the citizen is entitled to resist, by force if necessary, or by suing the police for compensation.

The principle is illustrated by the case of *Rice* v. *Connolly*. Police officers were patrolling at night in a burglary-prone area and noticed Rice loitering in the shadows. Sensibly enough, they asked him to account for his movements. He gave some doubtful information, so again quite reasonably they asked him to come down to the police station where it could be checked. Rice refused, and was arrested for obstructing the police in the execution of their duties. The Lord Chief Justice ruled that police had no power to insist upon answers to their questions or to detain Rice while they checked up on him.

> It seems to me quite clear that though every citizen has a moral duty or, if you like, a social duty to assist the police, there is no legal duty to that effect, and indeed the whole basis of the common law is the right of the individual to refuse to answer questions put to him by persons in authority, and to refuse to accompany those in authority to any particular place; short, of course, of arrest.[4]

It follows that the police have no power to compel citizens to assist them with inquiries into crime – either by detaining them or merely questioning them in situations where they are not suspected of any offence. There is no offence of 'refusing to help police with their inquiries' – a euphemism invented by the media to avoid libel actions from those arrested by police but not subsequently charged. 'Police officers either arrest for an offence or they do not arrest at all.'[5] If any citizen is detained against his or her will, in a situation falling short of an actual arrest, this is the wrong of false imprisonment, for which the victim can recover damages. Still less, of course, do police have power to insist that a witness visit the station to make a statement or answer questions, or indeed answer police questions at any time or place. Citizens can be served with subpoenas ordering them to attend as witnesses when a case comes to court for hearing, but that is all. They are entitled to ask an inquisitive policeman, 'Are you arresting me or not?' and, if not, to go their way unhindered.

The Police and Criminal Evidence Act (a clumsy title henceforth abbreviated to PACE) gives some statutory force to the common-law position by providing that people who voluntarily go to a police station to assist inquiries 'shall be entitled to leave at will' unless specifically told that they are under arrest.[6] Regrettably, it imposes no duty on the police to inform those they invite to assist inquiries that they are free to decline, or that, having arrived at the police station they are free to cut short their assistance and to leave at any point. This is a good example of the British reluctance to admit or to advertise 'rights' which may prove inconvenient to authority — it is better to keep citizens in ignorance than to encourage them to assert their rights at awkward moments. When this section of PACE was being debated in Parliament, a formidable case was made for an amendment which would have required police to be honest with citizens whom they invited to 'assist inquiries', but the Government claimed that this would impose 'an enormous administrative burden on the police'. In consequence, many suspects against whom there is insufficient evidence for arrest are inveigled to police stations in the hope that the atmosphere of confinement and interview will elicit an admission sufficient to justify an arrest.

In practice, of course, most citizens recognize a public duty to aid the detection of crime by giving the police all possible assistance. Innocent suspects will welcome the opportunity to clear themselves, witnesses will want to do their public duty, and most of them will probably not realize that the police have no compulsive power. Is it really an 'enormous burden' to require the police to explain either that no suspicion attaches, or, if it does, that attendance at the police station is voluntary?

Police accountability

The legal limits to police powers emphasize the importance of 'policing by consent': the community which has little trust in the police or is angered by policing policies will be reluctant to provide voluntary assistance. People will only give information which may incriminate neighbours if they are confident that police will use it fairly: they will not allow their homes to be used as surveillance posts if they believe that police hold unjust suspicions or routinely discriminate against certain classes of citizen. Regrettably, the independence of Chief Constables from any meaningful political or community accountability has, at least in some parts of Britain, hampered the partnership between the police and the public which is necessary for effective control of crime.

It is obviously desirable to keep the police politically independent, in the sense that their operations and the exercise of their discretions should not be dictated by or made in the interests of a particular political party. In Britain, however, this has been taken to an extreme, by endowing forty-one Chief Constables, together with the Commissioner of the Metropolitan Police and the City of London Police, with a freedom of action on questions of policy which cannot be called to account by central or local Government. As Lord Denning put it, in flourishing phraseology:

> I hold it to be the duty of the Commissioner of Police, as it is of every Chief Constable, to enforce the law of the land. He must post his men that crimes may be detected; and that honest citizens may go about their affairs in peace. He must decide whether or not suspected persons are to be prosecuted; and, if need be, bring a prosecution or see that it is brought; but in all these things he is not the servant of anyone, save of the law itself. No Minister of the Crown can tell him that he must, or must not, keep observation on this place or that; or that he must, or must not, prosecute this man or that one. Nor can any police authority tell him so. The responsibility for law enforcement lies on him. He is answerable to the law and the law alone.[7]

The law – or at least the judges who enforce it – will not call upon police chiefs to answer for very much. They will only interfere if satisfied that there has been an abdication of responsibility: in effect, a determined refusal to enforce the law. They will order a Chief Constable to think again about a policy, based on a misinterpretation of the law, of not enforcing gaming regulations,[8] and they will find a police officer guilty of misconduct for turning his back while a man was being beaten to death in a brawl.[9] But they will not pass judgement on the exercise of police discretion, for example by ordering a police chief to enforce more vigorously the law against pornography[10] or heeding a pacifist's complaint about political discrimination in the decision to arrest her for obstruction of the highway at a place where speakers with more acceptable messages had long been unmolested.[11] To say that police are 'answerable to the law alone' means that they are not answerable to anyone in the way they choose to enforce the law. They are free to take decisions and exercise discretions which may have dramatic consequences on the community (the clumsy 'Swamp 81' stop-and-search operation led to the Brixton riots) or on individuals, whose prospects of being prosecuted rather than cautioned for minor offences often depend upon where they are arrested. By 1987, for example, about half the police districts in England were cautioning first offenders for possession of small amounts of cannabis. The rest were prosecuting, or deciding whether to caution or prosecute on criteria which had no statutory basis. In Liverpool first offenders received a friendly lecture: in Leeds they received a criminal record. Some uniformity in deciding which cases to bring before the courts is achieved by the Crown Prosecution Service (CPS), but the all-important decisions about which cases to send to the CPS as appropriate for prosecution are still made by the police.

There is a deeply entrenched distaste for anything approaching a 'national police force', although some uniformity has been achieved through the device of the 'Home Office circular', advising all Chief Constables as to how particular policing tasks (e.g. the use of informers and surveillance devices) should be approached. These circulars do not have the force of law, and are merely 'guidance': there is no sanction for disobedience. The 'Codes of Conduct' which accompany PACE have provided a better basis for achieving uniform treatment of suspects throughout the country but they impose no constraint on police chiefs who adopt controversial policies, in relation, for example, to equipping their forces with rubber bullets and riot shields or mounting heavy-handed operations against pubs or clubs popular amongst ethnic communities.

Each police district has a 'Police Authority' comprising local councillors and magistrates: they appoint the Chief Constable and have a duty to maintain an 'adequate and efficient' force for their area.[12] But their powers are extremely limited and attempts by some police authorities to direct Chief Constables on matters of operational policy have been implacably rebuffed: Merseyside's Chief Constable laughed off his Police Authority's attempt to remove him with the comment: 'I have every Christian virtue except resignation.' ACPO, the Association of Chief Police Officers, has become the most powerful club in the country, promoting policies agreed amongst its members, resisting attempts to introduce measures for accountability and actively entering the political arena by lobbying against legislation which impinges upon policing methods. It operates the National Reporting Centre (NRC), a clearing-house for information about police problems which spill over several geographical areas (such as the 1985 miners' strike). It reports direct to the Home Secretary, and has the capacity to become a centralized intelli-gence agency, without any charter to limit its operations.

Few Western countries permit police forces such organizational independence. Most police chiefs in the USA must submit themselves for election and may be called for cross-examination by public repre-sentatives. In Europe, police are generally servants of Ministries of State which are themselves politically accountable. In Britain, Chief Constables can range in outlook from John Alderson, who shredded half the files of his Special Branch in Devon and Cornwall, to Manchester's James Anderton, who has claimed divine approval for his court-room crusades against the permissive society. Local communities have no say over what form of policing they would prefer: the Chief Constable is the expert on 'operational policy' who must not be trammelled in decid-ing whether to put bobbies on the beat with truncheons, or with sub-machine-guns.

In his report into the Brixton riots, Lord Scarman recommended the establishment of formal procedures for police consultation with rep-resentatives of the community, and Section 106 of PACE implements his proposal to the extent of requiring all local authorities to 'make arrangements' for obtaining 'the views of people in that area about matters concerning policing of that area' as well as 'securing their co-operation with the police in preventing crime'. Home Office guidelines now stress that while consultative groups cannot intervene in police operations they should work to enable 'decisions which are properly for the police (to) be more closely informed by the discussion of local needs'. This is a first, tentative step towards public accountability, and more should follow. Police Authorities should be entitled to demand more access to information and have more influence over policing policy, while the Home Office's secret circulars giving 'guidance' to Chief Con-stables should be published. The tradition which protects the police from overtly political control is not put at risk by requiring community con-sent to policies which otherwise risk alienating the community from the police.

ARREST

Personal freedom ends at the point of arrest. This is a formal act, by which the power to detain someone reasonably suspected of crime is exercised by a police officer or a citizen. If an arrest is made on insufficient or unreasonable suspicion, or if certain procedures are neglected, it will amount to an excess of power and the arrester will be liable to damages for falsely imprisoning the victim. 'Citizen's arrest', a relic of the pre-police days when every available member of the community was expected to join in the 'hue and cry' after a felon, is expressly preserved by P A C E in relation to murder, offences which may carry more than five years' imprisonment (such as theft) and a rag-bag of other 'arrestable offences' ranging from indecent assault and taking bribes to offences under the Official Secrets Act.[13]

In practice, the ancient right to perform a 'citizen's arrest' mainly serves as a protection for those who break up fights or answer the denuded shopkeeper's cry of 'Stop thief!' In the latter case, however, we act at our peril, as W. H. Smith discovered when one of its employees arrested a Mr Walters, believed to be stealing books from its King's Cross shop.[14] Walters was acquitted on the grounds that he intended to pay for them, whereupon he sued W. H. Smith for false imprisonment. He recovered damages, because of the rule that a citizen who arrests must not merely have reason to suspect his victim of committing an 'arrestable' crime, but that such a crime must in fact have been committed. Police powers of arrest are not limited in this way – an officer may arrest on reasonable suspicion, even if it turns out that no crime has in the event taken place.

This distinction between police and citizen powers is preserved in P A C E, and may be hard on a citizen who responds to the cry of 'Stop thief!' by tackling an innocent who flees from an unjust accusation. But it has the merit of obliging department stores to report suspects to the police if they wish to avoid the risk of damages for false imprisonment. Store detectives generally ask suspects to accompany them to the nearest police station, and supply their evidence to the police who make the arrest if they believe the evidence is sufficient to justify the charge. There is no obligation to assist a store detective with inquiries, much less to accompany him to a police station: the innocent suspect should insist on being made the victim of a 'citizen's arrest' to preserve a claim for damages against the store.

Police powers of arrest

The police have the power to arrest without a 'warrant' (i.e. an arrest authorization from a magistrates' court) in a wide variety of circumstances. Like the citizen, they may arrest for murder and for crimes carrying maximum sentences of five years or more and for the special 'arrestable offences' listed in Section 24 of P A C E. In addition, they may arrest for any offence, however minor, if they have reasonable grounds for *believing* (rather than *suspecting* – see later) that detention is necessary to prevent the suspect causing harm to himself or to anyone else, or damaging property or even obstructing the highway (Section 25). They may arrest rather than proceed by the more civilized method of summonsing the suspect to appear in court wherever this latter course would be impracticable – i.e. in cases where the suspect refuses to give a name and address, or provides a name or address reasonably believed to be false. Police may even use the power of arrest in order to stop a suspect committing an offence against public decency, in cases 'where members of the public going about their normal business cannot reasonably be expected to avoid the person to be arrested'.[15] (Those who wear T-shirts with rude messages can now expect to be thrown into the cells for a few hours while relatives or duty solicitors bring a change of clothing.) Before 1984, the police managed quite satisfactorily with a law which allowed them to deprive of liberty only citizens suspected of moderately serious crime: Parliament, by providing various statutory excuses for taking people off to the cells in the most minor cases, has unnecessarily diminished the liberty of the subject. Section 25, with its ominous title *General Arrest Conditions*, signals the change from a society where police powers were limited by reference to specific offences to a State where these powers may be exercised in most circumstances where the police find it convenient.

None the less, P A C E does not displace the traditional safeguards for every arrest: it must be based on reasonable suspicion, effected by no greater force than is necessary, and the suspect must be informed of the grounds for the arrest at the time it is made. Failure to comply with these requirements can give rise to civil liability in damages, and can provide a defence for any person charged with resisting arrest or assaulting or obstructing police in the execution of their duty. It is no part of an officer's duty to engage in an unlawful arrest: when police get it wrong, they have no remedy against physical violence inflicted on them by a suspect who attempts to escape. Others may come to the suspect's rescue, with all the force necessary to free him from the unlawful arrest. The force must, however, be directed to securing release from police clutches, and not to chastising the officers for abusing their powers. It is a curious liberty which entitles a citizen to punch a police officer who makes a mistaken arrest: it is, perhaps, the most dramatic reminder of the common law's insistence that every act of detention must be legally justified.

What constitutes 'reasonable grounds for suspicion'? The officer must act on more than a hunch, but not much more: 'suspicion' is no more than conjecture without hard proof, and a reasonable possibility, rather than the probability, of guilt is sufficient. The best definition has been given by Lord Devlin: 'The circumstances of the case should be such that a reasonable man acting without passion or prejudice would fairly have suspected the person of having committed the offence.'[16] This test allows the constable to take into account material as evidence which could never stand up in court – hearsay, gossip, tip-offs from informants and the like – and to apprehend the suspect at a point where the odds in favour of conviction would be much less than 50 per cent. But it does require a fair appraisal of existing evidence, subject to the circumstances (which may demand a hasty decision) and the application of common sense and logic. Common sense is not the same as common prejudice: judges these days are prepared to hold that it is not reasonable to arrest a man for dealing in drugs simply because he is black, drives a BMW and frequents The Mangrove restaurant in Notting Hill. Courts will decide whether an arrest is based on reasonable suspicion after hearing evidence of the objective facts and the constable's thought processes as applied to them at the time. In one recent case, a court held that a man wearing long hair and blue jeans, carrying a large canvas bag and loitering with a woman and a dog could not be 'reasonably suspected' of going equipped for theft, women and dogs being unlikely burglarious companions.[17] A jemmy protruding from the canvas bag would have been sufficient to make the suspicion 'reasonable', although had the bag been marked 'swag' it might have been unreasonable to suspect the man of going equipped for more than a fancy-dress party. 'Reasonable cause to *believe*' is a more stringent test, requiring greater certainty than 'suspicion', and this standard applies to judge the conditions required before an arrest can be made for a minor offence.[18]

The duty to give reasons

Suspects must be told that they are under arrest, and have the reasons for the arrest explained to them, either at the time or 'as soon as practicable' afterwards should they resist or attempt to run away. This rule, now contained in Section 28 of PACE, was established by the House of Lords in the leading case of *Christie* v. *Leachinsky*.[19] Leachinsky had attracted the sort of suspicion which frequently attaches to totters and rag-and-bone merchants – that of being in unlawful possession of stolen property. The police, who in fact had reasonable grounds for suspecting him of theft, arrested him under a municipal by-law which only applied when a suspect's name and address were unknown. Christie, the police officer, admitted that he knew Leachinsky and his address, but had found it 'more convenient' to arrest for the wrong reason. In 1947, before police convenience had become a factor to be reckoned with in the development of the criminal law, the House of Lords laid down a strict rule:

> If a policeman arrests without warrant upon reasonable suspicion of felony, or of other crime of a sort which does not require a warrant, he must in ordinary circumstances inform the person arrested of the true ground of arrest. He is not entitled to keep the reason to himself or to give a reason which is not the true reason. In other words a citizen is entitled to know on what charge or suspicion of what crime he is seized.

Leachinsky was entitled to damages against the police for false imprisonment. Although the police are not required to give technically precise or detailed reasons for arrest, 'in this country a person is, *prima facie*, entitled to his freedom and is only required to submit to constraints on his freedom if he knows in substance the reason why it is claimed that this restraint should be imposed'. The rule in *Christie* v. *Leachinsky* has the merit of requiring police to crystallize their suspicions prior to arrest sufficiently to give a reasoned statement, and permits the suspect to know the nature of the allegation which he can, if so minded, try to refute then and there. The arrest will be unlawful if no reasons for it are given, or if those reasons are irrelevant or insufficient or the power has been exercised for the wrong reason or in bad faith.

'Reasonable force'

In effecting an arrest, a police officer may use 'reasonable force, if necessary' – the notion of necessity shifting the burden to the police of justifying headlocks, handcuffs or the presence of loaded weapons.[20] Any show or use of force should be the minimum consistent with protection of the arresting officers in the circumstances, and police who shoot to kill without very good reason will often face murder charges if they can be identified. They will almost always be acquitted, however, because juries are understandably reluctant to bring back a verdict which will result in life imprisonment for a policeman or soldier who has acted in honest error as to the 'reasonableness' of discharging his weapon. The law, by applying too strict a test, allows those who respond excessively and unnecessarily to escape all punishment. There is need for an 'in-between' verdict of manslaughter in these situations, to bring British law into line with the European Convention which requires that no more force should be used in these situations than is *absolutely* (rather than 'reasonably') necessary.

The police have internal regulations about the use of firearms. With true British passion for secrecy, these regulations are contained in a confidential ACPO manual. In 1982, after a public outcry over the gunning down of Stephen Waldorf in mistake for a dangerous criminal, the inevitable 'Home Office circular' directed that firearms should only be used as a last resort, and should be issued only when a senior officer has reason to suppose that officers will have to face armed or very dangerous criminals.

This circular is no substitute for careful criteria governing the supervision and use of lethal weapons.[21] Britain can be justly proud that its police, at least on the mainland, go about most of their business unarmed: the bobby with truncheon and faintly ridiculous helmet is a genuinely reassuring figure compared with the pistol-packing cops who patrol the streets in many other countries. All the more reason, then, to draw up detailed and restrictive legal guidelines for lethal weapons. This reform has become urgent in the wake of allegations that the RUC have in the past operated a 'shoot to kill' policy, and after the controversial SAS killing of three IRA members in Gibraltar. It is unacceptable for the law to permit assassination in circumstances which are 'reasonable' rather than imperative.

Handcuffing is only justifiable when there is a reasonable apprehension that the prisoner would otherwise escape or turn violent, and if used unnecessarily will constitute a trespass to the person, even if the arrest itself has been lawful.[22] Public handcuffing is a degrading and humiliating action which should never be taken without good reason. The Metropolitan police rarely use handcuffs, but this B-movie tradition lingers in other police districts. The riot in St Paul's in Bristol in 1980 began with a police raid on a popular black café. The crowd which gathered was in good humour as the police carried away endless cases of Red Stripe beer from its unlicensed cellar, but the mood turned ugly at the sight of the proprietor, a popular and entirely peaceable figure in the local community, being led away in handcuffs. It was the spark which ignited a riot that caused £2 million damage. Parliament omitted to restrict the practice of handcuffing when extending police powers in 1984.

Summons as an alternative to arrest

Police have alternatives to arresting without a warrant. They can obtain an arrest warrant from a magistrate, or can simply summons the suspect to appear in court at a particular date to answer the charge. The extension of police power to arrest without a warrant (Sections 24 and 25 of PACE) has reduced the demand for magistrates' warrants: the detective's traditional doorstep greeting – 'I have a warrant for your arrest' – is now heard less frequently. (Search warrants, as we shall see in Chapter 3, are still keenly sought.) But why arrest at all, when there is no objection to bail and a summons sent by registered post will secure a court attendance by the defendant? Many suspects who are arrested and detained for a day or so could be quizzed at their home or at a solicitor's office and be subsequently served with a summons if the evidence warranted prosecution. That was the view of the Royal Commission on Criminal Procedure, which pointed out that 'arrest represents a major disruption in the suspect's life', and recommended that the option of arrest should be strictly limited to cases where detention was genuinely necessary (e.g. where police intended to oppose bail) and not be used routinely or for police convenience.[23] PACE, however, extended police powers of arrest generally, and hence provides no incentive to use the summons procedure.

Whether citizens will be summonsed rather than arrested may depend on who they are and where they are. Police are much more inclined to summons well-to-do persons than to arrest them. There was no question of arresting Mr Jeremy Thorpe, for example – he was interviewed, by appointment, in his solicitor's office and summonsed to attend court to face charges of conspiracy to murder without suffering the ritual indignities of searching and fingerprinting and a night in the cells. The Royal Commission, reporting in 1981, discovered that some police forces hardly ever use a summons (the Met and Greater Manchester in only 1 per cent of cases), while Derbyshire summonsed 72 per cent of its suspects and North Wales 53 per cent. The picture which emerges is that a summons can be used effectively, even in large cities, in about 50 per cent of cases: the enormous variations from police district to police district are unacceptable. Some police chiefs are hostile to the summons procedure because they prefer to play against their suspects on home ground – the police station. Arrested persons can be disoriented and frightened by the sights and sounds of police custody, and by the bare interview room and the long waits in cells reeking of tobacco, urine and cabbage. These atmospheric influences may be powerful inducements to confess, but not necessarily to make a true confession. As the Police Complaints Board has pointed out, many suspects unnecessarily arrested will be cleared after further inquiry:

> Arrest has occurred on the unsupported statement of a witness against persons of hitherto blameless character who have lived a settled life in the community for many years. Sometimes the arrest has been made without any attempt to make simple inquiries which could have been carried out on the spot and which would have confirmed the innocence of the suspect. We think that the police service is so involved with the process of arrest and detention that it fails at times to comprehend the sense of utter dismay felt by an innocent person who suffers such treatment.[24]

DETENTION

The period between arrest and charge is the time between the ending of personal freedom and the commencement of court-supervised custody. Persons reasonably suspected of crime are cautioned, interrogated, searched, often fingerprinted and photographed: in due course they will either be set free (if the accumulated evidence is insufficient to prosecute) or else charged and brought before a court, which will consider whether to grant bail or to remand them in prison pending subsequent stages in the prosecution process. It is a crucial time, in which their treatment is determined by a compromise between different public interests – the desirability of getting at the truth about an offence, the importance of the individual's 'right to silence', the need to maintain certain minimum standards of fairness and humanity, and the necessity of guarding against false confessions produced by fear or force or a simple desire to obtain bail. Occasionally police officers extract confessions by physical violence, although more often the inducement comes from offers of bail or threats to charge friends or relatives. The rules governing interrogation are designed to prevent such blandishments, which obviously render confessions unreliable. But a more subtle form of pressure is atmospheric. The very experience of being confined in a police cell, the fear – of police or of other prisoners – the disorientation, the smell, can all work to sap the will. So can lack of sleep – a common handicap for prisoners in police cells where lights burn all night. The psychologist who studied the mental impact of arrest and detention for the Royal Commission has described the 'softening-up' process that inevitably occurs:

> Say you are brought in for questioning and you are, in effect, a suspect. You're brought into the police-station yard, a door with a special locking device opens, you get out of the car, into the cell blocks, through another large iron door with a grille again with special locking devices, and you pass through into the charge room, where your property is taken from you. You will then be put in a cell which is a bare room, with bars that obviously are a guarded window, wooden bench, nothing much on it, or a lavatory next door, and the door is locked on you. There is a very small grating in the door, and you are obviously locked in, and very much alone, in a totally alien environment. You've got no shoes on by this time, and your belt has been taken away, and so have all your possessions – you no

longer feel in control of yourself, you are under somebody else's control and authority. That sets the scene for effective use of interrogation techniques of all kinds.[25]

This psychological softening-up, deriving from the very fact of police detention, makes many people an easy target for relatively simple interrogation techniques – the 'Mutt and Jeff' routines set out in police textbooks:

> The suspect may be placed in a chair with no arm-rests, probably fixed to the floor. The interrogator, behind a desk, endeavours to establish friendly relations and to draw the suspect out. If this fails he may change tactics, pretend that the case is sewn up by the discovery of an eye-witness or the confession of an accomplice, and suggest that the suspect's only course is to make a statement. Another routine is for the first, friendly, interrogator to be alternated by a verbal bully; or the interrogator may try to unnerve the suspect by addressing questions to him from behind.[26]

As the strongest pressure to confess undoubtedly derives from consciousness of guilt, is there any need for concern about oppressive atmospheres and techniques which fall short of torture or inhumane treatment? The problem for a society which rightly regards the conviction of the innocent as a greater evil than acquittal of the guilty is that oppressive circumstances can produce the very sort of false confession which juries find credible. Take the case of Albert Hudson, planning officer for Kensington and Chelsea Council. At 6.30 a.m. on a Sunday morning he was arrested at his home and taken to Chelsea police station, where he spent the next five days. Of that time, fifty hours were spent answering 700 questions from police officers. At the end of that period, he broke down and confessed to many things which simply could not have happened. 'Why should a man make an incriminating statement when the evidence was to the contrary?' asked the Court of Appeal, when it later quashed his conviction.

> The feeling of captivity starting with the police officers arriving at 6.30 a.m. at his house and arresting him; the fact that he was taken from his home in Farnham to Chelsea police station; the experience of being a prisoner in a police cell; the twenty-five hours of questioning; and the fact that he was always accompanied by a police officer except when he was in

his cell and was in custody out of his cell for fifty hours. All of that with a man of fifty-nine who had never been in trouble before would inevitably provide a strong inference of oppression.[27]

Length of custody

How long are police entitled to keep a suspect in their custody? The danger of the oppressiveness which bore down on Albert Hudson and others who have falsely confessed must be balanced against the need to give investigating officers a reasonable time-frame within which to conduct their inquiries. The Royal Commission on Criminal Procedure discovered that two-thirds of all suspects were processed within six hours, but that in London, over three months in 1979, there were 212 suspects who were kept in custody for more than three days before being brought before a court. It recommended that the law should provide a specific limit, which could be subject to a court-approved extension in complicated cases. That limit has now been set, by PACE, at twenty-four hours in the case of ordinary offences, and at thirty-six hours when 'serious arrestable offences' are being investigated and a senior police officer is satisfied that the additional time is necessary to secure evidence or to complete questioning. After thirty-six hours, the police must apply to a magistrates' court for a warrant authorizing continued detention, which may be extended for up to another thirty-six hours if the Justices are satisfied that the investigation is being conducted diligently and further detention is *necessary* to preserve or obtain evidence. The magistrates may extend the warrant for yet another period, so long as the total time spent in police detention by the suspect does not exceed ninety-six hours.

The 'serious arrestable offences' which may cause a suspect to spend up to four days in police custody include murder, rape, incest, causing explosions, using firearms, kidnapping, and terrorism. Regrettably, Section 116 of PACE adds to their number *any offence at all* which has serious consequences for public order, national security, or the administration of justice, or involves substantial financial gain or 'serious financial loss to the person who suffers it' (you can thus be held for four days on suspicion of picking a vagrant's pocket, but only for twenty-four hours on suspicion of stealing money from a millionaire who would not really miss it). This lack of clarity over what constitutes a 'serious arrestable offence' is a major defect in PACE, and one which could lead to many suspects being kept in custody for up to four days.

None the less, the Act does stress that extensions beyond the basic time must be *necessary* to secure evidence or complete interviews – not merely desirable, convenient or a good idea. But the system established by PACE pins its faith on the effectiveness of magisterial review after thirty-six hours. Local Justices, as we shall see, are more renowned for rubber-stamping police requests than for championing the liberty of the subject. In issuing a warrant for further detention they will at least have the suspect before them, with the right to have a lawyer to contradict and cross-examine the police case. Duty solicitors, when available at courts and police stations, are able in effect to make *habeas corpus* applications whenever called upon to resist an extension warrant. The writ of *habeas corpus* itself remains available to secure the release of any suspects held in breach of the time limits, although it is likely to take at least twenty-four hours to prepare the High Court application and have it listed for hearing.

A severe incursion into civil liberties is specially authorized in the case of suspects detained on suspicion of involvement in terrorism. They may be held incommunicado for two days, and the Home Secretary may grant a warrant to hold them for a further five days, in the course of which they may see a solicitor but only on condition that the interview is 'within sight and hearing' of a uniformed officer. These powers were extended in the angry aftermath of the Birmingham pub bombings in 1974, when twenty-one people were killed. The Prevention of Terrorism Act was then described as a temporary and emergency measure, but successive Governments have reimposed it. The Act proscribes membership of the IRA and INLA and permits the exclusion of suspects from the country, but it is doubtful whether its extended detention provisions have assisted the apprehension and conviction of persons who could not have been dealt with under existing police powers. Only 7 per cent of the thousands of suspects detained under the legislation have been charged with any criminal offence, and there is some evidence that the seven-day detention period is used more for low-level intelligence gathering on Irish activists.[28] The Home Secretary's warrant procedure is objectionable: the decision to detain for up to five days after the initial forty-eight hours should be decided by a court, and not by the prerogative of a party politician who in practice will rarely have the time or the ability to consider the police request with any degree of scepticism.

This was the view of the European Court, which decided in 1988 in the case of *Brogan* v. *UK* that holding persons under the Prevention of Terrorism Act for longer than four days without the approval of a judicial authority was a violation of Article 5(3) of the European Convention of Human Rights, which requires that all persons detained after their arrest 'shall be brought promptly' before a judicial officer. The Court made full allowance for the need for flexibility in response to terrorism, but refused to countenance this as an excuse for denying a fundamental right to have loss of liberty considered 'promptly' by a judicial authority independent of the State. The UK Government has threatened to derogate from the Convention on this issue rather than to implement its obligations by the simple step of amending the law to require a court, rather than the Home Secretary, to approve extended detention. The Government's determination to defy an authoritatively declared minimum standard of human treatment reflects its arrogance in the exercise of power rather than the exigencies of combating terrorism.

Official reports into the operation of the Prevention of Terrorism Act have drawn attention to the danger of police abusing the extra detention powers to fish for intelligence or obtain evidence of non-terrorist offences, and have recommended that the Act should only be used where no other police power is appropriate.[29] This recommendation has not been heeded, and police invariably arrest terrorist suspects under its extended powers. The official explanation is that hardened terrorists are trained in anti-interrogation techniques, so seven days detention may be necessary to break down their defences. This is not only an ugly admission that the end justifies the means, but an argument supported by neither logic nor evidence. Well-trained terrorists will easily withstand questioning for seven days, while innocent suspects may unreliably confess as late as day six or seven. Persons detained and then released without charge are, quite unjustly, not entitled to have their fingerprints or photographs destroyed, and police will retain photocopies of any interesting documents found in their possession for possible use against them later on. It is difficult to see how communication with a solicitor can be of much advantage when it takes place in the presence of a police officer. Of the 202 persons detained in 1986 only thirteen were charged with offences against the Act – statistics which call into question the need for a power which alone in English law may be exercised upon unreasonable suspicion, and which often involves periods of detention which amount to breaches of the European Convention.

The right to a lawyer

In the USA, the 'right to counsel' is absolute: suspects are told that they are entitled to have private access to a lawyer and that either their own will be contacted or one will be provided at State expense.[30] Section 58 of PACE begins with a similar flourish: 'A person who is in police detention shall be entitled, if he so requests, to consult a solicitor privately at any time.' That is subsection (1), however, and seventeen subsections later the entitlement appears far from absolute. Broadly speaking, access to a lawyer must be provided at the very latest after thirty-six hours of arrest for 'a serious arrestable offence'. Access may be delayed if police fear interference with evidence, hindrance to recovery of property or the alerting of other suspects as a result of notifying a solicitor or permitting him to consult with the arrested client. The same considerations also permit delay in giving effect to the right, established by Section 56 of PACE, of having one friend or relative notified of the arrest. In other words – which are certainly not the words with which the Section commences – a suspect may be held completely incommunicado in a police station for thirty-six hours. This is hardly an advertisement for Britain's commitment to civil liberties, or a comfort to families when a member 'disappears' without trace for the statutory period. But Parliament was swayed by the image of gang members disposing of drugs and gold bullion on hearing from helpful solicitors that one of their number had been arrested. Although the Law Society, on behalf of practising solicitors, undertook that its members would accept a solemn obligation in such exceptional cases to pass on no messages from the suspect, the risk was deemed too great.

The real reason, of course, why police are generally reluctant to contact a solicitor is their belief that a lawyer will advise the suspect to exercise the right of silence and refuse to answer their questions. The police belief is in many cases a misapprehension: solicitors frequently advise clients to put forward their explanation at the first available opportunity, and even if they counsel silence, that is merely reminding suspects of a right which they are fully entitled to use. The Code of Practice for police questioning[31] specifically states that access to a solicitor must not be denied on the ground that the lawyer might advise the suspect not to answer questions – which means in practice that police who do deny access must be able to justify their decision by reference to one of the three exceptions in Section 58. In any case where the suspect may have conspired with someone who has not yet been arrested, or where stolen property has not been recovered, a lawful justification will be claimed to exist. On this issue, Parliament sacrificed a fundamental right in favour of police convenience. The stark fact, after four years of PACE in operation, is that only 20 per cent of detained suspects are recorded as requesting solicitors. The so-called 'right' under Section 58 is avoided by police who conduct their interviews while driving the suspect to the police station, or who, once there, promise that if they cooperate by agreeing to an immediate interview they can go home rather than face a long wait in the cells before the solicitor arrives. Often suspects are simply not told that they have any 'right' to have a solicitor present. The only way that this right will become a reality for most suspects is if police are obliged, by an amendment to PACE, to obtain written authority from the suspect before the interview commences, waiving the right to legal advice.

Other physical restraints

What other powers do police have over suspects once they are in custody? Fingerprinting and photographing can sometimes be necessary to assist identification or to eliminate the suspect from the inquiry: before PACE was passed, however, these had become routine at many police stations even for the most minor offences. In 1981, the Divisional Court was shocked to find that police in Kingston upon Thames had insisted on fingerprinting 'a middle-aged lady of good character' after a trifling motoring offence, and issued a stern warning that such humiliating infringements of personal liberty should not be undertaken without good reason.[32] PACE now confines the compulsory taking of fingerprints to cases where a senior police officer has reason to believe that the prints would 'tend to confirm or disprove' the suspect's involvement in the crime. The code of conduct for identification procedures permits photographs to be taken for criminal-record purposes, but in cases where the suspect is released without charge or subsequently acquitted, any photographs or fingerprints must be destroyed, and the ex-suspect has a right to witness their destruction, although once again there is no duty to inform suspects of this right.

People are often misled by US films and television into thinking that police can put a suspect on a 'line-up' whenever they choose. In Britain, attendance at an identity parade is purely voluntary. It is a method devised, with careful safeguards, to test the most unreliable kind of evidence. Wrongful identification is a potent source of miscarriage of justice, and a parade offers a better means of checking it than such alternatives as inviting a witness (who may have had but a fleeting glimpse of the criminal) to associate the memory-image with a 'mug shot', or to identify a suspect who is sitting in a cell or a court dock. Where police believe that an identification check would be useful, they may ask the suspect to stand on parade, pointing out the less satisfactory alternatives. They are obliged to hold a parade if the suspect insists. Obviously the evidential value of any identification which takes place at a parade is destroyed if the witness has been shown a photograph of the suspect beforehand, or if the suspect's appearance is significantly different from that of all the other persons paraded. Police often have difficulty finding 'matching' members of the public to stand on the line, and although a defence solicitor is normally present there are often subsequent disputes in court over the manner in which the witness made the identification. Although the rules governing identification parades are as fair as possible to suspects in the circumstances, it would be a great help if all parades were filmed or videoed to enable a jury to make a better assessment of their reliability.

Some police practices relating to the search of suspects prior to the enactment of PACE and its codes of conduct were unnecessarily degrading. The courts were unimpressed by police claims that they were entitled forcibly to remove brassières from female suspects lest they do themselves an injury, and saw no need for custody officers to seize jewellery or watches.[33] PACE directs custody officers to record all items possessed by a suspect on entering the station: they can only be confiscated if there is reason to believe that they might be used for self-injury or to assist escape, or are otherwise relevant to the offence being investigated. An 'intimate search' of 'bodily orifices' may be conducted by a 'suitably qualified person' if there are reasonable grounds for believing that the orifice conceals a 'Class A' drug or something which could cause physical injury. This provision was made the subject of much agonizing debate in Parliament: while customs officers have similar powers to deal with suspected drug smugglers, there is no evidence that drug-dealers walk the streets with cocaine or heroin secreted in anus or vagina. This provision was inserted against original Government intentions as a result of back-bench hysteria about 'Class A' drugs, and affords an opportunity for police to invade personal integrity which is out of all proportion to the harm sought to be averted. The Act does not explain what classes of person are 'suitably qualified' to examine body orifices for non-medical purposes: the power is both degrading and unnecessary.

A more sensible and civilized approach is taken in relation to 'intimate bodily samples' such as blood, semen, urine or clips of pubic hair, which are sometimes required for forensic examination that may confirm or disprove the suspect's involvement with a crime. The suspect must consent before these can be taken, and a refusal will not be met by forcible extraction but by permitting the jury at the trial to hear of the refusal and to regard it, where appropriate, as an indication confirming other evidence of guilt. This provision will be of increasing importance with the development of 'genetic fingerprinting' techniques that enable semen taken from rape victims, or blood shed at a murder scene, to identify positively a suspect with the same unique configuration of DNA. It is a mistake to suggest that these provisions breach the rule against self-incrimination: refusal to allow a physical examination that could provide conclusive evidence of linkage to a crime can fairly be held against a suspect, while a refusal to answer police questions proves nothing.

POLICE INTERROGATION

The right to silence

Statements made to the police constitute the most important evidence in criminal detection, and the conduct by police of their interviews with arrested persons is a focal point in most criminal trials. Each and every interview must begin with the traditional caution: 'You do not have to say anything unless you wish to do so, but what you say may be given in evidence.' This is the one point at which the police are under a solemn obligation to remind suspects of a right – to stay silent if they so wish. If they do indicate a wish to stay silent, however, there is nothing to prevent the interrogator from attempting to goad or sting or prompt them into a response. There are certain well-established limits to efforts to coax a silent suspect: threats must not be made, nor promises of bail or favourable treatment held out as an inducement to 'spill the beans'. There must be no 'oppression' of the suspect, and no trick or other unfair practice employed, otherwise the resulting confession may not be allowed in evidence at the trial.

The caution embodies the 'right to silence' – the rule against self-incrimination which is one of the most notable features of British criminal law. Its origins go back to the nineteenth-century heresy trial of John Lilburn, the Leveller, who accused his judicial interrogators of 'trying to ensnare me, foreseeing the things for which I am imprisoned cannot be proved against me'. He was pilloried, but the House of Lords later condemned his treatment, holding it to be 'contrary to the laws of nature and the Kingdom for any man to be his own accuser'. While the rule undoubtedly can assist the guilty, it has also protected innocent suspects from making ill- considered explanations while disoriented after an arrest or in panicked responses to aggressive questioning. It places a premium on police *investiga- tion*, emphasizing the need to gather objective evidence rather than relying upon suspects to trip themselves up. The value of applying the rule to police questioning is underlined by the research conducted for the Royal Commission, which showed how the atmosphere of custody may exert a degree of oppression and confusion that can render unreliable confessions obtained after intensive questioning. There may be reasons for abrogating the rule in special circumstances, or in relation to special people. The Companies Act, for example, requires persons responsible for public companies which crash to answer questions about their stewardship put by Department of Trade Inspectors, and their answers may be used against them in subsequent criminal proceedings. They will, however, have had ample access to documents and legal advice before being called upon to respond. The suddenly arrested suspect has no such protection, and is entitled to decline to answer any or all of the police questions.

The 'right to silence' has stood out as one of the proudest boasts of Britain's commitment to civil liberties, contrasting most starkly with the forced interrogations and explanations required of suspects under inquisitorial systems. It has been adopted by Commonwealth countries, and in the United States the protection is entrenched in the Fifth Amendment to the Constitution. In Britain, however, its days are numbered: in 1988 the right was summarily abolished by the Government in relation to trials in Northern Ireland, and the Home Secretary announced that its curtailment would soon follow on the mainland. The Northern Ireland provisions, which are likely to be used as a model for British legislation, require suspects to answer specific questions put by police officers: their failure to do so permits the judge or jury to draw adverse inferences at any subsequent trial. Silence may, in addition, be used to corroborate evidence which would otherwise be insufficient to secure a conviction. Worse still, the jury is entitled to draw an inference of guilt from the refusal of an accused to testify at his trial. The result of these changes will be to make a severe inroad on the presumption of innocence, by establishing a virtual 'presumption of guilt' concerning any defendant who chooses to put the police or the prosecution to proof by refusing to answer questions or to give evidence. It will enable the prosecution to force defendants into the witness box to face cross-examination in cases where the evidence against them would otherwise be wholly insufficient to justify a conviction. It will be a devastatingly unfair amendment to the adversarial system of prosecution and trial, without the safeguards inherent in the inquisitorial system which operates in many European countries (where questions are initially put by magistrates rather than police, and testimony is assessed by judicial panels rather than juries). The change will become the leading example of how the IRA has succeeded in undermining British justice – the Government's reasons for it were related to the fight against terrorism and the difficulty of obtaining convictions against IRA members trained to withstand interrogation. Whatever may be the arguments for an emergency exception to the rule against self-incrimination in terrorist cases, they should not be allowed to demolish a fundamental pillar of a system of justice which is based on the notion that the prosecution carries the burden of proving the case that it brings. The prospect that the right to silence will be abolished in these circumstances serves as an emphatic example of how our most basic liberties have no constitutional protection, and remain at the mercy of any Government which commands a loyal parliamentary majority at a particular time.

The vast majority of suspects do speak, and it is crucial that their police interviews are accurately recorded. The greatest single reproach to English criminal procedure in recent years has been the vaudeville routine of the 'police verbal', in which officers present at an interview would, hours later, put their heads together and produce an allegedly verbatim account of what was said, only to be cross-examined endlessly in court at a later date about their presumed gift of total recall. Juries were rightly suspicious of the contents of police notebooks made up long after the interview, and circuit judges, in their evidence to the Royal Commission, blamed this imperfect recording practice as the major cause of acquittals of apparently guilty defendants. After one Old Bailey trial in which twenty days were taken up by suggesting to police officers that they had fabricated confessions which had never been made, an exasperated Court of Appeal declared: 'Something should be done, and as quickly as possible, to make evidence about oral statements difficult either to challenge or concoct.'

Relief had long been at hand, in the simple form of the tape-recorder, but irrational fears blocked experimentation until 1984. Police were afraid that suspects would be less likely to talk, or would record statements of the 'please stop beating me up' variety, or that defence lawyers would successfully allege that tapes had been tampered with. These fears have proved groundless, and police have been so delighted with the experimental schemes that the Government intends to introduce the tape-recording of suspects nationally by 1991. Suspects have shown no disinclination to talk into a microphone – on the contrary, this symbol of the *vox pop* society seems to be a positive encouragement to answer questions. Those who confess on tape generally plead guilty rather than seek acquittal by deriding 'police verbals'. A Home Office study released in 1988 concluded that experimental schemes had substantially increased conviction rates and had cut back the length of some trials. The advent of tape-recorders in police stations is another reason for discouraging the practice of interviewing suspects in police cars – a device currently in vogue to prevent the suspect taking legal advice prior to interrogation.

Confessions

There are three classes of confession which cannot be used in evidence against the maker:

1. *Confessions obtained by police oppression* – a concept which includes torture, inhuman and degrading treatment, and threats of violence (Section 76, PACE). The list is not exhaustive – overbearing behaviour designed to pressure a suspect to the point at which the will to claim the right to silence crumbles will amount to oppression. Bright lights and heavy-handed interrogation routines, and even the protracted interviewing periods to which Albert Hudson was subjected, may make any consequent confession unusable. 'Inhuman and degrading treatment' is a phrase taken from the European Convention on Human Rights. The European Court held that it covered the 'in-depth interrogation' to which the Royal Ulster Constabulary (RUC) subjected Irish internees in 1971. They were forced to stand for many hours spread-eagled against a wall, barefoot and hooded while listening to a high-pitched monotonous noise. They were deprived of sleep and kept on a diet of bread and water. These techniques were 'inhuman and degrading' because they caused physical and mental suffering and acute psychiatric disturbances, making use of fear and humiliation as a means of breaking down physical and moral resistance. They did not amount to 'torture' – a label reserved for very serious and cruel suffering.[34]

2. *Confessions which are likely to be unreliable as a result of anything said or done to the suspect* (Section 76, PACE). This overlapping test additionally catches more subtle inducements to confess. As an innocent suspect will want nothing more badly than to get out of the police station, an offer of bail in return for a confession is a potent incentive to tell the police what they want to hear, irrespective of the consequences. For the criminally experienced suspect, offers not to pursue more serious charges can have a similar effect. Where there is evidence which also implicates close family members (and especially where wives and girl-friends have already been arrested), offers to 'drop them out of it' frequently crack the most defiant of suspects. Whether the confession elicited by such improper ploys is 'unreliable' will be for the trial judge to decide on evidence as to what was said or done at the time (and many allegations of this sort made by defendants are rejected when the police deny on oath any impropriety).

3. *A confession which 'would have such an adverse effect on the fairness of the proceedings that the court ought not to admit it'* (Section 78, PACE). This is the general discretion to exclude unfairly obtained evidence, and it can be applied to confessions obtained by police through deceit or misrepresentations. An example of such malpractice is provided by *R.* v. *Mason*, a case remarkable not only for the dishonesty used to secure the confession but for the honesty of the police officer who admitted to it in the witness box.[35] He suspected Mason of fire-bombing a car, but had little evidence against him. So he arrested Mason and told both him and his solicitor that his fingerprints had been found on glass shards from the petrol bomb. 'This was play-acting – a trick,' he confessed proudly in the witness box. 'The fragments of the bottle had not even been sent for fingerprint testing at that stage. We set about "conning" the defendant. We had only a suspicion against him and we realized we needed more proof – I felt the only way to get the truth from him was to do this.' The trick worked – Mason's solicitor, conscious no doubt of the virtual impossibility of challenging fingerprint evidence, advised his client to give an explanation of any involvement in the incident, whereupon Mason confessed in reliable detail to having constructed the petrol bomb. His trial judge allowed the confession to go before the jury, which duly convicted and the defendant was imprisoned for two years. The Court of Appeal said that the trial judge was wrong to have allowed the confession into evidence. To hoodwink a suspect in this way was reprehensible, and it was even more reprehensible to hoodwink his solicitor. Although the confession was obviously true, it had been elicited by such serious misbehaviour on the part of the police that its admission into evidence adversely affected the fairness of the proceedings. The case is a timely reminder that the end of convicting the guilty cannot justify means which are patently dishonest. Police officers tempted to lie to suspects about the state of the evidence against them, in order to give the impression that 'the game is up', must be made to realize that their misconduct is likely to lose the case when it comes to court.

This approach can be justified on grounds of social morality: it is better that the guilty should walk free than that agents of the State should be permitted to play an ignoble part. Section 78 of PACE defines the court's discretion to protect a defendant against unfairness in terms of the moral imperative: was the evidence obtained so unfairly that the court *ought* not to admit it? Even when the accuracy of a confession which is inadmissible under Section 76 is confirmed by, for example, finding stolen property or a 'smoking gun' as the result of what the defendant has said, the fact that it was found as a result of what the defendant said should be withheld from the jury unless he goes into the witness box and gives an explanation at variance with the truth. This may not be much comfort if the defendant's fingerprints are found on the smoking gun, but even this devastating evidence might conceivably be kept from a jury if the court decides, under Section 78, that the police misbehaviour was so gross that no advantage whatsoever should be taken of it. If a policeman points a revolver at a suspected terrorist and threatens to shoot him unless he confesses the whereabouts of an unexploded time-bomb, the court should on principle exclude not only the ensuing confession and the fact that the bomb was found as a result of it, but also (under Section 78) any forensic evidence connecting the bomb with the defendant. The decision to exclude evidence under Section 78 is, none the less, a matter for the exercise of judicial discretion, and it is impossible to state hard-and-fast rules. Court of Appeal decisions in the first five years of PACE give little guidance on borderline cases (see later, page 61).

These rules not only serve to maintain minimum standards of fairness in the course of police questioning of suspects: they are designed as a safeguard against false confessions. The odds of suspects confessing to crimes they have not committed shorten when threats or promises are allowed to play on their minds. A special danger is encountered when the suspect is young or mentally handicapped – factors which were both present when three youths falsely confessed, in remarkably convincing detail, to participation in the killing of a man named Confait. They were convicted of murder as the result of a series of prosecution errors and oversights which began with police interviews held in the absence of any parent or solicitor. An inquiry by Sir Henry Fisher exonerated one youth and a subsequent confession to the murder by a man in prison for other offences has now made it clear that the other youths were innocent as well. Even after the publicity surrounding the Confait report, it appeared that police had not learned their lesson: the case against the person suspected of throwing Michelle Booth from a moving train collapsed when the judge excluded the confession he gave after police had grilled him for long periods despite knowing of his low IQ and mental handicap.[36]

The recommendations made in the Confait Report were taken up in the Code of Practice for interviewing 'persons at risk', namely juveniles and those who are mentally ill or mentally handicapped. They must be interviewed in the presence of an adult – either a parent or a person with some duty of care for the suspect. The adult must be allowed to advise the suspect and assist communication and interpretation of the questions and answers. The only exception permitted is in cases where urgent information is sought to prevent harm to others or serious damage to property. Section 77 of PACE requires trial judges to give a special warning to juries of the need for caution before convicting mentally handicapped persons on the strength of confessions made at interviews where no independent person is present. Unfortunately the Act does not require a special warning where confessions are made by persons who are under the influence of drink or drugs at the time, or of some temporarily incapacitating mental state such as hysteria or traumatic shock. There was some authority before the 1984 Act that courts would exclude confessions made in such circumstances, even though there had been no misbehaviour on the part of the police in obtaining them.[37] This discretion could still arise under the courts' general power to exclude evidence which has more prejudicial than probative value.

RELEASE FROM CUSTODY

Bail

Suspects must, by the end of twenty-four hours or any specially extended period, be either released or charged with an offence. Once charged, they must be brought before a court 'as soon as is practicable', at which stage they may make an application for bail. The magistrate may at this point remand the defendant in police custody for up to three further days, but only if and for so long as this is strictly necessary to allow inquiries to be made into other offences. The defendant has a right to bail, and the Bail Act of 1976 entrenches a statutory presumption in favour of liberty unless the court is satisfied that there is an unacceptable risk of failure to surrender to custody or the commission of further offences while on bail or interference with witnesses.

The Bail Act has measurably enhanced the liberty of the subject, and it provides ample scope for appeal to the Crown Court or to a High Court judge. There are occasional retrospective Press outcries when a person is convicted of an offence committed while on bail for a similar crime: the magistrates or the judge who granted bail are blamed in strident editorials for freeing a public menace. The benefit of hindsight is uniquely vouchsafed to the editors of popular newspapers: the court will on examination usually be found to have applied the law, and if blame is sometimes to be attached it generally rests on the prosecution for failing to apprehend the danger of the accused committing further offences. It is regrettable that bail hearings in the Crown Court and the High Court are not held in public: the Press would then have less excuse for the kind of ignorant opprobrium it heaped on a judge who quite properly freed on bail a man named Winston Silcott, who pending his trial participated in the murder of a policeman during a riot at Tottenham. The notion, much canvassed by back-bench MPs after that episode, that people on murder charges should never be given bail is unconscionable: many are acquitted, and many more have the charge reduced to manslaughter and (at least in 'mercy killing' cases or where there had been extreme provocation) are not judged to require any custodial sentence.

There is still a tendency for persons entitled to bail to be remanded in custody for a week or so after their first appearance in court. The Bail Act allows a court to refuse bail if it has not been practicable to obtain sufficient information to decide the issue, and this is an easy way out for magistrates when police object on the irrelevant ground that they have yet to complete their inquiries. The Divisional Court has held that a bail application, once made and rejected, cannot be renewed until the defence can show some change in the circumstances[38] – a ruling that encourages solicitors who have just met their client to wait a week and to gather the evidence for a considered application. The reluctance of courts to concede that circumstances have changed frequently means that a bail application, once made, cannot be renewed until committal.

The court may grant bail unconditionally, or on any conditions designed to secure the accused's presence at later hearings of the case. In appropriate cases, sureties may be required in considerable sums, passports may be confiscated and the accused can be required to report regularly to the local police station. These conditions are frequently 'offered' by the defence and 'accepted' by the prosecution – they must be designed reasonably to secure attendance or protect witnesses, and not as a pre-trial punishment. The 1688 Bill of Rights, which is still in force, provides 'that excessive bail ought not to be required', noting in its preamble addressed to William of Orange that his predecessor's 'evil judges' had 'required excessive bail of persons committed in criminal cases to elude the benefit of the laws made for the liberty of subjects'. This at least prohibits the absurd and distasteful device used by US judges to keep an accused person in custody by setting bail at astronomical levels.

Habeas corpus

The last resort to obtain release from custody is to apply for a writ of *habeas corpus*. This is a direction by a judge to anybody who has a person in custody to bring that person before the court so that the legality of the detention can be investigated. Traditionally, 'the great writ' has been regarded as being of the highest constitutional importance: the means whereby release from illegal detention is assured. The slave brought by ship into British territorial waters,[39] the demobilized Army officer pulled from his civilian bed for alleged military crimes over which the army no longer has jurisdiction,[40] the Polish seamen who feared punishment for their political opinions if they were not freed from their ship in the Thames before it sailed back to Poland,[41] the inmate of a mental hospital who was illegally detained there by the hospital authorities,[42] the woman imprisoned by the Vice-Chancellor of Cambridge University for 'walking with a member of the University'[43] – all secured their release upon a writ of *habeas corpus*. Even the validity of detention by order of either House of Parliament may be challenged in this way. An application for *habeas corpus* takes precedence over all other business before the court.

Valuable though *habeas corpus* can be, its limits must be noted. It operates only where there is no legal authority to detain. Prior to PACE, *habeas corpus* occasionally secured the release of suspects detained for unlawfully long periods in police stations. Now that strict time limits apply to detention, with provision for magistrates' court warrants to extend detention periods, there should be very little scope for *habeas corpus* applications in relation to suspects in police custody. However, if a suspect were held for longer than thirty-six hours without a warrant, or a warrant were granted in respect of an offence which was not a 'serious arrestable offence', an action for *habeas corpus* would still lie.

REMEDIES FOR POLICE MISCONDUCT

Rights only exist to the extent that they can be enforced when authorities abuse their power. In Britain, the citizen can sue for serious violations of personal liberty, and obtain damages as compensation for humiliation and indignity and even, in bad cases, as a measure of punishment for outrageous official misconduct. There is also a system for making complaints about police behaviour, which can in turn lead to disciplinary action within the police force against officers who have contravened codes of practice or behaved bloody-mindedly or from racist motives. Where there is evidence that officers have committed crimes, the Director of Public Prosecutions can bring them to trial. The rules which permit a court to exclude evidence of confessions extracted by oppression or unfairness are part of a general judicial discretion which can occasionally protect even guilty defendants from suffering punishment for an offence which police have themselves instigated or investigated in flagrant violation of suspects' rights. The families of those who have died in police custody or as a result of police action are entitled to be represented at the inquest, and police actions which have had serious social repercussions may be made the subject of a public inquiry.

At first blush, an impressive panoply of remedies seems available to the citizen: closer scrutiny demonstrates that some are in practice hedged about with unsatisfactory qualifications and restrictions. The police complaints machinery, for example, has many defects and does not enjoy public confidence, despite improvements made to it by PACE, and the role of the courts in excluding improperly obtained evidence is still largely undefined and discretionary. The constable, unaccountable to public representatives for the exercise of police duty, is still but imperfectly accountable to the law for doing constabulary duty wrongly.

Damages for civil wrongs

Actions for damages may be brought against Chief Constables when police under their command commit civil wrongs (torts). An arrest without reasonable suspicion is the tort of false imprisonment, and where force is used it will amount to the tort of assault as well. A prosecution brought against a person whom the police know to be innocent amounts to the tort of malicious prosecution; unlawful entry on to private premises will constitute trespass to land and (if property is wrongfully seized) to goods; police may additionally be sued for negligence which has resulted in the death of someone in their custody. The advantages for the citizen of taking civil action rather than (or in addition to) making a complaint are overwhelming: the case need be proved only on the balance of probabilities (rather than beyond a reasonable doubt), these actions can in many cases be heard by a jury, and there is the prospect of being awarded exemplary damages as a mark of public disapproval of intolerable behaviour.

One of the worst cases on record so far is *White* v. *Metropolitan Police Commissioner*, where a husband and wife received £40,000 exemplary damages for what Mr Justice Mars-Jones described as 'monstrously wicked' police behaviour, on top of £13,000 compensation for false imprisonment and malicious prosecution. The couple had been dragged out of bed in the early hours and beaten up 'in a brutal and inhuman way', then unlawfully arrested and detained for some hours at the police station. In order to cover up their own crimes, the police then fabricated charges of assault against the couple.[44] In most cases the damages will be limited to a few thousand pounds, although the Court of Appeal declined to interfere with a jury award of £12,000 to a woman who was detained for fourteen hours by police officers who had no reasonable cause to suspect her of crime.[45] Exemplary damages are awarded to punish police for conduct which is oppressive, arbitrary or unconstitutional, generally in circumstances where insult is added to injury. Thus a West Indian who had been unlawfully detained was entitled to punitive damages for a racist policeman's action in throwing peanuts into his cell with the words, 'Here you are, monkey.'[46] Even when circumstances justify an arrest, excessive force can provide the basis for a civil claim for assault. A middle-aged woman lawfully arrested for a minor traffic offence recovered damages for being subjected to a ju–jitsu 'hammerlock and bar' in which her wrist was held behind her back and twisted by the arresting officer until it fractured.[47]

Cases of this kind present such an unedifying picture of police conduct that considerable effort is expended in keeping them out of court and out of the public eye through a negotiated settlement. In 1984, for example, the Metropolitan Police settled 107 of the 181 civil claims made against them, paying total damages of £178,603. It should be important for the public to learn the details of such cases, and to be able to confirm that officers whose high-handed behaviour has led to the payment of public money in damages have been appropriately disciplined. Where secret settlements are made, however, such reassurance is not provided. The officers at fault do not pay the damages out of their own pocket, and while individual plaintiffs are doubtless happy to be compensated without the stress of a court action, the adverse publicity which serves to deter repetition of such conduct is lost. The £75,000 paid by police to the family of Blair Peach in order to avoid a trial had the consequence of suppressing details of the internal police investigation into reponsibility for the death, which was a matter of the gravest public concern.

Complaints against police

Civil actions will not lie against many kinds of police misconduct, including breach of most of the rules in the 'Codes of Practice'. Such matters fall to be dealt with, if at all, by internal disciplinary proceedings supervised in the case of public complaints by the Police Complaints Authority (PCA). This body was established in 1984 after widespread public criticism of the lack of any independent element in the investigation of complaints against the police. Lord Scarman, for example, was concerned by the evidence at his Brixton inquiry that 'there is a widespread and dangerous lack of public confidence in the existing system'. Public confidence has not been much enhanced by the PCA: it has no autonomous powers of investigation, which falls to be carried out by the police themselves, subject to the PCA's duty to oversee inquiries into serious complaints and to ensure they are conducted expeditiously, thoroughly and impartially.

The stumbling block in the campaign for an independent police complaints system has been the Home Office's implacable belief that you must set a policeman to catch a policeman: the notion of an outside investigative body, comprising lawyers, administrators, retired senior police officers and customs officials, has been repeatedly resisted on the unconvincing argument that detective skills are 'unique' to the police service. While there have been impressive examples – notably under Sir Robert Mark – of vigorous searches for 'rotten apples' in the police barrel, there have been equally notable failures, and the efficiency of inquiry teams in other public and professional areas refutes the notion that detective prowess is vouchsafed only to serving policemen. The clarity of PCA 'oversight' of police investigations may be doubted after its extraordinary failure to act on evidence produced by an inquest into the death of Cynthia Jarrett, who had collapsed from a heart attack during a police raid on her home in Tottenham, a factor which incited a serious riot on the Broadwater Farm Estate. The subsequent PCA report not only misunderstood the jury verdict, but took no action on matters which emerged at the inquest. A subsequent unofficial inquiry into the incident, chaired by Lord Gifford QC, concluded that, 'Given these failures in one of the PCA's first major investigations, it is not surprising if confidence in the new machinery is low.'[48]

The present procedure has at least the merit of simplicity: complainants set out their grievance and the investigation is conducted without further effort or obligation on their part. They may complain about a broad range of misconduct, from rudeness and indifference to breach of a Code of Practice or serious crime. Conduct which is disorderly or likely to bring discredit on the reputation of the police force is a disciplinary offence, as is any abuse of authority or behaviour which is racially discriminatory. Minor public complaints are made the subject of informal conciliation proceedings which can lead to explanations and apologies, while complaints substantiated after investigation are dealt with at disciplinary hearings before the Chief Constable or, in London, a disciplinary board. The complainant may attend, and can cross-examine accused officers if they elect to give evidence. Punishments range from reprimands to dismissal from the force. Although the procedure is internal, in the sense that all investigation and decision-making is done by police officers, the PCA has a duty to supervise the investigation of complaints which are serious (e.g. where death or injury has resulted from police action) or where the public interest requires some independent oversight. It has certain powers to direct reluctant Chief Constables to hold disciplinary proceedings or to send reports to the DPP for consideration of criminal charges.

Fewer than 10 per cent of all public complaints about police are upheld, and very few of these are by complainants from working-class and ethnic groups. One serious deficiency in the system is that it makes no provision for any compensation to successful complainants, even when they have suffered quantifiable loss. Another unhappy feature is that police officers complained against may sue the complainants for libel – their initial complaints are not covered by the absolute privilege from defamation action which protects statements made in court. The position is made intolerably unfair by the lack of any legal aid for libel defendants and by the willingness of the Police Federation to finance libel actions brought by its members. Although the complainant has a 'qualified privilege', the qualification (that the complaint was made without malice) can be expensive to establish in court, and there is no doubt that the possibility of being sued for libel has a powerful deterrent effect on potential complainants. It is right that there should be some punishment for complainants who can be proved to have fabricated their complaint: this can be achieved by prosecuting them for appropriate criminal offences.

One particular concern of potential complainants is that they may suffer reprisals from the police. The PCA has no power to investigate if victimization does occur, and the only remedy is by civil action. In 1985 a jury awarded £4,000 damages against Merseyside police for harassing a man without reasonable cause, allegedly because he had previously lodged a complaint against them.[49] One deplorable feature which follows from the internal aspect of the complaints system is that the PCA has no control over the use to which police may put evidence which they gather about a complainant in the course of investigating his or her complaint. After Cynthia Jarrett died of a heart attack while police were searching her home, her daughter cooperated with the investigation which was supervised by the PCA. Information she supplied was duly reported back to the Metropolitan Police Commissioner, and was used by the police at the inquest into Mrs Jarrett's death in an unsuccessful attempt to discredit the daughter's evidence. This incident is a glaring example of how the present complaints system can be perceived as partisan and of how the PCA is powerless to protect complainants from whatever use Chief Constables decide to make of their complaint. It is said that the police national computer contains a special entry for those who have made 'false complaints against the police'.[50] If 'false' means no more than 'not proven beyond reasonable doubt', then over 90 per cent of complainants will have a computer entry calculated to provoke any constable who calls to check their car registration.

The standard of proof for a disciplinary offence – beyond reasonable doubt – was applied reluctantly, and after pressure from the Police Federation. It puts the police in a privileged position compared with other employees, whose reason for dismissal need only be proved at an Industrial Tribunal on the balance of probabilities. For an occupation which should be above suspicion, and in relation to disciplinary charges which have no criminal consequence, this is a privilege which is not justifiable on public-interest grounds.

Another aspect of the complaints system which runs counter to the public interest, at least in cases which have aroused community concern, is the secrecy which attends all stages of the investigation. Inquiries supervised by the PCA cannot be published, even when Chief Constables wish to reassure the public by issuing the final report. Secrecy may be desirable in many inquiries in order to encourage witnesses to come forward, especially officers who 'break ranks' to give evidence against their fellows or their commander, but in cases where serious and apparently substantial allegations are publicly made against the police the community is entitled to demand satisfactory evidence of thorough investigation.

In some of the most controversial cases, there can be no disciplinary action at all because criminal proceedings have been brought unsuccessfully. This is another privilege unique to the police. It is based, inaccurately, on the rule against 'double jeopardy' – the principle that a person cannot be tried twice for the same offence. So where policemen kill a suspect and are acquitted of murder because they acted in self-defence or without intending to pull the trigger, they cannot be disciplined for careless handling of firearms. This rule overlooks the obvious fact that disciplinary procedures do not amount to a 'trial' – they may result in loss of seniority or even job, but not in a criminal record. Many police officers properly acquitted of criminal offences have nevertheless acted discreditably in the course of the incident and deserve to be disciplined. Other disciplinary bodies are not constrained by acquittals from probing discreditable conduct, and employees may suffer dismissal for behaviour which a jury finds to fall short of an actual crime. Frequently evidence which is inadmissible at a criminal trial may help to prove a disciplinary offence. While it would be wrong to subject police officers to special disabilities when confronted with accusations of misconduct, the present complaints and disciplinary system provides them with privileges other employees do not enjoy, which sit uneasily with their possession of unique legal powers.

Prosecution

Where there is clear evidence of a criminal offence, of course, police officers may face prosecution. There is a division of opinion, however, on the test to be applied in putting a policeman on trial. The DPP adopts the '51 per cent solution' – only if conviction is a better than even bet will he take action, and he is all too aware of a low conviction rate from juries which tend to prefer a policeman's word to that of his often unprepossessing accusers. Others maintain that the public interest of ensuring that those who enjoy authority do not abuse it demands prosecution whenever there is a clear, albeit not convincing, case. This debate masks the real question of how to go about producing a convincing case against those who abuse power within an institution whose members have a strong sense of solidarity and a professional awareness of their rights. During the investigation into the killing of Blair Peach, the right to silence became a right to *omertà*, as police officers who must have known the truth simply refused to tell it. The myth of the over-merciful jury makes the trial process a scapegoat for inadequate investigation and inability to prise open ranks which masonically close. In the United States, the special difficulties of unravelling police corruption are handed over to 'special prosecutors', who are senior lawyers with investigative powers. Company collapses, as we have seen, attract the special investigation powers of Department of Trade Inspectors, whose reports usually lead to successful prosecutions. Some day, we may come to recognize that an unsolved police murder of a political demonstrator is as worthy of special procedures as the death of a public company.

Inquests

Death, the ultimate loss of liberty, is made the subject of a special inquiry when it occurs in police or prison cells or as a result of police operations. The agency which seeks to satisfy the public conscience in such cases is the coroner, sitting with a jury whenever death results from an injury caused by a police officer.[51] In the Middle Ages, the coroner was given the task of inspecting dead bodies to discover the cause of death – a matter of great interest in those days to the King, who benefited from the estates of the slain. To assist him, in an age long before police forces and medical science, the coroner summoned a jury from the neighbourhood. The medieval coroner and his jury would squat around the body – often by a roadside or in a ditch – and look for tell-tale signs of disease or violence, or suicide. Pooling their local knowledge, they would often come up with the name of a likely suspect whom they would present for trial. Although these important functions were in due course taken over by professionals – policemen and doctors and lawyers – the coroner survived, as a public official appointed by local councils to investigate unnatural deaths. In this century, coroners lost most of their powers of criminal inquiry: in cases of suspicious death, they in effect unveil to the public the evidence upon which the police have failed to reach any conclusion.

Inquests are unlike any other judicial proceedings. Coroners need not be lawyers: they may be doctors of at least five years' standing. Unlike lay Justices, they do not have the assistance of a legally trained clerk. The closest equivalent at an inquest is a policeman who acts as the 'coroner's officer'. This does not help to create an appearance of impartiality where the death is alleged to have been caused by the police. In addition, an inquest does not follow the usual adversarial pattern of most legal proceedings, where the truth is expected to emerge from the clash of opposing evidence and submissions. Instead, the coroner takes the initiative and leads the investigation. The police collect the evidence and discuss it privately with the coroner, who is not obliged to show it to representatives of the deceased's family.[52] This means that lawyers are sometimes unprepared for the evidence which the coroner decides to call. It means, too, that at inquests where police misconduct is alleged, the police lawyers will have exclusive access to statements taken by police officers, and so have an unfair advantage over the deceased's family, who are further handicapped by the fact that legal aid is not available to pay for legal representation.

At inquests, no advocate may address the coroner or the jury on the facts. There are no final speeches. So the jury never hears the contentions of the parties about the cause of death put in a coherent account which is ever given to the public is provided by the coroner in the summing-up. This may be an unsatisfactory account, or even, as in the Helen Smith case, be a preposterous account.[53] But there can be no alternative, unless the Goverment is prepared to set up a proper inquiry headed by a High Court judge.

In cases where coroners sit with juries, public esteem for the jury system in criminal courts invests the 'verdict' with a degree of acceptability. But the most recent official inquiry into the coroner's system, the Broderick Report, concluded that the role of the coroner's jury today is no more than symbolic.[54] It conceded that the final verdict is usually dictated by the coroner. All the coroner's jury can do is to announce one simple fact – how the deceased met with death. The law requires a narrow answer to a narrow question, but in cases where police are responsible for death, the public rightly expects much fuller answers to a whole range of questions. Until 1980, a coroner's jury could add a rider to its verdict and make recommendations to prevent the recurrence of similar deaths, and the Blair Peach jury used this power to make several critical comments about the Special Patrol Group. (It recommended that the SPG should be better controlled by its officers, that its relations with local forces should be improved, that no unauthorized weapons should be available at police stations and that regular inspections should be carried out.) But an amendment to the Coroners' Rules has now taken away the jury's right to add a rider to its verdict.[55]

All these procedural handicaps work collectively to prevent a coroner's inquest from fulfilling public expectations as a mechanism for getting the truth out and for drawing lessons from it. There are cases – fortunately only a handful each year – which involve serious factual disputes and raise wider public-interest questions. Liddle Towers, Jimmy Kelly, Blair Peach, Colin Roach, Helen Smith and Cynthia Jarrett are examples of deaths which should have been investigated by High Court judges at public inquiries at which the families were legally aided and proper rules were followed. Such an inquiry could then end with a reasoned judicial conclusion as to the cause of death, setting out in detail any grounds for public disquiet, after all the evidence had been properly presented and put coherently into place first by advocates and then by the judge in his report. In 1988 the refusal of the British Government to hold a judicial inquiry into the killing by the Special Air Service (SAS) of three suspected IRA terrorists in Gibraltar, and the defects of the inquest which subsequently took place, received international condemnation. Any society which values civil liberties must take exceptional measures to examine why a life was lost through the actions of agents of the State: coroners' inquests, which serve useful purposes in uncontroversial cases, are inadequate for this task.

Unfair evidence

Should criminal courts play a part in punishing police misbehaviour by excluding improperly obtained evidence from the trial? This is a fundamental and very polarized debate. The US Supreme Court has long adopted the principle that it is better for the guilty to go free than for the State to play an unworthy part, a principle supported by the common-sense consideration that the only sure way to stop police obtaining evidence illegally is to remove the incentive by forbidding them to use it. Thus when a suspected drug dealer seen swallowing capsules was illegally stomach-pumped to force him to regurgitate the evidence, the capsules found in the vomit were 'fruit of the poisoned tree', and excluded from evidence at his trial. Orson Welles makes the argument in the film *Touch of Evil* through his portrayal of a corrupt police chief who frames only the guilty: his dying fall down a slippery river slope in the final scene symbolizes the reason for the rule. Once the courts start endorsing the principle that the end justifies the means, unfairness and illegality will become routine.

British law dodges the issue of principle by leaving the decision in the discretionary lap of the trial judge. There are special rules, as we have seen, for excluding improperly obtained confessions, but the admissibility of other sorts of evidence – obtained by illegal searches, for example – is decided by reference to Section 78 of PACE. Having regard to all the circumstances, including the circumstances in which the evidence was obtained, 'Would its admission have such an adverse effect on the fairness of the proceedings that the court ought not to admit it?' There was at first a fear that this statutory formulation would cut down the court's general discretion to exclude illegally obtained evidence by directing it to consider only the fairness of trial procedures. But appellate decisions since PACE came into operation have given Section 78 a much broader impact, and stressed that 'the circumstances in which the evidence was obtained', if attended by police misbehaviour, can provide a basis for exercising the discretion. Thus when police officers pursued a motorist into his own back yard and demanded that he take a breath test, knowing that they had no right to make this demand on private property, they were acting oppressively and in bad faith: the evidence that the breath test was positive was excluded under Section 78.[56]

When courts exclude reliable evidence like this because of police misconduct, it is difficult to accept that they are not in effect seeking to deter police misbehaviour by depriving them of its fruits. In *Mason*, the case described above where a true confession was obtained by pretending to the defendant and his solicitor that his fingerprint had been found on a petrol bomb, the Court of Appeal ended its judgement as follows: 'We hope never again to hear of a deceit such as the present being practised on an accused person and still less on a solicitor bound to advise.' Where misbehaviour is serious, exclusion of evidence is a mark of authoritative disapproval of a kind which too rarely comes from the PCA or police chiefs. Where the breach of proper standards or Codes of Practice is minor, the evidence will probably be allowed to stand, although the jury's view of police credibility may be shaken and make an acquittal more likely.

Court of Appeal judges have not been able to make up their collective mind about confessions obtained after suspects have been refused access to a solicitor in circumstances which amount to a breach of Section 58 of PACE. Sometimes the evidence is excluded, and sometimes not: cases in the Court of Appeal in 1988 had conflicting results, and no clear principles have emerged other than that trial judges should exercise their discretion according to the seriousness of the crime, the sophistication of the alleged criminal, and the character and likely advice of the solicitor whom the suspect has wished to summon.[57] It is unacceptable to make the exercise of a basic right (and perhaps the outcome of a serious trial) hinge upon a particular judge's assessment either of the suspect's worldly wisdom or of the 'trustworthiness' of his solicitor: the resulting confusion simply demonstrates why the Section 58 right should have been made unconditional in the first place. The alternative is an invitation to police to breach that particular law whenever they think the stakes are high enough.

The agent provocateur

In one respect, Section 78 of PACE may offer greater scope for trial courts to deter police misconduct. It supersedes a controversial House of Lords decision in *R. v. Sang* in 1980 that judges had no common-law power to exclude evidence obtained by police informers who act as *agents provocateurs*, encouraging defendants to commit crimes they would otherwise not have contemplated.[58] In Australia, such a discretion is well established,[59] and in the United States a positive defence of entrapment may be advanced 'when the criminal design originates, not with the accused, but is conceived in the minds of the government officers'.[60] Thus where a police informer befriended an ex-addict, and persuaded him to revert to heroin-taking in order to inform on him and so earn police favours, the Supreme Court quashed the conviction.

The entrapment defence helps to ensure proper standards in the exercise of Government power, but it has, regrettably, never been adopted in Britain. Although Lord Goddard once complained that 'it is wholly wrong for a police officer or any other person to be sent to commit an offence in order that an offence by another person may be detected', the only rules against permitting undercover policemen and informers to overstep the mark are contained in Home Office circulars. There have been several serious miscarriages of justice involving the imprisonment of men for robberies which were 'set up' and even led by police agents who were not charged, and much of the corruption which crippled Scotland Yard in the late sixties and early seventies stemmed from unhealthily close relationships between police officers and their criminal informants.

One case which the House of Lords disapproved in *Sang*, yet which may now, thanks to Section 78, return as a precedent is *R. v. Ameer*.[61] The defendant claimed he had been 'set up' by a man named Buckley, all trace of whom had disappeared from the prosecution evidence, along with much of the cannabis he had been possessed of when arrested. Buckley was subpoenaed by the defence to give evidence, and described himself as 'licensed' to deal in drugs on behalf of certain police officers. He claimed to be employed by these officers to 'set up' cannabis deals, and subsequently to sell part of the seizure. He told how he had befriended Ameer, given him cannabis on social occasions and originated the idea of a drugs deal, using 'every trick in the book' to obtain Ameer's participation. The judge was satisfied that Buckley had acted as an *agent provocateur*, playing a major role in drawing the defendant into a criminal enterprise which he would otherwise never have contemplated. The judge excluded all evidence relating to the cannabis and ordered the defendant's acquittal; subsequently, twenty-six other persons awaiting trial for drugs offences involving the same informer had all charges against them dropped.

The problem with the decision in *Sang* is that, without a discretion to exclude evidence obtained by unconscionable methods, conduct of the kind alleged in *Ameer* could never have been examined. Those who argue that criminal trials are not the place for inquiry into police malpractice ignore the fact that many of the worst cases of police corruption have only come to light as the result of barristers cross-examining police officers in the course of seeking to convince the judge to exercise a discretion to exclude unfairly obtained evidence.

The most dramatic example of the dangers of unsupervised informers is the story of Kenneth Lennon, a Special Branch agent who infiltrated an IRA team in Luton.[62] To maintain his cover, he was prosecuted on one occasion, with the evidence minimized to assist his acquittal without revealing his true role. The cover-up did not fool the IRA – Lennon was apprehended and executed, but not before he had made a 'confession' to the National Council for Civil Liberties (NCCL) alleging that he had been instructed by the Special Branch to act as an *agent provocateur*, setting up men for crimes which carried long prison sentences. The ensuing official inquiry published the secret 'Home Office circular' which purports to govern police relations with informants.[63]

Although it instructs police not to encourage informants to 'create' offences, the circular is not part of the law and in any event police are usually in no position to judge whether their informant has exceeded instructions. The practice of not disclosing the identity is apt to mislead the court and often to permit the trial to proceed on a false basis. As the Court of Appeal put it, in a case in 1969 where an informer's leading role in a burglary had been kept from all counsel and from the court,

> The judge was allowed to conduct his function blindfold, so that it is true to say that in this case, and let us hope to God it does not happen again, justice was blindfolded, and these men never had the chance to put forward the reality of the position.[64]

But over the next twenty years the courts retreated from this robust approach, and now generally refuse to allow questions relating to the identity of an informant.

There are many dangers inherent in accepting informer evidence as the basis for a criminal charge against a defendant who is not permitted, at his trial, to test it by way of cross-examination, or even, in many cases, to learn of its existence. Informer evidence may be obtained by fear, by guilt, by greed, by self-interest or by spite. The spy, secure in the knowledge that his version of events will normally go unchallenged, tends to supply his controllers with the information he feels they want to have, or at least will pay to obtain. He may feed them with stories that support his role, stress his own importance or perception and justify his continued employment. If, like Lennon, he is being paid on 'results achieved', he will have an incentive to achieve those results by using methods that he hopes will be undetected both by his masters and by his victims. The incentive to distort and exaggerate will be all the greater if he has become financially dependent on his controller, or if he needs a favour – immunity from prosecution or suppression of some dark corner of his past.

The question of whether a person guilty of crime should be acquitted if he can prove that he would never have participated without pressure and persuasion from a paid police agent goes to the crux of the balance between civil liberty and police power. We do not have quite the commitment to liberty to say, with the Americans, that entrapment should be a defence, but we are now inclined, by Section 78 of PACE, to let it in through the back door of judicial discretion. The Law Commission, reporting on a possible 'entrapment' defence shortly after the Lennon affair, said that the arguments were finely balanced, and the decision should be made at a political rather than a legal level. On one side is the view that informers ought to be protected at all costs even if there is a suspicion that they may have broken the rules and that people who succumb to temptation to participate in serious crime deserve to be punished anyway. The better view is that courts should not be misled, that rules against creating crimes where none would otherwise have been committed ought to be observed, and that it is a contradiction in terms for officials charged with maintaining the law to employ agents who arrange for it to be broken.

TWO

Public Protest

Demonstrations helped to win the democracy we enjoy today. The right to stand for Parliament, the right to vote and the right to join trade unions were all hastened by meetings and marches and protest movements. The right to assemble, to stand up and be counted among the believers in a cause or crusade, still marks the most obvious difference between liberal democracies and totalitarian States, where protest is banned and protesters are taken off to have their heads examined – and not only for bruises. Although public protest is still a powerful means of bringing the reality of grievance home to politicians and bureaucrats, it can also be high-pitched, brainless and brutal, spreading fear in minority communities, intimidating workers and clogging up traffic. More than any other freedom it comes at a price, and a price moreover which Governments are increasingly reluctant to pay. Despite much sentimental rhetoric, the right to protest has never been entrenched in English law: the police have always had power to stop speeches and demonstrations whenever a breach of the peace might occur. In recent years inner-city riots, violent clashes between police and striking miners, provocative racist marches by the National Front and the persistent defiance by the women of Greenham served as a backdrop to the Public Order Act of 1986, which enlarged police powers to control meetings and processions and to arrest those who cause alarm or distress to bystanders.

LACK OF POSITIVE RIGHTS

Although the virtues of peaceful protest are frequently extolled, there is in England no legal right of peaceful assembly or procession or (except at election time) even to hold meetings in public places. Cars and horses have more legal rights on the highway than people, as a small group of Islington social workers discovered when they were stopped by court order from spending their Saturday mornings distributing protest leaflets outside the offices of a local estate agent. They were complaining about the agent's tactics of 'winkling' working-class Islingtonians out of houses which were then profitably sold to the upwardly mobile. The demonstration was held with police approval and caused no obstruction, yet the Court of Appeal (over Lord Denning's vigorous dissent) put paid to any notion that there was a 'right to demonstrate' in English law.[1] The estate agents claimed the leaflets were libellous, and that the demonstrators were causing a 'nuisance' outside business premises: the court ruled that the 'balance of convenience' (i.e. the balance of business convenience) required that the protest should stop until these claims could be tried, a year or so hence. This case, *Hubbard* v. *Pitt*, is a regrettable example of how property rights can prevail over basic principles of free speech and assembly. The court asserted that the only right members of the public have on the highway is to move along it in a reasonable manner, otherwise the owner of the highway can sue in trespass.

Local authorities usually own the surface of main roads, so that they could sue in trespass anyone who used those roads for purposes other than that of passage. Other highways are usually owned by the owner of the land fronting the highway. The racehorse trainer who objected to Press racing correspondents timing from the highway his horses' practice gallops on his adjoining land,[2] and the landed duke whose pheasant shoot was interfered with by somebody deliberately opening and shutting his umbrella on the highway,[3] had their remedy in trespass. A landowner can also eject a trespasser with reasonable force after first requesting him to desist from the trespass. It is a criminal offence wilfully to obstruct free passage along a highway without lawful excuse, and policemen may arrest offenders without a warrant; the courts have decided that the offence may be committed although only part of the highway is obstructed, and even though no nuisance is committed. The scope of the crime is illustrated by what happened to Pat Arrowsmith: her conviction for obstruction was upheld although the area was frequently used for meetings, the police had been notified and she believed her meeting was lawful.[4] It follows that meetings on highways are always potentially unlawful: the owners of the appropriate part of the highway can always have the public removed, and any obstruction will constitute a criminal offence.

Restrictions on the right to demonstrate might be tolerable if there were a right to hold protest meetings in public places, like parks and open spaces. In the United States, for example, there is a constitutional *right* to use the streets and parks for purposes of public assembly. The Supreme Court has held:

> Wherever the title of streets and parks may rest, they have immemorially been held in trust for the use of the public, and time out of mind, they have been used for purposes of assembly, communicating thought between citizens, and discussing public questions.[5]

Compare that imaginative approach with the mean-spirited words of a former Lord Chief Justice in a leading British case on the right to demonstrate. It arose when a member of the National Council for Civil Liberties was arrested trying to address a group of people outside a Jobcentre. She was causing no obstruction, but the police thought that her speech might excite the unemployed and so lead to dissatisfaction inside the centre. The Chief Justice held this was ample ground to justify her arrest:

> There have been moments during the argument in this case when it appeared to be suggested that the court had to do with a grave case involving what is called the right of public meeting. I say 'called' because English law does not recognize any special right of public meeting for political or other purposes. The right of assembly is nothing more than a view, taken by the court, of the individual liberty of the subject.[6]

Most Western European countries permit meetings in public parks, and have laws requiring local authorities to hire halls to citizens for political meetings.[7] There is no equivalent in Britain, except for certain rights given to candidates at election times. Try to make a speech in the street, and you will be moved along, or, if you persist, arrested for obstruction of a police officer. In a park, your speech will probably be contrary to local by-laws forbidding meetings and distribution of literature in the interests of civic cleanliness. In most parks, dogs have more rights than demonstrators. You cannot even stand on a soap-box at Speakers' Corner or in Trafalgar Square – those world-famous symbols of freedom of British speech – without prior permission from the Department of the Environment. Organizations which have been refused permission to speak in Trafalgar Square – for no better reason than that their message was not acceptable to the Department of the Environment – include the Campaign for Nuclear Disarmament (CND), 'Save Greece from Fascism', the Northern Ireland Civil Rights Movement – and indeed, since 1972, *any* organization of *any* kind which has anything to say about Northern Ireland.

If a political group wants to hire a hall, the fate of its protest is in the hands of the local authority. Some local authorities will not allow the National Front to hire their halls – others have refused bookings from the Anti-Apartheid Movement. Indeed, Scarborough Council has preferred to pay large damages to the National Front by breaking a contract to hire its hall for a conference, rather than to permit the expression within its precincts of offensive political views.[8] These restrictions on protest are increasing. Until 1978, Oxford Street was a popular venue for processions. So was the route from Tower Hill to Westminster through the City. Quietly, without any fuss at all, the police have used their powers to close these areas off to marchers. The centre of consumerism and the citadel of capitalism may not be deaf to the voice of protest – they are just not permitted to hear it.

If a particular organization believed that it was being discriminated against by refusal of permission to hold a meeting, it is not clear what legal remedies, as distinct from the obvious political steps of having the matter raised in council and the local Press, would be available. It is a defect in the law that there is no clear-cut legal process for preventing political discrimination on the part of the local authority in controlling public meetings in its parks and open spaces. The citizen has no right to use premises belonging to local authorities for meetings, except a statutory right to use school or other premises controlled by the local authority upon payment of a reasonable fee for meetings organized by a candidate in connection with a parliamentary or local-government election. Of course, many local authorities habitually let meeting-halls to local associations and societies, but as the law stands this is purely a private business arrangement completely at council discretion. Ratepayers could secure the court's intervention if the local authority charged lower fees to one political body than to another, yet it is very doubtful whether they could have any legal remedy if the local authority systematically refused to allow particular associations the use of its premises on payment of the ordinary fee.

The citizen's rights seem inadequate here: the rights given in respect of elections could well be made of general application. There is much to be said for the proposal that English law should be brought into line with that of North America and most European countries, by the introduction of a statutory right to hold a public meeting, backed by a corresponding duty placed upon local authorities to set aside public land, or public halls, for such occasions. This recommendation was made by Lord Scarman in his report on the Red Lion Square disorders, but has been ignored.

The closest Britain has come to acknowledging a right to public protest is by accession to the European Convention of Human Rights, Article 11 of which guarantees 'the right to freedom of peaceful assembly and to freedom of association'. It is subject, of course, to considerations of public order and the rights of others, but these exceptions must be 'necessary in a democratic society'. When Parliament debated the 1986 Public Order Act, the Government was pressed to include a right of peaceful assembly to balance the extremely broad powers it was providing the police. The Government refused, but solemnly undertook to issue a 'Home Office circular' requesting the police to bear this 'right' in mind when exercising their new powers to control meetings and processions.[9] Whether that undertaking was given out of cynicism or naïveté it exemplifies Whitehall's ingrained fear of providing citizens with statutory rights, and illustrates the extent to which 'rights' are represented in England by polite letters to police chiefs rather than by rules of law.

PROCESSIONS

A political procession is a perfectly proper use of the highway, at least so long as it processes. The basic right to pass and re-pass along the highway exists for all reasonable users, and the Divisional Court had no hesitation in acquitting a CND official of incitement to obstruct the highway by directing a crowd to march down a particular route.[10] No obstruction or public nuisance is caused by a procession, whatever its size, unless, in all the circumstances, including the tradition of tolerating public protest, its use of the highway is unreasonable. Nevertheless, the Public Order Act 1986 gives police extensive powers to ban or reroute processions before they begin, however reasonable and peaceful their organizers' intentions, if public-order problems are expected.

Organizers of all 'political' processions – whether protests or campaigns or merely marches to commemorate historical events – must give notice to the police in writing of the time and route at least six days before the date, or as soon as reasonably practicable,[11] unless the decision to take to the streets is of the spontaneous, 'Let's march on the Town Hall' kind. The notice must designate at least one person as organizer, and a variety of footling offences are committed by organizers whose procession deviates from the route given in the notice or who fail to give notice at all or as soon as practicable. The notice requirement, imposed nationally for the first time by the 1986 Act, is of little value to public-order law. Over 80 per cent of marches were already being notified, and any demonstration large enough to pose a major public-order problem will obviously be known about well beforehand. The notice requirements merely discourage sensible people from volunteering to 'organize' a procession which would lay them open to a criminal charge if it took an unnotified turning or started an hour late because the band failed to arrive. The new offences may be committed in numerous petty ways, and there is ample scope for harassment of organizers of marches in support of controversial causes. The notice provision might have served some purpose had it provided that police approval of (or failure to request changes in) the notified route would be a defence to any marcher charged with obstructing the highway. This would have overcome the unfair decision in Pat Arrowsmith's case, when a brief and entirely unforeseeable obstruction caused by a meeting approved beforehand by police none the less resulted in her conviction for obstructing the highway.[12]

The 1986 Act gives senior police officers new powers to impose conditions as to the time or route of proposed processions if they reasonably believe that serious public disorder, serious damage to property or 'serious disruption to the life of the community' would otherwise result, or that the real purpose of the organizers is to intimidate others.[13] This power tilts the balance against civil liberties, in favour of the quiet life. Serious damage and disorder might be predictable as the result of a particular route, or a time which makes the march clash with a rival event, but 'disruption to community life' is an altogether too vague yardstick for ordering a protest march to keep to the back streets or the local playing fields, or to comprise no more than twenty demonstrators. Senior police officers are not required to consult representatives of the community whose life they allege will be seriously disrupted, and police decisions on this ground will inevitably involve political value-judgements. So too will the new power to impose conditions to avoid the intimidation of others 'with a view to compelling them to do or refrain from doing lawful acts'. If strikers decide to march to the place where 'scabs' are still working, the police power to route them elsewhere will depend on whether the strikers intend to use persuasion or compulsion – a distinction which is often difficult to make, even after the event.

Where a Chief Constable considers that his powers to impose conditions on a procession are insufficient to protect the area from serious public disorder, he may apply to the district council for an order banning all processions in the district for a period of up to three months.[14] The order must be approved by the Home Secretary (who approves it directly, without the interposition of any council, when requested by the Metropolitan Police Commissioner in London). At first sight, this seems reasonable enough: the Home Secretary is entitled, at the request of police and local councillors, to deny a particular organization the opportunity to march, at a particular time, if that would stir up serious public disorder. But if the Home Secretary does that, the law insists that a most remarkable and illogical consequence should follow: *all* marches in the area must be stopped, for a period which could be as long as three months. In other words, he is required to impose a *blanket ban* on all street marches, however harmless, in order to stop one particularly dangerous protest. These 'blanket bans' originated in the Public Order Act of 1936, which was rushed through Parliament when Mosley's Brownshirts were fighting pitched battles with Communists in the East End of London. Why, if only one march is going to cause a problem in one day, ban *all* marches on *all* days in the immediate future? That tactic may have made sense in terms of pacifying the East End battleground in 1936; it has no relevance to conditions today, when problems have mainly been caused by brief National Front sorties to different areas with high immigrant populations. The theory behind the law no longer makes sense – but the power unleashed *by* the law is formidable. In 1936, that power was justified on the basis that its very formidability would make Home Secretaries think twice before using it. And, sure enough, between 1936 and April 1980, there were only eleven bans imposed in Great Britain – an average of one ban every four years. But between April 1980 and June 1982 there were fifty-one total bans – prohibiting *all* marches in an area, sometimes for only a fortnight, sometimes for the full three months.

Most of these recent blanket bans have been imposed to stop just one march with a racist message. But a banning order is a scatter-gun which hits and hurts all sorts of innocent targets. For example, Friends of the Earth lost 5 per cent of their annual income when an entirely unobjectionable march against nuclear power, planned months in advance, had to be cancelled at the last moment because it fell within a banning period imposed to stop a National Front march. On another occasion, it lost a 'Save the Whale' rally for the same reason. Traditional events, like Trade Union May Day processions, have suffered the same fate. But even if the reasons for imposing a blanket ban are tenuous, the courts will not intervene to uphold the right to protest. That was discovered by the Campaign for Nuclear Disarmament, which became fed up with having its marches stopped because of other people's disturbances. After losing its seventh demonstration in five months, it marched into the Court of Appeal and sought to quash an order banning all demonstrations in London during the month of May 1981.[15] This particular blanket ban meant that there could be no wedding processions, no fairs on the common, no carnivals and no CND marches for four whole weeks in any part of the 786 square miles of Greater London. Although the court said that the police reasons for the ban were meagre, it could only overturn the order if there were no reasons for it at all. It is virtually inconceivable that judges would ever say that the Metropolitan Commissioner of Police and the Home Secretary had reached a decision which no reasonable person could make, so judicial review of banning orders is illusory.

Blanket bans have become an easy way out of difficult policing problems. But the consequence has been to give hooligans a new importance – a power, in effect, to dictate the terms upon which others may exercise their freedom to assemble. It is difficult to understand why the Government did not change the law when transferring it to the 1986 Act, so as to enable the Home Secretary to ban individual marches. The Minister of State claimed that Chief Constables were worried that a power to ban a single march would lay them open to charges of political bias – an illogical argument, since on every occasion a blanket ban has been imposed it has been well known which particular organization has triggered it. The first prosecution brought under the Act was against a demonstrator who shouted 'Apartheid murderers!' at visitors to a reception being held at South Africa House, and who refused to obey a police direction to move out of their earshot. The charge was dismissed after police admitted that the direction had been given merely to avoid discomfiture to the visitors.

PUBLIC MEETINGS

The most controversial new provision in the 1986 Public Order Act is Section 14, which extends to police officers the power to give directions to organizers or participants at public meetings of more than twenty persons. The power operates at two stages: before the demonstration, the Chief Constable may impose written conditions on the organizers; at the scene of the demonstration, the senior policeman present may impose them in any way he thinks fit. The power can only be exercised on the same grounds as the power to impose conditions on processions, namely on the reasonable belief that his direction will help to prevent serious public disorder or damage to property, or serious disruption to the life of the community, or deliberate intimidation. The conditions imposed can relate to the place of the demonstration, its length and the number of persons permitted to attend. Failure to comply with a police direction is an offence, punishable by up to three months' imprisonment, unless the failure arises from circumstances beyond the defendant's control. It is hard to see how an organizer could be held responsible for failing to comply with shouted directions lost in the tumult of an angry crowd, or with conditions which are broken by others who insist on swelling ranks beyond the allowed numbers or who refuse to disperse at the ordered time.

None the less, Section 14 is a recipe for conflict and confusion at demonstrations, as police officers shout directions, then wade in to arrest for non-compliance. It can permit Chief Constables to destroy the purpose of a protest in advance, by imposing conditions which make it futile. A vigil against apartheid outside the South African Embassy could be ordered to move across Trafalgar Square to the New Zealand High

Commission, a 'mass picket' at Wapping might be directed to reduce itself to twenty-one persons, and so on. The direction itself does not have to be reasonable or fair, so long as it subjectively appears to the particular police officer to be necessary at the time to thwart disorder or disruption or intimidation. The prospect of a gaol sentence makes it a more serious charge than obstruction of the highway, which carries only a financial penalty, and it is likely to become a regular police tactic to order demonstrators to move and then to arrest them under Section 14 for failure to comply with a direction. In effect, it provides the police with a new power to bring mass demonstrations to an end, by imposing a time limit by which the number of protestors must be reduced to below twenty. It remains to be seen how the power will be exercised in practice, but it has a potential for limiting severely the scope of demonstrations held in public places.

Section 14 was designed primarily to curb mass picketing. In some cases it will be possible for police to entertain a reasonable apprehension of serious public disorder or disruption to community life, but for the most part they will rely upon the ground that the purpose of the assembly is 'the intimidation of others with a view to compelling them not to do an act they have a right to do, or to do an act they have a right not to do'. Striking workers mustered at factory gates to deter others from working may have the object of persuading rather than compelling by intimidation: in *News Group* v. *SOGAT* it was held that 'abuse, swearing and shouting' did not amount to a threat of violence for the purpose of intimidation.[16] However, violent incidents accompanied by efforts to block entry will be sufficient to enable police to invoke their Section 14 powers to give directions.

The most unsatisfactory aspect of the Section 14 power, as of the power to ban or restrict processions, is the difficulty of appealing against restrictions. There is, in fact, no appeal from police decisions to impose conditions – only the possibility of having them reviewed for procedural errors or 'unreasonableness' in the High Court. To quash an order on the basis of 'unreasonableness' the court must be satisfied that it has been made by a police officer who has, in effect, taken leave of his senses. A preposterous condition – that print workers should hold their demonstration against Rupert Murdoch outside the offices of the *Morning Star* – might be struck down, as might a condition irrationally imposed on a traditional meeting which had never shown any signs of turning violent. But the High Court will never 'second guess' police apprehensions about public disorder, or apply a presumption in favour of freedom of speech and assembly: if there is some evidence, no matter how meagre, of potential dislocation, the belief will be upheld as one which a reasonable Chief Constable could entertain.[17] The potential of Section 14 conditions for diminishing the scope of permissible protest meetings requires some form of direct appeal, preferably to a judge at a Crown Court in the vicinity.

POWERS TO PREVENT DISORDER

The police and the magistrates have certain preventive powers at common law to restrain persons who are likely to create public disorder. The proper exercise of these powers turns upon whether there is a reasonable apprehension of a 'breach of the peace', in other words, behaviour which is likely to lead to harm to people or property or to put others in fear of suffering harm.[18] Mere annoyance or disturbance or insult is not sufficient: the peace is not broken by bad language or disobedience. The better view is that passive resistance will not amount to a breach of the peace, so long as protesters allow themselves to be removed without struggling, although one judge has noted that 'Even Mahatma Gandhi discovered to his sorrow that in the conduct of ordinary mortals passive resistance only remains passive so long as the resistance is successful.'[19] Those who sit down on highways can, of course, be arrested for obstruction, but police have no such power where the 'sit-in' takes place on private property. They are entitled to intervene only if there is forcible resistance to the owner's efforts to remove them. Police do have power to enter private property when they apprehend a breach of the peace, so they may attend public meetings (or even 'closed' meetings) on private premises, against the wishes of the organizers, if they believe that violence is likely to occur unless they are present. There is one case, *Thomas* v. *Sawkins* (1935), in which it was suggested that police could enter private premises without a warrant on the off chance that seditious speeches would be made.[20] This authority is unclear and has been much criticized: the better view is that police need an invitation or a warrant before entering meetings on private premises, unless a breach of the peace is reasonably apprehended. In this situation, the police do as a duty what any citizen is entitled to do by right, namely take reasonable steps to prevent breaches of the peace, if necessary by forcibly detaining the person whose conduct threatens public order.[21] That conduct must be 'likely', not 'liable', to breach the peace: the duty does not justify restraints on those who may possibly cause trouble.[22]

The police power to restrain breaches of the peace was used to controversial effect during the 1984 miners' strike, when police intercepted car-loads of picketers some miles from the collieries and forced them to turn back. The Divisional Court accepted that police were entitled to act because of recent violence from pickets at the colliery, and the likelihood of a breach of the peace by reinforcements was real, imminent and immediate.[23] Police pushed the decision considerably beyond these limits by stopping car-loads of picketers at the Dartford Tunnel, several hundred miles from the destined demonstration.

Another device used by the courts during the miners' strike for limiting the right of individuals to join flying pickets was to impose a condition of bail on those arrested for a public-order offence that they should not henceforth engage in picketing other than at their own place of work. Such conditions involved a presumption of guilt prior to trial, and were particularly objectionable when imposed by magistrates as a routine policy rather than by reference to the facts of individual cases. A person who commits another public-order offence while on bail risks a much higher sentence at the second trial, and this fact should itself serve as a deterrent to misconduct, without the need to impose bail conditions which prevent the exercise of the right to assemble and express opinion. The Divisional Court, which approved the application of these bail conditions on men of good character upon their first arrest for a minor public-order offence, made no reference in its judgement to such right: it accepted police evidence that all the mass pickets invoked violence and intimidation, and that Justices were therefore entitled to decide there was a 'real risk' that defendants would commit offences by returning to the picket line.[24]

Bind-overs

Magistrates may make an order binding over any person in their court to keep the peace in future. This power was given to lay Justices in 1360 as a means of containing the depredations of drunken soldiers roaming the country after the French wars, and it still has valuable uses to calm neighbourhood disputes and to prevent domestic violence. It does not count as a conviction, and may be imposed without any trial at all, so long as the magistrates foresee future misbehaviour. Refusal to accept a bind-over may be punished by up to six months in prison – a fate some protesters are prepared to suffer rather than fetter their future conduct. In 1961, Bertrand Russell and some of his distinguished CND colleagues were sent to prison for refusing to be bound over, and in 1969 Pat Arrowsmith became Britain's first 'prisoner of conscience' when she was gaoled for six months for refusing to provide sureties for future good conduct after participating in an anti-Vietnam demonstration. They had not been convicted of any offence: they simply refused to put themselves in a position which would make it more difficult for them to organize or participate in future demonstrations.

There have been several unedifying cases of the bind-over power being inflicted by country Justices on anti-hunting demonstrators appearing as prosecution witnesses against huntsmen who have beaten them up. The latter were given discharges or small fines for assault, and the witnesses were sent to prison for refusing the magistrates' demands to be bound over. Not even Kafka envisaged a judicial proceeding where the victim is gaoled and the assailants go free, yet that is exactly what has happened in recent years in courts in Rye and Market Bosworth.[25] Anti-hunt campaigns may be provocative, but it is wrong to seek to deter further protest by demanding that participants who have not themselves been proved to have breached the law should submit to a bind-over. It is especially unjust that protesters should be gaoled, not merely in circumstances where they have committed no offence, but where the offence that the court fears they might otherwise commit is minor and would only result in a small fine.[26]

PUBLIC-ORDER OFFENCES

The two offences most commonly charged against demonstrators are obstructing the highway and obstructing police in the execution of their duty. Section 137 of the Highways Act makes it an offence wilfully to obstruct the free passage along a highway without lawful authority or excuse. The test is invariably one of reasonableness, and the court must consider the length of time the obstruction lasted, whether any passers-by were forced to detour, whether any request was made by police to clear the area, and so on.[27] It is not unreasonable to stand on a street corner holding a placard or making a political speech, and it is entirely reasonable to demonstrate, even in large numbers, until police seek to clear the road to make way for vehicles or pedestrians. The Divisional Court quashed convictions of animal rights protesters who had been handing out leaflets condemning the fur trade in a shopping precinct: the prosecution had failed to prove either that pedestrians had actually been obstructed in going about their business or that the protest had been conducted in such an unreasonable manner that there was no 'lawful excuse' for it.[28] But note that the fur shop might well have succeeded in obtaining an injunction against the demonstrators on the authority of *Hubbard* v. *Pitt*.

The offence of obstructing the highway cannot be committed on private property or on a road to which some members of the public have been denied access: a 'highway', in law, entails 'the right of all Her Majesty's Subjects at all seasons of the year freely and at their will to pass and repass without let or hindrance'. This caused difficulties for the police when they made use of statutory powers to divert vehicular traffic from the roads leading to Rupert Murdoch's plant at Wapping, and then sought to arrest demonstrators for obstructing those roads – which had ceased to be 'highways' in law as a result of the restricted access.[29] A test case involving Tony Dubbins, Secretary of the NGA, ended when he was acquitted of obstruction on the basis that he had not heard the police order to clear the road and had sat down for his own safety when police charged and attacked those who ran away. Whether or not the road was a 'highway' at the time, he had acted reasonably in the circumstances.

The offence of obstructing police in the execution of their duty is committed by any action which makes it more difficult for them to do their job – by resisting arrest, for example, or trying to hinder the arrest of someone else. Contested cases generally turn on whether the police were in fact acting in the execution of their duty, as a citizen is entitled to use reasonable force to resist an unlawful arrest. Thus it will be a good defence to charges of obstruction or assault if the police action which provoked them cannot be justified on grounds either of reasonable suspicion of an 'arrestable offence' or of reasonable apprehension of a breach of the peace. At industrial disputes, many arrests for obstruction of both the highway and the police arise from attempts by pickets to 'persuade' drivers and workers to turn back. There is nothing to stop pickets from communicating their case; equally, there is nothing to oblige drivers to stop and listen to it.[30] When reason prevails, police will allow pickets to stop and converse briefly with drivers, and then move them back when the driver indicates that he wishes to proceed. Unless some such system is agreed between police and picket organizers, ugly confrontations are likely, in which pickets can be charged with obstructing the highway by blocking the passage of vehicles, and obstructing the police by refusing to budge or by resisting arrest. Obstruction offences are difficult to prosecute, at least in courts which apply the proper standards of proof, because the evidence will inevitably reflect the confusion of the mêlée, and it may be difficult to determine which side has acted the more reasonably.

A more effective weapon against pickets has been found, in recent industrial disputes, in civil actions for injunctions against the unions to which they belong. Especially where there is evidence of workers being intimidated or assaulted, or commercial contracts being interfered with by the turning away of lorries, the High Court is generally prepared to grant injunctions which oblige the union to restrain its members from such actions, on pain of heavy financial punishment for contempt of court and further damages payable to the employers. It is now customary for the courts, in recognition of traditional 'rights', to exclude from the ambit of the injunction 'peaceful, disciplined and orderly marches' and 'pickets, provided they do not exceed six in number, at the entrance to the main gate for the purpose of peacefully obtaining or communicating information'.[31] These exceptions define the 'right to protest' in industrial disputes. The number of six is taken from the Employment Code of Practice (1980) and is inevitably arbitrary. Unfortunately, it is becoming a magic number for police-approved picketing on non-industrial matters.

There is an important difference, which some civil libertarians are reluctant to recognize, between mass pickets organized and financed by trade unions as part of a battle to obtain better conditions for members, and political demonstrations which touch the conscience rather than the hip pocket of those who attend. This is not to deny that there may be a certain nobility in trade unionists who fight to get back their jobs on the *Sun*, but they lack the disinterested quality of those who keep twenty-four hour vigils outside South Africa House. Whatever reason there may be to limit to six the number of pickets stationed to communicate with strike-breaking drivers, it is wrong to put any limits on the numbers who wish to picket as an act of conscience, so long as there is no imminent danger to public order.

A new rod for the backs of violent pickets was fashioned by the offence of 'violent disorder' in Section 2 of the 1986 Public Order Act. This makes it unlawful for three or more persons to use or threaten violence in a way which would cause 'a person of reasonable firmness present at the scene to fear for his personal safety'. No 'person of reasonable firmness' need be present at the time, although police officers, as persons of unreasonable firmness, will generally give observation evidence of strike-breaking workers being spat upon and threatened with violence. Threats uttered when there is a strong police presence would be unlikely to cause reasonable fears for personal safety, and 'abuse, swearing and shouting' will not be sufficient of itself to constitute the 'use or threat of violence' necessary to obtain convictions.[32] A single demonstrator who makes a physical (as distinct from simply a verbal) threat of violence which would intimidate a reasonable person present at the scene can be prosecuted for the new offence of 'affray' contained in Section 3 of the Act.

Both violent disorder and affray are triable in magistrates' courts (where the maximum penalty is six months' imprisonment) but the defendant may elect trial by jury – the greater chance of acquittal being counterbalanced by the prospect of a heavier sentence (five years maximum for 'violent disorder' and three years for 'affray'). As the two offences will often overlap with the less serious crimes of obstruction, assault on police and 'insulting and threatening behaviour', which do not carry a right to jury trial, Crown prosecutors will generally prefer to charge the latter offences so as to have the charges dealt with more speedily by magistrates. This is the preferred approach where picketing is likely to continue for some time. Where serious violence has occurred, however, the prosecution may well decide that the case is grave enough to require a Crown Court trial.

The most serious public-order offence is riot, which carries a maximum penalty of ten years' imprisonment. It is committed by any person who uses unlawful violence for a common purpose shared by at least twelve persons, whose collective conduct would make the hypothetical 'person of reasonable firmness' fear for his personal safety. The offence was retained in Section 1 of the Public Order Act, although Parliament's sentimental attachment to the word and the concept overlooked the historic tendency of juries to acquit alleged rioters with political motivations, from trade unionists at the turn of the century to Fascists in the 1930s to miners in the 1980s. Over 600 miners were charged with riot or 'unlawful assembly' (now abolished) as a result of the 1984 strike: overwhelmingly they were found 'not guilty' or had the charges dropped. A prosecution of nineteen persons for riot after the disturbances in St Pauls, Bristol, in 1980 hindered efforts to 'let bygones be bygones' in that community, and the long trial cost half as much as the damage done by the disturbances before the defendants were acquitted. Riot is a blunderbuss of a charge, posing great difficulties for prosecutors in associating particular defendants with a 'common purpose' or in proving that they used unlawful violence in pursuit of it or at all. It invites 'political' defences: the miners charged with riot put the police tactics on trial, and the Bristol riot trial jury heard about the history of racial oppression in the area from the days of the slave trade.

One significant fact to emerge from recent riot trials is the lack of consensus on what constitutes the 'reasonable force' with which police are entitled to quell a riot. At Wapping and at strike-bound collieries crowds were dispersed by mounted police advancing into the crowd at a canter, and a secret Association of Chief Police Officers manual of 'riot tactics' advocates a police advance 'striking in a controlled manner with batons about the arms and legs and torso' of suspected stone-throwers and ringleaders.[33] This notion of 'controlled striking' needs further examination, especially by reference to evidence of quite unbridled police violence presented to juries during the riot trials arising from the miners' strike, and similar photographic evidence of police attacks on demonstrators at Wapping in 1987. The latter incident led to a lengthy investigation which resulted in charges being laid against a number of police officers alleged to have brutally beaten protesters.

CS gas was first used on the mainland in Brixton in 1981, and the

Home Secretary in that year announced that stocks of CS canisters and plastic bullets and water cannon would be held in a central store, 'available to chief officers of police for use in the last resort and under strict conditions in situations of serious public disorder' – these 'strict conditions' being defined, presumably, in secret Home Office circulars. In 1986 the Home Office offered to supply Chief Constables direct from the central store if their local police authorities withheld approval for purchasing CS gas and plastic bullets. The Court of Appeal rejected an application by a Labour-controlled police authority to stop the Home Office from going behind its back: it ruled that the Government is entitled to supply police forces with any weapons appropriate for dealing with breaches of the peace, and the decision to use those weapons is entirely one for the Chief Constable, uncontrolled by court or local council.[34] On these matters, local police authorities have no authority whatsoever.

THE LIMITS OF PROTEST

There is a fundamental conceptual question which is raised throughout the law relating to public order. To what extent are police entitled to restrict lawful protest because of disorder apprehended from lawless reactions by others? In the USA, the right to protest is absolute: those who exercise it cannot be stopped merely because they are provocative. In Britain, the approach has been much more pragmatic. In the last century the courts protected obstreperous Christians who provoked attacks, but the same tolerance was not vouchsafed in the 1930s to left-wingers and pacifists whose speeches provoked Fascist wrath. These latter decisions were meanly argued and much criticized, but they provided a basis, in the 1970s, for police actions which turned the historic tables and stopped the National Front from flaunting its racist doctrines in the face of ethnic communities and provoking angry attacks from left-wing organizations. The European Court of Human Rights has now held that States must take positive action to protect demonstrators from fear of physical violence from counter-demonstrators, and to enable lawful demonstrations to proceed peacefully. However, it ruled that Austrian police had fulfilled this duty by separating opposing groups only when tempers had risen to the point at which physical violence became likely:

they were not obliged to intervene to protect the original demonstrators from lesser forms of disruption.[35]

The leading British case of *Beatty* v. *Gillbanks* arose from Salvation Army processions in Weston-super-Mare in 1882.[36] Their object, 'lawful and laudable', was to 'reclaim and draw away from vicious and irreligious habits' those hitherto dead to religion. They regularly clashed with 'The Skeleton Army', a jeering mob egged on by the brewery trade, and on several occasions 'free fights, blows, tumult, stone-throwing and disorder' erupted. The burghers of Weston-super-Mare objected to the disruption of the customary quiet of the town, and the Justices bound the Salvation Army captains to find sureties to keep the peace – in effect, putting an end to their participation in processions which would be sure to disturb it. The Divisional Court quashed the order, on the principle that persons acting lawfully could not be held responsible merely because others were thereby induced to act unlawfully and create a disturbance. Had the Salvationists been more directly responsible for the disturbances – by abusing and insulting their opponents – the bind-over might have been upheld.[37]

A less principled result was reached in *Duncan* v. *Jones* (1936) where a speaker was arrested for obstructing a police officer who ordered her down from her soap-box outside a training centre for the unemployed.[38] A year previously there had been a restlessness amongst the unemployed after the same speaker had addressed them, and the police claimed they feared repetition – the topic, ironically enough, was the threat to free speech posed by the Incitement to Disaffection Bill. The Divisional Court had no hesitation in holding that the police had reasonable grounds for apprehending a breach of the peace, and that the speaker wilfully obstructed them by refusing to desist from what was otherwise lawful conduct. *Duncan* v. *Jones* is a miserable decision for civil liberties, all the more so because the judges purported to find no difficulty of principle in it. Australian courts have recently refused to follow it in a case involving women who protested on Anzac Day (a hallowed remembrance of war dead) against the propensity of soldiers to rape in wartime.[39] Although they refused a police order to desist from a demonstration which would probably have provoked old soldiers to breach the peace, they could not be convicted of obstructing police because they were committing no offence themselves. The remedy – as the court had pointed out in *Beatty* v. *Gillbanks* – was for the police to arrest those who allow themselves to be provoked into violence by lawful demonstrations.

Protesters may none the less break the law if their actions are calculated to goad bystanders beyond endurance. Even in the USA, the right falsely to shout 'fire' in a crowded theatre is overridden by considerations of public order and safety. The British Parliament redefined the permissible limits of protest in Sections 4 and 5 of the Public Order Act 1986 and showed a distinct preference for curbing speech and behaviour which could end in violence or tears. Section 4 makes it an offence punishable by up to six months in prison to use threatening, abusive or insulting words or behaviour towards another person, or to distribute threatening, abusive or insulting pamphlets, either with the intent that others should fear or be provoked to violence or in circumstances where it is likely that such fear or provocation will result. The key adjectives – 'threatening', 'abusive', 'insulting' – are 'all very strong words'[40] which must be given a common-sense interpretation: vigorous, distasteful, unmannerly, offensive and annoying words and behaviour are permissible. When anti-apartheid protester Dennis Brutus disrupted a tennis match at Wimbledon featuring a South African player, the audience was provoked to fury – fists were shaken and attempts were made to hit him. But the House of Lords held that he had been wrongly convicted under the predecessor of Section 4, because his conduct had not in any ordinary sense been 'insulting', let alone abusive or threatening.[41] But if this test is satisfied, speakers take their audiences as they find them, and British Fascists have been convicted for proclaiming that 'Hitler was right' in speeches at Trafalgar Square which insulted and were likely to provoke to violence Jews and Communists who happened to be in the audience.

Section 4 requires the insulting words to be used 'towards another person', so there can be no conviction unless the speaker directs his diatribe towards people likely to take offence, or be put in fear of violence. It is not enough, of course, merely to prove that the speaker is abusive or insulting: the prosecution must prove that, in the circumstances in which the words were uttered, people addressed would either be provoked to unlawful violence or would be likely to believe that unlawful violence would be used against them. The standard abuse hurled at those who walk to work through picket lines will not be sufficient, although belief in an imminent attack would be justified if similar abuse had been followed, on previous occasions, by attacks on workers. It is not clear how the Australian women protesting against wartime rape would fare under Section 4 at the Cenotaph with their placards 'Patriots Kill' and 'Heroes Rape': it would be for the court to decide whether these words were insulting and liable to provoke violence from those present at the time. By 'court' is meant the local magistrates: Section 4, like most public-order offences, carries no right to jury trial. For all our rhetoric about the jury as guardian of liberty, successive Governments have been careful to avoid having to submit fundamental free-speech issues to juries. Magistrates are assumed, with some reason, to be more likely to convict. Yet the question of whether we should tolerate a protest which causes deep offence and anger to those remembering the war would be more acceptably decided by a jury rather than a lawyer-magistrate or a group of lay Justices.

The women against rape would probably fall at the last hurdle set up by Section 5 of the 1986 Public Order Act, the catch-all offence of using threatening, abusive, insulting words or behaviour, 'within the hearing or sight of a person likely to be caused harassment, alarm or distress by the above conduct'. This minor offence of 'disorderly behaviour' carries a maximum fine of £400, and police can only arrest after having first given a warning to desist which has not been heeded. This new offence was introduced in 1986 ostensibly to give the police power to deal with hooliganism and rowdy late-night behaviour, but the notion of 'disorderly behaviour' is so elastic that police could use it to victimize people in the community who cause alarm and distress by acting differently rather than dangerously. The wide words of the statute make it applicable to many peaceful protests, especially those with banners and placards which abuse Governments and politicians and employers, and cause distress to bystanders with different political perspectives. 'Distress' is a weak and weasel word: a lot of art and literature, and speeches at political meetings, are designed to distress those responsible for or indifferent to injustice or poverty or oppression. The Crown Prosecution Service covered itself with ridicule during the 1987 general election by its unsuccessful attempt to use Section 5 against students displaying a satirical poster depicting Mrs Thatcher as a sadistic sexual dominatrix.

It is a defence under Section 5 'for the accused to prove that his conduct was reasonable' – which could lead to some interesting, if long-winded, political exercises in magistrates' courts. Could Greenham women argue that the horror of nuclear Armageddon makes a disorderly or abusive protest against cruise missiles entirely reasonable? Once again it will be magistrates rather than juries who decide. When anti-Vietnam demonstrators set a match to an American flag in Grosvenor Square in 1969, they were convicted of the crime of 'insulting behaviour' – on the basis, according to the Marlborough Street magistrate, that it would anger American tourists. Yet that very same action for the very same reason, if it were committed outside the White House in Washington, would under American law be a form of symbolic speech, protected by the First Amendment. In the words of the Supreme Court in a flag-burning case, 'We are unable to sustain a conviction that may have rested on a form of expression, however distasteful, which the constitution tolerates and protects.'

INCITEMENT TO RACIAL HATRED

There are few issues in the field of human rights that are more difficult to resolve than the head-on collision between the right to express unattractive ideas and the right to live free from racist vilification. In 1974 the US Civil Liberties Union lost a substantial proportion of its funds and many of its members by supporting the right of the American Nazi Party to march through the predominantly Jewish town of Skokie; ten years later the National Council of Civil Liberties in Britain was condemned by many of its most distinguished members when it took the opposite position by refusing to support the civil rights of a racist political party, the National Front. There is no easy answer to the dilemmas posed for a tolerant society by racial intolerance.

Freedom of expression entails the right to entertain ideas of any kind, and to express them publicly. The mode or the manner of the expression, however, may properly be regulated in the interests of the freedom of others to go about their business in public without being gratuitously assaulted or defamed, and may properly be curtailed in order to avoid public disorder which may follow provocative dissemination of racist ideas. This was the basis of the first anti-incitement laws, passed in Britain in 1965 after several years of racial violence of the most serious kind, by a Labour Government whose commitment to freedom of speech was weakened after the infamous Smethwick by-election, in which a Labour majority evaporated in the face of the slogan, 'If you want a nigger for a neighbour, vote Labour.'

This law has been amended on several occasions – the 1986 Public Order Act being the last – in an effort to make convictions easier to obtain. Nevertheless prosecutions, which can only be brought with the Attorney-General's consent, are comparatively infrequent. There were only twenty-eight between 1976 and 1982; in 1983 there were four, and fifteen in 1984. The Attorney-General applies the 'more than 50 per cent chance of conviction' test with particular nervousness, because of the counter-productive consequences of acquittals.

Section 18 of the 1986 Act makes it an offence to use threatening, abusive or insulting words or behaviour with the intent of stirring up racial hatred or in circumstances where racial hatred is likely to be stirred up. 'Racial hatred' means hatred against a group defined by colour, race, or national origin, thereby including Jews, Sikhs (but not religion) and Romany gypsies, but excluding Zionists, Muslims and gypsies in general. The offence can be committed via any of the media other than radio and television broadcasts supervised by the BBC, IBA or the Cable Television Authority – these institutions have rules and statutory duties which disincline them to transmit racist material other than to condemn racism. Nevertheless, an election broadcast in 1983 by the National Front raised a troublesome issue: if political parties obtain sufficient support to qualify for unvetted broadcasts, any incitement to hatred in those broadcasts will not be capable of prosecution.

The offence can be committed by the performance of a play, although a drama's propensity to stir up racial hatred is to be judged with regard to all the circumstances and 'taking the performance as a whole'. Racist abuse heaped on Shylock and Othello by Shakespearian characters is therefore defensible, and there have been no prosecutions of stage plays since the offence first appeared in the Theatres Act of 1968. However, the Royal Court Theatre's cancellation of the play *Perdition* in 1987 after pressure from Jewish interests shows that the question may not be of entirely academic interest in the future.

Further potential for inhibiting free speech is contained in the offence of possessing racially inflammatory material with a view to its publication in circumstances where racial hatred is likely to be stirred up. Authors and journalists who collect such material in order to condemn it will not be at risk, but it might be argued that uncritical displays of Nazi memorabilia or unvarnished publications of *Hitler Diaries* and the like could revive old hatreds. The protection for books of genuine historic interest is provided, not by the words of the Act, but by the need to obtain the Attorney-General's consent to prosecution. It is unfortunate that Parliament did not make these Sections of the Act subject to a defence that the play or the publication or collection was in the interests of drama, literature, history or other subjects of general concern.

When the offence of inciting racial hatred was first introduced it was severely criticized as a counter-productive attack on the right to free speech. Since then, it has been enlarged and stretched to what may be hoped will be its limit, although some want it further amended to catch racist ideas expressed without threat or insult or abuse. Has the advent of the crime helped or hindered race relations? Few would assert that it has measurably diminished racism in British society, although it has provided a standard for condemning racist utterances. It has helped to stigmatize racists as persons involved in anti-social behaviour, and has been used to justify deployment of police resources in monitoring their organizations and plans. Although prosecutions have been few, the majority have been successful, because successive Attorney-Generals have adopted the policy of only prosecuting when there is a very strong case. Some of the most crude and hurtful racist utterances have been removed from the public domain, and the editor of a National Front magazine for schoolchildren has been sent to prison. (Whatever view may be taken of the right of racists to put their doctrines on display in a free market-place of ideas, attempts to indoctrinate schoolchildren with specially tailored propaganda are hardly defensible on free-speech grounds.)

However, the incitement-to-racial-hatred law in Britain has had a number of counter-productive consequences. It has changed the *style* of racist propaganda: by making it less blatantly bigoted, it has made it more respectable. As a Home Office review of the law pointed out:

> Whilst this shift away from crudely racialist propaganda and abuse is welcome, it is not an unmixed benefit. The more apparently rational and moderate is the message, the greater is its probable impact on public opinion.[42]

There is no doubt that the law has a potential for punishing the expression of genuine political statements, albeit couched in crude or insulting terminology. This can apply particularly to activists from oppressed minorities, whose rhetoric is designed to jolt what they perceive as white complacency. In Britain the law was used, at least in its first decade of operation, more effectively against Black Power leaders than against white racists. The first person to be gaoled for a race-hatred offence was Michael X, convicted by a white jury in 1967 for some fairly routine black-consciousness rhetoric of the period.[43] Although prosecuting authorities have taken care to avoid creating martyrs, the publicity attendant upon acquittals has been counter-productive. When members of the Racial Preservation Society were acquitted for publishing a newspaper claimed to be 'innocently informative' rather than 'intentionally inflammatory', they derived benefit from the publicity surrounding the trial and reissued the edition, overprinted 'Souvenir Edition – the paper the Government tried to suppress'. There was an increase in this type of quasi-educational racist literature after the acquittal. Similarly, racists were encouraged by the acquittal of a National Front speaker who 'joked' in reference to the murder of an Asian immigrant, 'One down, one million to go.'

Laws against inciting racial hatred create more expectations than can be fulfilled by prosecution authorities anxious to avoid giving racist utterances the publicity of a trial and the endorsement of an acquittal. There is no objection in principle to prosecuting racist speeches or writings which either occasion a real threat of public disorder, or which are forced on citizens in public places or in their homes against their wishes in terms so gross as to cause serious affront to reasonable people. In such cases, freedom of speech is not at stake: what is being prosecuted is not the idea behind the utterance, but the occasion chosen for making it. Suggestions that the law should go further, by punishing opinions which favour discrimination, would make too great an inroad on the principle of freedom of expression. Once protection is denied to one socially unacceptable belief it can be denied to others: sexism, communism, anarchism or whatever. Any abuse is hurtful, whether on grounds of race, sex, religion or physical or mental handicap: racism is a special case because of its particular propensity to cause public disorder, but a law which does not confine its operation to that particular mischief offers a cure which may well serve only to promote the disease.

OFFENSIVE WORDS

Protests are usually collective expressions of anger and outrage, and individual protesters may give vent to their feelings in unrestrained language and offensive slogans. They can fall foul of various laws against public indecency, which courts in Britain will judge according to the circumstances of the utterance rather than by the high-flown jurisprudential principles deployed in the USA to decide, for example, that a 'Fuck the Draft' badge enjoyed constitutional protection. The leading case on bad political language is *Wiggins* v. *Field*, which arose from a public reading of Allen Ginsberg's poem *America*, including the line, 'Go fuck yourself with your atom bomb'. The reader was charged with using 'indecent language' in contravention of a local by-law, but the Divisional Court said that the case ought never to have been brought.

> Whether a word or phrase was capable of being treated as indecent language depended on all the circumstances of the case, the occasion, when, how and in the course of what it was spoken and perhaps to a certain extent what the intention was.[44]

It decided that in the work of a recognized poet, read without any intention of causing offence, the word 'fuck' could not be characterized as 'indecent'. The same robust attitude was expressed by the court in quashing a doctor's conviction for using indecent language when he described workmen as 'a pair of stupid bastards' for making a noise outside his surgery. 'It is quite impossible to say that the word in this context was indecent.'[45]

A message will be 'indecent' if it outrages the sensibilities of reasonable people – a quality which it is not always easy for prosecutors to prove beyond reasonable doubt. Slogans on T-shirts have come in for some attention: the arguably political (or at least defiantly apolitical) message 'Fuck Art, Let's Dance' has been acquitted, but the more commercial message, on a T-shirt issued by Stiff Records, 'If it ain't stiff it ain't worth a fuck', resulted in a conviction. In 1977 the promoters of a record album entitled 'Never Mind the Bollocks, here's the Sex Pistols' were acquitted of indecent advertising, after the court heard evidence from a professor of English who traced the etymology of the word 'bollocks' from its original meaning of 'testicles' to its modern connotation of 'rubbish'. The turning-point apparently came with the King James edition of the Bible, which had replaced 'bollocks', used in the original sense in earlier editions, with the word 'stones'. The acquittal relieved the promoters from retitling their album 'Never Mind the Stones, here's the Sex Pistols'.

The circumstances of the protest can make all the difference. In 1966 a group of anti-Vietnam protesters interrupted a church lesson being read by the Foreign Secretary, Mr George Brown, with cries of 'Oh you hypocrite. How can you use the word of God to justify your policies?' The Divisional Court upheld their conviction for indecent behaviour, on the grounds that 'an act done in a church during divine service might be highly indecent and improper, which would not be so at another time'.[46] This principle is unexceptionable, although it may be doubted whether the court applied it correctly in the actual case, which arose from a church service at a Labour Party conference where Government Ministers were ostentatiously displaying their piety for the benefit of television cameras. Lord Soper, a defence witness, testified to 'the tradition of vigorous disputation in Methodist churches', and it would be unfortunate if politicians or partisan clerics could be protected from reasonable interjections by delivering their messages in a church. Normally, of course, religious feelings do deserve special protection when they are being solemnly celebrated in places of public worship, and public-order laws have been used to punish racists who intruded a pig into a Muslim mosque. A range of arcane laws punish disturbers of 'decent and quiet devotions' and those guilty of 'riotous or indecent behaviour in church precincts', 'molesting vexing or misusing preachers' and 'unauthorized addresses at the graveside' (Hamlet and Laertes would face two years' imprisonment under the Burial Laws Amendment Act 1880).[47] These laws are all justifiable when used to punish the deliberate disturbance of religious devotions, although the rise of political preachers in the USA underlines the need for some protection for peaceful protest on occasions that are more political than religious.

BROADCASTING BANS

In October 1988 the Government used its powers over radio and television broadcasting to order that no interviews should be transmitted with representatives of Sinn Fein and other Irish organizations which have supported the political use of violence, or statements which incite support for such organizations. This is the first peacetime prohibition on public statements by or about lawful organizations, and it serves as a clear example of how the IRA has succeeded in diminishing liberties traditionally enjoyed in Britain. The ban applies to interviews with elected local councillors (of whom Sinn Fein has sixty) and with Gerry Adams (the Sinn Fein MP) as well as with persons who manifest support for Sinn Fein or the Ulster Defence Association. It does not apply to candidates at election times, or to parliamentary broadcasts, but it operates to prevent any representative of these organizations from being heard on the electronic media discussing local political issues far removed from terrorism, such as voting intentions on rate increases or measures to prevent dogs from fouling the pavements. It prevents the broadcast media from using direct quotations as part of an analysis (even a historical analysis) of such organizations, and it prevents the public from hearing representatives cross-examined about any aspect of their policies. It is a measure of direct political censorship, denying the air waves to specific organizations whose policies, however unattractive, none the less command some support in Northern Ireland. The early days of the ban produced much confusion, as broadcasters had to censor reactions to the ban itself amongst those it affected, and even (quite unjustifiably) stopped programmes which featured persons claiming that defendants had been wrongfully convicted of terrorist offences.

The Home Secretary's reasons for imposing the ban were that such interviews caused outrage to many viewers, and gave 'a spurious authority and respectability' to interviewees. These reasons are, of course, self-contradictory: viewers who are offended are unlikely to respect the person causing them offence. The philosophy of a free market-place of ideas which underpins the 'freedom of expression' guarantee in the European Convention is based on the principle that citizens should be entitled to judge for themselves the odiousness of politicians and their platforms, and the great value of television interviews is that it enables this judgement to be made by seeing and hearing representatives under a form of cross-examination. (A *World in Action* programme severely dented the credibility of Gerry Adams precisely because it was able to put him under interrogation.) The very fact that up to 100,000 people in Northern

Ireland vote for Sinn Fein at local elections makes its representatives and their policies a matter of public interest in the United Kingdom, however 'offensive' such interviews may be to the Government (the evidence suggests that viewers, on the whole, are not offended by the fact that such interviews have been screened in the past). The ban operates a political censorship which is unnecessary and unjustifiable in a democratic society. Citizens are entitled to form and promote organizations which are not conspiracies to break the law, and it makes no sense for Governments to deny them one outlet for expressing their opinions merely because the power to shut off that outlet exists fortuitously in the law which regulates broadcasting. It may be that the ban will in due course be struck down, or at least restricted in its scope, by the European Court: a total prohibition on television and radio appearances by representatives of a lawful political organization, for example where they are elected local councillors speaking about domestic issues, can hardly be justified on the grounds of national security or prevention of public disorder. One of the first casualties of the ban was a song recorded by an Irish pop group with lyrics claiming that the 'Guildford 4' were innocent. The Home Secretary, who shortly afterwards referred the 'Guildford 4' conviction back to the Court of Appeal, must at least have shared their doubts, but the IBA still refused to allow the record to be played on radio or television.

THREE

Privacy

The right to privacy has many applications: it can mean freedom from snoopers, gossips and busybodies; or being treated by State officials with a measure of decency and dignity; or being entitled to indulge in harmless activities without observation or interference. At base, it is a right to be left alone, to be able to live some part of life behind a door marked 'do not disturb'. The guarantee in Article 8 of the European Convention of Human Rights, that 'Everyone has the right to respect for his private and family life, his home and his correspondence' reflects both the individual's psychological need to preserve an intrusion-free zone of personality and family, and the anguish and stress which can be suffered when that zone is violated. We shall see that the fond boast that 'an Englishman's home is his castle' needs revision in an age when the battlements are defenceless against electronic surveillance devices, journalists have no difficulty getting their foot in the drawbridge, and several hundred different kinds of officials are endowed by law with power to walk on the water of the moat.

EAVESDROPPING

The first recorded protection for personal privacy is a 1360 statute, still in force today, which provides that

> such as listen under walls or windows, or the eaves of a house, to hearken unto discourse, and thereupon to frame slanderous and mischievous tales, are a common nuisance, and are punishable by finding sureties for their good behaviour.

It is occasionally invoked to deal with those who install bugging devices in their neighbours' bedrooms, although a bind-over to keep the peace is hardly a satisfactory punishment for perverts whose activities have caused their neighbours to suffer nervous breakdowns. The absence of any modern statute incriminating prurient or malicious invasion of privacy makes Britain something of a haven for the peeping or listening Tom with access to infinity bugs (which pick up any conversation in a room), metallic contact bugs which can tap any telephone, stethoscope microphones which listen through walls, directional microphones which pick up conversations at fifty paces, infra-red cameras which see in the dark, microwave antennae which pick up and translate vibrations on window panes, and so on. These devices have been on open sale for many years, through specialist shops or mail-order advertisements in *Exchange & Mart* ('James Bond type bugging devices which listen to conversations up to 50 yards away without the person's knowledge – dangerous but what fun – only £19.00 each'). There is no law against the use of surreptitious surveillance devices, whether for fun or for profit, unless the device uses wires to intercept messages or to transmit electronically in a way that might interfere with a radio channel, in which case a minor offence will be committed against the Wireless Telegraphy Act 1949. In 1985 it was made an offence to intercept a telephone conversation without a Home Secretary's warrant, although the Interception of Communications Act does not cover bugging and other forms of surveillance which are used far more frequently than intercepts to monitor electronic communications.

The general legal principle is that everything is permitted which is not expressly prohibited, as Lord Bernstein discovered when he failed to stop aerial photography of his home.[1] The court did say that harassment by constant aerial surveillance and photographing of the plaintiff's every movement would be 'such a monstrous invasion of his privacy' that it might award damages for nuisance, but there is no law which deters surveillance by telephoto cameras and wireless listening devices which do not involve any trespass on private land. Most civilized countries have such laws, and a series of official reports from the Younger Committee on Privacy in 1972[2] to the Law Commission in 1981[3] have recommended criminal prohibitions against obtaining information and photographs by improper use of secret surveillance devices. But we still have no real deterrent against those who spy for prurience, profit or politics. The shadowy hypothetical presence of the electronic eavesdropper has made 'debugging' a growth industry – many company boardrooms are now swept not only by cleaners, but by counter-espionage experts.

The professional privacy-invader, the private detective, operates lucratively in an area where law is either non-existent or inadequate to deter abuse. Individuals cannot complain if they are profiled from public sources or observed going about their business, but many private investigators – of whom there are 10,000 employed in the UK – have no difficulty tapping into the Police National Computer, the DVLC, and repositories of confidential information in DHSS and other Government departments. If money is paid for the information then offences of corruption are committed, but many private detectives offer the service to clients none the less. Some private detectives have criminal convictions, and others are ex-police officers who resigned under a cloud, but there is no agency empowered to license, regulate or discipline them. While the Government is understandably reluctant to issue 'licences' which could easily be misrepresented to gullible members of the public as official sanction for requests to snoop, most Western countries have found ways to contain the behaviour of private detectives by regulatory authorities which can discipline or expel those whose conduct or methods involve unacceptable invasions of privacy. Such an agency would not, of course, be able to stop practices which are permitted by law: the use of lie detectors and 'psychological stress evaluations' to screen candidates for employment, for example, or the circulation amongst employers of 'black lists' of persons with records of trade-union activism. One private organization, the Economic League, supplies information on 'left-wingers' in trade unions to over 2,000 employers who subscribe to its black-list services. The failure of British law to develop any general right to privacy has allowed these practices to grow without any check.

In the United States, the courts have moulded the common law so as to award damages whenever a person's interest in seclusion, or in personal dignity and self-respect, or in being free from emotional upset, is interfered with by conduct which is regarded as intolerably anti-social. They have awarded damages in the following situations: installing tape-recorders secretly in hospital wards in order to hear the account given by the victim of an accident to her relatives; publishing lurid photographs of the victim of a car accident; publishing X-ray photographs of the deformed pelvis of a woman celebrity; photographing the body of the plaintiff's dead husband; photographing a plaintiff's mother's Siamese twins and publishing the picture. In none of these cases would the English courts be likely to afford any remedy to the victim.

Private information which is accurate may be circulated and published without any redress, unless it involves a breach of copyright (e.g. by the publication of family photographs without payment or permission) or a breach of confidence. The scope of this action is unclear: the few cases decided in relation to domestic confidences have mainly been brought by members of the Royal Family (who succeed) and pop stars (who fail). Thus the Duchess of Argyll was able to stop the Duke from publishing sordid details of their marriage,[4] and the Prince of Wales obtained an injunction against the publication of purported tape-recordings of pre-marital and long-distance conversations with Lady Diana, but John Lennon,[5] Tom Jones,[6] and Soraya Kashoggi[7] all failed to ban stories of their marital and extra-marital dalliances. No sensible distinction has emerged from those cases between public interest and public prurience, with the result that 'kiss and tell' stories are now staple fare of Sunday newspapers. The pop stars, television personalities and sports stars, the details of whose sexual performances are sold by erstwhile partners to the *News of the World*, must suffer in silence, victims of a new form of blackmail. Indeed, the crime of blackmail has become redundant with the rise of Rupert Murdoch: those possessed of sordid secrets about celebrities now offer them lawfully to newspapers for much larger sums of money.

This is just one of the disquieting developments as entrepreneurs take commercial advantage of the lack of any real remedy for breach of privacy. The courts are reluctant to act against them, on the principle that 'England is not a country where everything is forbidden except what is expressly permitted'.[8] There have been occasional legislative initiatives against the worst abuses – the Rehabilitation of Offenders Act withdraws protection from libel actions in the case of malicious publication of truthful details about very old criminal offences, and the Unsolicited Goods and Services Act makes it a criminal offence to send brochures describing or illustrating human sexual techniques to unsuspecting households, but successive Governments have consigned recommendations for more fundamental law reform to the 'too hard' basket. It may be that the courts will develop the common law, as in America, to provide

a more satisfactory remedy, and injunctions have been granted to stop
publication of confidential material (such as Myra Hindley's application
for parole and jockey John Francome's tapped telephone conversations)
when the information is of minimal public importance and has been
obtained by illegal methods.[9] There is also the possibility of victims of
invasion of privacy suing for wilful infliction of physical harm, if the
nervous shock occasioned by the invasion was foreseeable and has caused
long-term suffering.[10] It would take courage, however, for victims to
relive the trauma by bringing test cases, and the results, as the law now
stands, may not be worth the effort. When one plaintiff successfully sued
his neighbour for trespassing in his house to install a bugging device (so
that his bedroom conversation could be 'listened to and chuckled and
chortled over'), the court awarded damages of only £52.[11]

PRESS COUNCIL RULINGS

'The shortest and most satisfactory definition of privacy' Harold
Wilson suggested to the most recent Royal Commission on the Press,
'would be a clause which said "Newspapers will accord to the general
public the same rights of privacy they accord to their own proprietors, or
even the proprietors of other newspapers".' His cynicism was immediately justified by the refusal of journalists and editors to participate in
a confidential Royal Commission survey of their earnings and political
ties – even the editor of the *News of the World* had the effrontery to
complain that the survey invaded his privacy. The Royal Commission
found ample evidence, in the operations of the *News of the World* and its
ilk, of unsavoury snooping, deception, 'flagrant breaches of acceptable
standards' and 'inexcusable intrusions into privacy'.

The Royal Commission, which reported in 1977, castigated the
Press Council for failure to maintain proper ethical standards and pointed
out that no satisfactory form of discipline or redress exists to combat
wanton violation of a basic human right. The importance of these findings
is not confined to the public; they underline how journalists are sometimes forced to degrade themselves and their profession by editors prepared to sacrifice common decency on the altar of circulation. While
Russell Harty lay dying in hospital, one journalist posed as a doctor in an
attempt to obtain his treatment notes, while another sent messages to

fellow patients on the intensive-care ward offering large sums of money in return for information about the television star's condition.

Press Council adjudications and declarations on privacy carry little or no weight amongst the editors of national newspapers. The Council is a private body, funded by newspaper proprietors as a useful pretence that the Press is capable of self-regulation. It has no powers to award compensation to victims or to discipline editors or journalists other than by making disapproving noises when one of the routine breaches of its rules causes a public protest.[12] It has published a *Declaration of Principle* on the subject of privacy, the nub of which is:

> The publication of information about the private lives or concerns of individuals without their consent is only acceptable if there is a legitimate public interest overriding the right of privacy . . . The public interest . . . must be a legitimate and proper public interest and not only a prurient or morbid curiosity.

This *Declaration* has had no impact, and the tendency to invade personal privacy for stories of no genuine public interest has increased since it was promulgated. Pictures and stories which detail the romantic entanglements or private griefs of people who are not public figures are published with regularity, but whether they receive the censure they deserve will often depend on whether a public-spirited individual or a local welfare organization is sufficiently appalled to overcome the obstacles of the complaints procedure. The Press Council shows much more vigilance in its efforts to protect members of the Royal Family. It has even met in emergency session to condemn the hounding of Prince Charles and Princess Diana, and to condemn publication of pictures of the pregnant Princess on a Caribbean beach out of bounds to all but the telephoto lenses of the Fleet Street *paparazzi*. But its actions have had no effect. The *Sun* did apologize for the incident, taking the opportunity to reprint the controversial pictures to illustrate its apology, under the banner, 'THIS IS WHAT THE ROW'S ALL ABOUT FOLKS!' It then proceeded to demonstrate the genuineness of its concern for Royal privacy by selling the pictures to newspapers around the world.

There are numerous other examples of regular defiance of Council rulings in the sphere of privacy. It has repeatedly ruled that 'it is neither fair nor acceptable for newspapers to publish detrimental information about a child just because his parents are well known', yet the expulsion from school or the arrest or merely the interviewing by police of any child of a famous person is inevitably attended by Press publicity. In 1980, after Professor Harry Bedson's suicide was partly attributed by the coroner to Press harassment after an outbreak of smallpox in his Birmingham University department, the Council declared that people under stress as the result of bereavement or involvement in a public crisis should not be put under pressure by the Press.[13] In 1981 it upheld a complaint that a newspaper had harassed the family of the donor for a child heart-transplant, and directed newspapers to cooperate in arrangements to relieve the cumulative effect of inquiries on people suffering severe personal grief. In 1983, it was driven to conclude that both the 'Yorkshire Ripper's' wife and the relatives of his victims 'were harassed by the media ferociously and callously'.[14]

The Council has failed to give workable guidance on the 'public interest' exception to its privacy rule. In the Maureen Colquhoun case, for example, it announced that 'members of Parliament are entitled to a degree of protection in their private lives'. Maureen Colquhoun lost this protection because she was an MP 'who has taken a very strong stand on feminist issues'. The public was therefore 'entitled' to know that she was sharing a house with another woman. Since this seems perfectly consistent with feminism, wherein lay the genuine interest, of the sort which might have been aroused had she taken up residence with a notorious male chauvinist? Her relationship, the Council pompously declared, was a matter of public interest because it was 'capable of affecting the performance of her public duties'. If this is the test, then clearly MPs (and other public figures) have no right of privacy at all. Any private or family matter is 'capable' of affecting public performance: the correct test for publication should be whether there is reasonable evidence that it has *in fact* affected ability to do a public job.

Of course, the scope of private matters which do not bear on public performance is necessarily limited: the hypocrite who preaches a return to Victorian values whilst committing adultery, the left-wing politician who takes advantage of private medical treatment, the bankrupt financier who lives it up in casinos and the dowager who charters an airliner to fly her pet dogs to a tax haven are all fair game. Social butterflies can hardly complain if their activities provoke gossip – there is a difference between snooping and recording the obvious. What powerful people do with their money or their credit is always a matter for the public domain, although what they do to each other in the privacy of their own houses deserves some veil of secrecy.

However, it must by now be clear that the Press Council is utterly incapable of deterring unjustifiable invasions of privacy by the popular Press, wherever the interests of circulation or partisan politics are at stake. The abuses are growing worse: in 1986 the *Sun* published, over three full columns on its front page, a picture of the victim of a rape at an Ealing vicarage, taken as she was leaving her church the following Sunday. The victim's family told the Press Council that the thin black line masking her eyes still left no doubt of her identity, and the *Sun*'s coverage had been deeply distressing. A year later, the Council condemned the newspaper for taking and publishing the photograph. 'Both were insensitive and wholly unwarranted intrusions into privacy at a time of deep distress for the subject and neither served any public interest.' The *Sun*, of course, showed no remorse. Its managing editor had told the Council, with more than the usual display of humbug, that the newspaper had a duty to present rape as a sordid crime and the picture was published to highlight the victim's 'ordinary, girl-next-door qualities'.[15]

Such abuses make a strong case for a legal right to privacy, enforceable in courts empowered to compensate victims for the distress they have suffered. A Press Council which had real power, either by statute or contract, to censure breaches of its *Declaration of Principle* by front-page condemnations published in the offending newspaper, and to oblige the payment of compensation to victims, might provide a satisfactory alternative. But since newspaper proprietors fund the Press Council, there is little prospect that they will ever allow it to affect their profits. In other countries, a remedy has been found by establishing an ombudsman or Privacy Commissioner, with powers to conduct investigations into abuses. But despite occasional initiatives by MPs there is little Government resolve to do anything about the unjustifiable publication of sensitive private information: 'sneaking' on personal behaviour is a much-enjoyed national pastime (as the circulation figures of the *News of the World* and *Private Eye* attest), which is ironic in view of the punishments reserved by the Official Secrets Act for those who sneak on official misconduct.

CONTROLLING THE DATA BANKS

There are over a million people in Britain employed in the business of collecting information on fellow citizens – not by spying or snooping, but simply by gathering facts and forms and feeding them into files and computerized data banks. The average adult has private information about him- or herself on over two hundred separate files, and by 1982 Government departments alone boasted 220 different computerized data banks. From birth certificate to death certificate, our lives are printed out on school and NHS records, tax and VAT returns, insurance, mortgage and credit ratings, social-security files, motor-vehicle licences, police records and the like. The proposed poll tax will require computerized registers of all adults in Britain, accumulating personal details and enabling everyone's movements to be monitored.

The gossip of neighbours has nothing like the potential for damage of the chattering of computers, as they link and match scraps of information from different data banks to build up an incomplete jigsaw of the individual on record. As computer technology enters its fifth generation, processing psychological and motivational analysis to determine fitness for jobs or promotion, the implications for privacy become particularly serious. There may be data so sensitive that they should not be on file – details of sexual behaviour or past illnesses or voting habits. The data may be out of date, such as a psychiatric report on teenage depression or an old criminal conviction, raked up to tip the odds against being offered a job or a loan. The data may be inaccurate: it is common for individuals to be recorded as bad credit risks after they have simply refused to pay for defective goods, or have been confused with people of similar name who have criminal records. The more that hard facts rub shoulders with unchecked gossip and ill-considered opinions, the more the prospects for fair evaluation of an individual recede. We look to the law to provide adequate guarantees that confidential data will not be transmitted without permission, that there are safeguards against information being used for purposes for which it was not provided, and that data which have been collected are accurate and up to date.[16]

Information is not property which can be 'stolen' for the purposes of the law of theft, so no offence is committed by tricking banks and insurance companies and hospitals into giving information about their client accounts.[17] In 1982, a newspaper hired a private investigator for £500 to report on the private life of an MP: in a matter of days he was able to obtain access to criminal records, bank statements, credit-agency reports and insurance files. Subterfuge thrives on the negligence of data handlers – one survey in the *Lancet* concluded that anyone wearing a white coat and stethoscope could obtain any record he cared to name from an NHS hospital. A social-work lecturer conducted an experiment by having students call up different agencies on various pretexts to obtain information about his clients, and only once was the request refused. The Law Commission has, since 1974, consistently pointed out this gap in the criminal law: to the relief of the private-investigation industry there has been no attempt to fill it by creating an offence of dishonestly obtaining sensitive private information.

The Data Protection Act

In 1984 major legislative action was at last taken to regulate data banks. The Data Protection Act owed more to EEC pressure than Orwellian fears: the Council of Europe's Data Protection Convention required signatories to withhold transmission of data to countries which had no laws to protect it, and British firms had started to lose overseas contracts which involved the swapping of information, because European businesses were not permitted to deal with firms in countries which could not guarantee the confidentiality of computerized information. The Act requires all companies which process or use computerized personal data to register their operations with the Data Protection Registrar in sufficient detail to enable his office to be satisfied, if necessary after inspection, that use of computerized data is in accordance with principles laid down in the Act. Citizens may inspect the Register, and may apply, on payment of a small fee, to inspect any information which is being held about them and may apply to a court to order correction or removal of any factual errors.

The 'data-protection principles' which all companies should observe, on pain of being struck off the Register and hence unable to use or collect computerized personal data, are:

1. The information to be contained in personal data shall be obtained, and personal data shall be processed, fairly and lawfully.

2. Personal data shall be held only for one or more specified and lawful purposes.

3. Personal data held for any purpose shall not be used or disclosed in any manner incompatible with that purpose.

4. Personal data held for any purpose shall be adequate, relevant and not excessive in relation to that purpose.

5. Personal data shall be accurate and, where necessary, kept up to date.

6. Personal data held for any purpose shall not be kept for longer than is necessary for that purpose.

7. An individual shall be entitled:

    (a) at reasonable intervals and without undue delay or expense:

        (i) to be informed by any data user whether he holds personal data of which that individual is the subject; and

        (ii) to access to any such data held by a data user; and

    (b) where appropriate, to have such data corrected or erased.

    8. Appropriate security measures shall be taken against unauthorized access to, or alteration, disclosure or destruction of, personal data and against accidental loss or destruction of personal data.

The Act requires all data users who 'process personal data automatically' to register, giving details of the kind of information they collect, their purpose, sources, and the persons or organization to whom it may be disclosed. The Registrar may (subject to an appeal to the Data Protection Tribunal) refuse to register where insufficient information is provided, or where he is satisfied that the data-protection principles are not being observed, and any business which processes personal data without being registered commits a criminal offence, punishable by an unlimited fine at Crown Court. The Registrar has certain powers to inspect the premises of data users, to obtain search warrants for this purpose, and to serve an 'enforcement notice' as a warning before taking de-registration proceedings. The Act's provisions relating to rights of citizen access allow 'data subjects' (in the unlovely computerspeak terminology adopted by the statute) to make a request to see copies of information held about them which is not exempt, does not identify other individuals who have provided the information, and relates to facts and opinions but not to the 'future intentions' of the data user (e.g. prospects for promotion of the data subject). The business must respond within forty days: if the information turns out to be inaccurate, the applicant can obtain compensation for any harm suffered and a court order to correct factual errors and erase opinions and assessments made on the basis of facts which are false.

There are, needless to say, broad exemptions for citizen access to information held by police, prosecution authorities and tax departments, and the Home Secretary may exclude any review of 'information as to the physical or mental health of the data subject' held by Government departments or local authorities or voluntary agencies. 'National Security' is a catch-all exemption from the Act, decided conclusively by a ministerial certificate.

The Data Protection Act came into full operation in November 1987, and it is too early to judge how effective it will be in encouraging professionalism and caution in the handling of data and permitting rights of access and correction. Its overwhelming defect is that it applies only to computerized information: data users who wish to breach every principle in the Act can continue to do so with a manual filing system. There is ample scope for companies to make applications for access difficult, by delaying any response for the full forty days and insisting on extravagant requirements for applicants to prove their identity. The compensation provisions are grossly inadequate, as damages may only be awarded for inaccurate information compiled directly by the data user, and not for inaccurate material supplied to the user by malevolent or incompetent third parties. This kind of rumour and gossip is, of course, precisely the kind of information which is likely to prove most damaging. The Home Office justified this exemption by asserting that 'Where a data user records inaccurate information supplied by someone else, the data are accurate. They are an accurate record of what someone else said'[18] – a distinction of which Pooh-Bah would have been proud. The result is that the victim of false information maliciously provided to a data user cannot either obtain compensation from the user for circulating it, or obtain the name of the malicious person who provided it in order to sue for defamation.

Some serious deficiencies have already become apparent in the Data Protection Act's 'protection'. The most dangerous data errors are in criminal records, motor-vehicle registration details, and 'wanted person' information transferred to the Police National Computer (PNC) to which subjects are allowed no access at all. Yet official access to the PNC is vouchsafed to Government departments and authorities and to numerous professional bodies and organizations ranging from the BBC to the National Gallery, and improper access is obtained by many private-detective agencies. Almost 120,000 calls are made to the PNC every day, but very few are monitored to ensure that the request is *bona fide*, despite the inevitable 'Home Office guidelines'. Moreover, local police computers store information provided by 'collators' at each station, which includes gossip and innuendo about persons who are not even suspected of crime. These compilations fall outside the provisions of the Act.

The Data Protection Act permits access only to personal information held on computer. There is, however, a legally enforceable right of access to information held on any personal file by credit agencies,[19] and the 1987 Access to Personal Files Act will allow individuals to inspect and correct manual files held on them by local council social services and housing authorities. This Act covers all factual data and personal opinion recorded since it was passed (although not statements of future intentions) and it provides that the Home Secretary may make regulations to include other local-authority records within its ambit.

Security data

Special problems arise in relation to data which are collected by Special Branch and by MI5 on persons who are thought to harbour 'subversive' thoughts or intentions. MI5 is said to have a central registry with dossiers on 500,000 citizens, and the Special Branch (with whom it works closely) has some 2,000 officers throughout the country collecting information. Both services have computers, which are outside the provisions of the Data Protection Act, and access to the fruits of telephone-tapping, mail interception, electronic surveillance, infiltrators and the GCHQ monitoring of overseas communications. The secret directive establishing MI5 in 1953 invites its Director-General to 'arrange to have such access to the records of Government departments and agencies as you may deem necessary for the purposes of your work' and to 'arrange that all Government departments and agencies submit to you for inclusion in your records all information bearing on security which may come into their possession'.[20] This directive would suggest that security-service files on individuals will contain material from the Inland Revenue and DHSS, together of course with reports from informers, agents and 'assets' in different walks of life.

The collection and transfer of information about individuals by the Special Branch (and, for that matter, by GCHQ, military intelligence and MI6) falls outside the provisions of the Data Protection Act and is entirely unregulated by law. There are serious questions about the criteria upon which targets are chosen and the basis upon which information is divulged to those parties. In 1981 Madelaine Haigh, a teacher who had no political involvements, wrote to her local paper complaining about the lack of controls over American nuclear missiles on British soil. In consequence, she was clumsily investigated by her local Special Branch, who gained entry to her home under a subterfuge and lied about the reason for their interest in her. The Chief Constable criticized them for 'unprofessional' behaviour, but strenuously defended their right to investigate anyone with views which might lead them to participate in public protests. Another Chief Constable, John Alderson, has admitted to discovering that 40 per cent of the information on the files of his Special Branch related to persons who posed no security or criminal threat, but who were merely outspoken on public issues or members of pressure groups. In 1985 the Home Secretary disclosed the inevitable 'Home Office guidelines' which recommend against data collection on persons 'solely' because they espouse unpopular causes, but as Madelaine Haigh's case shows, the blanket label of 'potential subversive' may be attached simply by assuming that those who feel strongly enough to write to newspapers may one day be prepared to break the law in the same cause.

The collection and dissemination of secret information on individuals by MI5 is to be 'regulated' by the Security Service Act (see later, page 155) which the Government introduced in 1989. This measure came about as a direct response to applications to the European Court of Human Rights by Harriet Harman MP and Patricia Hewitt, who had been NCCL officials at a time when that organization, like CND and various trade unions, had been targeted by MI5 as 'subversive'. In 1984 an ex-MI5 officer named Cathy Massiter revealed this surveillance on a television programme, and the victims complained to Strasbourg that it breached their right to privacy guaranteed by the European Convention.

It was apparent from recent European Court decisions that they would succeed: their right to privacy had been invaded by secret collection of information on them by an organization which had no legal powers or even legal existence, and against whose behaviour they had no remedy. The Government introduced the Security Service bill in an effort to meet the minimum standards required by the Convention, and in the hope of allaying fears generated by publication of *Spycatcher*, in which Peter Wright confessed to 'burgling and bugging his way around London' in the service of MI5. Wright and his cronies had by this time been shown to have collected private (and often inaccurate) information about a large number of left-wing politicians, trade-union leaders and friends of Harold Wilson, and to have used this in attempts to destroy or damage their careers. It transpired that even in the late 1970s MI5 paranoia had been secretly and irresponsibly at work in the BBC, stopping the employment of the respected journalist Isabel Hilton because she had as a student been Secretary of a China friendship association regarded as subversive, and trying to stop Anna Ford from reading the news on the BBC because an ex-boy-friend had been a Communist. It is highly unlikely that the Security Service Act will provide satisfactory safeguards against resurgence of such McCarthy-like behaviour, and it is doubtful whether it satisfies the minimum requirements of the European Convention.

Under the Act, MI5 is entitled to collect and to use information to the extent that is necessary for the protection of 'national security'. This term is not defined other than by examples (which are not exhaustive) including 'actions intended to overthrow or undermine parliamentary democracy by political, industrial or violent means'. The notion of undermining Parliament by political means seems a veiled invitation to maintain surveillance on political agitation outside the mainstream parties – even the campaign to introduce a Bill of Rights has been described by the Prime Minister as 'undermining parliamentary democracy'. The definition of 'national security', of course, may be very much wider – the Government White Paper in 1985 which led to the Interception of Communications Act defined 'the interests of national security' to include steps taken 'in support of the Government's defence and foreign policies'. The only limitation on the security service is that it must not 'take any action to further the interests of a political party' – a clause inserted as a result of Wright's admission to participating in a plot to bring down the Wilson Government and Massiter's claim that information collected on CND found its way to Conservative politicians bent on discrediting Labour's defence policies. The Act recognizes that MI5 may need to trespass, burgle and steal to obtain information: such actions merely require the Home Secretary to sign a warrant. MI5 is free to use the private information it collects as it sees fit in the national interest, except to influence employment decisions, in which case it must follow procedures which the Home Secretary will authorize. The Minister will not be required, under this clause, to approve specific MI5 blackballs on individual careers, but only the procedures by which they are thrown (presumably, we will insist that such decisions are made at a senior level within the service).

The Act, in effect, serves to legitimize every complaint hitherto made about the operation of MI5, other than its involvement in promoting party-political interests. There are new safeguards, modelled on the scheme established in 1985 for the supervision of telephone tapping (see later, page 120). A tribunal of senior lawyers shall be appointed to receive and investigate complaints from members of the public who believe they have been burgled or black-listed or have otherwise suffered as targets of MI5. The complaint will only be upheld, however, if the targeting was based on information that MI5 had no reason to believe was true, or (in the case of a Home Secretary's warrant) that it was granted for reasons that no Minister in his right mind could conceive was really necessary in the interests of national security. The tribunal's function is so restricted that it offers no meaningful oversight – the bill specifically provides that it is 'reasonable' to target entirely innocuous complainants if they happen to be members of a group 'regarded by the service as requiring investigation'. (Madelaine Haigh would on this basis have no cause for complaint if she were monitored by MI5, so long as it regarded CND as 'requiring investigation'.) The tribunal has certain powers to refer targeting decisions to a senior judge, who will be appointed to review the working of the Act and to report to the Prime Minister, although any part of his report which might be prejudicial to the functioning of the service (including, presumably, revelation of any targeting decision) will not be made public. In short, the complaints procedure to be established by this Act offers no remedy for persons who are victims of mistaken judgements rather than mistaken facts. Even those who are targeted as a result of clerical errors and administrative confusion of names will rarely have cause to complain, for the simple reason that the Government's new Official Secrets Act of 1989 (see later, page 139) makes it a crime to reveal any detail at all of MI5's operations, even when such revelations (e.g. of mistakes in targeting) are in the public interest. There will be no more Cathy Massiters: the Government's 1989 legislative package is designed to outlaw the very class of revelation which forced it to bring MI5 within the law in the first place.

POLICE SEARCHES

The great boast that 'an Englishman's home is his castle' goes back to a court case in 1604,[21] and was much embellished by several splendid decisions in the 1760s when the courts awarded damages to John Wilkes and his radical supporters who had their homes ransacked by Government officers in search of evidence to connect them with seditious newspapers. These decisions were based, not on any considerations of personal privacy, but upon the pre-eminent respect that English law has always accorded rights of property ownership,[22] although they inspired William Pitt's famous declaration:

> The poorest man may in his cottage bid defiance to the Crown. It may be frail – its roof may shake – the wind may enter – the rain may enter – but the King of England cannot enter – all his force dares not cross the threshold of the ruined tenement.

The modern council flat is a good deal less sacrosanct, however, since police need do no more than obtain the rubber stamp of a lay Justice on warrants permitting them to enter, search and seize property related to a myriad of possible offences. The heady defiance of John Wilkes is no longer permitted to his journalistic successors like Duncan Campbell, whose personal library was entirely uplifted by a police pantechnicon in 1978 and whose films about *The Secret Society* were removed from the cutting rooms of the BBC in 1986. The modern counterparts of the eighteenth-century printers and booksellers who could slam the door on 'the King's messengers' are powerless to withstand the warrants and 'writs of assistance' (see later, page 118) displayed by police and customs officials to remove dangerous books from their shelves: 'Operation Tiger' in 1985 denuded one Bloomsbury bookshop, Gay's the Word, of its stock of literature by Gore Vidal, Oscar Wilde, Jean Genet and Christopher Isherwood.

The Police and Criminal Evidence Act (PACE) 1984 now largely governs official search-and-seize operations, and confirms the police power to enter private premises whenever there is reason to believe there may be evidence of serious (and certain not-so-serious) offences within. Although it discourages 'dawn raids' and ensures that searches are carried out reasonably and without obvious provocation, it pins far too much faith on the ability of lay Justices to control the extensive police power which a search warrant represents. From the viewpoint of the citizen, the drawback of PACE is not so much that it awards greater powers to search and seize, but that it fails (except in its special provisions relating to confidential material) to provide a proper system of review.

The eighteenth-century cases of *Entick* v. *Carrington* and *John Wilkes* v. *Lord Halifax* at least established the permanent principle that no State official may enter a citizen's premises without the authority of law. Halifax, convinced by the informers he interviewed that Wilkes had written a seditious attack on the King and his Government, himself issued a warrant for Wilkes's arrest and for the search of his home to remove all his papers. Wilkes sued for trespass, and was awarded £1,000 in damages (the equivalent of £200,000 today) while crowds in the street roared their approval of 'Wilkes and Liberty'. The court ruled that Lord Halifax, as Secretary of State, was not a Justice of the Peace and had no legal power to issue a warrant. Moreover, the 'general warrant' to seize any evidence of any crime by anybody was itself illegal: search warrants had to specify the kind of material which was sought, and only material of that specific description could be seized.[23]

What is left of 'Wilkes and Liberty' more than two centuries later? It remains the case that police officers who enter without a warrant are liable for damages for trespassing on private property unless they either enter by invitation, or to make or follow up an arrest, or to put down a breach of the peace. Of course the police, like all members of the public, have an implied licence to go up the garden path to the front door of a house to make legitimate inquiries: they become trespassers if they refuse to leave within a reasonably short time of being ordered out by the occupier or owner.[24] The case of *McArdle* v. *Wallace* illustrates these restrictions: One night policemen found new car parts in a passage outside a factory. They proceeded along the passage to the yard of a café in order to pursue their inquiries about the parts, which they reasonably believed to have been stolen. The café proprietor's son ordered them off the premises, but they did not leave and asked further questions about car parts, whereupon the son struck the policemen. The son was prosecuted for assaulting the policemen in the execution of their duty. The court pointed out that the policemen had no reasonable grounds for expecting to find and apprehend the thief on the premises, so that they had no right to remain once somebody acting with the authority of the occupier asked them to leave. Accordingly the son was not guilty – indeed, the café proprietor could successfully have sued them for trespass.[25]

In other respects, however, the chant of 'Wilkes and Liberty' has failed to echo down the corridors of legal time. In 1763, the Chief Justice declaimed

> that to enter a man's house by virtue of a nameless warrant, in order to find evidence, is worse than the Spanish Inquisition . . . the Government sought to exercise arbitrary power, violating Magna Carta, and attempting to destroy the liberty of the Kingdom with the general search warrant.

More recent court decisions, extended by PACE, have virtually turned every search warrant into a general warrant. Section 19 of the 1984 Act, ominously headed 'General Power of Seizure', is precisely that: once lawfully on private premises, police may seize anything they reasonably believe to be evidence of any offence, whether or not related to the offence under investigation and whether or not that offence was committed by the person under investigation. The only condition is that they must believe that seizure is necessary to prevent the evidence being 'concealed lost altered or destroyed' – a belief which will normally be entertained about any evidence of crime. Section 19 undermines the 'search warrants – safeguards' section of PACE, with its requirements that in applying for such warrants police shall 'identify so far as is practicable, the articles or persons sought', that entry should if possible be at 'a reasonable hour', and that the search 'may only be a search to the extent required for the purpose for which the warrant was issued'.

The fundamental weakness of the search-warrant procedure is that it relies on lay Justices to safeguard citizens' rights. Lawyers have long known what academics are just beginning to discover from research, namely that lay Justices almost invariably 'rubber stamp' police requests to sign search and arrest warrants. Indeed, many police stations select a few favoured local Justices who can be relied upon to issue warrants at any time of the day or night without asking difficult questions, and direct all warrant requests to them. Justices of the Peace are not lawyers, but local worthies who do not critically examine police requests – often made on their doorstep late at night – to issue warrants on 'reliable information'. PACE requires that warrant applications shall be supported by 'an information in writing' – generally a formal document providing little actual information – and that constables must answer on oath any questions that JPs may ask. A recent study of thirty-two separate warrant applications revealed that only in two cases were serious questions asked, and in most areas it is virtually unheard of for a JP to refuse to sign a warrant.[26] (If one does, he or she is unlikely to be asked again.)

It is unfortunate that Parliament grasped at such a weak reed to support its 'safeguards' for searches of private homes. In 1968, there was a great fuss about a JP who acted as a 'mere formality' in granting a warrant to search Lady Diana Cooper's home for drugs, after police had received an anonymous telephone call that turned out to be a hoax. Although it is technically possible to quash a warrant that has been issued without adequate scrutiny, and to sue for trespass where a warrant has been wrongfully obtained, a successful legal action is made virtually impossible by the paucity of detail required on the 'written information', and the fact that Justices are not required to give written reasons for signing the warrant. As the leading work on the law of search and seizure concludes,

> The lack of any record of reasons undermines the protection for citizens which a judicial procedure for vetting applications for warrants is designed to provide: it becomes difficult to make the officer or the magistrate accountable for their behaviour ... the warrant is likely to be uninformative, and the provisions in the Act do not adequately protect an individual's civil law remedies.[27]

Seizure of confidential material

The protection of scrutiny by a Crown Court judge rather than a magistrate is required in cases where police wish to seize confidential papers – including medical and social-work records, journalistic material and personal records created in the name of any business or profession. Where such documents are sought for the purpose of a police investigation into a 'serious arrestable offence' (see earlier, page 35), a Crown Court judge must be satisfied that police have reasonable grounds to believe that they are likely to be of substantial evidential value and that their seizure under a warrant is likely to be for the public benefit. (Certain documents of a highly confidential nature are classed as 'excluded material', and can only be seized if the judge is satisfied that a warrant would have been granted under an enactment prior to PACE.) The importance of the protection awarded to 'special procedure' and 'excluded' material is not only that a Crown Court judge rather than a magistrate decides whether to issue a warrant, but that the owner or occupier is entitled to be represented at the hearing, which may be in open court, to argue that the warrant should not be granted.

These are complicated provisions, but their very existence has been an encouragement to law-enforcement agencies to make use of them to obtain information in circumstances where, prior to PACE, no search power existed or where social scruples might have stayed the police hand. It was hardly surprising that newspapers were the first to experience the 'special procedure' provisions, as police in Bristol went on a fishing expedition to obtain all photographs, whether published or not, taken by Press photographers who had covered a 'riot' in the St Paul's area of the city. Prior to PACE, media organizations had refused to hand over untransmitted film and photographs taken at public-order disturbances, fearing that cameramen could be put in danger if they were perceived by the mob as agents of the police. This argument cut no ice with the judge: there was reason to believe that pictures of a fast-moving series of incidents would help to identify persons committing serious crimes, and the public benefit from handing them over to the police outweighed any added danger to photographers or the possibility that sources in the area would no longer cooperate with the Press.[28] ITN protested loudly when its untransmitted film was seized by South African security police investigating black protesters, but the Bristol decision shows that the same result would be reached in Britain. What the decision means in practice, of course, is that photographers and news media will now destroy untransmitted film of riots and violent demonstrations rather than run the risk of being subjected to an order to hand it over to the police.

In all cases involving contests between confidentiality and police applications for access, there will be a clash between the right of privacy and the demand to prosecute serious offences effectively. Crown Court judges will have to weigh the testimony about 'public benefit' presented on each side. The only class of material which is exempt from seizure under any circumstances is that relating to communications between lawyer and client, or between lawyers and third parties (such as potential witnesses) in relation to legal proceedings. Documents covered by 'legal professional privilege' are sacrosanct: the law, understandably, regards it as the highest possible good that citizens should be entitled to take legal advice without fear that their confessions should be made public.

'STOP AND SEARCH' POWERS

By far the most controversial police power to invade personal privacy has, at least in recent years, been the power to stop and search citizens in the street. 'Operation Swamp', which preceded the Brixton riots of 1981, involved 943 stops on suspicion of theft – over half of black people, more than two-thirds of whom were under twenty-one. The arrest score was one burglary charge, one attempted robbery and twenty minor thefts. When two young police officers noticed a black minicab driver put money in his sock, they suspected – with no more evidence – that it might be the proceeds of drug dealing. So they searched him, in full view of a gathering crowd, while he laughingly explained that he kept his money there for safe-keeping. Undeterred by finding him 'clean', they began to search his car, while the crowd started to mutter about 'police harassment'. This incident, against the background of hostility engendered by 'Operation Swamp', sparked off the worst rioting Britain has seen this century. The two young policemen, Lord Scarman observed, acted without judgement or discretion.[29]

Although the power to search for stolen goods is necessary to combat street crime, there must be safeguards against police officers acting on 'hunches' which are no more than prejudices. The power to stop and search for drugs has been especially open to abuse: in the sixties, long hair and beards or attendance at a pop festival was enough to provoke police suspicion, and ten years later it was being young and black and standing on a street corner (or driving a BMW). Studies done shortly before PACE revealed that about one third of all police stops were random, in the sense that there was no cause to suspect the individual detained, other than that he was black or young or walking in a neighbourhood associated with drug deals. Fewer than 10 per cent of those stopped and searched were found to be in breach of any law, and generally the offences uncovered were trivial (such as possession of a small amount of cannabis).

PACE does not, unfortunately, confine the power to cases where possession of stolen property or 'Class A' drugs is suspected. However, the Act has introduced a number of safeguards by requiring constables to justify their decision to stop, both to the suspect at the time and subsequently in a written report. The Code of Practice stresses that 'reasonable suspicion' must be founded on fact, and have a concrete basis which can be evaluated objectively. Suspicion must relate to a fact about the individual, and not to the group or class to which he or she belongs.

> A person's colour of itself can never be a reasonable ground for suspicion. The mere fact alone that a person is carrying a particular kind of property or is dressed in a certain way or has a certain hairstyle is likewise not of itself sufficient. Nor is the fact that a person is known to have a previous conviction for unlawful possession of an article.[30]

The extent to which this Code of Practice has been put into practice is doubtful: the temptation to 'show them who's boss' in city areas frequented by defiant young blacks is difficult for police to resist, especially where there are resident complaints of real street crime such as mugging and burglary. At least police stops in public must now be carried out with a minimum of decorum: the power only permits them to remove a suspect's outer coat, jacket and gloves.[31] Any more intimate search will require the exercise of a power of arrest, and consequent detention.

OTHER SEARCH POWERS

Several hundred different officials have been given statutory powers to enter private homes, generally after court orders and usually for entirely acceptable purposes like reading the gas and electricity meters or checking up on the welfare of children. VAT inspectors have the most draconian powers of search and seizure, but only after obtaining a warrant from a High Court judge. The Court of Appeal was very critical of the zeal with which dawn raids were conducted on the homes of those suspected of revenue offences in the *Rossminster* case,[32] when the bedrooms of five-year-olds were turned over in search for cheque-books, although others may feel this is an occupational hazard for very young children who have active trading accounts.

One constitutional anomaly which invites abuse is the 'writ of assistance', an ancient prerogative granted to customs officers searching for contraband. This curious document, couched in what was doubtless common parlance when it originated 300 years ago (it begins 'To all and singular our officers and Ministers – Greeting') is issued by the 'Queen's Remembrancer' at the beginning of each reign, and contains a blanket power for every customs officer carrying a copy to search any premises at any time and to seize smuggled goods. It is a general warrant which is executed, without any judicial or magisterial scrutiny, on about 500 occasions each year, often for no better reason than that customs officers (who have the alternative power to obtain a magistrate's warrant) have a sentimental attachment to this relic of despotic royal power. On over half the occasions on which the writ is run, no smuggled goods are discovered – which suggests that it is being abused to conduct raids on suspicions which a court, if asked, might not find reasonable. There are no 'codes of practice' to govern the execution of the writ, which was used as the basis for the Customs and Excise assault on books by, for or about homosexuals imported by Gay's the Word bookshop. The 'writ of assistance' has produced one great historic consequence, namely the American Revolution. Oppressive use of these writs by British customs officials to raid Boston merchants in efforts to extract revenue for George III was, according to the US Supreme Court, 'perhaps the most prominent event which inaugurated the resistance of the colonies to the oppression of the mother country'.[33]

In recent years the Chancery Division of the High Court has provided a means whereby private plaintiffs in civil actions can search the homes of defendants and seize disputed property. This exceptional remedy was developed to enable film and record companies to deal with 'pirates' who produce counterfeit articles or simply run off copies of tapes and cassettes in direct breach of copyright. Until 1983, film and video piracy was a minor offence and police were not much interested in it: the producers had to band together to take civil action against persons who were capable of selling or hiding the pirate copies long before the action came to trial. The courts, with good intentions but without the ability to control the consequences (a defect which commonly character-izes judicial law-making), sat in secret to issue *Anton Pillar* orders (which required suspected pirates to admit the plaintiff's solicitors to their prem-ises to inspect their stock and carry off items relevant to their breach-of-copyright claim) and *Mareva* injunctions (which froze the bank accounts of the alleged pirates). Solicitors were generally accompanied by private detectives, and these raiding parties sometimes resulted in the closing down of High Street video shops and the ransacking of premises allegedly used for copying tapes.

In 1985 the High Court, in the first contested case resulting from an *Anton Pillar* raid, awarded £10,000 damages in trespass against solici-tors who had over-zealously executed the order and Mr Justice Scott expressed serious misgivings about the manner in which such orders had been applied for and carried out.

> What is to be said of the *Anton Pillar* procedure which, on a regular and institutionalized basis, is depriving citizens of their property and closing down their businesses by orders made *ex parte*, on applications of which they know nothing and at which they cannot be heard, by orders which they are bound, on pain of committal, to obey, even if wrongly made? . . . even villains ought not to be deprived of their property by proceedings at which they cannot be heard.[34]

The court emphasized the need for applicants to produce overwhelming evidence of piracy causing considerable damage and of imminent danger of destruction of evidence before *Anton Pillar* orders could be made. The remedy should henceforth be confined to highly exceptional cases, and should not be granted at all where there is an allegation of criminal conduct capable of proper police investigation. The need for widespread *Anton Pillar* action only arose because police forces did not perceive copyright theft as criminal behaviour: legislation in 1983 which massively increased the punishment for piracy has changed that perception, and there should now be less scope for court-approved invasions of privacy by private litigants.

TELEPHONE TAPPING

Telephone tapping and mail interceptions are conducted by Post Office employees at the request of police and security-service officials who have obtained a warrant from the Home Secretary authorizing the intercept for a particular period of time. The Home Secretary is a party politician whose ministerial duties leave little time for proper discharge of the serious responsibility of authorizing State invasion of the privacy of many thousands of citizens each year. Although there were only 252 telecommunications warrants and 72 postal intercept warrants in force at the beginning of 1988, many of these related to organizations and it has been estimated that up to one million private communications are intercepted each year.[35] There can be no doubt that the State requires powers of interception in order to gather information about serious crime and terrorism, but these powers are not limited by law to acceptable and definable targets. As a result, interception as practised in the UK has three disadvantages: it is not used to convict criminals; there is insufficient independent safeguard against abuse; and there is a good deal of unnecessary paranoia amongst those whose telephones malfunction.

Given the historic principle of *Entick* v. *Carrington* that an official has no power to interfere with a citizen unless that official can prove affirmatively that the law confers on him such a power, it is surprising that the first inquiry into telephone tapping, conducted by a group of Privy Councillors led by Lord Birkett in 1957, was not more concerned about a practice for which it could find no clear legal sanction.[36] In 1937 the Home Secretary had secretly begun to issue warrants for intercepting telephone calls to detect breaches of exchange-control and emergency food regulations and the posting of Irish sweepstake tickets in violation of the Lotteries Act. In 1951 a secret 'Home Office circular' was issued, stating that intercept warrants could only be issued where serious crime was suspected or the national interest was at stake. The Birkett Committee approved these principles, and recommended that transcripts should not be passed on to persons outside the public service. It criticized as 'mistaken' the Home Secretary's decision to pass to the Bar Council intercepts of communications between a barrister and a target criminal, although it did not criticize the Bar Council's decision to disbar the barrister for 'unprofessional behaviour' on the strength of the intercepts.

After the Birkett Committee's report, Post Office interception of mail and telephones continued under a Home Secretary's warrant (other forms of surveillance, such as bugging devices, required no authority at all). The warrant procedure still had no legal sanction, and the authorities were careful never again to reveal that any particular intercept had taken place. Even when telephone taps provided the clearest evidence of guilt, they were not revealed, as a matter of policy, to a court. But in 1979 a young police officer, giving evidence in a case against Mr James Malone involving theft of antiques, made a historic oversight. Under cross-examination he produced his police notebook, in which he had scribbled some extracts from an intercept authorized by the Home Secretary on Malone's telephone. This provided sufficient evidence for Malone to challenge the lawfulness of the Home Secretary's warrant procedure in the High Court. The judge, Sir Robert Megarry, reluctantly concluded that he had no power to intervene, but he was scathing about the lack of legal safeguards: 'This is not a subject on which it is possible to feel any pride in English law ... telephone tapping is a subject which cries out for legislation.'[37] Malone took his case to the European Court of Human Rights in Strasbourg, which held that the warrant procedure violated the Article 8 guarantee of privacy in the European Convention. The lack of adequate or effective safeguards and indeed the total absence of any rules governing tapping or any remedy against abuse, meant that interceptions were not carried out 'in accordance with the law' – a pre-condition required by the Convention before official invasion of privacy can be justified to combat crime or protect national security.[38] This ruling obliged the British Government to introduce legislation, which took the form of the 1985 Interception of Communications Act.

This Act gives statutory effect to the Home Secretary's warrant procedure, establishes a Commissioner to keep it under review and a Tribunal to consider complaints from persons who believe their telephone may have been tapped or their mail interfered with. The entire purpose and effect of the legislation, however, is to remove official interception from any independent examination, and to ensure that the embarrassment caused by the violation of Malone's privacy tap can never happen again. Section 9 outlaws any evidence or questioning in court proceedings which might tend to suggest either that any public servant or Post Office employee has been guilty of the offence of intercepting a communication without authorization, or indeed that any interception warrant has ever been issued. In other words, the subject of State interception is henceforth taboo in British courts: there can be no questioning of police as in the *Malone* case, no affidavits by persons like Cathy Massiter, an ex-employee of MI5 who has accused the Home Secretary of granting warrants for party political purposes. With a genius for turning defeat into victory, the British Government has sought to fulfil its obligation to protect privacy by the simple expedient of ensuring that violations of privacy are henceforth not to be mentioned.

The quid pro quo for demolishing any possible remedy in the courts against unauthorized or unjustified tapping is a tribunal of five senior lawyers empowered to investigate a complaint from any person who believes that he or she may have been the subject of an intercept. But their powers to 'investigate' are confined to considering whether a warrant has been issued, and if so whether, 'applying the principles applicable on an application for judicial review', it was properly issued. This formula means that they cannot critically examine the evidence available to the Home Secretary: so long as there was some information before him from which a reasonable person could conclude that a threat to national security or a serious crime needed investigation, the Tribunal can take no action. They merely inspect the Home Secretary's paperwork, and make no examination of the reality or reliability of police or security-service assertions. An application to tap a telephone in relation to an utterly trivial crime, or an innocent activity which it would be wholly perverse to regard as a threat to national security, would enable the Tribunal to quash the warrant and compensate the victim. But no senior policeman or security official would be so stupid as to make a written application on perverse grounds, and in 1984 it took a senior judge only a few days to satisfy himself that the 6,129 warrants issued since 1970 had been formally in order. Whether the evidence upon which a formally correct application is based is sufficient or reliable involves questions that the Tribunal will be unable to consider. Nor, remarkably, does it have any power to investigate *unauthorized* interception. Not surprisingly, given its limited terms of reference, the Tribunal found no contravention of the Act during its first eighteen months of operation. The Act provides for a senior judge to be appointed as 'Commissioner', a part-time officer with a roving brief to assist the Tribunal and generally to monitor the warrant procedure. He has no obligation to examine the background to every application, but merely makes 'random checks', and on discovery of any contravention of the rules he is to notify the Prime Minister in secret and not the victim. His public reports have been uninformatively reassuring, disclosing no more than the rare occasions when clerical errors have led to taps being placed on the wrong phone.

The sum total of these arrangements is: to stop the courts from ever providing any redress to victims of unauthorized or wrongly authorized interceptions; to permit a number of senior lawyers to read transcripts of private conversations, without having the power to do anything about them unless the warrant application is perverse; and to pretend to the public that the system is working fairly because a senior judge is keeping an eye on the paperwork it generates. The complainant, of course, will hardly ever discover whether his telephone has in fact been tapped: the uninformative response from the Tribunal will normally be to deny that it has discovered any contravention of the Act. (The only way to discover with any certainty whether your telephone is tapped is not to pay the bill: the State's appetite for information being greater than its appetite for money, disconnection will not automatically follow.)

Whether the 'safeguards' satisfy the requirements of Section 13 of the European Convention, which requires an effective remedy for every violation of a right, is open to doubt, although it will be some years before the court in Strasbourg will pass judgement upon them. In *Klass* v. *Federal Republic of Germany* it barely approved a much more effective system which operates in the Federal Republic of Germany, where a phone tap may only be installed when a judge is satisfied that there is imminent danger of serious crime.[39] The transcripts are handed to the judge, who releases to police only such portions as he considers relevant to their investigations, and are destroyed when the surveillance comes to an end. The suspect is notified once surveillance has ended, and the entire system is supervised by an all-party Committee of MPs. The Royal Commission on Criminal Procedure recommended in 1981 that no warrant should be issued until the Official Solicitor, on behalf of the unsuspecting suspect, has had an opportunity to consider and to question in court the grounds for the application.[40] While these proposals may not be appropriate to national-security intercepts, there would be obvious advantages in adopting them where warrants are sought to obtain information about crime. The faith reposed in the Home Secretary, who does not have the time and may not have the relevant experience to consider judicially whether an application fulfils the stated criteria, is wrong in principle and misplaced in practice. Moreover, it has led to the absurd consequence that evidence of serious criminal conspiracies contained in intercepted letters or on transcripts of telephone conversations is never produced in court. The obsession with secrecy is such that the State prefers criminals to walk free rather than have them convicted by revealing the secret transcripts which contain the evidence of their guilt. If intercept warrants were, like search warrants, issued by courts (preferably, by High Court or at least Crown Court judges) there could be no objection to introducing the transcripts as part of a prosecution case. Indeed, American experience suggests that this class of evidence can be crucial to the conviction of Mafia leaders and 'inside dealers'. The British obsession with secrecy, in this respect, is a positive handicap to effective law enforcement.

The Interception of Communications Act sets out three grounds on which a warrant may be issued:

(a) in the interests of national security;

(b) for the purpose of preventing or detecting serious crime; or

(c) for the purpose of safeguarding the economic well-being of the United Kingdom.

Ground (c), according to the Home Secretary when moving the bill, is not concerned with promoting British trade but rather with securing supplies of essential commodities and with obtaining information about significant threats to the national economy.[41] It would, however, seem to justify the interception of the telephones of trade unionists who organize strikes in major industries. (The 'person' against whom a warrant may be granted 'includes any organization and any association or combination of persons'.) A crime is 'serious' if it is likely to result in a

sentence of more than three years' imprisonment, or in substantial financial gain, or if it involves the use of violence or conduct by 'a large
number of persons in pursuit of a common interest'.[42] This formula too
would permit the tapping of the telephones of those involved in large-
scale political protests. The Government defines 'the interests of national
security' to include combating 'terrorist, espionage or major subversive
activity' and supporting 'the Government's defence and foreign
policies'.[43] This affords a broad scope for intercepting communications
between those concerned with peaceful protests against the politics of
the Government of the day. Cathy Massiter, the MI5 'case officer' on
CND, claimed that the real reason for the application she had been
instructed to make for a warrant to tap the telephone of John Cox, a
member of CND's executive, was to gather information which might
help the Defence Minister, Mr Michael Heseltine, to discredit the peace
movement for political purposes. In the application, she had alleged that
Cox's membership of the Communist Party indicated a subversive intent:
in reality, she claimed, he was chosen because he lived in Wales and
frequently communicated by telephone with the executive members.

In 1986 CND brought a High Court action based on Massiter's
evidence, arguing that the repeated Government statements and White
Papers promising that tapping would be confined to subversives and
would not be used for party political purposes had created a 'legitimate
expectation' that the court could oblige it to honour. Mr Justice Taylor
agreed that the courts were entitled to review unfair actions by Government stemming from failures to live up to 'legitimate expectations'
aroused by repeated publication of policy criteria, even in areas such as
phone tapping where it had no obligation to hear representations on
behalf of a proposed victim. (This principle marks a significant extension
of administrative law's ability to protect the liberty of the subject, and
may in due course enable the courts to review official actions taken in
breach of Home Office 'guidelines' and 'circulars' which are so often
used as substitutes for law.) He succinctly stated the principles which
should govern security-service surveillance:

> The function of the Security Service is the defence of the realm as a
> whole from, *inter alia*, the actions of persons who and organizations which
> may be judged subversive to the State. Subversive activities are those

which threaten the safety or well-being of the State and which are intended to undermine or overthrow parliamentary democracy by political, industrial or violent means. A warrant to intercept should issue only where there is reasonable cause to believe that major subversive activity is already being carried on and is likely to injure the national interest. The material reasonably likely to be obtained by the interception must be of direct use to the Security Service in its functions which include keeping up to date its information about subversion. Normal methods of investigation must either have failed or be unlikely to succeed. Interception must be strictly limited to what is necessary to the Security Service's defined function and must not be used for party political purposes or for the purposes of any particular section of the community.

On the facts, CND's case was rejected, as Massiter's evidence did not exclude the possibility of other and more legitimate reasons, of which she was unaware, being given to the Home Secretary to justify the issue of the warrant. None the less, the decision stands as an important authority on the limits of State interception, especially as it is unlikely ever to be repeated. Section 9 of the Interception of Communications Act puts an end to any further applications to the court, and requires these to be considered only by the Tribunal. Ironically, Mr Justice Taylor rejected the Government's argument that national-security considerations should have stopped the court from hearing the case at all:

> I do not accept that the court should never inquire into a complaint against a Minister if he says it is his policy to maintain silence in the interests of national security ... Totally to oust the court's supervisory jurisdiction in a field where *ex hypothesi* the citizen can have no right to be consulted is a dangerous and draconian step indeed.[44]

It is precisely this 'dangerous and draconian step' which the Government has taken by enacting the Interception of Communications Act. That Act, of course, applies its 'safeguards' only to intercepts authorized by a Secretary of State. GCHQ operates a microwave system which scans overseas telephone calls and scoops up those containing 'key words', and reportedly has facilities which intercept telex and facsimile messages, at home or from abroad. In 1967, it was revealed that the security services were reading all foreign telegrams – a disclosure which the Government sought to prevent by a 'D' notice. There is a vast array of electronic bugs and surveillance devices available to security agencies and police which require no authorization at all. Peter Wright went 'burglaring and bugging' his way round London for MI5, without the Home Secretary's approval, and in 1982 security officials were interrupted while installing a bug on a public telephone serving a council estate in Wales.

In 1979 a hidden video camera was discovered in the bar of a Hartlepool pub: the publican disclaimed any knowledge, so it was commandeered by a group of his customers. They were later arrested and held for a day before the police owned up to planting the camera in an attempt to obtain evidence of small-scale trafficking in cannabis.[45] This was a breach of the inevitable 'Home Office circular' recommending that the use of secret surveillance devices be confined to the investigation of serious crime, but as a senior officer commented in a similar case a few years later, they could not see any reason why they should respect 'an obscure piece of paper brought out five or six years ago'. Fresh guidelines were issued by the Home Office in 1984 to 'regulate' use of aural and visual surveillance devices, recommending (since 'guidelines' and 'circulars' are not legally binding on anyone) that use be confined to the investigation of serious crime (or obscene telephone calls) where more routine methods would be unlikely to succeed, and that attention must be paid to the risk of interfering with privacy, especially when devices are placed in homes or hotel bedrooms. The use should be approved at Chief or Assistant Chief Constable level, and bugging devices should not be used to pick up telephone calls in a way which would circumvent the Home Secretary's warrant procedure.

Surreptitious surveillance is now a regular incident of policing, and is entirely beyond control by the courts. Telephone and mail intercepts cannot be mentioned, let alone challenged, in any court, and breaches of 'Home Office guidelines' do not give rise to any action for damages. The warrant procedures which offer some safeguards in respect of telephone and mail intercepts have no application to other forms of electronic surveillance. In the case of suspected crime, there is little to be lost and much to be gained by obliging police to obtain judicial warrants before deploying surveillance devices of any sort in places not open to the public. The criteria set out in the Interception of Communications

Act and in the Home Office guidelines are best applied by a judge: the Home Secretary lacks the time and the qualifications for the role of objective scrutineer of police suspicions. If intercept and surveillance warrants were applied for and granted by courts on the same basis as search warrants, there could be no objection to the fruits of that surveillance (subject to the 'fairness' provisions of Section 78 of PACE) being used as relevant evidence of criminal conduct or conspiracy. The gathering of national-security information does present problems with which courts are less familiar, but the abuses alleged by Cathy Massiter and Peter Wright make it difficult to maintain confidence in a secret procedure authorized in certain cases by a Government Minister and in others by anonymous senior civil servants in the security service. If 'national interest' surveillance were in every case to be undertaken upon a warrant issued by a senior judge, overseen by an all-party committee of Privy Councillors, there would be less cause for disquiet. The US Supreme Court has convincingly refuted the executive's claim to a unique ability to authorize secret surveillance on those suspected of domestic subversion:

> We cannot accept the Government's argument that internal security matters are too subtle and complex for judicial evaluation. Courts regularly deal with the most difficult issues of our society. There is no reason to believe that federal judges will be insensitive to or uncomprehending of the issues involved in domestic security cases. Certainly courts can recognize that domestic security surveillance involves different considerations from the surveillance of 'ordinary crime'. If the threat is too subtle or complex for our senior law enforcement officers to convey its significance to a court, one may question whether there is probable cause for surveillance ... By no means of least importance will be the reassurance of the public generally that indiscriminate wiretapping and bugging of law-abiding citizens cannot occur.[46]

Official Secrecy

'Can you shed any light on the disappearance of Burgess and Maclean?'

'No I can't . . . I am debarred by the Official Secrets Act from saying anything which might disclose to unauthorized persons information derived from my position as a former government official.'

> Mr Kim Philby at a Press conference
> in 1956 after being cleared by the
> Prime Minister of any taint of
> disloyalty

Secrecy, said Richard Crossman, is the British disease, and it has reached epidemic proportions. No other Western democracy is so obsessed with keeping from the public information about its public servants, or so relentless in plumbing new legal depths to staunch leaks from its bureaucracy. The laws and practices which are examined in this chapter have cast a blanket of secrecy over 'official information' irrespective of its triviality, or its importance for public health and safety, or its revelation of bungling and incompetence. There is no compelling legal reason why much of this information should not be revealed: successive Governments, advised by successive bureaucrats, have simply made political decisions to protect it from Parliament, Press and public, other than by way of 'authorized' disclosures through departmental Press releases and ministerial statements, or by dishonestly briefing journalists on non-attributable 'lobby' terms. This has obvious advantages for the party in power, because it can control the flow of information so as to reduce political embarrassment for senior civil servants, whose performance is not subject to sensible public scrutiny until they are long retired or deceased. One of the most remarkable sights Britain has to offer is the annual queue of journalists and historians waiting at Kew for the Public Record Office to open its doors and reveal the secret papers which will explain how and why the British Government acted as it did thirty years before. The occasion deserves to be a tourist attraction: it symbolizes the governance of modern Britain a good deal more accurately than the Trooping of the Colour.

The cult of secrecy amongst our mandarins is not entirely explained by self-interest: there is a genuine belief that decisions are made better if made without publicity. (As Sir Humphrey Appleby felicitously puts it, 'Open Government is a contradiction in terms. You can be open, or you can have Government.') The difficulty of squaring this belief with any acceptable view of democratic accountability leads them to shelter behind a political fiction called 'Ministerial accountability' which holds that information emanating from Whitehall should only come from or with the approval of a responsible Minister. But the truth is that Ministers neither control nor are in practice answerable for thousands of decisions made by middle-ranking bureaucrats – decisions which may vitally affect individuals. Freedom of Information legislation, which allows inspection of information accumulated by and acted upon by officials, is fast becoming a defining characteristic of democracy in countries throughout Europe, North America and Australasia, underpinned by Madison's vision of representative Government:

> Knowledge will forever govern ignorance. And a people who mean to be their own governors, must arm themselves with the power knowledge gives. A popular Government without popular information or means of acquiring it, is but a prologue to a farce or a tragedy, or perhaps both.[1]

The evidence shows that public participation in government leads to better Government. But when the Freedom of Information Campaign was launched in 1984, it was condemned by Mrs Thatcher: a Freedom of Information Act, she proclaimed, is 'both inappropriate and unnecessary . . . Ministers' accountability to Parliament would be reduced, and Parliament itself diminished.' The notion that Ministers would be less accountable if there was more information about Department blunders for them to account for is curious, to say the least, and it is not clear how Parliament would be diminished, other perhaps than by a fuller public appreciation of how little influence it has on civil-service decision-making. None the less, constitutional fictions like 'Ministerial accountability' and 'Parliamentary sovereignty' are invariably paraded in opposition to proposals to increase citizens' legal freedoms: left-wing politicians, as we shall see, oppose a Bill of Rights by reference to a view of Parliament as protector of civil liberties which is just as absurd as Mrs Thatcher's.

THE CLIMATE OF SECRECY

The first Official Secrets Act was passed in 1889, after a clerk in the Foreign Office had passed details to the *Globe* of a secret treaty between Britain and Russia. He had, sensibly, committed these details to memory, and much embarrassment was suffered by the authorities when he was duly acquitted of the only available offence, that of removing a State document. In an era where secret treaties were necessary to effect imperialist ambitions, some protection against the disclosure of such high policy matters did not seem unreasonable. A much more significant protection was afforded by the Prevention of Corruption Acts of 1889 and 1906, which make it a criminal offence for any employee to receive bribes or kickbacks as an inducement to use his position to favour an outsider. This covers the selling of information derived from an office or employment, and is a much more satisfactory method of prosecuting public servants who have tainted motives for disclosing official information. It only applies while the employee holds office, and so does not catch those who write reminiscences in retirement, nor those impelled to speak out, without payment, by reason of conscience or political belief. It was this that worried civil-service chiefs at the beginning of the century and they prepared legislation – secretly, of course – to gag any public servant who might feel morally impelled to talk to the Press. The law which was to become Section 2 was recognized by its sponsors to be a draconian infringement of civil liberties: they bided their time, waiting for a suitable opportunity to slip it through Parliament.

That opportunity was provided in 1911, when German 'gunboat diplomacy' at Agadir caused national panic, and coincided with sensationalized newspaper stories about German spies posing as tourists and photographing the fortifications at Dover harbour. The Government, to the acclaim of the Press and the opposition, instantly produced the

Official Secrets Act as a measure to protect the nation from enemy agents. Astoundingly, the bill passed through all its parliamentary stages in one day, with no more than one hour's debate, in the course of which Section 2 – cunningly inserted between sections dealing with espionage – was not mentioned once. Until 1989 Section 2 forbade any of our one million public servants, or any of the further one million civilians employed under Government contracts, from revealing any information about their jobs, or any information obtained in the course of their jobs, if the disclosure had not been 'authorized' by a superior. In legal theory, it was a crime to reveal the number of cups of tea consumed each day in the MI 5 canteen.

In 1989 the Government introduced a new Official Secrets bill to replace Section 2, which would make it the clearest possible criminal offence to reveal the number of cups of tea served in the MI 5 canteen on any day in the eighty-year history of the security service.[2] The purpose of this legislation is to refurbish the criminal law as a weapon for punishing leaks from the intelligence community or which relate to defence and foreign policy, by removing or narrowing potential defences that may have been available under the old Section 2. In practice, as we shall see, the new law would make it easier to convict all persons who had in the past been controversially prosecuted under Section 2, and would enable the State to gaol people like Cathy Massiter whom it had not previously dared to prosecute because of the public importance of their revelations. The impact of the 1989 legislation can be appreciated in the context of what the State had previously thought it necessary to punish under Section 2.

Section 2 was for many years taken quite seriously. An early decision confirmed that, despite its title, it did not apply to information which was 'secret', and in 1932 the distinguished author Compton Mackenzie found himself in the dock of the Old Bailey for publishing a collection of reminiscences about his intelligence activities in the First World War. The Crown conceded that the book had not prejudiced the public interest, other than by revealing the names of long-retired intelligence officers who, it was argued, might be brought back from retirement in the event of another war. Mackenzie pleaded guilty in return for a promise of a small fine, and heard the Attorney-General explain to the judge that his worst crime had been to reveal the dangerous consonant – 'C' – by which the Chief of the Security Service was known, and that the position had been occupied by Sir Mansfield Cumming. 'Surely this officer's name was perfectly well known during the war, Mr Attorney, in clubs both you and I belong to?' asked the astonished judge. The Attorney-General demurred, and was unable to explain what secret occupation Cumming was currently engaged on until the defendant, from the dock, reminded the court that 'C' had died ten years previously.[3] Mackenzie was none the less fined £100, a sentence which did not deter *Daily Telegraph* journalists from publishing the Government's secret plans to arrest Mahatma Gandhi. They were held in custody and interrogated about their source, until their proprietor let it be known that the source for the story was the Home Secretary himself. (Under the 1989 Official Secrets Act, Mackenzie would have no defence at all to the charge of disclosing information learnt in the course of long-past intelligence activities.)

Needless to say, politicians have never been prosecuted. In 1934 no action was taken against Labour MP George Lansbury, who gave a Cabinet paper to his son (who published it and was fined), and two years later J. H. Thomas, a Cabinet Minister who should have been prosecuted for leaking Budget secrets, was allowed to resign in disgrace. Parliament protects its own: in 1938 the Attorney-General was criticized by the Privileges Committee for threatening Mr Duncan Sandys MP (described in a secret War Office memo as 'a slippery young gentleman who is certainly backed up by Winston') with an Official Secrets Act prosecution for obtaining and disclosing information about the lack of anti-aircraft defences in London.[4] (Under the 1989 Act, the MP's source would be guilty of the crime of revealing information about defence equipment.) Parliamentary privilege will protect any MP from prosecution for disclosing an official secret, even when it is alleged to affect national security: Kim Philby's treason and Colonel 'B's identity were disclosed by questions in the House, and recently a former Labour Minister was said to have damaged the national interest by blurting out the fact that Britain had been intercepting Argentinian Government communications for many years before the Falklands War.

When in office, Ministers are assumed to have the power to authorize themselves to disclose secrets, however deviously or improperly. This 'self-authorization' doctrine saved J. H. Thomas, and doubtless Mr (now Sir Leon Brittan QC when he flagrantly violated convention by leaking to the Press the Solicitor-General's opinion on an aspect of the takeover bid for Westland Helicopters, in order to damage the credibility of a fellow Minister. There was a half-hearted police investigation when Ms Sarah Keays claimed that her lover, Mr Cecil Parkinson, had spilled intimate details of the War Cabinet proceedings during the Falklands conflict: Section 7 of the Official Secrets Act (which is not repealed by the 1989 law) makes it an offence to 'knowingly harbour' a person you have reason to believe is about to communicate an official secret, so Miss Keays may herself have committed an offence by allowing her Cabinet lover to stay the night. Such speculations are in practice idle: the Attorney-General's consent is required for any official secrets prosecution, so Cabinet Ministers and/or their mistresses are unlikely to be seen in the Old Bailey dock.

The decline of Section 2 dates from the prosecution in 1970 of Jonathan Aitken, a journalist and Parliamentary candidate, who came by a secret Army document about the state of the Biafran war which contained information at variance with Prime Ministerial statements to Parliament. He was given it by a general, who had received the report from a colonel attached to the British Embassy in Nigeria. Aitken, to the general's embarrassment, arranged for it to be published in the *Daily Telegraph*. The Attorney-General authorized a Section 2 prosecution of the colonel, Aitken and the editor of the *Daily Telegraph*, with the general cutting a sorry figure as chief prosecution witness. Various technical defences were canvassed, based on the prosecution's difficulty in proving that original disclosure by the colonel to the general, his former commanding officer, was 'unauthorized'. Both journalist and editor additionally claimed that they had a moral duty to make the information public in order to rectify false statements in Parliament. The defence claimed the case was a 'political prosecution', initiated by a petulant Labour Government, and the trial judge in a sympathetic summing-up told the jury that it was high time that Section 2 was 'pensioned off'. All defendants were acquitted. (Under the 1989 reforms, all defendants would have been guilty of making disclosures about army logistics and deployment which would be likely to jeopardize British defence interests abroad.)

The outcry provoked by the Aitken prosecution led to the establishment of a committee headed by Lord Franks to examine Section 2 of the Official Secrets Act. It condemned the width and uncertainty of the section, and urged its replacement by a law narrowly defining the categories of information which deserved protection. The Government, in a White Paper in 1976, accepted that mere receipt of secret information by the Press should not amount to an offence.[5] But its White Paper promise was almost immediately betrayed by its prosecution the following year of investigative journalist Duncan Campbell, for interviewing an ex-soldier about his work many years before at the GCHQ base at Cyprus. The 'ABC' case as it came to be known (after the defendants Crispin Aubrey, John Berry and Duncan Campbell) marked the first public admission that the function of GCHQ, which had been established in 1920, was to intercept communications. Campbell, who was then working for *Time Out*, faced not only a Section 2 allegation but two 'spying' charges laid under Section 1 of the Act and carrying fourteen years' imprisonment apiece. The Government (a Labour Government, be it noted) was determined to put behind bars for a very long time a twenty-four-year-old journalist with a discomfiting ability to read between the lines of glossy Ministry of Defence handouts and to conjure official secrets out of telephone books. Although his entire library had been transferred by pantechnicon to Scotland Yard, the Section 1 charge accusing him of 'collecting information' collapsed as it became apparent that all the information was available from public sources (for example the microwave facilities alleged by the prosecution to be 'top secret' were all shown on a map issued to Aeroflot pilots by the Department of Civil Aviation). The judge threw out the second Section 1 charge as 'oppressive',[6] Campbell and his fellow journalist Aubrey were given conditional discharges for breaching Section 2, and John Berry received a suspended sentence: a counter-productive result of a case which had done little more than to put GCHQ on the public, as well as the Aeroflot, map.

Duncan Campbell has not been deterred by his prosecution from probing official secrecy. In 1984, when he fell off his bicycle, a policeman helped him to hospital while others helped themselves to the contents of his saddle-bags, confiscating his copy of *The Army Manual on Personal Protection* with its secret 'Instructions on Defecating in the Arctic'. The following year, Campbell was retained by the BBC to make a series of films about *The Secret Society*, with results which will shortly require examination. (Much of Duncan Campbell's journalism can be made the subject of prosecution under the 1989 law, because it includes the use of information of a class regarded as 'likely to damage' the intelligence services or the defence establishment.)

In the meantime, however, the cases of Sarah Tisdall and Clive Ponting re-emphasized the counter-productive consequences of using Section 2 to punish those who leak from motives of conscience or concern for democratic accountability. Tisdall, who pleaded guilty to sending the *Guardian* documents revealing the date of cruise-missile arrivals at Greenham Common, was gaoled for six months, a sentence which many believed to be harsh for an impulsive act taken when she read in them that the Defence Minister planned to dodge questions in the House and that there was official concern that American military personnel might shoot at women who stormed the base in protest at the arrival of the missiles. Many journalists, mortified that the evidence against her had been provided by the *Guardian* itself, in obedience to a court order to hand back the documents, vowed henceforth to destroy such documents immediately after use.

Tisdall's fate did not deter Mr Clive Ponting OBE, a senior MoD official, from priming Tam Dalyell MP with information which undermined the truth of Ministerial answers to questions he had been asking in Parliament about the sinking of the *Belgrano*. (When confronted in court with these Parliamentary fibs, the Minister's private secretary riposted that 'one man's ambiguity is another man's truth' – a worthy precursor, in the Whitehall book of euphemisms for lying, to Sir Robert Armstrong's more notorious phrase about 'being economical with the truth.') Ponting was prosecuted under Section 2, and acquitted. It was very much a 'sympathy verdict' – in which sympathy for Ms Tisdall's fate may have played some part, together with a feeling that Ponting had a duty to expose Ministerial evasiveness. A jury, of course, has a constitutional right to acquit a defendant irrespective of the evidence, and the only defence open to Ponting under Section 2 – that Dalyell was 'a person to whom it is his duty in the interests of the State to communicate (the information)' was in effect foreclosed by the judge's controversial ruling that 'the interests of the State' referred to the policies of the Government of the day. The jury presumably took the view that Ponting had a moral duty to let MPs know that answers provided by Ministers, and drafted by their civil servants, had been positively parsimonious with the truth.[7] (The 1989 law forecloses any defence based on 'moral duty' or public interest.)

The message that juries could not be trusted to convict where apparent breaches of Section 2 had been motivated by conscience came through loud and clear, and no attempt was made to charge Cathy Massiter when she revealed details of MI5 operations against trade unionists, civil libertarians and the peace movement in a Channel 4 programme tauntingly entitled *MI5's Official Secrets*. The IBA loyally postponed the screening of the film for a month to give the Government an opportunity to prosecute its makers, an action which only served to have the transcript published widely in the Press while video-cassettes of the film were marketed by Virgin Records under the label 'The Programme That Couldn't be Shown'. The purpose of the 1989 law is to ensure that any person like Cathy Massiter shall have no defence at all to charges of disclosing information about the work (however controversial or even unlawful) of the security services.

The current climate of secrecy in Britain is not a legacy of Section 2, which has been discredited since the Aitken prosecution in 1970 and the Franks Committee Report. It is a permanent state of the official mind, represented by a Prime Minister who adamantly rejects Freedom of Information legislation and calls in Scotland Yard whenever a 'leak' of any major policy document embarrasses her Government. The courts have assisted by allowing the civil remedy of breach of confidence to be used to injunct the media from publishing documents which have escaped from Whitehall, even when an official secrets prosecution would never be contemplated. There are over one hundred separate statutes which make it a crime to disclose specific information obtained by Government agencies, for the most part relating to health and safety. Within the civil service, incompetence and mismanagement are lesser evils than boat-rocking: secrecy is enforced by disciplinary proceedings or, most influentially, by failure to promote those who speak out. Willingness to take a form of loyalty oath by 'signing the Official Secrets Act' is becoming a pre-condition for appointment to public office and Government advisory committees, creating the danger that 'the great and the good' are more often the hack and the placeman.

All civil servants and most experts who sit on Government committees go through the routine of 'signing the Official Secrets Act' (a legally pointless exercise, as they, like everyone else in Britain, are bound by it anyway). Although the likelihood of prosecution is negligible in the case of disclosures which are not made corruptly or are not damaging to national security, this ritual conduces to an atmosphere in which outspokenness and open debate are officially discouraged. To take but one example, a detailed and disturbing study of the eating habits of British schoolchildren, completed in 1983, was kept under wraps until it was leaked in 1986. The scientist who had conducted it, by then retired from Government service, was warned by DHSS lawyers that she could not publicly discuss it – her obligation of confidence continued even unto the grave. The need for open debate on food policy is obvious, given the 'behind the scenes' influence of the agriculture and food-processing industries, yet independent scientists seconded to DHSS committees are still required to 'sign the Official Secrets Act' and to hold their tongues. The media's absorption with the debate about national security leads it to overlook how the absence of a Freedom of Information Act prevents disclosure of information relating to pesticides and radiation and petrol and drugs and microwaves and housing and education and product testing and welfare benefits and so on – all areas of vital concern to individuals whether as consumers or voters or as human beings who simply want to go on living.[8]

The Official Secrets Act offers remarkably extensive powers of search and seizure which sidestep some of the safeguards in PACE. This came dramatically to public attention in 1987, when Special Branch Officers raided the BBC offices in Glasgow and seized all master tapes of Duncan Campbell's *Secret Society* series, raided the homes of three *New Statesman* journalists and spent over four days examining files in the offices of that magazine.[9] Because the London warrants were issued under Section 2 of the Official Secrets Act, the normal requirement in PACE that 'special procedure' applications for journalistic material shall be preceded by a notice to the person in possession of it, so that the application can be contested in court, did not apply.[10] Because the information was alleged to be covered by a secrecy law, and was in the possession of persons who were journalists and therefore likely to disclose it, the search warrant could be granted at a secret court hearing without representations from the *New Statesman*. The same result would follow under the 1989 law, which makes no change to search and seizure provisions. In addition, both Campbell and the BBC would have committed the new crime of conspiring to make a damaging disclosure relating to 'defence policy and strategy, and military planning and intelligence'.

The whole episode related to Duncan Campbell's exposure of 'Project Zircon', a £5-million spy satellite being planned by the MoD to put Britain in the business of eavesdropping from space. Campbell's argument, supported by BBC executives, was that public interest required debate over both the politics of the decision – which arguably distorted the defence budget in merely replicating US technology – and the fact that its cost had been hidden from the Parliamentary Accounts Committee. The Government's case for suppression was undermined both by the fact that the project seemed to be common knowledge amongst defence contractors and by the impossibility of keeping the satellite a secret from the Russians once it was launched. (This last consideration has never weighed with the defence establishment. The 'D' Notice Committee once tried to expunge references in a book by Tom Driberg to the disastrous SIS (Secret Intelligence Service) attempt to overthrow the Albanian Government. When Driberg protested that Philby and Burgess had told the KGB all about it at the time, the committee's secretary replied, 'Good heavens, old boy! It isn't the Russians we worry about, its the British public we don't want to know about it.')[11] With similar logic, the Treasury Solicitors tried to stop other newspapers from referring to the transcript of the Zircon project, which had been published by the *New Statesman*, and the Government stopped the BBC from transmitting it by the simple expedient of keeping the master tape. No charges were ever brought under Section 2, which had been used as a pretext for searches and seizures of journalistic material unparalleled in peacetime since the 'King's Messengers' went in search of John Wilkes and his seditious newspaper more than two centuries before.

The 1989 reforms

The British Government unveiled new plans for reforming Section 2 in a White Paper published whilst it was still smarting from its *Spycatcher* defeats. A High Court judge had pointed out that the absolute protection it was seeking in that case 'could not be achieved this side of the Iron Curtain', but the Official Secrets Bill of 1989 certainly made the attempt. Its primary purpose is to deter all leakage of information about security and intelligence matters by making disclosure and publication of insider information an absolute criminal offence, without any scope for acquittal on grounds of public interest or even on the common-sense basis that the information had already been published, in Britain or abroad. In addition, a range of new criminal offences was created to punish the disclosure or publication of information about defence, foreign policy, police operations and relations with other countries and international organizations. To obtain a conviction in relation to disclosures in these categories, the prosecution must at least prove that they are likely to be damaging, but the statutory tests for determining damage are exceedingly broad and much easier to satisfy than the 'serious injury' test proposed by the Franks Committee. The new law threatens imprisonment for up to two years not only of civil servants who make such disclosures, but of journalists and editors who encourage them or publish their information with reason to believe that it has been divulged 'without lawful authority'.

The litigation associated with *Spycatcher* demonstrated that the judiciary, however supportive of the Government in granting injunctions, would at the end of the day apply a 'public interest' standard to permit important disclosures made in breach of confidence. So the Government could not rely on civil litigation to deter media organizations which could afford to fight for freedom of expression in the Courts. A serious risk of imprisonment was necessary to frighten editors and television executives, yet juries could be expected, after the *Ponting* trial, to acquit them unless Section 2 was replaced with offences which made a defence difficult or indeed impossible. The 1989 legislation was designed to achieve this level of deterrence, by making convictions more likely (and in some familiar cases, unavoidable) while at the same time removing from entirely theoretical liability under Section 2 a host of disclosures which the Government would never have dreamed of prosecuting in the first place.

The Government launched its new legislation with extravagant and dishonest claims that it would usher in a new era of openness. But it does nothing for freedom of information – not a single document will be released as a result of its enactment. It narrows the absurd breadth of the discredited Section 2, but leaves the disclosure of everything that the Section previously covered by penal sanctions to be dealt with by specific secrecy laws, disciplinary offences and civil actions for breach of confidence. In the armoury of criminal sanctions, it replaces a blunderbuss with an Armalite rifle, trained on those who disclose precisely the kind of information which has caused political controversy and embarrassment in the past. The most objectionable new offences are those which allow of no defence at all, namely revelations about any aspect of intelligence work by persons engaged, or formerly engaged, in it. Not only must all employees take their secrets − however trivial or however scandalous − with them to the grave, but so too must any person who is 'notified' by the Home Secretary that he is bound by this absolute duty. Anyone who comes into contact with the Security Services − by being approached to work as a spy, or by witnessing a bungled operation − may be silenced for ever by a Home Secretary's notice. The duty of absolute secrecy extends to the revelation of serious crime, or breaches of the Security Service Act, or to any information obtained by telephone taps or burglaries authorized by the Home Secretary's warrant. It will not only be an offence to blow the whistle, but even in some circumstances to hear it: journalists who conspire to obtain security-related information or 'aid abet counsel or procure' any divulging of it to them can be prosecuted as accomplices. If they publish such information with grounds for believing it has been disclosed to them without official approval, they will also be guilty. Under these arrangements, it will be virtually impossible to learn anything of security and intelligence operations other than what the Government chooses to make public.

The disclosure of other categories of information is punishable only if 'damaging', but this test is readily satisfied by statutory assumptions that 'damage' is occasioned by any act which 'endangers the interests of the United Kingdom abroad' or 'damages the capability of any part of the armed forces' or 'impedes the prevention or detection of offences'. Once the prosecution proves this level of damage, the burden shifts to the defendant to prove that he or she had no reasonable cause to believe that the disclosure would have any such consequences. Reversal of the burden of proof in a criminal statute restricting freedom of expression is objectionable, but at least gives some scope for mounting a defence. In practice, however, the odds will be stacked in favour of the Government, which has access to senior military and police experts who will be permitted to make damage assessments in closed court-rooms. The difficulty of making good a defence will itself have a chilling effect on what the media are prepared to risk publishing in relation to material within the forbidden categories: legal caution will prevail in respect of any potentially important disclosures, and anxious consultations between editors and senior civil servants, the 'D Notice Committee' and the Attorney-General's Department can be expected. Prosecutions under the Official Secrets Act can only be brought with the consent of the Attorney-General, and no doubt many nervous editors and television executives will prefer to submit material to his office for 'vetting' rather than to run the risk of criminal prosecution by publishing. That the new law will institutionalize this form of back-door Government pre-censorship may well turn out to be its worst consequence.

The scope of the 1989 legislation, while not the theoretical dragnet of the old Section 2, is none the less considerable. Revelations about defence which are potentially actionable include any disclosure about the 'size, shape, organization, logistics, order of battle, deployment, operations, state of readiness and training of the armed forces of the Crown'; anything relating to the research or development or operation of weapons and equipment, 'defence policy and strategy' and plans for civil defence. Publishers will be guilty if their information comes from a civil servant or Government contractor and if it 'prejudices the capability of the armed forces' or 'endangers the interests of the UK abroad or seriously obstructs the promotion of those interests by the UK'. Stories about deficiencies in protecting the Falklands, or projected troop withdrawals from Hong Kong, or plans to send more ships to the Gulf, or the development of sinister weapons at Aldermaston, or British involvement in the 'Star Wars' project, or plans to reintroduce internment in Northern Ireland, might all be held to satisfy the standard for guilt by juries instructed to ignore any public interest which might be served by the story. It will be a crime to publish information from police sources which 'impedes the prevention or detention of offences' – even if such information additionally promotes the public interest of learning about police corruption or controversial operational policies or breaches of data protection principles by the Police National Computer.

The most confusing and potentially important category of information protected by the new criminal law is that described simply as 'relating to international relations'. Any unauthorized disclosure which 'endangers the interests of the UK abroad' or 'seriously obstructs the promotion or protection by the UK of those interests' is deemed to be 'damaging' and hence prosecutable. This includes disclosure of any information provided in confidence by the Government to any foreign country or international organization. This new offence may severely limit media coverage of foreign policy and diplomacy, much of which is informed by unauthorized leaks from embassies and from within the Foreign Office. It is here that the 'damage' defence looks most threadbare, in light of the White Paper's insistence that any leakage of information 'endangers the UK's interests abroad', because it will make foreign governments and organizations more reluctant to trust British diplomats. If 'damage' is ascertained by reference to diplomatic embarrassment, there will be few revelations that can be made about dangerous alliances and dubious deals with dictators. One of the great scandals of the 1970s – how British Ministers and Foreign Office officials connived with oil companies in busting the Government's own sanctions policy against Rhodesia – would fall within the prohibition, and so would any revelation of a British equivalent of the 'Irangate' scandal in America.

Section 5 of the new law makes it a specific offence for journalists and editors to publish information which they know is protected by the Act, although the prosecution must additionally prove that they had reason to believe that the publication would be damaging to the security services or to the interests of the United Kingdom. If charged under Section 5, editors can at least testify as to their state of mind in deciding to publish, and will be entitled to an acquittal if the jury accepts that there was no rational basis for thinking that the disclosure would damage British interests. This defence will not be available, however, if they publish information from former or serving members of the security services (or 'notified' persons), and are charged instead under Section 1 with aiding and abetting, or conspiring with, such persons to disclose information about their secret work. Any editors minded in the future to publish information derived from the likes of Cathy Massiter and Peter Wright – or even from defected agents like the late Kim Philby – run the risk of being charged as accomplices, with no defence.

In the course of Parliament's debates on the new law, most attention was focused on the need for a public-interest defence. The Government adamantly and successfully resisted amendments which would have provided a defence where the information revealed the existence of serious misconduct (defined as 'crime, fraud, abuse of authority or neglect in the performance of official duty') in circumstances where the benefit of revelation outweighed any damage which might be caused by it. (Civil servants, to make good the defence, would have had to show that they had taken all reasonable steps to bring the misconduct to the attention of the authorities, but to no avail.) The consequence of rejecting this amendment is that disclosure of a public scandal – such as corruption in naval procurement or lives negligently lost in the course of a secret army mission – will be a criminal offence if it is 'damaging' as defined by the Act (e.g. by revealing details of 'secret' military movements or equipment). The virtue of the disclosure and the social value of its consequences will be irrelevant: in official secrecy law, hereafter, nothing can matter more than the needs of defence, intelligence and foreign policy.

It would have been possible to reform Section 2 by confining its operation to information of real security importance. In Canada, this was achieved quite simply when the courts ruled, in relation to an identical Act, that its very title required it to be confined to information which was truly 'secret' and which had not already been made public.[13] The criminal law need extend only to information the disclosure of which would be liable to cause serious injury to the national interest: any document classified 'secret' or 'top secret' would be presumed to fall into this prohibited category unless it could be proved that the classification was mistaken. Unauthorized disclosures of the kind made by Sarah Tisdall and Clive Ponting can be dealt with by disciplinary action within the public service, the 'trade secrets' and commercially sensitive material which government departments frequently receive is protected by the civil law of confidence, and information which is leaked for reward is punishable under the Prevention of Corruption Act. The 1989 legislation rejects this sensible reform in favour of a blanket ban on security disclosures and wide-ranging offences 'damaging' rather than 'seriously injuring' defence, policing and foreign policy. Its three most objectionable features are its failure to provide any public-interest defence for the media, its failure to provide a defence for the civil servant impelled by a moral duty to reveal dishonesty or malfeasance, and its failure to provide any basis at all for citizens to request the release of a single Government document.

FREEDOM OF INFORMATION

The Government adamantly refused to incorporate in the 1989 reforms a legal right of access to information collected or generated by civil servants. This, in most Western democracies, is the function of a Freedom of Information Act, which generally works to require departments of State to publish annual lists of all their reports and surveys and advisory opinions and working files. These Acts establish a procedure for applying for copies of desired documents, and a time limit of a month or two within which a request must either be granted, on payment of a small fee, or else refused by reference to a category of exemptions set out in the legislation. Applicants whose requests are refused in whole or part may then appeal to a court or tribunal, which inspects the document and decides whether the refusal has been properly made. Exemptions are usually on grounds that disclosure would prejudice national security or foreign relations, impede law enforcement, invade the privacy of individuals, disclose trade secrets or commercial confidences, or reveal Cabinet discussions. FoI legislation assumes that citizen access to bureaucracy records is a right rather than a privilege: the exceptions are narrowly defined, although public servants whose opinions are disclosed are immune from libel or other legal action as a result of any opinions they have expressed in the course of their duties. Applicants in Australia and Canada tend to be successful about 70 per cent of the time, and partly successful in most of the remaining cases. They include journalists and MPs, historians and authors, interest groups, consumer organizations, research scientists, businesses, parties to litigation and individuals seeking access to records about their own personal affairs or simply wanting to know how a decision affecting them has been made. FoI is not merely a minority interest: there are 25,000 applications a year in Australia and 250,000 in the United States. The costs are considerable, although overseas experience suggests they would be about half of the £27 million the British Government spends each year on its heavily controlled Press and information services.

FoI is becoming almost a defining characteristic of accountable democratic government elsewhere in the world, at a time when it is implacably opposed by the British Government and its senior bureaucrats. Their objections on grounds of cost have been much exaggerated.

Their objection of principle is based on the 'Ministerial accountability' theory. But Ministerial involvement in departmental decisions occurs only at levels of high policy: Ministers neither control nor are in practice answerable for thousands of decisions made by middle-ranking departmental officers, which may vitally affect individuals and communities. It is often claimed that civil servants would be less candid in offering advice and writing reports if they knew their words would be publishable within a year or so rather than after thirty or fifty years' anonymity which the Public Records Act currently provides. This argument does little credit to the civil servants who advance it, and overlooks the fact that statutory privilege from libel action will give no cause for them to fear about frankness.

Overseas experience suggests that the prospect of early public scrutiny does concentrate the mind in helpful ways: judgements are more careful and considered, and advice is not tendered lightly. FoI provides, in fact, an incentive to perform better, to produce analysis that will withstand contemporary public scrutiny and may often receive accolades a good deal more genuine than the honours routinely handed out in the Queen's Birthday list. There is, of course, a congenital fear of having to defend secrecy decisions in the courts, and no amount of logic will convince Ministers and mandarins that a High Court judge might be in a better position to determine the public interest than they are. None the less, the skies have not fallen on Westminster-style democracies in Canada and Australia with the advent of FoI: on the contrary, most public servants there have not only come to terms with the legislation, but even come to like it. Tax and social-security forms contain messages about FoI rights, telephone books contain basic instructions on how to make an application and media campaigns promote awareness of the Act. Not content with merely making memoranda available to the public, in 1978 the USA provided legal protection for civil servants who take the initiative in revealing misconduct. The Civil Service Reform Act of 1978 – known as 'the Whistleblowers Act' – protects civil servants from any form of retaliation, legal action or demotion if they disclose wrongdoing or malpractice. Thanks to this legislation, US civil servants are protected if they disclose, to Congress or, through the Press, to the people, any evidence of: violation of any law, rule or regulation; mismanagement; gross waste of funds; abuse of authority; or any substantial or specific danger to public health or safety.

What has Britain missed in not having had FoI? In the USA, the public have been able to measure rules of official thumb, through access to guidelines used by tax inspectors; the Parole Board's guidelines and decisions; military rulings on internal discipline; criteria used by law-enforcement agencies in deciding whether to prosecute; environmental impact statements and other submissions by corporations; internal policy directives on immigration control; contracts between government departments and private contractors; guidelines and manuals on drug analysis, highway management and supervision of social-security benefits; and reports by the Government analysts on food additives, pesticides and vitamin pills. Documents disclosed under the Act have revealed: radioactive contamination of state water supplies; an increasing incidence of cancer among workers in nuclear plants; risks inherent in the use of silicone in cosmetic surgery; and potentially corrupt connections between public servants and big business. The Freedom of Information Act has assisted spectacular Press revelations of illegal and ignoble activities by Government agencies. It provided evidence of the perverted mind of J. Edgar Hoover, who bugged Martin Luther King's bedroom and gloatingly played the tapes to his cronies. It exposed the CIA programme of LSD experiments on unsuspecting citizens (one of whom died as a result) and CIA plots to assassinate Castro, Trujillo and other Third World political leaders. The army report on the My Lai massacre has been disclosed, and the public was informed for the first time of their Government's interpretation of the Vietnam peace agreements when a judge ordered the legal opinion to be released pursuant to the Act. The FBI's programme of illegal harassment and disruption of dissidents and left-wing groups came to public attention when courts ordered production of Bureau documents.

If reform of Section 2 had been accompanied by the enactment of FoI, we would have three classes of official information: a 'secret' category of facts and material the revelation of which would attract a criminal sanction; an intermediate category of sensitive information (e.g. trade secrets supplied under legal obligation by companies) which would not be disclosable under FoI and could be protected by breach-of-confidence actions or by prosecution under the Prevention of Corruption Act if leaked for reward; and the remaining, largest category, which would be discoverable pursuant to an FoI application. The effectiveness of such a system would depend on a sensible classification policy – and since it is unlikely that any policy concocted in Whitehall would be sensible, the system would need to be defined by law and be reviewable by the courts. Classification categories should correspond to realistically apprehended injury to the national interest – reviewable in the spirit of Justice Stewart's injunction to government in the *Pentagon Papers* case:

> The very first principle [of a wise security system would be] an insistence upon avoiding secrecy for its own sake. For when everything is classified, then nothing is classified, and the system becomes one to be disregarded by the cynical or the careless, and to be manipulated by those intent on self-protection or self-promotion. I should suppose, in short, that the hallmark of a truly effective internal security system would be the maximum possible disclosure, recognizing that secrecy can best be preserved only when credibility is truly maintained.[14]

SPIES' STORIES

The United Kingdom has, at every level, an extraordinary obsession with spying, which makes it particularly difficult to draw acceptable distinctions in law between the interests of freedom of expression and the real interests of national security. The code-breakers of Bletchley helped to win the last war, and even today an increase in tank traffic on some benighted border, picked up by a GCHQ monitoring station strategically located in some former colony, may signal the commencement of new hostilities. Signals Intelligence (Sigint) is by far our most valuable intelligence asset, and is shared with the United States, Australia and Canada under the UK/USA agreement of 1946. Human Intelligence (Humint) is a distinctly more dubious commodity, and the list of traitors, ideological and mercenary, since the last war is long and embarrassing. It is, none the less, the stuff of which spy novels are made, and the popular imagination which has been gripped by Smiley's people and James Bond's women is easily and lucratively attracted to 'truths' about MI5 which seem stranger than the fiction. 'Insiders' who have been privy to secret work want to write autobiographies for all sorts of motives: money, boastfulness, the settling of old scores, a natural desire to put one's life in perspective for one's grandchildren, a burning sense of duty to alert the public to security lapses or Communist infiltration, and so on. There will be a variety of obvious public benefits from such revelations, but there may also be detriments: disclosure of information which may still be security sensitive, invasion of privacy and accusations against those who cannot answer back.

In the United States, which has intelligence secrets that are more vital to the West than Britain's, these conflicting interests are sensibly resolved contractually, by requiring ex-CIA officers to submit their manuscripts to a Publications Review Board, which requests deletion of disclosures that would damage national security. By the end of 1986 there had been 430 manuscripts submitted, and none had ever been rejected in whole or substantial part – any changes required were modest. The penalty for failure to submit a book is not an injunction preventing publication: the US Supreme Court has ruled in the *Pentagon Papers* case that the First Amendment prohibits such prior restraint, save in cases so serious that lives would be lost or wartime troop movements disclosed. In Britain, however, the Government claims that books by 'insiders' are by very definition damaging to the national interest, and it has invited the courts of this and other countries to develop the elastic doctrine of breach of confidence to prohibit all of them.

The principle of a total embargo has been slow to emerge, and did not really crystallize until the case against Peter Wright concentrated the minds of the Government's legal advisers. Until then, Section 2 of the Official Secrets Act had been fitfully invoked to intimidate publishers, although quite a few memoirs slipped through its net. The turning-point came in 1976, with the threatened publication of Richard Crossman's diaries, which detailed discussions in Cabinet. The Government, reluctant to take proceedings under the Official Secrets Act against the executors of its own former Minister, chose instead to argue that Cabinet meetings were confidential. The Lord Chief Justice agreed that, in principle, the law against breaches of confidence could be invoked to restrain publication of confidential Government material, although he found Crossman's diaries such heavy going that he declined to suppress their 'stale' secrets.[15] None the less the principle was established, and the Treasury Solicitors who lost that particular battle were soon using it to claim that other 'insiders' were bound by contract or by moral obligation to keep their activities secret for ever.

The first casualty was a book by Jock Kane, a former security officer at GCHQ stations, who had resigned in order to campaign against the corruption and incompetence he had discovered hiding beneath the veil of Sigint secrecy. Kane was an archetypal 'whistleblower' – a man of unquestioned loyalty who had (as the Prime Minister conceded in Parliament) done much to improve security at GCHQ. He had taken his evidence of petty corruption and lack of security consciousness to all available departmental channels, and tried to go public only when he believed his complaints had fallen on deaf ears. Interestingly, the Government put its case against his book on two separate grounds: it listed in its pleadings a number of revelations which it maintained would compromise national security, and it then made the general argument that Kane was debarred by his conditions of employment from ever publishing *anything* about his years of service. Clearly, a sensible compromise could have been reached by making the 'national security' deletions, but the Treasury Solicitor was determined to press the broader claim.

That claim was made and considered in the litigation about *Spycatcher*[16]. The background to the book and its author is of some importance. Wright entered MI5 as a 'boffin' – an electrical engineer initially seconded from Marconi because he was a dab hand at bugs and concealed microphones. Wright's scientific expertise was employed on bugging embassies and diplomatic residences and international conferences – an activity contrary to the Vienna Convention but engaged in as a matter of course by most Governments. In 1963 his pre-eminence as an eavesdropper, and a severe shortage of qualified staff, led to his rapid promotion to interrogator and then to chairman of an internal committee inquiring into Soviet infiltration of the security services. Wright and his cronies were convinced that MI5's record for incompetence and bungling in the fifties and sixties was only explicable on the basis that it was still infiltrated, at the top, by Soviet double-agents. This embarrassing thesis was at least convenient, as it avoided the alternative and more embarrassing hypothesis that MI5 was indeed full of incompetents and bunglers.

Wright's suspicions settled on the head of MI5, Roger Hollis. He was formally interrogated, but no evidence of any substance was discovered. Meanwhile, with an obsession matching that of Senator Joe McCarthy, Wright proceeded to discover reds under the pre-war beds of Cambridge and Oxford colleges. He interrogated hundreds, hounded some out of Government jobs and caused at least one of his suspects to commit suicide. Consumed with the presumption of guilt, Wright and his colleagues managed to convince Harold Wilson that one of his best junior Ministers was a security risk because his wife had once been a Communist: Wilson, to his discredit (and one hopes his subsequent mortification), arranged for the man to leave Parliament. Wright, by now a chief interrogator, amassed copious files and used them to damage individuals who disturbed his overly suspicious mind.

It was only a matter of time before the paranoia exemplified by Peter Wright took an insidious political turn. Accepting a view of the world in which things are the opposite of what they seem (Dubček was a KGB agent and the Sino–Soviet split a KGB disinformation plot), Wright came to believe that Harold Wilson himself had been installed by the KGB, which had poisoned Hugh Gaitskell, and that victory by the Labour Party at the 1974 elections would not be in the national interest. He fomented a half-baked plot hatched at this time to feed anti-Labour gossip and tittle-tattle from MI5 files to pro-Conservative newspapers. He retired from 'the service' and left the country in 1976 because there were 'too many blacks' – which was not a problem in Tasmania, whose aborigines had all been massacred in the previous century by English settlers and convicts. His Tasmanian stud farm was on the brink of bankruptcy when Lord Rothschild summoned him back to Britain and introduced him to Chapman Pincher. Wright had brought with him a dossier of his case against Hollis, and went into partnership with Pincher to exploit the material. The security services were well aware of the contents of Pincher's book, *Their Trade is Treachery*, before it was published, but deliberately did nothing to stop it, doubtless preferring that the allegations against Hollis, if they had to surface, should do so through the perspective of a Chapman Pincher rather than a Duncan Campbell. Wright was not satisfied with the result – a Prime Ministerial statement in Parliament to the effect that Hollis had been 'cleared' – and he broke cover in 1984 in a television interview to voice his conviction that Hollis was guilty. This led to his own book, *Spycatcher*, in which he developed the case against Hollis and gave his version of the plot against Wilson.

The Government claim that a book by an 'insider' is more damaging than a book containing the same information which has been written by a journalist has at first blush a certain force: to a lawyer, first-hand eyewitness evidence is always preferable to hearsay. But the evidential rule against self-serving statements reflects the fact that autobiographies are notoriously unreliable – vitiated by memory lapses, self-interest, and skewed perspectives. The historian and the investigative journalist, sifting numerous sources, are better placed to produce approximations to the truth than individual participants in events. And autobiographies by patriotic ex-security officials pose a particular problem for the reader who really matters – the KGB analyst assumed to weigh every word in his office in the Kremlin. How much is truth, and how much is disinformation? (Applying Wright's own system of intelligence analysis – what might be termed the Little Buttercup approach to a world in which things are seldom what they seem – the whole furore over *Spycatcher* appears as a carefully laid disinformation plot, in which the British security services have planted Wright as a novel kind of double-agent, defecting not to the Soviets but to the Press, and endowing his 'revelations' with a spurious credibility by deliberately bungled legal attempts to stop them.) Of course it must be conceded that an 'insider', however security-conscious, may expose a detail or an identity which could prejudice current security operations. This is why it is so much better to have a CIA-style Publications Review Board which can require the deletion of such material. Wright and Kane would have been perfectly happy to submit their manuscripts to a sensible vetting process, and indeed offered to do so. By imposing a blanket ban on publication of any kind by an 'insider', and refusing to negotiate deletions, the Government has adopted an 'all or nothing' policy which damages national security when unexpurgated books are published abroad.

A more weighty objection, underplayed by the Government in the *Spycatcher* case, is based on invasion of privacy. The information which Wright was marketing related to the private lives of individuals he had, for the most part inconclusively, investigated for 'disloyalty'. Using the special, above-the-law position of MI5, he had spent much of his life prying into the backgrounds of many people who were not under suspicion of any crime, but whose past associations might or might not have made it undesirable for them to hold security-related positions. Quite apart from the unattractiveness of Wright's mercenary motives, there is a strong public interest in protecting, even after death, the reputations of those whose private peccadilloes may have found their way into secret police files. In the best of possible legal worlds, public curiosity would be no excuse for publishing details of inconclusive loyalty investigations other than by way of access to files granted either to the subject of the investigations or in the fullness of a time sensibly fixed for releasing historical records.

The genuine public interest which overrides the claim to privacy lies precisely in the revelation of how individual privacy was invaded, for purposes which had little to do with the defence of the realm, by people like Wright whose appreciation of the 'national interest' was distinctly warped. In any proper study of whether the security service has worked effectively to combat genuine enemies, the paranoia of Peter Wright must be exhibit number one. How and why did this technical assistant come to don the mantle of grand inquisitor, to an extent that gave him an apparent hold over Lord Rothschild, and drove one of his targets to suicide? How many 'spies' did he really catch, and how many honourable careers did he ruin by passing on gossip and innuendo? If there was a genuine fear about high-level penetration, why was it not fully and properly investigated by a special commission, rather than allowed to drag on in a part-time committee staffed by conspiracy theorists? In this sense, the real public interest in Wright's book lay not in its accusations against Hollis (which even Wright's co-author has rejected) but in what it revealed about the mentality of its author, and the standards within MI5 which allowed people with that mentality to occupy positions of power outside any legal or democratic control.

The Wright case serves to show the absurdity of a blanket ban on security-service memoirs, in a world where British court writs do not run beyond the three-mile limit. Those who serve the State should not thereby lose their right of self-expression for all time: the interests of national security can be safeguarded by obliging them to submit manu-scripts to a Committee empowered to delete only those disclosures which would cause serious damage to current security operations, with a right of appeal to a High Court judge. The present policy of objecting to any publication by an 'insider' can have absurd results: in 1986 it successfully stopped publication in Britain of *One Girl's War*, a Mills & Boon-style account of how a débutante secretary working in MI5 during the war fell in love with her boss, only to find her romantic hopes dashed by the dawning realization that he was happier in the arms of men. The book was published in Ireland, where a British Government attempt to suppress it was laughed out of court.[17]

CONTROL OF THE SECURITY SERVICES

The Wright and Massiter revelations have served to emphasize the need for some oversight and accountability in the security services, to ensure that its practices and policies really do protect the country from external enemies and internal subversion, and do not go beyond what is strictly necessary for that purpose. There can be no doubt that the operational activities of MI5 and GCHQ require secrecy: the IRA is a permanent threat to British soldiers and civilians, and London has had more than its share of international terrorist outrages. There can be no objection to the gathering of information about individuals or organizations which espouse extreme or violent views, so long as there are clearly defined limits to the use to which such information is put. Citizens cannot demand to know what is going on, but should at least be able to live in confidence that it is going on effectively and fairly. This can only be achieved by setting independent guards to watch over the guardians, representing a public which has a right, if not to know, at least to be positively reassured.

The security service was established in 1909 by Royal Prerogative as part of the defence forces of the realm. Its purpose was carefully spelled out by Lord Denning in his Profumo report:

> The cardinal principle is that their operations are to be used for one purpose, and one purpose only, the *Defence of the Realm*. They are not to be used so as to pry into any man's private conduct, or business affairs: or even into his political opinions, except in so far as they are subversive, that is, they would *contemplate the overthrow of the government by unlawful means*.[18]

These principles are clear enough, but are they complied with? The constitutional position of the security service could scarcely have been more carefully devised to remove its operations from democratic scrutiny. The Director-General has direct access to the Prime Minister if he wishes to discuss a particularly sensitive matter, but Ministers are specifically enjoined not to inquire into its day-to-day operations. MI5 directs the operations of the Special Branch, which is part of the Metropolitan Police Force, whose Commissioner is responsible to the Home Secretary on matters of general policy. The courts have held that in operational matters, police discretion cannot be interfered with by Ministers of State. In 1964 the Government set up a Security Commission – a panel of public figures from the judiciary, the armed forces and the civil service. It is chaired by an eminent judge, but activated by the Prime Minister only to examine particular scandals that have come to public notice. The Ombudsman is specifically excluded from examining any action taken for the purpose of protecting the security of the State.

In 1989 the Government introduced legislation to establish MI5 on a statutory basis, in an effort to forestall condemnation by the European Court of Human Rights (see earlier, page 108). This measure merely provides that MI5's function shall be to protect national security, 'in particular' to guard against espionage, terrorism and sabotage and actions 'intended to overthrow or undermine parliamentary democracy by political, industrial or violent means' and 'to safeguard the economic well-being of the United Kingdom' against actions by foreigners. This is a very much broader definition of 'subversion' than that provided by Lord Denning 'contemplating the overthrow of the government by unlawful means'), but his definition has demonstrably been ignored in the past by a service that was not properly accountable. Given that any functional definition in this area is bound to be elastic and to require the application of subjective judgement, what matters is accountability and oversight. In this respect the Security Service Act is notably deficient. It provides for a director-general to be appointed by the Home Secretary and enjoins him to ensure that no information is collected or passed on 'except so far as be necessary' for safeguarding national security or detecting serious crime. How far is 'necessary' is again a question of judgement. The courts regard the term as denoting something more than 'expedient' and less than 'indispensable'. So what is really needed in the interests of national security will remain a matter for the judgement of those within the service in deciding which targets to select as 'subversive' and which of those 'subversives' to subject to deceptive or illegal measures. That their judgement has not always been acceptable in a democratic society is demonstrated by their targeting of NCCL officials, trade-union leaders, 'left-wing' journalists and politicians, CND members and a host of other citizens whose careers, it now transpires, have been damaged or put in jeopardy by judgements made within M I 5 to collect information about their private lives and to use it to block their employments or appointments. As one former Home Secretary, Roy Jenkins, said in 1988: 'I am convinced now that an organization of people who live in the fevered world of espionage and counter-espionage is entirely unfitted to judge between what is subversive and what is legitimate dissent.'

The Security Service bill, however, ensures that such judgements will not be subject to the kind of democratic scrutiny which operates in the United States, Canada, Australia and European countries other than the UK. The Government resisted all proposed amendments to have the service overseen by a Select Committee of Parliament or even by an appointed body of Privy Councillors. Nor was it prepared to allow independent oversight in the form of an Inspector-General, who functions in Canada and Australia (in addition to parliamentary committees) as a watchdog empowered to monitor all aspects of security operations to ensure that they are within the law and respect civil liberties. Instead, the Security Service Act provides merely that a senior judge will serve as a part-time 'Commissioner', with the limited task of 'reviewing' the Home Secretary's decisions to grant warrants allowing M I 5 to trespass and burgle. He is not permitted to question the Home Secretary's judgement in signing the warrant, but merely to consider whether his action was procedurally proper – i.e. whether he had before him some material, however slight, that justified the exercise of judgement. It is difficult to believe that this will provide any real measure of control: in the unlikely event that the Commissioner concludes that the Home Secretary has taken leave of his senses by signing a warrant, his only power is to report the fact to the Prime Minister, who may exclude any mention of it from the Commissioner's annual report to Parliament. The Commissioner's other function is to investigate in the event that the secret tribunal established to consider complaints from possible victims of M I 5 operations stumbles across unreasonable behaviour within the service. The likelihood of such reference is minimal, given the severe restrictions on the scope of the tribunal itself (see earlier, page 110). But even if a reference is made and the Commissioner concludes that M I 5 has acted unreasonably, he has no power to do anything about it. He can only report the matter to the Home Secretary, 'who may take such action in the light of the report as he thinks fit' – and the Home Secretary may, of course, think it fit to take no action at all. To describe the Commissioner as a 'safeguard' is to argue in a circle: his remit is limited to a small area of MI5's operations and any malfeasance he uncovers can merely be reported to the Prime Minister or Home Secretary who need neither correct it nor bring it to public attention.

The only statutory limit imposed on MI5 operations by the Security Service bill is that the Director-General is placed under a 'duty to ensure that the service does not take any action to further the interests of a political party'. Since the 1989 official secrets reform prohibits any revelations at all about MI5 actions, it is difficult to envisage a breach of this duty ever becoming public, unless an officer were to publish memoirs from abroad. The duty is in theory enforceable by the High Court at the behest of a disfavoured political party, although it would have to show that the Director-General was unreasonable in his belief that the objectionable action was not designed to promote party-political interests. When what is being furthered is the interests of the Government and its policies (especially in defence and foreign relations), the courts would be unlikely to intervene. Given the difficulties of obtaining credible evidence, the duty is for all practical purposes unenforceable in law, and if the Commissioner stumbles upon a breach of it his only remedy is to report to the Prime Minister, who may well be the leader of the party which is being favoured. It is no secret that individual MI5 officers 'leak' private information on political figures to chosen journalists, or by way of anonymous contributions to *Private Eye*. The practice is long-standing (in 1924 no less than four different security officials leaked copies of the 'Zinoviev telegram' to discredit the Labour Party). Such practices will only cease by the encouragement of an ethos of professionalism and impartiality within the service – a task that would be assisted by independent oversight, but to which part-time commissioners and tribunals will make little contribution.[19]

MI5, with its estimated staff of 2,000 and a budget of about £200 million, remains effectively beyond parliamentary control. The security services have had notable achievements in recent years against the IRA and terrorist groups, and have attracted several important KGB defectors. It is difficult to see how this legitimate work would be compromised by independent oversight which provides reassurance that the secret services are not targeting trade unionists and civil liberties groups as 'subversive', or leaking information obtained by invasions of privacy for party-political purposes, or conducting internecine feuds of the kind which have been alleged in recent controversies over the disciplinary proceedings against John Stalker or the whispering campaign against the late Sir Maurice Oldfield. In the USA, a satisfactory degree of control and accountability for the CIA has been achieved by the enactment of a legally binding charter, and inquiries conducted by Congressional committees into activities which may be in breach of it. The Australian and Canadian intelligence communities have has been placed on a firm democratic footing as the result of Royal Commissions which discovered numerous inadequacies and malpractices. There is no evidence that national security performance in these nations has been damaged by democratic controls over forces whose methods of operation and selection of targets can vitally affect the liberty of the subject.

'D' NOTICES

A curious institution known as the 'D' Notice Committee was established in 1912 – the year after the Official Secrets Act was passed – for the purpose of applying behind-the-scenes pressure on editors in relation to national security issues. The Committee comprises a handful of representatives from the media together with civil servants and officers from the armed forces, and it worked for forty years before the Press dared even to mention its existence. In 1963 Mr John Profumo tried unsuccessfully to have it issue a 'D' Notice to stop the publication of Christine Keeler's memoirs, and in 1967 it fell into some disrepute when the *Daily Express* published the identities of the heads of MI5 and MI6 in contravention of a 'D' Notice and revealed MI5's practice of monitoring all overseas cables. The Secretary of the Committee, Colonel Sammy Lohan, had taken journalist Chapman Pincher to lunch in an attempt to persuade him not to publish the cable-monitoring story: when it did emerge, Lohan resigned his job and became restaurant critic of the *Evening Standard*. There are now only eight 'D' Notices, and they warn in general terms against publication of details of defence plans and equipment, nuclear weaponry, codes and communication interceptions, the security services, civil defence and the photography of defence installations.

It is important to appreciate that a 'D' Notice has no legal force whatsoever, and 'guidance' from the Committee or its secretary is not conclusive. In 1980 the *New Statesman* published a series of articles by Duncan Campbell about telephone tapping, despite a warning from the Committee's secretary that this contravened a 'D' Notice, yet no prosecution followed. Conversely, an editor who assiduously follows the Committee's advice is not guaranteed immunity from prosecution under the Official Secrets Act. The editor of the *Sunday Telegraph* faced charges along with Jonathan Aitken for receiving the Biafran War report, although the secretary of the 'D' Notice Committee had told him that its publication would create no danger to national security.

In 1980 a House of Commons Committee reviewed the system and published a damning indictment. It reported that major newspapers had stopped consulting 'D' Notices; that the foreign and fringe Press had never received them; that the Notices were so vaguely worded as to be meaningless; that the Notices had not been amended in the previous ten years; and that some categories of sensitive information were not covered by the Notices.[20] The Conservative majority of the Committee (which had finally split on party lines), thought the system could be reformed. It was supported by both the BBC and the IBA, on the grounds that they welcomed 'official' advice. Evidence to the contrary was given by the *Sunday Times*, *World in Action* and the Press Association, which argued that the freedom of the Press is incompatible with the cosy cooperation which the 'D' system envisages. They convinced the Labour MPs who recommended in a minority report that the Committee should be abolished.

Should the media continue to cooperate with, and indeed to be represented on, a Committee which applies informal pressure in favour of censorship? The representatives of the BBC and the IBA who gave evidence to the Parliamentary Committee were a poor advertisement for media freedom, accepting that there were matters of national security on which the Government knows best. The programme-makers who opposed the system were able to point to specific occasions on which the Government had been proved, in retrospect, to have known very little. In 1986 a 'D' Notice was placed on publication of the name of the legal adviser for MI5, who had been mentioned in open court in the *Spycatcher* case. The reason for the Notice – that he might become a target for terrorist attack – seemed acceptable until it was pointed out that his name and position had figured prominently in a recent book about the IRA. There is no doubt that the Committee is welcomed by some nervous media executives who view it, mistakenly, as an insurance against costly prosecutions and injunctions. It may one day develop into a 'Publications Review Board' on the US model. But at present its 'guidance' is heavily influenced by the military's predisposition in favour of secrecy, and its Secretary has his offices in the Ministry of Defence. Moreover, it offers no protection to those who accept its invitation to submit articles or manuscripts – it has, in one recent case, handed a book immediately over to the Government so that it could consider whether to prosecute the author. In 1988 the Secretary of the Committee tried to put a 'D' Notice on certain names mentioned in books by David Leigh and Rupert Allison MP. Some were dead, and others had served with Philby, who blew their cover forty years ago. Both authors insisted that their books be published with the names intact.

MEMORABILIA

Former Ministers, retired civil servants, ex-police chiefs and even the public hangman have sought to write accounts of their stewardship in office. Many of these books will be freed from the threat of criminal prosecution by the abolition of Section 2, but may none the less be subject to civil injunctions for breach of confidence. What Whitehall bureaucrats are desperately anxious to suppress are comments or criticisms on their own performance, and premature revelation of differences of opinion in Cabinet discussions. Such differences emerge in unattributed 'leaks' to newspapers by Ministers and their advisers at the time, but an insider's account is believed to carry greater credibility and to undermine the constitutional fiction of 'collective responsibility' whereby all members of the Cabinet are assumed fully to support decisions against which they have, in real life, fought tooth and nail. The public interest is alleged to be served by suppressing the truth for many years: Ministers will feel inhibited in what they say at Cabinet meetings if they know that one of their Cabinet colleagues might publish a version of the meeting as soon as they return to the opposition benches. These assumptions do not accord with political reality, but none the less form the basis of the legal argument that what happens in Cabinet and at top levels in Whitehall is confidential, and revelations can be stopped by breach-of-confidence actions.

In 1975 these arguments were accepted, up to a point, by the Chief Justice in the breach-of-confidence action brought against the publishers of Richard Crossman's diaries. He ruled that Cabinet discussions were confidential, although the public interest in suppressing first-hand accounts of them lapsed with time, and an eight to ten-year embargo was the maximum period which the law would uphold in the absence of any danger to national security.[21] He rejected the claim that civil servants should be immune from criticism, and that the Permanent Secretary to the Cabinet has any legal power of censorship over Ministerial memoirs. None the less, the case proved a watershed, unleashing a powerful current of civil law which had hitherto been confined mainly to trade secrets. As the criminal sanctions of Section 2 fell into disrepute, injunctions granted by civil courts (backed by criminal sanctions for contempt in the event of disobedience) became a powerful weapon in the hands of the Whitehall mandarins. The 'bottomless purse' of the Treasury Solicitor, who could mount expensive legal actions and carry them through to the House of Lords, was a threat which few publishers could ignore, as memoirs of civil-service life, however interesting for political scientists, were unlikely to sell in sufficient numbers to justify the risk of losing a costly legal action. Now, whenever the Government can satisfy a judge that a contemplated breach of confidence is against the public interest, it can have publication stopped – and by seeking an injunction from a High Court judge it will prevent the Press from having trial by jury.

All this is in sharp contrast with American law, as the *Pentagon Papers* case of 1971 shows. *The New York Times* obtained volumes of top-secret documents on the history of the Vietnam war and began publishing. The US Supreme Court refused the Nixon administration an injunction; only if disclosure would surely result in direct, immediate and irreparable damage to the nation would freedom of the Press to publish documents from Government sources be interfered with by US courts. It is also significant to contrast the speed of the US decision (so that publication plans were not impeded) with the long period during which the *Sunday Times* had to wait before it could publish the *Crossman Diaries*.

The Government was not satisfied with the amount of secrecy – extensive though it is – which the Crossman decision brought within the law's protection, and it set up a Committee of Privy Councillors on

Ministerial memoirs. In 1976 that Committee, chaired by Viscount Radcliffe, made proposals which were gratefully and immediately accepted by the Government, which laid them down as new 'Conventions' (not laws) which should govern Ministerial memoirs.[22] Everything which the Government failed to have decided in its favour in the *Crossman Diaries* case was duly enshrined in the following constitutional conventions:

No Minister past or present is to reveal the opinions or attitudes of colleagues as to Government business with which they have been concerned. He is not to reveal advice given to him by civil servants. He is not to make any public comment on the capacity or competence of civil servants who have worked for him. On assuming office he will be told of these conventions and required to sign a declaration that he will follow them. Whenever an ex-Minister contemplates making public an account bearing on any aspect of his Ministerial life he must show the Secretary of the Cabinet in advance the full text of what he proposes to say. He is to follow these guidelines even for letters to and interviews in the Press, and for appearances on television and radio. If clearance is refused by the Secretary for reasons of national security or the preservation of international relations, the ex-Minister may appeal to the Prime Minister, whose decision is final. If it is refused on the ground of 'confidential relationships' the Minister must make his own decision whether to publish in the face of that refusal. An author is free to disregard the above principles relating to 'confidential relationships' fifteen years after the events which they describe, except that in respect of a reference to a civil-service adviser, the embargo period is fifteen years or the remainder of the service life of that adviser, whichever is the longer. There is no fifteen-year limit for questions of national security and international relations. Ministers should leave instructions to their executors in their wills that posthumous publication of their diaries should not take place in breach of these conventions.

These guidelines have clearly been drawn to protect senior civil servants from criticism by the Ministers with whom they have dealt, and to remove high-level policy information from public exposure until long after public criticism can have any impact. They exemplify the secrecy obsession of successive British Governments, advised by senior civil servants motivated more by protecting their own backs than by any desire to protect the public. They are not laws – neither the Labour

Government which accepted them nor its Conservative successors have dared to submit them to Parliamentary debate – but they take the form of a 'gentleman's agreement' which can be relied upon in any future breach of confidence action. Whether the courts would hold fast to the *Crossman Diaries* criteria, or would find that the Radcliffe conventions have enlarged the ambit of confidentiality, remains to be seen. Ministers can choose to ignore them, and indeed the former Arts Minister Hugh Jenkins refused to delete criticisms of civil servants from his book *The Culture Gap*, which was published shortly after he left office.

Civil servants are subject to the same rules as those concerning Ministers. When clearance for their books is refused, no reasons will be given and the author is given no opportunity to argue his case before those who decide – indeed, their identity is concealed from him. This is yet another example of a matter which can affect a person's livelihood being decided by unknown civil servants according to undisclosed rules without the citizen having any opportunity to present argument or test the reasons for refusal. The usual Government apologia – Ministerial responsibility for a collective department decision, accountability to Parliament, necessary anonymity of civil servants, decisions of policy, matters of security and so forth – are unconvincing.

PUBLIC RECORDS

Most civil-service records are transferred after thirty years to the Public Record Office at Kew, where they can be inspected by historians and journalists. The Government has the power to 'weed out' and with-hold records which it thinks should be kept for a longer time, whether fifty or one hundred years, or for ever. The main categories are: distressing or embarrassing personal details about living persons or their immediate descendants, information received by the Government in confidence, some papers on Ireland and 'certain exceptionally sensitive papers which affect the security of the State'.[23] The weeders are super-sensitive to national security and until very recently refused to release any papers which so much as mentioned the existence of MI5 or MI6. The records of these services are not available for inspection, and never will be if civil servants have their way.

By what right does Whitehall withhold the raw material of history for a century or even longer? The Public Records Acts provide that Government papers shall not be available for general inspection until they have been in existence for thirty years 'or such other period as the Lord Chancellor may provide'. In 1967 Lord Gardiner was prevailed upon to grant a 'dispensation' for some forty categories of documents, including all records relating to civil defence, overseas defence planning, atomic energy and the security services. He assumed that documents in these categories would be released as and when they lost any contemporary security significance, but the Cabinet office has interpreted the 'dispensation' as a blanket authorization to withhold all records for as long as it wishes. Hence the documents relating to MI5 activity between the wars and the defections of Burgess and Maclean have never been released. There is no basis for legal challenge: the Lord Chancellor has an unreviewable discretion, and there is no guidance given by the Acts as to what documents should be suppressed.

The British obsession for secrecy is well illustrated by the 300 feet of official volumes (some 5 per cent of the total) stored at Kew which cannot be opened for fifty to one hundred years. Amongst the official memoranda listed in January 1989 as being closed for a century are: prison reform and lengths of sentences (1910–34); forcible feeding in reformatory schools (1910); the sterilization of mental defectives (1911–30); imprisonment and forcible feeding of suffragettes (1913); imprisonment of Emily Pankhurst (1913–17); internment of Sinn Fein leaders (1918); industrial unrest and strikes (1918); experiments on animals with poison gas (1913–16); instructions to police on sedition charges against Socialists (1912–18); Home Office practice in dealings with criminal lunatics (1913); coal-miners' strike (1919); flogging of vagrants (1919); decisions against prosecuting James Joyce's *Ulysses* (1924); Fascist marches (1936); police reports on the activities of the National Council for Civil Liberties (1935–41); opposition to British interests in Palestine (1938); Tibetan relations with China (1938–45); dental service for police in wartime (1939); war crimes – lists of suspects and reports on atrocities (1941–7); interrogations of prisoners of war in London (1942–4); British scorched-earth policy in Malaya (1943); the relief and repatriation of allied internees (1946); and the Albert Speer file (1946).[24] These topics need only be listed to demonstrate how the notion of 'embarrassment to descendants' is being manipulated to cover 'embarrassment to the descendants of civil servants'. Closure for a century of files relating to official treatment of suffragettes, prisoners and mental patients prior to the First World War cannot conceivably be justified on privacy grounds. Records of field executions in the First World War were withheld for seventy years, ostensibly to avoid embarrassment to relatives of the long-dead soldiers, but when these documents were finally released, it became clear that the secrecy had been used to avoid exposing the arbitrariness and brutality of justice in the trenches. Quite apart from the absurdity of sealing files about arrangements for police dental treatment during the Second World War, the above examples illustrate how a good deal of information of historical significance in relation to British foreign policy is being suppressed, together with material of contemporary importance about the investigation of war crimes. Home Office material about police surveillance of strikes and civil libertarians in the 1930s is being withheld, for no conceivable reason other than that it will present an unedifying picture of official intolerance, especially when compared to the more permissive attitudes taken towards Fascists, the files about whom are similarly being suppressed.

A recent departmental committee recommended more liberal access.[25] It criticized the practice whereby the Lord Chancellor can order an entire class of documents to be kept secret for a century, without considering the specific documents which make up that class. It proposed that more files should be released before the thirty-year embargo is up, that 'embarrassment' should no longer be a ground for suppression, that the power to keep files secret for ever should be abolished, and that there should be a right to appeal from secrecy orders. The Government, of course, rejected the report.[26] But what good reason can there be for withholding routine Government records from scholars and historians for longer than the ten years thought appropriate for Cabinet records by the Chief Justice in the *Crossman Diaries* case? The 'thirty-year plus' rule is a typical feature of British public life. A British student of government will often learn more from a short period in Washington about the US administrative process than he can learn about his own from a lifetime in England. The Government and the senior members of the Opposition have been agreed on one thing: that the less the public knows about the process of decision-making the better.

The irony is that many of the documents withheld from the public in the UK are sent, under bilateral arrangements, to other countries where they become immediately open to inspection. Modern British historians like Professor Geoffrey Warner are becoming more familiar with the US Freedom of Information Act than with our own Public Records Office. He had to go to America to obtain British files and British reports, compiled by British officers, about the occupied territories during the Second World War. The Public Records Office would not let him see them – although they were more than thirty years old. Although the Government has recently confirmed that all security and intelligence-related records will never be released to the Public Records Office, MI5 files have occasionally been copied to the CIA, where they may be inspected at the US National Archives. Professor Bernard Wasserstrom, a respected US historian, was recently refused access to the MI5 file on an agent who had dealings with British security sixty years ago. Fortunately, he found some of the material in Washington: it had been collected by the British Special Branch in Shanghai before the war, and had been passed to the CIA by the Nationalist Government shortly before its fall in 1949. Utterly harmless, yet historically fascinating, material of this sort is for ever foreclosed to British historians on bogus 'national security' grounds. Decisions to suppress innocuous documents of this kind are made in order to reinforce a cardinal principle of civil-service administration – that Government must be carried on in secret. As Lord Devlin has put it, 'The danger of the system is that it installs as judges of what ought to be revealed men whose interest it is to conceal.'

VETTING AND PURGING

To what extent is the State entitled to probe the private life and political views of its employees to eliminate security risks? In 1952, after the defection of Burgess and Maclean and the conviction of several scientists for supplying nuclear secrets to the Russians, a 'positive vetting' (PV) procedure was introduced to enable closer scrutiny of employees with access to security information. A measure of the extent to which the 'Secret State' has grown is provided by the increase in positively vetted employees, from 1,000 at the time the system was introduced to 68,000 in 1982. The system is expensive and time-consuming, and the vast number of checks has undoubtedly contributed to reduce their comprehensiveness and has led to such spectacular failures as MI 5's Michael Bettany (who flaunted Fascist beliefs at Oxford), GCHQ's Geoffrey Prime (who sexually molested small children) and Commander Trestrail, the Queen's bodyguard who openly consorted with male prostitutes. The PV procedure involves interviews of the employee, his referees and his previous employers, and checks into family background, associations and life-style. Security clearance is denied if there is an indication of 'unreliability', such as sympathy with a subversive organization, or 'character defects' which may expose the employee to blackmail or to temptation offered by foreign security services. The MoD regards as 'character defects' the following: 'Major indiscretion, drunkenness or drug-taking, dishonesty, conviction for serious crime, having substantial financial difficulties, being vulnerable as a result of irregular sexual behaviour and significant mental illness.'

Positive vetting is a necessary precaution for members of the security services, although the definition of a 'character defect' is open to debate. The Security Commission has recommended that homosexuality should not be an absolute bar to a security clearance, and the revelation in 1981 that Sir Maurice Oldfield, the most distinguished of spymasters, was that way inclined serves only to emphasize the wisdom of this approach. Regrettably, the Prime Minister greeted the revelation with distress, and other politicians who sometimes pretend concern for civil liberties, such as Dr David Owen, sought to make it into a scandal. What really matters is whether a civil servant who is subject to an adverse PV report has an effective means of challenging it – and this is far from the case. Where the civil servant is refused clearance on the basis of alleged character defects, his appeal is merely to the permanent Head of Department, who is hardly an independent judge, and the Courts will not intervene even if the appeal is unreasonably turned down. One young data processor had worked at GCHQ for some years before he recognized his homosexuality. He immediately disclosed it, and in consequence lost his PV clearance on the grounds that he might be subject to blackmail.[27] This was an irrational decision, since his openness about his sexuality would preclude him being blackmailed on that ground alone. None the less, the High Court held that it was not entitled to interfere with 'positive vetting' procedures other than to check that they had been conducted with basic fairness. The Government was entitled to hide behind 'national security', irrespective of whether the decision had been made unreasonably, irrationally or in bad faith.

When security clearance is denied on the basis of suspected Communist or Fascist links, the employee has the right to invoke what has become known as the 'purge procedure', and to state his case to 'Three Advisers'. Until 1962, an accused person was not allowed any formal representation: since then, he has been permitted to bring a 'friend', who could be a lawyer or trade-union official, but who has no right of audience. The civil servant is given no opportunity to confront or cross-examine his accusers, and no power to subpoena witnesses. 'Chapter and verse' of the allegations is very rarely provided, on the ground that to do so might compromise sources. The Three Advisers meet and report in secret, they do not see witnesses, and the Minister is not bound to accept their recommendations.

This 'purge procedure' was revised in 1957 as a result of an inquiry set up after the Burgess/Maclean defections. The inquiry – a committee of seven Privy Councillors – decided that the Three Advisers had been too fair to civil servants of doubtful loyalty, because they had adopted too high a standard of proof. Henceforth, the Government announced, the Advisers were to 'tilt the balance in favour of offering greater protection to the security of the State rather than in the direction of safeguarding the rights of the individual'.[28] The sole question that the Advisers should ask themselves was, 'Are there or are there not reasonable grounds for supposing that the individual has or has recently had Communist sympathies or associations of such a type as to raise legitimate doubts about his reliability?' The Privy Councillors indicated that marriage to a Communist or Communist sympathizer would be sufficient to raise such doubts, and ICI was forced by the Minister of Supply to dismiss their assistant solicitor, Mr J. Lang, or suffer cancellation of all Government contracts. Lang's wife had once belonged to the Communist Party, although she had disaffiliated before her marriage. The Minister refused to tell Lang of the allegations against him, or to explain to Parliament why he should be debarred from drafting contracts relating to secret work. In 1962 the Radcliffe Committee extended the 'purge procedure' to independent contractors working for Government departments.[29]

It is the consistent policy of British Governments to avoid putting themselves under judicial controls whenever possible. If a person is not accorded the protection, such as it is, allowed by the arrangements already described, there is no court to which he can complain. This defect is particularly important in cases pivoting upon vague words like 'security'. 'Security' is an abstraction, and the citizen is at the mercy of administrators who will define it as they please. To tilt the scales against liberty in favour of security is serious enough – when 'security' is undefined, the threat to the citizen is manifest.

The justification is always the same: Ministerial responsibility. In the words of Lord Kilmuir, then Lord Chancellor, the balance 'must be struck by a Minister who is responsible to Parliament . . . and who is there to be shot at'.[30] The value of this protection can be measured by looking at the proceedings of the House of Commons ten days previously. The Minister of Supply was asked on what grounds he had denied access on the part of Lang to secrets: he refused to answer. What is the point of stressing the right to ask a question on matters of security when the Minister can be relied on never to answer? The political accountability of a Minister does not extend to security matters, and is a completely inadequate substitute for the right to take one's case before the courts. The rules laid down by the Government in 1957 do not envisage the employee being given details of the allegations or permit him to be represented at the hearing before the Advisers, or to cross-examine the evidence against him.

It may well be that these manifestly unjust aspects of the purge procedure will be the subject of future challenge in the courts, which have in recent years developed broader powers to review administrative actions and to strike them down on grounds of unfairness. The 'Three Advisers' system is also available to aliens threatened with deportation on national-security grounds, and was challenged by American journalist Mark Hosenball when he was made the subject of a deportation order in 1977 (see later, page 326). The Court of Appeal accepted that the procedure was unfair, but upheld the order on the grounds that national-security considerations justified a shortfall in the rights which could be accorded to an alien suspect.[31] A British citizen whose job is at risk falls into a different category, and in 1984 the House of Lords was prepared to insist that there should at least be some evidence of a security threat before the Prime Minister was entitled to prohibit civil servants at GCHQ from joining trade unions.[32] The court is not prepared to evaluate evidence relating to national security, but will use its powers of judicial review to ensure that the basic rules of natural justice have been complied with. In the case brought by the homosexual data processor against GCHQ, the High Court confirmed that it would supervise the 'fairness' of dismissals on grounds of national security, ensuring that employees were given at least an indication of what was alleged against them and an opportunity to present arguments against their sacking. In the light of this case, it may be that courts would strike down a dismissal or refusal of security clearance where legal representation had not been afforded or no reasons at all had been forthcoming.

Individual litigants cannot expect British courts, as presently minded, to look very closely into Government claims that actions taken against them are based on national security. Unlike breach-of-confidence actions (where such claims must at least be weighed against a specific public-interest defence) judicial review is strictly limited to ensuring that proper procedures are followed and that there is *some* evidence – however slight and however dubious – that national-security interests were at stake. All assessment of that evidence will be left to the executive, no matter how much the decision strikes at civil liberties. The Government's ban on trade-union membership at GCHQ was a plain denial of the right of freedom to associate. It was struck down by a High Court judge on the basis that the Government had acted unfairly in imposing it without giving the unions the opportunity for consultation that they had a legitimate right to expect. On appeal, however, the Government succeeded by arguing that a national-security consideration had been present in its decision, because the monitoring centre had been adversely affected by union strike action several years previously. This was hardly an impressive argument: the Government had not thought to make it in the initial proceedings, and the unions were in any event offering a 'no strike' agreement which would have guaranteed no further disruption. The Government could not prove that its ban was necessary, or even justifiable, in the interests of national security, but the House of Lords required merely to be satisfied by some evidence (a passage in an affidavit by Sir Robert Armstrong) that the decision had been motivated by security concerns. Judges are often accused of being too deferential to the Government in this area, and there is no doubt that they could go a little further, within the constraints of judicial review, by requiring national-security decisions to be made rationally. But this test is easily satisfied, and it is unfair to expect the courts to protect civil liberties unless they have the power to judge whether a withdrawal of a fundamental right is *necessary* in the interest of national security. That is the test applied by the European Convention of Human Rights for abrogating rights to freedom of speech and assembly, and only by enactment of the Convention as part of British law would we enable the courts of this country to safeguard citizens from losses of liberty by unjustifiable invocations of 'national security'.

OTHER POLITICAL OFFENCES

Section 1

Section 1 of the Official Secrets Act makes it an offence punishable by fourteen years' imprisonment to enter top-secret establishments or to collect, publish or communicate any official document or information which might be indirectly useful to a potential enemy, if such acts are done 'for any purpose prejudicial to the safety or the interests of the State'. These are very wide words, and the Act has special provisions designed to reverse the burden of proof if secret information has been found in a defendant's possession, and which enable a jury to draw an inference of intention to prejudice State interests merely from evidence about a defendant's character and associations. Suspects have no 'right to silence' – police have special powers to oblige them to answer questions in the course of a Section 1 investigation, and the trial itself may be held wholly or partly in secret. Section 1 is the most oppressive law on the statute-book, and its provisions which reverse the burden of proof, permit guilt by association and abolish the right of silence are impossible to justify.

Although Section 1 is headed 'penalties for spying', it has on two occasions been used in cases which had nothing to do with espionage. In 1962 a group of anti-nuclear protesters were convicted under Section 1 for immobilizing an airfield used by nuclear bombers: it was State policy to keep the base on constant alert, and the jury was not permitted to hear argument that the immobilization of nuclear weapons might safeguard rather than prejudice the interests of the nation.[33] In 1977 Duncan

Campbell was alleged to have breached Section 1 by collecting information for publication in *Time Out* – a purpose claimed to be as prejudicial to the interests of the State as selling the information to the Soviet embassy. This prosecution was a breach of parliamentary assurances in 1920 and 1949 that Section 1 was aimed at spies in the employ of foreign powers, and caused considerable dismay in the publishing world.[34] An A–Z of London, after all, is 'indirectly useful to a potential enemy' – could its publisher be punished for 'prejudicing the interests of the State'? Mr Justice Mars-Jones correctly described Section 1 as 'oppressive', and these charges were in due course abandoned.

It is interesting to note that even with its oppressive features Section 1 charges are still capable of being rejected by a jury. Seven young servicemen were acquitted in 1985 of passing secret information to enemy agents in Cyprus in return for sexual favours, despite their extremely full confessions. A subsequent inquiry found that military police had extracted these confessions by unfair questioning, and recommended that in future servicemen suspected of spying offences should be treated like any other suspect under police interrogation. Michael Bettany was convicted in the same year of attempting to pass information about his work in MI5 to Soviet diplomats. Both the Cyprus and the Bettany trials took place in secret, although the Press was allowed to report sections of the prosecution's opening address. While Section 1 cases may sometimes involve evidence which deserves to be kept secret, it is hardly fair to publish the prosecution's allegations of treason without lifting the veil on the answers provided by the defence.

Although the dice are loaded in favour of the prosecution, it is noteworthy that Section 1 was not used against either Blunt or Philby. Both men were offered an immunity from prosecution in return for a confession, the security services apparently believing that the public interest would be better served by hushing up their treachery than by punishing them for it. Blunt was allowed to live in peace for fifteen years until exposed by a journalist (in a book which could not have been published had the 1989 secrecy legislation been in force), while Philby made a brief confession to an MI5 colleague in Beirut and then departed for Moscow. These immunities were later justified on the grounds that Blunt and Philby might volunteer useful information in return for the promise not to prosecute, although the real reason for offering them a secret amnesty was doubtless to avoid public and political embarrassment.

Treason

The crime of treason has played a lurid part in British history ever since the Treason Act of 1351 made it a capital offence for British citizens to give aid and comfort to the King's enemies. This Act remains on the statute-books and the crime still carries the death penalty, although in 1790 Parliament substituted hanging for the traditional punishment of beheading in the Tower. There has not been a treason trial since William Joyce (Lord Haw-Haw) was convicted in 1946 for making Nazi propaganda broadcasts. Those proceedings did little credit to British justice: Joyce was an American who was convicted on the technicality that he had once possessed (but never used) a British passport, and he was executed in defiance of the principle that the death penalty should not be exacted where there is a dissenting appellate judgement.[35] Treason is broadly defined to include 'compassing or imagining' the death of the King or the heir apparent, slaying the Chancellor, the Treasurer, or any judge or magistrate, or having sex with 'the King's companion, or the King's eldest daughter unmarried, or the wife of the King's eldest son and heir'. (Anne Boleyn, it will be recalled, lost her head for being an accomplice in her own treasonable adultery.) In 1848, much disturbed by the republican revolutions in Europe, Parliament passed the Treason Felony Act which makes every person who shall 'compass, imagine, invent, devise or intend to deprive our most gracious Lady the Queen ... from the style, honour or Royal name of the Imperial crown of the United Kingdom ...' liable 'to be imprisoned for the term of his or her natural life'. In theory, the publication of arguments in favour of abolishing the monarchy constitutes an offence under this legislation.

These laws are historical anomalies, and serve no useful purpose other than by exciting the occasional back-bench MP to demand that IRA bombers be hanged for treason rather than sent to prison for life for murder or conspiracy to cause explosions. It is inconceivable that treason would be charged as a means of bringing back the death penalty for politically motivated murder, or that any outspoken republican would face imprisonment 'for the term of his or her natural life'. As the Law

Commission has commented, with its usual understatement, 'It is our provisional view that there is no need for the retention of any treason-type offence to deal with violation of the royal ladies.'[36] In 1977 it recommended that all treason statutes should be abolished and replaced with a crime of engaging in conduct likely to help an enemy country with which we are at war.

Sedition

Sedition is the political crime *par excellence*, used in the eighteenth and nineteenth centuries in direct attempts to silence critics of Government. The crime is broadly defined as promoting ill-will between different classes of citizens, raising discontent and disaffection among the people, and bringing the Government or the laws into hatred, ridicule or contempt. In 1764 it was used against John Wilkes and the printers of radical papers, who assailed George III with such seditious remarks as 'You have never been acquainted with the language of truth until you heard it in the complaints of your subjects.'[37] The King's judges, and notably Lord Mansfield, were determined to obtain convictions from juries who shared the popular dislike of George III and his Ministers, so they themselves ruled that the writings were seditious and instructed their juries that the only issue was whether defendants had published them or not. Juries ignored these directions to convict, and emerged from court to the cheers of crowds who had gathered to celebrate the acquittals. Charles Fox and his Whig supporters finally pushed through Parliament the Libel Act of 1792, which established that it was the province of the jury and not the judge finally to decide whether a particular piece of writing was seditious. The Lord Chancellor and his judge predicted at the time that the Act would lead to 'the confusion and destruction of the law of England' – in fact, it legitimized 'sympathy acquittals' in seditious libel cases and deterred subsequent Governments from using this particular law to muzzle political criticisms of their policies.

Subsequent generations of judges have been less subservient to the Government, and have narrowed the scope of the offence so that it is now virtually useless as a weapon against writers and agitators. In 1886, John Burns and other Socialist speakers were acquitted of sedition at the Old Bailey, after the judge had ruled that the crime required a determined intention on the part of the defendant to incite people to violence – speeches critical of the Government which aroused class hatreds and might lead to violence were not seditious if actuated by 'an honest desire to alleviate the misery of the unemployed' or by a genuine desire to promote lawful reform.[38] The last case of sedition was brought in 1947, against the editor of a local paper who had justified violence against British Jews who refused to condemn Zionist outrages in Palestine. Mr Justice Birkett ruled that it was not enough to show that ill-will and hostility had been provoked: the prosecution had to prove an intention to stir up 'public disorder, tumult, insurrections or matters of that kind'.[39] Sedition now serves no purpose in the criminal law: any legitimate target is amply covered by offences in the Public Order Act.

Incitement to Disaffection

We have seen in this chapter how the power of the jury to return a verdict of acquittal, irrespective of the evidence, has been a significant deterrent to 'political' uses of Section 2 and sedition charges. A further example of the power of a jury to 'unmake' a bad law is provided by the acquittal in 1975 of fourteen pacifists who were charged at the Old Bailey with inciting troops to disaffection by distributing a leaflet explaining how they could conscientiously object to service in Northern Ireland or, as a last resort, desert. The Incitement to Disaffection Act was passed amid great controversy in 1934 – indeed, several of the leading cases on public order examined in Chapter 2 arose from meetings held in protest against this legislation. It punishes those who 'endeavour to seduce' military personnel from their 'duty or allegiance', and aroused understandable fears at the time that it would be used against those who merely distributed pacifist literature or who urged soldiers to disobey orders to fire on striking workers. Those fears have proved unfounded, although the notion of 'duty' is unjustifiably wide, and could theoretically catch both the wife who persuades a husband to stay back from barracks and a protester who urges soldiers to disobey orders on the grounds of conscientious objection to executing them. In neither case would 'allegiance' (in the sense of 'loyalty') be affected, and since the Incitement to Mutiny Act of 1797 punishes any attempt to seduce military personnel from their 'duty *and* allegiance', it is questionable whether the 1934 Act serves any real purpose. It has not been used since the Old Bailey acquittals in 1975, and the then Attorney-General, Sam Silkin, expressed regret that this much-publicized case was ever brought. The most powerful incitement to disaffection was made during the 1987 election campaign by the Prime Minister, Mrs Thatcher, who announced that service chiefs should consider resigning in protest if the Labour Party were elected and sought to implement its non-nuclear defence policy. It will henceforth be difficult to convince a jury that pacifists should be punished for urging lesser ranks to consider leaving the services in protest against having to implement Government policies on nuclear defence or Northern Ireland.

There are other unjustifiable pieces of legislation which are embarrassing, oppressive and of no contemporary significance. The Aliens (Protection) Amendment Act of 1919 makes it an offence for an alien to attempt any act likely to cause sedition or disaffection or industrial unrest in an industry where he has not been employed for at least two years; and in the same year it was also made an offence to do any act calculated to cause disaffection in the police force or to attempt to induce any policeman to go on strike. Like the laws against sedition and incitement to disaffection, these pieces of legislation have fallen into disuse, and any attempt to revive them would be highly controversial. The Police Federation has certainly not shrunk from inciting disaffection over pay and conditions, and it is difficult to see why aliens should not be permitted to participate in industrial action which is not otherwise unlawful. Attempts to enforce these laws against peaceful protests would probably now be in breach of the European Convention on Human Rights, and the most remarkable thing about them is that the Government has not taken the many opportunities which have been available to have them repealed. Has this been the result of oversight, or of a feeling that they may one day be gainfully deployed?

FIVE

Censorship

We live in an age where one person's obscenity is another person's bedtime video. The deep division in society over the appropriate limit to sexual permissiveness is mirrored by an inconsistent and largely ineffectual censorship of material which may offend or entertain, corrupt or enlighten, according to the taste and character of individual readers and viewers. The problem of where (if anywhere) you draw the line has been with us since the invention of printing: the exploits of Fanny Hill and Constance Chatterley gained a cinematic dimension with the advent of Linda Lovelace, and now page 3 titillation arrives with the morning milk on millions of breakfast tables. The arguments for and against censorship have worn well throughout the ages: 'Let us renounce the effort to reconcile these two irreconcilable things – art and young girls' exclaimed the Victorian novelist George Moore as his works were personally removed from the bookshelves of Mr W. H. Smith after complaints from elderly ladies in the provinces. The censorship of art and literature in Britain until the nineteen-sixties at least had the one great merit of bringing James Joyce and Henry Miller and D. H. Lawrence to the excited attention of generations of schoolchildren: the ideologically vapid rubbish which it is now necessary to travel to the Continent in order to procure hardly seems worth investing with the special thrill of the taboo. Britain, at least, can still boast the best obscenity trials. *Lady Chatterley's Lover* was a tension-packed seminar on English literature, the *Oz* trial produced more letters to *The Times* than the Suez crisis, and during the *Gay News* blasphemy trial readings from the Bible were interrupted by the judge announcing the cricket score while the prosecutrix led prayer meetings in the corridors of the Old Bailey.

The traditional pro-censorship lobby has recently found some strange bedfellows amongst the feminist movement (although, as we shall see, obscenity laws have been much used against outspoken women) while at the same time a new public explicitness about sexual behaviour has been officially sanctioned to help combat the spread of AIDS. The main battleground has shifted to television drama – from *EastEnders* to the plays of Dennis Potter and the late-night movies on Channel 4: the Government, in its 1987 election manifesto, promised to change the law to enable television producers to stand in the dock of the Old Bailey, at risk of up to three years' imprisonment for broadcasting obscenity. The trial of *EastEnders* will be something to look forward to.

HISTORY OF OBSCENITY

The history of obscenity provides a rich and comic tapestry about the futility of legal attempts to control sexual imagination. The subject-matter of pornography was settled by 1650: writers in subsequent centuries added new words and novel settings, but discovered no fundamental variation on the finite methods of coupling. The central irony of the court-room crusade – what might be termed 'the *Spycatcher* effect' – is always present: seek to suppress a book by legal action because it tends to corrupt, and the publicity attendant upon its trial will spread that assumed corruption far more effectively than its quiet distribution. *Lady Chatterley's Lover* sold three million copies after its prosecution in 1961. The last work of literature to be prosecuted for obscenity in a full-blooded Old Bailey trial was an undistinguished paperback entitled *Inside Linda Lovelace*. It had sold a few thousand copies in the years before the 1976 court case: within three weeks of its acquittal 600,000 copies were purchased by an avid public. That trial seems finally to have convinced the DPP of the unwisdom of using obscenity laws against books with any claim to literary or sociological merit.

The first censorship in Britain was decreed by the Star Chamber, and implemented by the Stationers' Company. Its charter, in 1559, required all serious books to be approved by the Queen, her Archbishops, or the Chancellor of Oxford or Cambridge University. The cost of licence fees alone deterred many publishers from submitting their books, and in 1640 the whole system fell with the abolition of the Star Chamber. In 1643, however, it was reintroduced by Cromwell, moving Milton to utter his immortal cry for freedom of the Press, the *Areopagitica*:

> Promiscuous reading is necessary to the constituting of human nature. The attempt to keep out evil doctrine by licensing is like the exploit of that gallant man who thought to keep out the crows by shutting his park gate . . . Lords and Commons of England, consider what nation it is whereof ye are: a nation not slow and dull, but of a quick, ingenious and piercing spirit. It must not be shackled or restricted. Give me the liberty to know, to utter and to argue freely according to conscience, above all liberties.

Milton's plea fell on deaf ears, and the country was saddled with no less than twenty-seven censors, who seem to have been no more effectual than their predecessors. One of their victims was, predictably, Milton himself (his *Defensio* was burned by the public hangman). The Lord Protector's protection was designed to save his subjects from political error rather than lusty thoughts, and Milton's *Paradise Lost* almost fell victim in 1667, but only because it suggested that an eclipse of the sun 'with sudden fear of change perplexes monarchs'. Licensing finally ended in 1695 when Parliament uncovered widespread corruption in its operation. Fraud, extortion, favouritism and intimidation by licensers and their agents had made the whole system a scandal.

During the reign of Charles II, the King's judges wrested control over disorderly conduct from the moribund ecclesiastical courts. To do so they asserted an inherent power, independent of parliamentary or ecclesiastical authorization, of superintending public morality by punishing deviations from what they considered to be desirable standards of conduct. The watershed case, in 1663, involved the poet Sir Charles Sedley, who had been responsible for a breach of the peace one night in Covent Garden. Sedley and his fellow revellers, 'inflamed by strong liquors', had climbed to the balcony of the Cock Tavern, 'and putting down their breeches they excrementiz'd in the street: which being done, Sedley stripped himself naked, and with eloquence preached blasphemy to the people'. A riot almost ensued, and some windows were broken – evidence of a breach of the King's Peace, and therefore appropriately tried by the Court of the King's Bench. But in rejecting Sedley's demands to be dealt with by the more lenient church courts, the Court of the King's Bench announced that it possessed an inherent power to punish moral subversion, whether or not there was a judicial precedent or any law in force against the particular brand of immorality alleged. 'This court is the custodian of the morals of all the King's subjects,' the court ruled, 'and it is high time to punish such profane conduct.'[1] Sedley's case was to become the precedent for the creation by English judges of the offence of obscenity and the crimes of corrupting public morals and outraging public decency. In 1989 the case was used as a precedent for convicting an artist who had exhibited ear-rings made out of human foetuses. The fact that he did so in an art gallery provided no defence.

The crime of obscenity began in 1727 when the court declared that publication of an erotic book entitled *Venus in the Cloister* was a common-law misdemeanour because it tended to 'weaken the bonds of civil society, virtue and morality'.[2] At first the new crime brought no new prosecutions: it was not activated again until 1763, as part of an attempt to silence the political radical John Wilkes. His popular polemics excoriated George III and his Ministers, but he had privately circulated a robust parody of Pope, on the theme that '. . . life can little more supply / Than just a few good fucks, and then we die'. This *Essay on Woman* was solemnly read to the House of Lords by Lord Sandwich, a casualty of the publisher's polemics, and when one peer protested the others shouted, 'Go on, go on.' They ultimately resolved that the poem was 'a most scandalous, obscene and impious libel'.

The law of obscene libel created by the judges in 1727 failed to make an impact on the circulation of erotica. By the middle of the eighteenth century the classic of English pornography, *Fanny Hill*, was on sale, with its lurid, if decorous, descriptions of rape, sodomy, flagellation and most other forms of sexual deviation. It was not until 1857 that Britain acquired an Obscene Publications Act, which gave the police powers to take books before local Justices to have them 'forfeited' and destroyed for obscenity. The task of defining obscenity was left to the courts, and Chief Justice Cockburn, in the 1868 case of *R. v. Hicklin*, obliged with a formula which has influenced the subject ever since:

> I think the test of obscenity is this, whether the tendency of the matter charged as obscenity is to deprave and corrupt those whose minds are open to such immoral influences, and into whose hands a publication of this sort may fall.[3]

Armed at last with a definition of obscenity, Victorian prosecutors proceeded to destroy many examples of fine literature and scientific speculation. James Bradlaugh and Annie Besant were convicted for advocating birth control in *An essay on the Population Problem*, Havelock Ellis's pioneering classic *Sexual Inversion* was destroyed, and a massive assault was mounted on the works of the 'French pornographers' Zola, Flaubert and de Maupassant. In 1888 Henry Vizetelly, a distinguished bookseller, was brought to the Old Bailey charged with publishing their books. A fortnight before the trial Zola was appointed to the French Legion of Honour for his services to literature and freedom, but this failed to save Vizetelly from a heavy fine. *The Times* gloated that 'In future, anyone who publishes translations of Zola's novels and works of similar character will do so at his peril, and must not expect to escape so easily as Mr Vizetelly.' It was right, of course. Next year Vizetelly, a sick man of seventy, was gaoled for three months for publishing further books by Zola and de Maupassant.

Despite the new law, pornography thrived in the Victorian underworld as never before. This was the time of the great *œuvres* of Victorian prurience: *The New Lady's Tickler* (1860), *Lady Bumtickler's Revels* (1872), *Colonel Spanker's Experimental Lecture* (1879), *The Story of a Dildoe* (1880), *My Secret Life* (1885), not to mention one epic entitled *Raped on the Railway: A True Story of a Lady who was First Ravished and Then Flagellated on the Scotch Express* (1894). Such titles found a new and avid readership as illiteracy declined from thirty per cent in 1861 to an estimated five per cent in 1893. These new readers were held to require the protection of the obscenity law. In the first twentieth-century obscenity case, the Common Serjeant of the Old Bailey could confidently assert that a book which sold at 1s. 11d. would 'clearly tend to the corruption of morals ... In the Middle Ages things were discussed which if put forward now for the reading of the general public would never be tolerated.'[4]

Under the old law of obscene libel, almost any work dealing with sexual passion could be successfully prosecuted. The *Hicklin* test focused upon the effect of the book on the most vulnerable members of society, whether or not they were likely to read it. One 'purple passage' could consign a novel to condemnation, and there was no defence of literary merit. D. H. Lawrence's *The Rainbow* was destroyed in 1915, and *The Well of Loneliness* suffered the same fate in 1928 at the hands of a magistrate who felt that a passage which implied that two women had been to bed ('And that night they were not divided') would induce 'thoughts of a most impure character' and 'glorify a horrible tendency'. (In 1974 *The Well of Loneliness* was read as a 'Book at Bedtime' on BBC's Radio 4.) The operation of the obscenity law depended to some extent upon the crusading zeal of current law officers. There was a brief respite in the 1930s, after a banned copy of *Ulysses* was found among the papers of a deceased Lord Chancellor. But in 1953 the authorities solemnly sought to destroy copies of *The Kinsey Report*, and in 1956 a number of respectable publishers – Secker & Warburg, Heinemann and Hutchinsons – were all tried at the Old Bailey for 'horrible tendencies' discovered in their current fiction lists. The Society of Authors set up a powerful lobby, which convinced a Parliamentary Committee that the common law of obscene libel should be replaced by a modern statute which afforded some protection to meritorious literature. The Obscene Publications Act of 1959 was the result.

The 1959 Act emerged from a simplistic notion that sexual material could be divided into two classes, 'literature' and 'pornography', and the function of the new statutory definition of obscenity was to enable juries and magistrates to make the distinction between them. The tendency of a work to deprave or corrupt its readers was henceforth to be judged in the light of its total impact, rather than by the arousing potential of 'purple passages'. The readership to be considered was the actual or, at least, predictable reading public, rather than the precocious fourteen-year-old schoolgirl into whose hands it might perchance fall – unless it were in fact aimed at or distributed to fourteen-year-old schoolgirls, by whose vulnerability to corruption it should then be judged. It was recognized that a work of literature might employ, to advance its serious purpose, a style which resembled, or had the same effect as, the pornographer's: here the jury was to be assisted to draw the line by experts who would offer judgements as to the degree of importance the article represented in its particular discipline. Works of art or literature might be obscene (i.e. depraving or corrupting) but their great significance might outweigh the harm they could do, and take them out of the *prima facie* criminal category established by Section 1 of the Act.

In fact, the 1959 Act has worked to secure a very large measure of freedom in Britain for the written word. It took two decades and a number of celebrated trials for the revolutionary implications of the legislation to be fully appreciated and applied. The credit for securing this freedom belongs to a few courageous publishers who risked gaol by inviting juries to take a stand against censorship, and to the ineptitude and corruption of police enforcement. The first major test case – over D. H. Lawrence's *Lady Chatterley's Lover* – enabled the full force of the reformed law to be exploited on behalf of the recognized literature. In 1968 the appeal proceedings over *Last Exit to Brooklyn* established the right of authors to explore depravity and corruption explicitly described. The trials of the underground Press in the early seventies discredited obscenity law in the eyes of a new generation of jurors, and acquittals of hard-core pornography soon followed. These came in the wake of apparently scientific evidence that pornography had a therapeutic rather than a harmful effect. Popular permissiveness was reflected in jury verdicts, and the repeal of obscenity laws in several European countries made it impossible for the authorities to police the incoming tide of eroticism. And if pornography did not corrupt its readers, it certainly corrupted many of those charged with enforcing the law against it. Public cynicism about obscenity control was confirmed when twelve members of Scotland Yard's 'dirty squad' were gaoled after conviction for involvement in what their judge described as 'an evil conspiracy which turned the Obscene Publications Act into a vast protection racket'.[5]

After the acquittal of *Inside Linda Lovelace* in 1976, the authorities largely abandoned the attempt to prosecute books for which any claim of literary merit could be made. The Williams Committee, which reported on the obscenity laws in 1979, recommended that all restraints on the written word should be lifted – a position which they thought had already been achieved *de facto*.[6] Since the Williams Report, the only books which have been prosecuted have either glorified illegal activities, such as the taking of dangerous drugs, or have been hard-core pornography lacking any literary pretension or sociological interest. However, the boast of British literary artistic freedom cannot be made with confidence, given a vague law and a swinging moral pendulum. The forces of feminism have done more than the cohorts of Mrs Whitehouse to challenge public acceptance of erotica: there can be no guarantee that some future legal onslaught against sexually explicit art and literature would not succeed. In 1988, the DPP seriously considered a test-case prosecution against the works of Henry Miller.

'Censorship' is itself a dirty word for most civil libertarians, and its history in the courts has been comical in retrospect. But there are a number of entirely reasonable claims that can be made in favour of some degree of public reticence about sexual matters. Whatever the claims of 'dirty old men' to dilate over sexual fantasies in private, the colourful display of erotic magazines at local shops and news-stands is offensive to many. Would there be any loss of liberty to require them to be encased in Cellophane, and placed on racks above the reach of children or be confined for sale in licensed sex shops? This is the kind of administrative control that operates in many countries, and avoids the problems of deciding whether particular magazines are likely to deprave and corrupt or be grossly offensive to reasonable people. Although there is no proven link between availability of pornography and sexual crime, many senior judges have little doubt that rapes and indecent assaults increasingly involve behaviour that defendants have read about and are in consequence encouraged to try. What is necessary, of course, is to build up societal inhibitions against any form of forcible sex, but although the courts have increased the prison sentences for rape to the point where they approximate to the punishment for armed robbery, this does not seem to deter men whose minds have been warped by something rather more fundamental than the reading of dirty books.

Attitudinal changes are difficult to enforce by criminal laws against publishers who arouse lust in men. The page 3 phenomenon has certainly done more to promote callous salacity than any amount of smuggled Scandinavian pornography, but would a law which banned pictures of nude women in national newspapers be enforceable, or would it merely result in provocative but partly clothed page 3 poses? The lesson to be drawn from the history of obscenity prosecutions is that criminal trials are counter-productive. They polarize opinion and publicize the book, and they only succeed in bringing the law into disrepute. Britain is one of the last countries in the Western world which still occasionally tries to gaol publishers for lapses of taste. Other nations adopt point-of-sale restrictions based on classification systems, whereby material which is apt to give offence is not banned but put out of sight and out of mind.

THE TEST OF OBSCENITY

The definition of obscenity is contained in Section 1 of the Obscene Publications Act:

For the purposes of this Act an article shall be deemed to be obscene if its effect or (where the article comprises two or more distinct items) the effect of any one of its items is, if taken as a whole, such as to tend to deprave and corrupt persons who are likely, in all the circumstances, to read, see or hear the matter contained or embodied in it.

In any trial, the prosecution must prove beyond reasonable doubt that the material is obscene. It has a number of hurdles to surmount.

The tendency to deprave and corrupt

'Deprave' means 'to make morally bad, to pervert, to debase or corrupt morally' and 'corrupt' means 'to render morally unsound or rotten, or destroy the moral purity or chastity of, to pervert or ruin a good quality, to debase, to defile'.[7] The definition implies that the tendency must go much further than merely shocking or disgusting readers.[8] Thus 'obscene', in law, has a very different, and very much stronger, meaning than it possesses in colloquial usage. The convictions of the editors of *Oz* were quashed because their trial judge had suggested that 'obscene' might include what is 'repulsive, filthy, loathsome, indecent or lewd'. To widen its legal meaning in this way was 'a very substantial and serious misdirection'.[9] 'Corrupt' is a strong word, implying a powerful and corrosive effect, which goes further than merely 'leading morally astray', and the courts have recalled the Book of Common Prayer reference to 'where rust and moth doth corrupt'.[10] In one case, however, the Law Lords pointed out that corruption could be all in the mind – it need not take the form of overt sexual misbehaviour. It was a crime to sell pornography to an addict, no matter how far gone in depravity, because dirty old men could be corrupted more than once (a ruling which was no doubt greeted with relief by dirty old men).[11] At the end of the day, the 'deprave and corrupt' test really calls upon the jury to decide whether the material is harmful to likely readers and viewers.

The aversion defence

One important corollary of the decision that obscene material must have more serious effects than arousing feelings of revulsion is the doctrine that material which in fact shocks and disgusts may *not* be obscene, because its effect is to discourage readers from indulgence in the immorality so unseductively portrayed. Readers whose stomachs are turned will not partake of any food for thought. The argument, however paradoxical it sounds, has frequently found favour as a means of exculpating literature of merit. Thus *Last Exit to Brooklyn* presented horrific pictures of homosexuality and drug-taking in New York. Defence counsel contended that its only effect on any but a minute lunatic fringe of readers would be horror, revulsion and pity. It made the readers share in the horror it described and thereby so disgusted, shocked and outraged them that instead of tending to encourage anyone to homosexuality, drug-taking or brutal violence it would have precisely the reverse effect. The failure of the trial judge to put this defence before the jury in his summing-up was the major ground for upsetting the conviction.[12]

The most valuable aspect of the aversion defence is its emphasis on the context and purpose of publication. Writing which sets out to seduce, to exhort and pressurize the reader to indulge in immorality is to be distinguished from that which presents a balanced picture, and does not overlook the pains which may attend new pleasures. For over a century prosecutors thought it sufficient to point to explicitness in the treatment of sex, on the assumption that exposure to such material would automatically arouse the libidinous desires associated with a state of depravity. Now they must consider the overall impact, and the truthfulness of the total picture. Books which present a fair account of corruption have a defence denied to glossy propaganda.

The target audience

An article is only obscene if it is likely to corrupt 'persons who are likely, having regard to all relevant circumstances, to read, see or hear the matter contained or embodied in it'. Thus the Act adopts a relative definition of obscenity – relative, that is, to the 'likely' rather than the 'conceivably possible' readership. The publication in question is judged by its impact on its primary audience – those people who, the evidence suggests, would be likely to seek it out and to pay the asking-price to read it. The Act rejects the 'most vulnerable person' standard of *Hicklin*, with its preoccupation with those members of society of the lowest level of intellectual or moral discernment, and focuses on 'likely' readers and proven circumstances of publication. A work of literature is to be judged by its effect on serious-minded purchasers, a comic book by its effect on children, a sexually explicit magazine sold in an 'adults only' bookstore by its effect on adult patrons of that particular shop.

The 'significant proportion' test

The 1959 Act requires a tendency to deprave and corrupt 'persons' likely in the circumstances to read or hear the offensive material. But how many persons must have their morals affected before the test is made out? The answer given by the Court of Appeal in the *Last Exit to Brooklyn* case is that the jury must be satisfied that a *significant proportion* of the likely readership would be guided along the path of corruption. The 'significant proportion' test has been applied at obscenity trials ever since. It protects the defendant in that it prevents the jury from speculating on the possible effect of adult literature on a young person who may just happen to see it, although it does not put the prosecution to proof that a majority, or a substantial proportion, of readers would be adversely affected. If the jury feels that a considerable number of children would read or see the article in question, and would be corrupted by the experience, it may decide that this number constitutes a significant proportion of the class which comprises the likely audience.

The dominant effect principle

In obscenity trails before the 1959 legislation it was unnecessary for juries to consider the overall impact of the subject-matter on its likely readers. Prosecuting counsel could secure conviction merely by drawing attention to isolated 'purple passages' taken out of context. The Select Committee on the Obscene Publications Act had stressed the importance of considering the 'dominant effect' of the whole work and this recommendation was duly embodied in the 1959 statute, which provided that 'an article shall be deemed to be obscene if its effect . . . is, if taken as a whole, such as to tend to deprave and corrupt . . .'

The effect of the 'dominant impact' test is to enable the courts to take account of the psychological realities of reading and film viewing, in so far as the audience is affected by theme and style and message, so that isolated incidents of an offensive nature are placed in context. The injunction that an article must be 'taken as a whole' will apply to books and plays and films: in the case of magazines, however, which are made up of separate articles, advertisements and photographs, the 'dominant impact' principle has less force. In such cases the publication is considered on an 'item by item' basis: the prosecution may argue that obscenity attaches only to one article or photograph, and that the other contents are irrelevant.

THE PUBLIC GOOD DEFENCE

Section 4 of the Act provides that the defendant to an obscenity charge 'shall not be convicted' – despite the fact that he has been found to have published an obscene article – if 'publication of the article in question is justified as being for the public good . . .' The ground upon which the defence may be made out is that publication, in the case of books and magazines, is 'in the interests of science, literature, art or learning, or of other objects of general concern'. Section 4 (1) looks to the advancement of cultural and intellectual values, and the expert opinion as to the 'merits of an article' must be able to relate to the broader question of 'the interests of' art and science. A publication of obscene primitive art may lack objective merit, but none the less may be defended on the grounds of its contribution to art history. (The DPP once considered a complaint about the ancient drainage ditch at Cerne Abbas, which forms the outline of a giant with a truly giant-size erection. In the interests of history, and the interests of the local tourist trade, he declined requests to allow grass to grow strategically over the offending area.)

In both the *Oz* and *Nasty Tales* cases underground comics were accepted as 'art' for the purpose of a Section 4 defence. Rupert Bear cartoons, it was said by Mr Feliks Topolski, were art of a sort, and when an underground comic superimposed private parts on the much-loved nursery creature, this was satiric art of a high order. In 1975 the New Zealand courts held that drawings of toilet fittings were 'artistic works' – a conclusion which the surrealist school would never have doubted.

In *DPP* v. *Jordan* the House of Lords ruled that the psychiatric health of the community allegedly served by 'therapeutic' pornography was not an 'object of general concern' for the purposes of Section 4, which referred to objects of general concern similar to those aesthetic and intellectual values specifically enumerated in Section 4. Among the 'objects of general concern' advanced on behalf of *Lady Chatterley's Lover* were its ethical and Christian merits and the Bishop of Woolwich testified to the book's contribution to human relations and to Christian judgements and values. Other witnesses testified to its educational and sociological merits, and the editor of *Harper's Bazaar* was called as an expert on 'popular literature'. In the *Last Exit to Brooklyn* case the Court of Appeal conceded that 'sociological or ethical merit' might be canvassed. Other objects of general concern which have been relied upon at obscenity trials include journalism, humour, politics, philosophy, history, education and entertainment.

The last, and undoubtedly the worst, 'serious' book to be prosecuted was *Inside Linda Lovelace* in 1976 – its sociological merits were endorsed by a leading feminist and by the Oxford Professor of Jurisprudence. 'If this isn't obscene, members of the jury, you may think that nothing is obscene,' said the judge. The jury acquitted.

How is a jury to decide whether a work which it has already found to be obscene is none the less justified as being for the public good? It must undertake a 'balancing act' described by the Court of Appeal in the *Last Exit to Brooklyn* case:

> The jury must consider on the one hand the number of readers they believe would tend to be depraved and corrupted by the book, the strength of the tendency to deprave and corrupt, and the nature of the depravity and corruption; on the other hand, they should assess the strength of the literary, sociological or ethical merit they believe the book to possess. They should then weigh up all these factors and decide whether on balance the publication is proved to be justified as being for the public good.[13]

Unfortunately, 'corruption' and 'literary, sociological or ethical merit' do not admit of meaningful comparison, and the balancing act is a logical nonsense. 'Depravity and corruption', a predicted change for the worse in the characters of a significant number of readers, cannot be quantified, and even if it could, its quantity could not meaningfully be compared with literary ability, or scientific value. No book exists in a vacuum: one of the merits of *Oliver Twist* was to awaken the public conscience, and the value and purpose of Greek tragedy was to purge an audience with pity and terror. Nor is it logically possible to 'weigh' such disparate concepts as 'corruption' and 'literary merit'. Is an ounce of depravity-spreading more or less potent than an ounce of artistic merit? Even if the jury manages to find a common measure, the outcome may well be foreclosed against the defendant by the jury's reluctance to find that it could *ever* be in the public interest to spread depravity. 'The publication of this book is for the public good, although it will deprave and corrupt a significant number of its readers' is a verdict any jury would be reluctant to deliver.

PROSECUTION PRACTICE

The enforcement of the obscenity laws is now directed largely at 'hard-core pornography'. This has no legal definition, although juries are often told that 'pornography is like an elephant. You cannot define it, but you know it when you see it.'

Despite the uncertainty of the law, there is some consistency in prosecution targets. Descriptions of sexual deviations are much more likely to be attacked than accounts of 'normal' heterosexual behaviour. In practice prosecuting authorities ignore the message of an article, and concern themselves instead with the physical incidents photographed or described. Stories may degrade women, 'do dirt on sex', by depicting them as objects to be manipulated for fun and profit, but obscenity for most prosecutors hangs on simpler things. DPP officials have their lines to draw, and they draw them fairly consistently at the male groin: nudity is now acceptable and even artistic, but to erect a penis is to provoke a prosecution. Bizarre strains of pictorial pornography depicting extreme sexual violence, simulated necrophilia and human excretory functions do exist in Scandinavia and are sometimes imported into Britain, where distributors are almost invariably convicted. Juries which are sometimes inclined to support freedom for voyeurs are less keen to promote freedom for ghouls.

There is no indication in the debates which surrounded the Obscene Publications Act that 'obscenity' pertained to anything but matters of sex, but the courts have interpreted the statutory definition of 'obscene' to encompass encouragements to take dangerous drugs and to engage in violence.[14] In 1984 there was an obscenity blitz on American drug books, and the publishers of *Cooking with Cannabis*, *The Pleasures of Cocaine* and *How to Grow Marihuana Indoors under Lights* were prosecuted in a four-week trial at the Old Bailey. The prosecution failed to convince the jury that drug-taking was necessarily a depraved activity, given the widespread use of cannabis, or that books which provided factual information about both the pains and the pleasures of drugs would necessarily encourage people to experiment. Some twenty books were acquitted, and only one, a pamphlet which mindlessly promoted the free-basing of cocaine, was found obscene. The Court of Appeal, in an interesting development of the law, approved the calling of expert witnesses to explain the effects of the drugs.[15] Any publication which deals with drug-taking would be well advised to emphasize repeatedly both the physical dangers and the criminal penalties which attach to drug usage.

Any material which combines violence with sexual explicitness is a candidate for prosecution. Yet there are many gradations between a friendly slap and a stake through the heart, and most 'spanking' books and articles escape indictment. 'Video nasties', however, which combine pornography with powerful scenes of rape and terror have been successfully prosecuted. More difficulty is experienced with the depiction of violence in non-sexual contexts. The Divisional Court in one case approved the prosecution of a manufacturer of children's swap cards depicting scenes of battle, on the theory that they were capable of depraving young minds by provoking emulation of the violence portrayed.[16] In 1955 Parliament, in doubt as to whether the obscenity test covered non-sexual violence, passed a special law against 'horror comics' which might deprave and corrupt children. This legislation is rarely invoked, and comics which showed horrific scenes of the 'Green Berets' in action in Vietnam were never taken to court. In 1976, Southampton magistrates acquitted *The Adventures of Conan the Barbarian*, after a child psychiatrist pointed out that the Conan legend would be perceived as moral and even romantic by children inured to the adventures of *Starsky and Hutch*.

The Obscene Publications Act gives a broad discretion to prosecuting authorities to take action against any publication which a jury might consider to 'deprave and corrupt'. In order to achieve some national consistency in prosecution targets, decisions are referred to the DPP, who has been reluctant since the acquittal of *Inside Linda Lovelace* to prosecute the publisher of books and films which have any claim to merit. But the law allows two methods of avoiding a major 'test case' trial. One way is to prosecute the shop-owner who stocks the book or the video, rather than its publisher. The shop-owner will not have the commitment or the resources to mount full-blooded opposition, and will probably rely on a special defence that he had not examined the article and had no reason to believe it obscene. In 1983 the DPP sanctioned a large number of obscenity prosecutions against video shops for stocking so-called 'video nasties' – the results were chaotic, as juries in different parts of the country reached different decisions in respect of the same video title, and major distributors were powerless to intervene to defend their works as they would have wished. In an effort to reduce confusion, the DPP issued an index of some sixty titles which he regarded as candidates for prosecution. Some of these films had claims to merit, but shopkeepers took fright and refused to stock them. The distributors once again were powerless to protest against this back-door State censorship: the DPP was reluctant to prosecute them, but sought to have their films withdrawn from sale by a form of intimidation. The particular problem was resolved by the Video Recordings Act, which requires every video to be submitted to the British Board of Film Classification (BBFC) for classification, and it is to be hoped that law-enforcement authorities never again succumb to the temptation of imposing censorship by threat rather than by prosecution.

The other deficiency in the 1959 legislation is that it permits police to avoid jury trial entirely by seizing books and magazines from local stores and applying for 'forfeiture orders' at local magistrates' courts. This procedure, under Section 3 of the Act, is used in some areas to destroy material which the police are well aware would never be convicted by a jury. Local Justices are less broadminded, and can generally be relied upon to make forfeiture orders against 'adult' magazines on national sale.

Section 3 may well have been appropriate to meet the situation where a bookshop or street-stall proprietor stocks only a few obscene books, perhaps inadvertently, and does not deserve to be convicted of a criminal offence. But the forfeiture power has been exploited in a number of cases for the wholly objectionable purpose of depriving publishers of their right to trial by jury. Books – in some cases, many thousands of books – have been seized from publishers who did wish to defend them to the hilt, and condemned by local Justices after the most cursory of hearings. The Justices of Stony Stratford bankrupted Maurice Girodias and his Olympia Press (which after the war published in Paris the works of Samuel Beckett, Jean Genet, J. P. Donleavy and William Burroughs for the benefit of British tourists who would smuggle them through customs). Thirty-four different novels were condemned, after the Justices had retired to read them all in ninety minutes.[17] This was an abuse of the forfeiture power, and was contrary to an undertaking given in Parliament in 1964 that Section 3 would not be used to deprive serious publishers of the right to trial by jury.[18]

To effectuate the 1964 undertaking Section 3 should be amended so that booksellers or publishers who give notice of their wish for a jury trial can be re-charged under Section 2 of the Act, or else the forfeiture proceedings dropped entirely. (As Mr Roy – now Lord – Jenkins put it in 1964, 'I should not have thought that to put upon somebody the right to opt to be prosecuted and to run all the risks, including the risk of prison, was conferring very excessive liberty of choice upon any individual.') This is a difficult choice for publishers to make; nevertheless *they*, and not the State, should be given the right to make it. That, at least, was the conclusion of the Committee on the Distribution of Criminal Business, which reported in 1975 that:

> It seems to us especially desirable that a person charged with an offence involving an obscene or indecent publication should have a right to have the matter decided by a jury, which can better reflect contemporary public attitudes towards obscenity and indecency than can a stipendiary magistrate or a bench of lay justices.[19]

Magistrates and Justices frequently approach their censorship task under Section 3 in a cavalier fashion, and their decisions are not precedents which carry any weight outside their own locality. A vast amount of police time is currently expended on raiding corner shops, seizing and forfeiting magazines which are on open display in other shops in the same locality. What purpose does this sort of action serve, beyond wasting public time and public money in order to harass publishers of sexually explicit magazines which, however awful, are none the less lawful? The publishers may be unprepossessing people, out to make money by exploiting interest in sex, but there would be a major outcry if such arbitrary destruction of property were visited upon tobacco companies or wine merchants (whose products, by contributing to death rather than to lust, may be the more harmful). If action is to be taken against sexually explicit magazines on open sale, it should be taken nationally (by test-case prosecutions of publishers, or by a classification system which consigns such material to sex shops) and not by having local Justices engage in periodic burnings of magazines they do not like.

SHOULD THE LAW BE CHANGED?

The 'deprave and corrupt' test has become a focus for law reform, and the uncertainties in its application remain a matter for concern, both for libertarians who believe that British citizens should have the same right as Europeans and Americans to obtain pornography from discreet suppliers, and for those who believe that the 'soft porn' available from local newsagents is degrading to women and morally dangerous. The problem is to find a better alternative. The best that anti-pornography campaigners could do in 1986 was to draw up a 'laundry list' of activities, the pictorial representation of which would be 'deemed' to deprave and corrupt. Their bill received an enthusiastic second reading in the House of Commons, but the 'laundry list' was withdrawn after sober realization that it would ban the display of Grecian urns, 'safe sex' guidelines, *King Lear*, videos of the Falklands War and David Attenborough's film about the courtship rituals of the praying mantis.

In 1987, Parliament gave a second reading to a bill which would introduce an entirely new concept of obscenity, namely 'whatever a reasonable person would regard as grossly offensive' in dealing with any matters relating to sex or violence or drug-taking. This test would create more problems than it solves. At least the 'deprave and corrupt' formula makes harm the criterion for guilt. The test of 'gross offensiveness' is conceptually very different. It focuses on what might be termed 'gut reaction' – the instant response of shock or disgust to particular written or visual images. The respondent is described as 'a reasonable person', but since magistrates and jurors invariably regard themselves as 'reasonable', they will test the material according to their subjective and immediate response. 'Offensive' merely means that to which offence is taken, whether on grounds of morals or politics or aesthetics; 'gross' would probably be interpreted by the courts as 'obvious' rather than 'extreme'. Thus a reaction of shock and disgust, as distinct from mild disapprobation, would plainly satisfy the new criterion. In this sense, it would cast a very wide net indeed. British criminal law has generally distinguished between actions which harm and actions which err in taste. The former are banned, the latter are contained by nuisance laws which prohibit the public display of indecent pictures or words. The use of such a broad test is justified to protect citizens from gratuitous offence which they do not seek out: the mischief of the 1987 bill was that it sought to apply the 'offensiveness' concept to material which some citizens choose to view, and judge it according to the artificial reactions of others who might never choose to view it.

Thus, the test of 'gross offensiveness' is far too vague and subjective to be a fair or proper criterion of guilt for an offence which carries up to three years in prison and which is aimed at regulating artistic freedom. It is a fundamental principle of criminal law that it should be sufficiently certain to enable citizens to regulate their conduct so as to avoid committing crimes. The 'gross offensiveness' test would entirely fail to provide that necessary measure of certainty, and lead to total confusion as to what could be published without shocking the hypothetical 'reasonable person'. In reality reasonable people have very different thresholds of dismay: the new test would enable juries to choose whether to convict material which shocked a person as reasonable as Mrs Mary Whitehouse, or acquit material which failed to shock a person as reasonable as Mr John Mortimer.

Is it possible to produce a different sort of legal definition which will encapsulate what is commonly seen as the real evil of pornography, namely its reduction of women to little more than objects of male lust? A section of the feminist movement in North America has devoted much energy to promoting a law which would punish

> the sexually explicit subordination of women, graphically depicted whether in words or in pictures, where
>
> (i) Women are presented dehumanized as sexual objects, things or commodities,

(ii) Women are presented in postures of sexual submission,

(iii) Women's body parts are exhibited, such that women are reduced to those parts,

(iv) Women are presented as whores by nature.

Is this a workable legal definition? If it is illegal to degrade women by treating them as submissive sex objects and to perpetuate notions about women's inferiority and limited role within society, then many newspapers and films become candidates for prosecution. Vast entertainment and advertising industries have been built on these very presumptions. It is difficult to see how pornography infringes women's rights to *equal* treatment, where the actors are as degraded as the actresses and the context is the fantasy enactment of sexual charades. Admittedly, pornography generally attracts a male audience and projects male sexual fantasies, but to justify prohibition the equality argument must go further, and show that women are treated less fairly or favourably in a community which permits men to dilate over pornographic fantasies. This is difficult to maintain, given the fact that many societies which permit pornography are the very societies which also protect women's rights, precisely because they accord a high value to everyone's civil liberties. The notion that obscenity trials should be occasions for judges and juries to scrutinize the texts of novels to decide whether female characters are presented as 'whores by nature' or 'commodities' is asking too much of the criminal law.

The feminist case has been accepted to some extent in Canada, where a recent Royal Commission recommended that material depicting violence against women or female submissiveness should be banned.[20] It argued for a distinction between 'good clean pornography' which would be publicly available as 'erotica', and 'bad dirty pornography' which should be punished by heavy prison sentences. This distinction is being applied, with some difficulty and at enormous expense, by an army of customs censors who carefully scan every word of rubbishy US magazines for innuendoes derogatory to women. It remains to be seen how effectively this well-intentioned censorship works in practice – there is something unedifying and prurient in obliging State officials to decide which sexual fantasies are to be 'authorized' and which are to be turned back at the border. Ultimately, perhaps, it makes the mistake of taking pornography too seriously, dignifying some sexual fantasies with official approval while placing a political ban on certain instincts and imaginings which have always been with us.

The basic problem with any obscenity law which applies a legal test to methods of expression is that it calls for a judgement of *opinion* rather than a finding of fact. Whether the test is 'deprave and corrupt' or 'grossly offensive to reasonable people' or 'derogatory to women', it will inevitably be applied according to the subjective views of the tribunal, which will be unpredictable at the time of publication. Thus obscenity trials reflect the inability of traditional modes of criminal adjudication to comprehend the issues which can arise in the decision to censor. Criminal law has developed as a method for obtaining the truth in a world of fingerprints, alibis, police informers, bloodstains, and the dog that doesn't bark in the night. These are facts able to be tested: the evidence can be weighed; the credibility of witnesses can be shaken by confrontation. The machinery of the criminal law is geared to adjudicate disputes about *facts*. Obscenity cases call for decision, not about truth or falsity, but about which of two plausible opinions is to be preferred. And that is the case, whether they depend upon ambulatory notions of 'community standards' or whether they turn into debates about 'artistic merit'. The only rational solution is to find a system which works by classification rather than censorship, removing public offence by confining clearly defined material to discreet outlets and making the decision for the court a simple question of fact (whether the material has been sold in defiance of a prohibition) rather than an occasion for debating social morality.

In Britain, the case for rational law reform was advanced by the 1979 Report of a Home Office Committee chaired by philosopher Bernard Williams. The philosophical axis of the Williams Report is the principle that conduct should not be suppressed by law unless it can be convincingly demonstrated to carry a real prospect of harm to others. An almost clinical fidelity to John Stuart Mill keeps the report on a narrow course. The siren slogan of 'free speech' is set aside: the nasty and dirty pictures which formed the subject-matter of this inquiry were ideologically vapid and wholly lacking in communicative content. Equally, a deaf ear is turned to rhetorical thunder about 'moral pollution': causation of harm is carefully distinguished from a cultural phenomenon symptomatic of what may (or may not) be an undesirable change in moral standards.

The question is whether the availability of pornography demonstrably contributes to anti-social conduct, and the answer emphatically is 'not according to the evidence'. Pornographic books and magazines, the Committee concluded, can be vile and stomach-turning and trashy, but only when their actual production involves the exploitation of persons under sixteen or the infliction of physical harm on participants should they be banned outright. Restriction – to adults who are prepared to search them out in specialist shops – is the only answer consistent with Mill's principle, in that it removes public offence from a trade which cannot otherwise be proved harmful. The Committee would sweep soft-core sex magazines from the counters of corner newsagents and place them on sale, together with pornography of much harder core, in soberly fronted 'adults only' sex shops. What the public eye does not see, the public heart will not grieve over.

The present obscenity law assumes that some books and magazines conduce to a particular kind of harm: namely corruption of the mind. The Williams Report found insufficient evidence to support this assumption, and sought to replace it by a law which would punish the sale of pictorial material when production has involved actual harm to young or maltreated models, and a system which restricts to sex shops magazines with pictures prone to give offence to reasonable people if displayed in public. Thus the legal focus would be shifted from speculation about the working of susceptible minds to speculation about reactions in the reasonable mind's eye. The new mischief is aesthetic outrage, not psychological damage: pictures which turn ordinary stomachs must be sought out by those constitutionally capable and desirous of digesting them. The corner newsagent who wishes to continue dispensing sweets and comics must dismantle his shelf of *Mayfair* and *Men Only*. The Williams Committee offered something for everybody: pornography *aficionados* will have access to pictures dirtier than ever before, the clean-up campaigners will have nothing visible to complain about, and the public will have a sensible and workable law commanding general support. These proposals have not, however, been received with gratitude. The consumers of 'men's magazines', who appreciate the delicacy with which local newsagents carefully fold their 'adult' purchases inside a copy of the morning news paper, do not want the indignity and embarrassment of searching them out in a sex shop. Clean-up campaigners are outraged at the very *idea* that pornography should be lawfully dispensable, even behind drawn shutters.

For those who see censorship as a reflection of society's lack of confidence in itself, the Williams reforms deserve considerable support. Those who fear that tolerance of pornography will demean and diminish the quality of life may not be much impressed by a proposal to legalize the availability of sexually explicit material for consenting adults. But the principle of prohibiting profit-making enterprises from advertising sexual wares in a manner calculated to embarrass citizens going about their ordinary business is unexceptionable, and sexually explicit material on a shelf of a soberly fronted sex shop is hardly an environmental threat. The Williams Committee recognizes that such literature may serve as a boon to the lonely, the ugly, the aged, and those who are forced by circumstances or by personal unattractiveness to live without love and companionship. A system of control which requires responsible management of bookshops presenting a modest front to a public street far from schools, churches and council flats deserves a try, based on a law which echoes the sentiments of Mrs Patrick Campbell: 'It doesn't matter what you do in the bedroom as long as you don't do it in the street and frighten the horses.'

SEX-SHOP CONTROL

Although the Williams Committee Report has not been implemented, its philosophy of 'out of sight, out of mind' is apparent in legislation passed in 1982 giving local councils special powers to license sex shops and sex cinemas in their areas. Sex-shop chains proliferated in Britain in the seventies, to the extent that they threatened to rival Mothercare on local high streets. An Indecent Displays (Control) Act of 1981 cleaned up window displays, obliging them by law to refuse admission to persons under eighteen and to erect a large warning notice in their windows stating that 'persons passing beyond this notice will find material on display which they may consider indecent'. This was hardly an imposition, as it tended to attract rather than repel custom. The Local Government (Miscellaneous Provisions) Act of 1982 was another matter, because it empowered local councils to refuse a licence to shops 'used for a business which consists to a significant degree' of selling books, magazines films, videos and artefacts which portray, encourage or are otherwise used in connection with sexual activity. A licence may be refused if the applicant is unsuitable, or if the 'character of the locality' makes the presence of a sex shop undesirable. The local council may decide the number of sex shops which are appropriate for the locality, and the legislation specifically provides that 'nil may be an appropriate number'.

The effects of the legislation have varied from council to council: some have decided not to exercise the powers at all, others have used them to ban sex shops altogether, while most have taken the opportunity to extract large licensing fees, limit the number of shops, and lay down rules which exclude them from residential areas or proximity to schools and churches. Sex-shop operators have suffered, but not all that much: licensing has reduced competition rather than demand, and led to some ingenious avoidance devices, such as selling sex articles through 'Tupperware parties' in private homes and reopening sex shops as 'birth-control centres' which solemnly promote 'items which are manufactured as masturbatory aids as an alternative method of birth control'.

The legitimate concern that local-council licensing powers might be used as a form of censorship is somewhat reduced by the fact that 'sex shops' are confidence tricks, selling magazines and videos that may be obtained from local newsagents and video stores, exotic lingerie available at a fraction of the price in Marks & Spencer, and contraceptives and vibrators which are found in most pharmacies. It may be doubted whether these lawful items, when sold under the same roof, really justify the inordinate amount of public time and money which is spent on inspection and application hearings. If (as Williams recommended) pornography of all kinds was confined to such outlets, then some such system of control would be necessary. The legislation has some unattractive features: it permits no appeal from local-council decisions other than on procedural grounds, and it allows local councils to levy quite extortionate annual licence fees (which range from £10,000 in Westminster to £12.50 in South Kesteven, Lincolnshire). Some over-enthusiastic inspectors have tried to extract licence fees from newsagents and bookshops whose erotic publications form a small part of their trade, but the Divisional Court has now ruled that the 'significant degree of business' test is not satisfied in such cases.[21] The legislation has spawned a great deal of planning litigation, but does not seem to have reduced the national turnover in sexual impedimenta (one million vibrators were reportedly sold each year by one sex-shop chain in the early 1980s). It is interesting that a law which was designed to enable local councils to drive sex shops out of town seems to be working to give them some measure of respectability, as local councillors and council officials up and down the country warm to the task of deciding precisely at what distance from a church one may be permitted to purchase an inflatable rubber doll.

THE THEATRE

Theatre censorship was originally imposed in 1551 to curb opposition to the Reformation, and no play was to be performed without a licence from the Master of the Revels, an officer of the Lord Chamberlain At first, the royal licence afforded protection from puritan hostility: theatre was an aristocratic entertainment, and so long as no insult was offered to Church or State, dramatic invention was unrestrained. Shakespeare was patronized by the Lord Chamberlain – his sexual candour caused no contemporary offence because his political themes did not overtly challenge the existing social order, and bawdy Restoration drama pandered to the tastes of the King and his court clique. It was Prime Minister Walpole who, goaded beyond endurance by caricatures of himself in the plays of Henry Fielding, first introduced legislation empowering the Lord Chamberlain to close down theatres and imprison actors as 'rogues or vagabonds' for uttering any unlicensed speech or gesture which offended against 'decency and good manners'. The first victim of the Lord Chamberlain was, predictably, Henry Fielding, who stopped writing plays after a series of licence refusals and turned his talents to the novel.

In 1843 a new Theatres Act was passed to consolidate the Lord Chamberlain's power to prohibit the performance of any stage play, or any scene of any stage play, for as long as he thought necessary, 'whenever he shall be of opinion that it is fitting for the preservation of good manners, decorum or of the public peace so to do'. Repressive licensing was in some measure responsible for the sterility of British drama in the nineteenth century. *La Dame aux Camélias* and Oscar Wilde's *Salomé* were refused licences, and in 1892 the performance of Ibsen's plays was banned 'in the permanent interests of the stage'. The Lord Chamberlain's Examiner of Plays explained:

> I have studied Ibsen's plays pretty carefully, and all the characters . . . appear to me to be morally deranged. All the heroines are dissatisfied spinsters who look on marriage as a monopoly, or dissatisfied married women in a chronic state of rebellion against not only the condition which nature has imposed on their sex, but against all the duties and objectives of mothers and wives; and as for the men, they are all rascals or imbeciles.

Many serious writers eschewed the drama, and those few who persisted suffered intolerable restrictions. *Mrs Warren's Profession* was banned from 1894 to 1925, and not even Gilbert and Sullivan were sacred: in 1907 licences for all performances of *The Mikado* were withdrawn for one year to avoid offence to a visiting Japanese prince. The Lord Chamberlain operated a broad definition of 'indecency', and excised all vernacular references to intercourse, genitalia, birth control and venereal disease. Homosexuality could not even be hinted at, and casualties included Lillian Hellman's *The Children's Hour*, Sartre's *Vicious Circle*, Arthur Miller's *A View from the Bridge* and Robert Anderson's *Tea and Sympathy*. Irreverent references to Fascist dictators were suppressed throughout the thirties, and even in 1939 a revue song was banned on account of its opening line: 'Even Hitler had a mother'. This obsessive deference to heads of State extended in the sixties to satires on the Kennedy family, and to aspersions on long-deceased relatives of royalty – as late as 1960 Sadler's Wells Opera were forced to rewrite the libretto of Edward German's *Merrie England* to remove scenes in which Elizabeth I conspired to poison a rival. Commercial managements accepted political discipline without demur, but State-subsidized companies had no profits at stake, and the Royal Shakespeare Company launched an all-out attack after the Lord Chamberlain objected to the play *US* on the grounds that it was 'beastly, anti-American and left-wing'. In 1966 the Joint Committee on Theatre Censorship commenced its deliberations. Dramatists, State theatre companies and drama critics overwhelmingly demanded abolition of the Lord Chamberlain's powers, and convinced the Joint Committee that pre-censorship provided a service neither to playgoers nor to dramatic art. Its recommendations were embodied in the 1968 Theatres Act. The 1843 Act was repealed, and the test of obscenity installed as the sole basis for theatre censorship.[22]

Section 8 of the Theatres Act duly provides that proceedings shall not be instituted 'except by or with the consent of the Attorney-General'. But when Howard Brenton's play *The Romans in Britain* was first performed at the National Theatre there was considerable critical comment about a scene which called for a simulated homosexual rape, perpetrated by three Roman soldiers upon a young Druid priest. Mrs Mary Whitehouse, the 'clean up' campaigner, asked the Attorney-General to prosecute under the Theatres Act: the DPP investigated, and reported that no prosecution would be likely to succeed. The Attorney refused his consent to allow a private prosecution to go forward, whereupon Mrs Whitehouse sent her solicitor to view the play, and he convinced a magistrate to issue a summons against the director, Michael Bogdanov, under Section 13 of the Sexual Offences Act. This section is directed at male persons who masturbate themselves or others in public toilets and parks, and punishes males who procure the commission of acts of gross indecency in public. The allegation against Bogdanov was that he, being a male, 'procured' a male actor playing the part of a Roman soldier to commit an act of gross indecency with another male, namely the actor playing the young Druid. The artificiality of the proceedings is demonstrated by the fact that had any of the participants been female, Section 13 could not have been applicable.

The prosecutrix had discovered a loophole in the law, applicable in a very limited way to plays directed by males which contain scenes calling for simulation of homosexual activity which a jury might find to be 'grossly indecent'. Although the intention of Parliament was to abolish all residual offences in relation to the staging of plays, the section of the Theatres Act designed to achieve this was not comprehensively drafted. It abolished common-law conspiracy offences, obscene and blasphemous libel and the like, but it overlooked the existence of Section 13. The prosecution evidence was that the act of gross indecency consisted in one male actor holding his penis in an erect position, advancing across the stage and placing the tip of the organ against the buttocks of the other actor. This was the testimony of Mrs Whitehouse's solicitor, who had been seated, appropriately enough, in the gods – some seventy yards from the stage. He admitted, under cross-examination, that he might have mistaken the top of the penis for the actor's thumb, adroitly rising from a fist clenched over his organ. Shortly after this admission the prosecution was withdrawn, relieving the jury from further consideration of a 'thumbs up' defence which might have provided a complete answer to the charge. The jury might also have acquitted on the basis that the actor's performance had not been 'procured' by the director, or that the scene, a necessary part of a highly moral play, was not 'grossly indecent'.

Local councils retain control over front-of-house displays, which they require to remain within the realms of public decency, and they are entitled to withhold licences from theatres which do not comply with fire regulations or other health and safety requirements. They are not, however, permitted to impose any licence conditions relating to the content of plays performed in the theatre. In 1987 Westminster Council contemplated action against the Institute of Contemporary Arts for staging a theatrical performance which featured a 'female Lenny Bruce', but had to accept that it could not use its licensing powers as a back-door method of censorship. The Theatres Act has only been used on one occasion, in 1971, to gaol the promoters of a 'live sex' performance which lacked even the veneer of merit claimed by *O Calcutta*. In 1987, a much more erotic production by the RSC, *Les Liaisons dangereuses*, was performing to packed houses without any public protest, while *No Sex Please, We're British* ended a fifteen-year run which had been justified by little more than its title.

POSTAL AND CUSTOMS OFFENCES

It is an offence against Section 11 of the Post Office Act to send 'indecent or obscene' articles through the post. 'Indecency' has a much wider meaning than 'obscenity' (it may include anything that 'offends the modesty of the ordinary person') and there is no public-good defence or right to trial by jury, so it is possible for prosecuting authorities to avoid the safeguards of the Obscene Publications Act in relation to books and magazines supplied by mail order. The 1971 Unsolicited Goods and Services Act specifically proscribes the unsolicited sending of books or leaflets 'which describe or illustrate human sexual techniques' (the word 'human' being added at the insistence of the Ministry of Agriculture to protect its flow of breeding information to farmers). Most people regard the unwelcome arrival of advertisements for pornography as an intrusion on their private life, and the 1971 Act was passed after a public outcry when a leaflet advertising *A Manual of Sexual Technique* was posted indiscriminately to recipients who included schoolchildren and nuns. On the other hand, it is difficult to see why the postal regulations should prevent people from ordering 'indecent' material which, because it is not 'obscene', may lawfully be sold over the counter. This point was made by the Director of Public Prosecutions, and endorsed by the Attorney-General, in 1981 to justify their failure to prosecute a distinguished diplomat who had been sending indecent material to his friends. The DPP indicated that henceforth, as a matter of prosecution practice, prosecution under postal indecency laws would be confined to cases where indecent material was written on the outside of the envelope or sent to unwilling recipients.

Section 49 of the British Telecommunications Act 1981 makes it an offence to 'send any message by telephone which is grossly offensive or of an indecent obscene or menacing character'. This offence appeared in the earlier Post Office Acts, doubtless to deter unpleasant and unsolicited calls. (Although whether it is apt to catch one breed of telephone nuisance, the 'heavy breather', depends upon whether exhalation of breath amounts to a 'message'.) This Section acquired a new importance when the privatization of British Telecom led to the introduction of telephone services which provided allegedly erotic recorded messages at an expensive dialling rate. The exploitation of a former state monopoly to provide crude entertainment was condemned in the Press and in Parliament, although providers of this service, carefully supervised by British Telecom, were in fact offering messages so anodyne that to advertise them as 'erotic' was probably a breach of the Trade Descriptions Act. None the less they attracted considerable custom, and became a lucrative service for which telephone subscribers were charged at the same rate as a dialled call to the Republic of Ireland.

In response to public criticism, in 1986 British Telecom required its 'telephone information and entertainment providers' to abide by a special Code of Practice, monitored by an independent committee empowered to receive complaints and to discontinue any service which breaches the Code. The Code of Practice excludes 'extreme political or religious messages', establishes careful ground rules for messages designed for persons under sixteen, and provides that in relation to 'adult services', messages should not 'offend against the good taste and decency of reasonable people'.

The 'reasonable people' test would allow some latitude to information services about sexually transmitted diseases, but otherwise the Code is more restrictive than Section 49, confining telephonic jokes to the current level of television situation comedy. In practice, the Code operates to dilute the content of messages designed to titillate, although regrettably it does not stop the misleading advertising of these services. Impersonation of living persons is not permitted if the message is 'grossly offensive to reasonable people'. All these restrictions have been justified by reference to the novelty of the British telephone system being used to provide entertainment as well as information, and by the danger of children using their parents' telephones to hear suggestive messages. There is nothing to stop callers in Britain who wish to experience international dirty-talk from dialling ISD to verbally explicit services in the USA or Europe which are available to credit-card holders.

Customs officers have powers to intercept 'obscene or indecent' articles and commercial smugglers of large quantities can be gaoled for up to two years. In 1985 no fewer than thirty-seven customs officers were involved in 'Operation Tiger' directed against Gay's the Word, a small Bloomsbury bookshop which imported a wide range of literature by or about homosexuals. The operation seems to have originated from the actions of zealous customs officers who seized parcels addressed to Gay's the Word for no better reason than that 'Gay' signified to them abnormality, and books by Oscar Wilde, Gore Vidal, Christopher Isherwood and Jean Genet were enthusiastically impounded. Some seventy books, mainly American novels, were selected for prosecution: the bulk of them were alleged to be 'indecent' rather than obscene, and indeed several had for some years been published within the United Kingdom. The proceedings were withdrawn in 1986, shortly before the trial was to commence, as a consequence of the EEC Court of Justice ruling in *Conegate Ltd* v. *Customs and Excise Commissioners* that British customs law could not apply a more stringent test (that of 'indecency') to imported goods the domestically produced equivalent of which were permitted to circulate freely because they were not obscene. The practical consequences of the *Conegate* decision have been to remove the prospect of discriminatory use of customs legislation to prohibit merely 'indecent' material, and to confine its operation to material which would clearly be subject to conviction under the Obscene Publications Act because it depraves and corrupts. Illogically, the Court of Appeal in 1988 refused Gay's the Word permission to call expert evidence to show that 'obscene' books it wished to import could be protected by a public-good defence if printed in England.

Conegate was a sex-shop chain which had imported 'life-size rubber dolls of a sexual nature' from the Continent. A Crown Court judge had found them to be 'indecent' articles, and thus liable to forfeiture, notwithstanding that they could be marketed within Britain subject only to laws relating to public display and control of sex shops. The EEC Court held that the Treaty of Rome requires 'broadly comparable' moral standards for domestic and imported goods: the UK Government could not defend the customs prohibition on 'indecency' when it was not an offence to sell 'indecent' material over the counter.[23] The decision in *Conegate* has had major implications for customs operations. It has been the major liberalizing development in censorship in recent years, achieved not by Parliament, which has become impervious to any reform smacking of 'permissiveness', but by virtue of our accession to the EEC. In strict law it applies only to importations from Common Market countries, but the Commissioners of Customs and Excise took a policy decision to apply it across the board – it would have been impractical to apply different tests to imports from different countries, and would simply have caused determined American importers to route their goods through Europe. It is likely that a policy will develop of prosecuting importers who smuggle commercial quantities of hard-core pornography, while permitting representations to be made by those who have honestly imported 'borderline' material. Where no agreement can be reached on whether an article is likely to be regarded as 'obscene' if marketed domestically, the question could be tested by allowing the articles entry and leaving it to the DPP to decide whether to bring an obscenity prosecution.

THE COMMON LAW

There are several arcane common-law offences which are occasionally revived 'to guard the moral welfare of the State against attacks which may be more insidious because they are novel and unprepared for'. The case of Sir Charles Sedley (see earlier, page 179) was relied upon by the

House of Lords judges in 1961 when they approved the use of a charge of 'conspiracy to corrupt public morals' to convict the publisher of the *Ladies Directory* – a 'Who's Who' of London prostitutes. In ringing tones, the majority affirmed the right of the courts to punish behaviour which was prejudicial to the public welfare, even though Parliament had not legislated against it. ('No one may foresee every way in which the wickedness of man may disrupt the order of society.')[24] This judicial presumptuousness is directly opposed to any democratic theory of government, and has attracted widespread and powerful criticism (as Lord Reid put it in his dissent, 'Where Parliament fears to tread it is not for the courts to rush in'). The Law Lords defended the inherent power of the courts to punish immoral (but otherwise lawful) behaviour on the grounds that guilt would be decided by a jury, although this is clearly contrary to the principle, enshrined in the European Convention of Human rights, that no penalty should be imposed for actions which are not understood to be illegal at the time they are committed. As Lord Reid pointed out, 'The law will be whatever any jury may happen to think it ought to be, and this branch of the law will have lost all the certainty which we rightly prize in other branches of our law.'

In one remarkable case in 1967, the defendants were found guilty of conspiring to corrupt public morals by 'producing and offering for sale certain whips, leg irons, wrist irons, arm restrictors, belts, straps, chains, gags, hoods, masks, head harnesses, chastity belts, restrictive equipment and other articles, rubber and leather garments ...' The high-water mark of 'swinging London' was undoubtedly reached when men were convicted at the Old Bailey for conspiring to sell chastity belts.

The law against corrupting public morals is predicated upon the hypothesis that there is one all-embracing moral code to which all classes of the community subscribe – a notion which sociologists have demonstrated to be wishful thinking. Moreover, this assumed moral consensus is further assumed by the conspiracy law to be so vulnerable that a single publication is capable of jeopardizing it. It is not illegal to take advantage of a prostitute's services, but to facilitate this, to help short-cut the sordid and possibly dangerous process of tramping red-light districts by publishing a prostitute's telephone number, may be a serious crime. By allowing juries in effect to make law by deciding what constitutes a corruption of public morality, the criminal law is thrown into an unacceptable state of uncertainty. 'Conspiracy to corrupt public morals' is such a vague and drag-net charge that it is impossible to predict the scope of the law's operation before a jury returns its verdict.

In 1971 the House of Lords reconsidered such drag-net offences as 'conspiracy to corrupt public morals' and 'conspiracy to outrage public decency' and confined them to conduct which was 'reasonably analogous' to conduct which had been punished by prosecution of these offences in the past.[25] The Law Officers have given an undertaking that these conspiracy offences will never be used against any publication which could raise a 'public good' defence if prosecuted under the Obscene Publications Act. None the less, it would be far preferable for Parliament to deal comprehensively with 'contact advertisements' in the course of its reform of the law relating to prostitution rather than by occasional and unpredictable prosecutions against magazine publishers. In 1986, publishers of a contact magazine in Birmingham were convicted of conspiracy to corrupt public morals – the first recorded case for over a decade, and perhaps a harbinger of the revival of common-law charges to punish other 'ways in which the wickedness of man may disrupt the order of society'.

The common-law offence of 'outraging public decency' was revived in 1989 to punish an artist and the proprietor of an art gallery who exhibited a surrealist work featuring ear-rings which had been fashioned from human foetuses. This prosecution was a breach at least of the spirit of the Law Officers' undertaking, since there were a number of distinguished artists and critics prepared to testify that the work had artistic merit. The jury was not permitted to hear anything about art, and the exhibitor's intentions were ruled to be irrelevant. The judge directed the jury to put aside logic and reason and to set standards of public decency by reference to whether the display outraged their emotions. Although the facts of this case were highly exceptional, it showed how the protections for art and literature solemnly enacted by Parliament in 1959 could be circumvented by the device of charging an offence at common law. The test of 'outrage' is vague and subjective, calling for a value-judgement verdict which will depend not on any provable public standard or any deliberate intention to outrage, but on the 'gut reactions' of the jurors who happen to be empanelled to try the case. The majority-verdict procedure, which allows a conviction despite two dissenters, further undermines the protection for minority tastes and views – it is not surprising that in the 'foetal ear-rings' case, the *Oz* trial and the *Gay News* blasphemy prosecution, conviction was by a 10–2 majority. If we are to have crimes which pivot upon subjective moral reactions, the least we can ask is that a 'guilty' verdict be unanimous.

BLASPHEMY

The crime of blasphemy was created by the courts in 1617 in order to punish a madman, John Taylor, for denouncing Christ as a whore-master and orthodox religion as a cheat. In those days, a crime against religion was a crime against the State, and

> ... to say, Religion is a Cheat, is to dissolve all those Obligations whereby the Civil societies are preserved, and that Christianity is a parcel of the Laws of England and therefore to reproach the Christian religion is to speak in subversion of the law.[26]

Taylor was set in the pillory, wearing a placard inscribed: 'For blasphemous words tending to the subversion of all Government.'

Until the Darwinian revolution in the latter part of the nineteenth century, the offence was regularly used to punish attacks upon articles of Anglican belief, on the principle that strange gods might subvert familiar government. The evangelical fervour of the Vice Society coincided with fear of French revolutionary atheism to produce a rash of prosecutions against free-thinkers and publishers of the works of Thomas Paine. Blasphemy was irreverence irrespective of motive: in 1840 the Attorney-General secured the conviction of a bookseller named Hetherington for publishing an attack on the violence and obscenity of the Old Testament, 'careless of the effect it might have on the morals of the unthinking working class'.[27] If workers needed protection against the unexpurgated Old Testament, it seemed only fair that literary salons should be protected from the heretical imaginings of great poets, so Hetherington emerged from prison to secure the conviction of a respected bookseller for selling copies of Shelley's *Queen Mab*.[28] The stringency of the blasphemy law became an embarrassment to the Government: in 1851 the Law Officers reluctantly advised the Home Office that John Stuart Mill was liable to prosecution for expressing mildly agnostic views in a public lecture, although 'we should in this case consider it highly inexpedient for the Government to institute any such proceedings'.

Judges had made the law, and in the late nineteenth century it was the judges who changed the law to serve different social conditions. They altered the gist of the offence from an attack upon the Christian faith to the mode of expressing that attack. Christianity might be challenged, so long as this was done in moderate and respectful language. There were no blasphemy prosecutions at all between 1922 and 1978, when *Gay News* was charged by Mrs Mary Whitehouse with 'unlawfully and wickedly publishing a blasphemous libel concerning the Christian religion, namely an obscene poem and illustration vilifying Christ in his life and in his crucifixion'.[29]

The Old Bailey had never quite seen the like of *Whitehouse* v. *Lemon and Gay News*, and may not do so again. The prosecutrix led prayer meetings in the corridors; the Bible replaced *Archbold* as the basic forensic reference; the jury (all of whom had taken the Christian oath) were supplied with Test-match scores by the judge – who later wrote a book congratulating himself, the deity and Mrs Whitehouse on the result. He confessed an 'extraordinarily unreal sensation' in writing and delivering his summing-up, which he attributed to his 'being guided by some superhuman inspiration'. One would expect Divine inspiration to have produced a summing-up rather fairer to the defence: at any event sales of the newspaper soared after the conviction, and the Law Commission discovered a number of practising Christians who were so disgusted with the prosecution of *Gay News* that 'they ceased to be communicant members of the Church of England'.[30] The Commission, in two comprehensive reports on the blasphemy law, found little to commend the tests which the trial judge had directed the jury to apply in determining whether an offence had been committed:

– Do you think God would like to be recognized in the context of this poem?
– Did it shock you when you first read it?
– Would you be proud or ashamed to have written it?
– Could you read it aloud to an audience of fellow-Christians without blushing?
– Is the poem obscene?
– Could it hurt, shock, offend or appal anyone who read it?

The fundamental defect in the blasphemy law is that it is so uncertain that it is impossible to establish in advance whether a particular publication would constitute an offence. The crime hinges upon the finding by a particular jury that material is unacceptably 'scurrilous', 'abusive' or 'insulting' in relation to the Christian religion, and as the Law Commission points out:

> It is likely to be difficult if not impossible to prophesy in any particular case what the verdict may be . . . since the law is so uncertain in ambit, it becomes, to say the least, difficult for any legal advice to be given as to whether or not a jury in whichever part of the country a prosecutor (who may be a private prosecutor) institutes proceedings will find a particular publication blasphemous.

The Law Commission's criticism of the uncertain ambit of the offence was borne out by the experience of the publishers of the film script of *Monty Python's Life of Brian*. Three QCs gave markedly different opinions as to whether it could be published. One said the whole work was blasphemous, and the others advised cuts, some of them substantial. The publishers took the risk of publishing an unexpurgated edition, which was not, in the event, prosecuted.

Another fundamental defect of blasphemy is that, anomalously, it affords protection only to Christianity and the Established Church in a society which is both secular and multi-religious. Lord Scarman has suggested that the way forward for a plural society is to extend the law to cover all religious beliefs – a development which the Law Commission resists on grounds both of principle (religious beliefs are no less firmly held than those which relate to politics or patriotism) and pragmatism (special protection would discredit the law and encourage objectors to seek an easy martyrdom). These objections are surely justified: the identification of Church and State in Iran, for example, would mean that political protest against recent decrees in that country could constitute a blasphemous 'insult' to Islamic beliefs. Moreover, a law criminalizing the wounding of feelings of adherents to any religious group could hardly avoid protecting practices which merit investigation, and possibly condemnation or ridicule. The Law Commission has despaired of any definition which could make workable distinctions between Baptists, Scientologists, Rastafarians, Anglicans and Moonies.

Is it necessary to attempt such a daunting task? Even if it could be accomplished to general satisfaction, a reformed law of blasphemy would serve no purpose necessary to modern society. The claims of public order, morality, and the rights of individuals provide insufficient justification for any offence additional to the existing public-order prohibitions which protect against possible breaches of the peace. This conclusion is reinforced by the absence of prosecutions for blasphemy in England between 1922 and 1977; the withering away of the crime in Scotland (there are no recorded cases since the 1840s, and it is doubtful whether the offence any longer exists); and the demise of prosecutions in Northern Ireland, despite the sectarianism in that society. The scope of the offence in Wales is uncertain, as a consequence of the disestablishment of the Welsh Church in 1920.

The very existence of a blasphemy law is calculated to encourage some Christians to believe they can enforce a conventional presentation of sacred themes in the arts. Martin Scorsese's film *The Last Temptation of Christ* led to demands (most notably from the retired *Gay News* trial judge) that its distributors should be prosecuted. Whilst its presentation of Christ's humanity was challenging and unorthodox, the film lacked any element of vilification or scurrility, and on this basis the BBFC classified it as appropriate for screening to adults and the DPP declined to prosecute. None the less, religious activists prevailed on some local councils to use their powers to prevent it from being screened in some parts of the country, and the distributors had no protection against private prosecutions which could have been brought. If they had been, the defence could not have called evidence as to the film's seriousness of purpose or cinematic merit (there being no 'public good' defence to blasphemy) and the punishment, in the event of a conviction, could have been an unlimited fine or sentence of imprisonment. The episode reinforces the view that a criminal law which holds a publisher strictly liable for an artistic work liable to shock the Christian on the Clapham omnibus is inappropriate to an age in which the creeds of passengers to Clapham, if they have any, are many and various.

The unfairness of a law which protects only Christian sensibilities was highlighted in 1989 by the outrage felt amongst the Muslim community by the publication of Salman Rushdie's celebrated novel *The Satanic Verses*. This grievance was legitimate only to the extent that Muslims could correctly claim that the blasphemy law in Britain discriminated against their religion. But had it been extended to cover all faiths, Rushdie could have been prosecuted without the right to a literary-merit defence, and without even being given an opportunity to argue that he had no intention to blaspheme. He would have been at risk of conviction merely by proof that the book was likely to outrage and insult believers – which it most certainly did. To punish him in these circumstances would have been offensive to justice, but no more so than the punishment of the editor of *Gay News*. The incident exploded into an international and diplomatic crisis after Rushdie and his publishers were barbarically 'sentenced to death' by Iran: the British Government was unable to take a satisfactory stand on the principle of freedom of speech precisely because it was compromised by a law which had been used in recent years to condemn poetry offensive to Anglicans.

Regulation: Film, Video and Television

Before the children's greedy eyes with heartless indiscrimination are presented, night after night ... terrific massacres, horrible catastrophes, motor car smashes, public hangings, lynchings. All who care for the moral well-being and education of the child will set their faces like flint against this new form of excitement.

'Cinematography and the Child', *The Times*, 12 April 1913

The recent history of moral and political censorship in Britain has been characterized by a move from criminal law to statutory regulation. The process began, visibly, in 1954, when the inauguration of commercial broadcasting was deemed to require the establishment of a monitoring body, the Independent Broadcasting Authority, with statutory duties to ensure that political coverage was balanced and that programmes did not contravene the boundaries of good taste. Equivalent obligations were soon voluntarily accepted by the BBC, with the consequence that all radio and television broadcasting is subjected to a regime of institutional censorship, with rules and 'guidelines' which are of powerful effect, although they lack the force of direct law. More recently the Government, distrustful of television executives, has moved to regulate the regulators, superimposing both a complaints authority and a standards commission to exert another level of disciplinary pressure on programme-makers. The film industry had, at an early stage of its development, established a voluntary scheme known as the British Board of Film Censors (BBFC): its certificate carried no legal immunity from prosecution, but in practice deterred police action and smoothed distribution problems with local auth orities. In 1984, the BBFC became the official censorship body fo video-cassettes, charged by Parliament with the task of cutting out any scenes not suitable for viewing in the home. The following year a Cable Authority was established with the duty of ensuring that bad taste and indecency did not embarrass subscribers to cable services.

There are several reasons for the retreat from law in respect of the new media industries. The criminal law is a blunt instrument, incapable of being framed to take into account the nuances of visual presentation. Moreover, the new media are big business, attracting leading directors and substantial investors who have no desire to see their reputations and their profits at risk in the Old Bailey. For Government, of course, there is the great attraction of avoiding trial by jury: good men and women and true are prone to acquit programmes which can be suppressed, or better still not made at all, by winks and nods from State-appointed licensers. There is, in addition, a deeply felt fear that a free market will lower standards: regulation is necessary to ensure that the public is provided with what it ought to like. These arguments, variously appealing to the industry itself and to politicians from all sides of the spectrum, have produced licensing systems for the new media the like of which have not, since the days of Cromwell, been visited upon books and newspapers. They can cause severe difficulties for makers of films and broadcast programmes, because they set up a form of institutional censorship against which there is little or no appeal. For example, there is nothing that can be done about BBC directives, other than by processes of negotiation within the Corporation. Complaints Commission adjudications are un-appealable. Films which are denied certification by the BBFC can be shown if the distributor is prepared to run the risk of an obscenity prosecution, although distribution outlets will be severely limited. Most videos cannot be distributed at all without BBFC approval. The most effective form of appeal will not be to the courts, which have little or no jurisdiction, but to the public through stories leaked to the Press. Censorship is news, and some decisions which appear firm when first made within an institution have been rescinded or ameliorated as a result of public criticism. Executives in the higher echelons of broadcasting organizations generally affect liberal sympathies, and dislike the social embarrassment which follows upon publicity about their decisions to censor.

A licensing system is, by definition, a restriction on freedom of expression, although the guarantee of that right in Article 10 of the European Convention is subject to a crucial proviso: '*This article shall not prevent States from requiring the licensing of broadcasting, television and cinema enterprises.*' This exemption permits the establishment of licensing systems, but it does not underwrite specific censorship decisions made by regulatory bodies. Such decisions, if unchallengeable in the English courts, might be taken direct to Strasbourg if they have had the effect of preventing the dissemination of controversial ideas or opinions.

FILM CENSORSHIP

Film censorship today operates on three different levels. The distributors of feature films may be prosecuted under the Obscene Publications Act if the Director of Public Prosecutions deems that audiences are likely to be 'depraved and corrupted' by their offerings. Irrespective of the DPP's decision, district councils may refuse to license controversial films for screening within their jurisdiction. Most councils rely upon the advice of the BBFC, which may insist upon cuts before certifying the film's fitness for the public screen or for certain age groups, or may refuse to issue any certificate at all. Additionally, as a result of new powers granted in 1982, councils may limit the number of 'sex cinemas' in their locality, or prohibit such cinemas altogether. Neither theatre producers nor book publishers suffer institutional restrictions laid down by trade censors or local councillors. Many district councils, prompted by evangelical pressure-groups, have devoted a good deal of public time and money to reviewing films already certified by the Board, so that controversial releases such as *The Life of Brian, Clockwork Orange* and *The Last Temptation of Christ* have been banned in some districts and licensed in others, sometimes only a short bus-ride away. Local film censorship has been delegated to magistrates or entrusted to standing committees: some district councils rely upon their fire-brigade committees to extinguish any flames of passion which may have escaped the BBFC hose, while one Cornish borough solemnly bans films despite the fact that there are no cinemas within its jurisdiction. Some local councils prohibit 'sex cinemas' entirely, while others allow a reasonable number to operate. The paternalistic axis of the BBFC and the local authorities

operates haphazardly, but it does produce a great deal of both nation
and regional censorship. Chief beneficiaries of this arrangement are th
commercial interests involved in film distribution, which are generall
happy to obey BBFC directives to expurgate films with the assurance
in practice if not in theory, that certified products will not attract lega
action.

The BBFC was established in 1912 in an attempt to protect the
new cinema industry from claims that it was destructive of morality.
Local councils discovered that they had power to license cinemas in
order to protect against fire hazards, and started to use these powers
against moral and political hazards as well. The first film to be banned in
Britain was an American newsreel of a boxing championship, although
the ban had less to do with violence than with the fact that the film
showed a Negro defeating a white man. The duty of the British Board of
Film Classification (it changed the 'C', somewhat disingenuously, from
'Censors' to 'Classification' in 1984) was to induce confidence in the
minds of the licensing authorities, and of those who have in their
charge the moral welfare of the community generally. In 1924 the
BBFC received its judicial imprimatur when the Divisional Court
upheld the validity of a condition that 'No cinematograph film . . .
which has not been passed for . . . exhibition by the BBFC shall be
exhibited without the express consent of the council.'[1] So long as a
council reserved the right to review BBFC decisions, it was entitled
to make the grant of a cinema licence contingent upon the screening
of certified films.

The cutting-room counsels of the BBFC avowedly err on the side
of caution, in an effort to protect the established film industry from
criticism as well as from prosecution. Although the BBFC is (save for
its role in approving video-cassettes) an unofficial body, unrecognized by
statute and financed through fees imposed upon every film submitted for
censorship, it exercises a persuasive and in most cases determinative
influence over the grant of local-authority licences. 'I freely admit that
this is a curious arrangement,' conceded the Home Secretary, Mr Herbert
Morrison, in 1942

but the British have a very great habit of making curious arrangement
work very well, and this works. Frankly, I do not wish to be the Ministe

who has to answer questions in the House as to whether particular films should or should not be censored.[2]

The present classification, endorsed by all local councils and by the Home Office, is:

U   Universal: Suitable for all.
Uc   Universal: Particularly suitable for children.
PG   Parental guidance: Some scenes may be unsuitable for young children.
15   Passed only for persons of fifteen years and over.
18   Passed only for persons of eighteen years and over.
18R   Passed only for restricted distribution through segregated premises to which no one under eighteen is admitted.

The BBFC has effectively become the authorized censor for feature films in cinemas and on television, and for those marketed on video-cassettes. Its position derives, not from the law, but from an understanding it has reached with prosecuting authorities, local councils and the Home Office. The basis for this understanding was admitted by the DPP to the Select Committee on Obscenity in 1957:

> If I wished to prosecute a film – and it has been suggested on two occasions to me that certain films that had passed the British Board of Film Censors were obscene – my answer would be, as it was in those two cases, I shall have to put the British Board of Film Censors in the dock because they have aided and abetted the commission of that particular offence. So it inhibits me to that extent. As long as I rely on the judgement of the British Board of Film Censors as to the suitability, under the various categories, of films for public showing, which I do, I do not prosecute.[3]

On this basis, the DPP has not prosecuted certified films in connection with cinema screenings, and several private prosecutions have come to grief. A case against *Last Tango in Paris* under the Obscene Publications Act 1959 failed on technical grounds, and a prosecution of the exhibitors of *The Language of Love* for the common-law offence of gross indecency (now abolished in relation to the cinema) was rejected by an Old Bailey jury. Feature films which are certified in the '18' and '18R' categories do not receive the same practical immunity from the obscenity law when marketed on video-cassettes, because there is no control over the age of the audience which may view them in the home. For this reason the DPP has authorized prosecutions against distributors of video-cassette versions of *The Evil Dead* and *The Burning*, certified films which have played without objection to over-eighteen audiences in cinemas.

Films rated '18' are suitable for general release in cinemas which exclude entry to persons under that age. Films rated '18R' are suitable for screening only at film festivals, in private clubs for cinema buffs or in cinemas which are licensed as 'sex cinemas' by local authorities pursuant to the provisions of the Cinemas Act 1985. It is an offence, punishable by the somewhat extravagant maximum fine of £20,000, to use unlicensed premises for film exhibitions. The Cinemas Act allows local councils to restrict, on environmental grounds, the number of cinemas devoted to screening films with explicit sexual content; to ensure that such cinemas are sited well away from schools, churches and private homes; to control public advertising; and generally to impose conditions enforceable by a system of licensing. The '18R' certificate will be granted to films which would not previously have qualified for an X certificate on the grounds of their sexual explicitness, and will generally imply a judgement by the BBFC that the film, although sexually explicit, would survive a prosecution under Section 2 of the Obscene Publications Act. The film will therefore be judged as a whole, in the context of current jury decisions: material which appears to justify or glamorize harmful, illegal or anti-social actions will not receive an '18R' certificate.

It follows that films which encourage the taking of dangerous drugs, or depict extremes of sexual perversion, brutality or sadism, will not be certified. On the other hand, films which show a degree of sexual explicitness within a normal human relationship, whether heterosexual or homosexual, with scenes which are photographed with care and taste, may well receive an '18R' certificate. A more liberal test will be applied to films of recognized social or cinematic merit: by analogy with the 'public good' provisions of the Obscene Publications Act, such merits may redeem an otherwise unacceptable film so that its '18R' certificate will permit it to be shown to members of a cinema club. Pasolini's *Salo* and Oshima's *Empire of the Senses* (*Ai no Corrida*) are examples of meritorious films which have been made available by this route. However, the lack of '18R' cinemas in most areas means that distributors will rarely be interested in obtaining this classification, but will prefer to cut large chunks of scenes and dialogue in order to obtain an '18' certificate, or even more in order to attract the larger audience able to view a film with a '15' certificate. This means that the British adult public sees less in many major feature films than cinema-goers in other countries.

The one argument in favour of the BBFC is that of keeping hold of nurse for fear of finding something worse – in the form of idiosyncratic prosecutions and an upsurge in local-authority bans. The Board has stood up for some films of genuine worth which have been assailed by 'clean-up campaigners'. As the hysteria mounted to prosecute *The Last Temptation of Christ* it organized special screenings for churchmen, obtained legal opinions and issued authoritative statements rebutting suggestions that the film was blasphemous. Its efforts failed to convince many local authorities, which succumbed to lobbying from well-organized evangelical pressure groups, but its firmness did ensure that the film was screened without cuts in some parts of the country.

The system of classifying films as not suitable for showing to various age groups is entirely justifiable, but why impose censorship on adult films above and beyond what the law of obscenity demands? The answer, of course, lies in the archaic powers of local authorities to license cinemas, and to object to the content of films. These powers involve not merely a waste of local councillors' time and ratepayers' money, but the constant attention of the BBFC in editing movies so that a BBFC certificate remains acceptable to local councillors. This 'curious arrangement' may protect Ministers from being questioned in Parliament about film censorship, although their answer could take the reasonable form of referring the matter to the DPP. The arrangement today is not so much curious as eccentric, and means that the cinema, alone of art forms, is subject to moral judgement by local councillors. Regrettably the 1985 Cinemas Act left local licensing powers in place. It would be sensible to restrict their exercise to health and fire hazards, and to give the BBFC statutory powers to classify films as suitable for screening to particular age groups. It should have no power to ban or to expurgate films for adults: this task should be left to film-makers and distributors, who would at the end of the day be answerable to a jury in the event of an obscenity prosecution.

THE ADVENT OF VIDEO

The home video market in Britain has been a remarkable success: by 1986 there were over 30,000 outlets selling or renting almost 10,000 separate video titles for home viewing. Although video-cassettes were not in existence at the time the obscenity law was passed in 1959, the Court of Appeal soon held that they could be prosecuted in the same way as books and cinema films: the question is whether their contents, taken as a whole, would tend to corrupt people likely to see them.[4] In determining the potential audience, juries could consider the fact that they were designed for screening in the home, and decide whether children were likely to obtain access to them as a result. Pornographic videos presented no additional problems to those posed at trials of sexually explicit books, magazines or 8-mm films. But fears of this novel technology – its fascination for children, the ability to freeze-frame and to replay favourite episodes, and its mushroom growth – were exploited in a manic Press campaign against 'video nasties', which led to the Video Recordings Act of 1984.

Only 10 per cent of the feature films available in 1983 on video cassette had been certified by the BBFC as suitable for universal viewing. Many had been granted an 'X' certificate for cinema screening, and many more had never been certified at all. Amongst these were many run-of-the-mill horror movies, for which there was an early video vogue: to capitalize on it, distributors promoted videos which explicitly depicted violence and brutality. The label 'video nasty' was used indiscriminately, but it reflected the prevailing fear that meretricious movies which dwelt on rape and mayhem would affect the minds of young children permitted to watch them by negligent parents. The Obscene Publications Act was a suitable tool for prosecution of such films, where there was any prospect that a significant number of children might view them, and in 1983 a jury convicted the distributors of *Nightmares in a Damaged Brain* on account of its detailed depictions of sex and violence. But the campaigners – led by the Festival of Light and the *Daily Mail* – saw the opportunity to erect a new censorship apparatus which went far beyond the scope of the Obscene Publications Act. With a remarkable talent for passing off propaganda as scientifically valid research, they convinced politicians and newspapers of the accuracy of such claims as '37 per cent of children under seven have seen a "video nasty"' and that 'the nasty video has replaced the conjuror at children's birthday parties'. 'Scientific' research purportedly showed that very young children in working–class homes up and down the country were watching sadistic sex while their parents were away from home. Sensationalized research claims, timed to coincide with important stages of the Video Recordings bill, created a mild form of hysteria among politicians of all parties and the bill was rushed through with only two Tory MPs and one Labour peer dissenting. Subsequently, the much-publicized 'research' was heavily criticized, but it had served the purpose for which it was apparently designed.[5]

Meanwhile, the climate engendered by the campaign against 'video nasties' affected police forces throughout the country, who were raiding video shops and prosecuting owners for 'X'-certified horror movies perceived as 'nasties'. There was a two–year period of utter confusion, and a few video traders went to prison for stocking films which had been seen by thousands when on previous cinema release. Under heavy pressure from organizations representing the retail trade, the Attorney-General finally issued a 'list' of some sixty film titles which the DPP regarded as obscene because of depictions of violence. Retailers who wished to avoid police seizures could collect a copy of the list from their local police station and remove any offending titles. The 'DPP's list' was the first modern example of an 'Index' in Britain: video traders greeted it with relief, although many of the films on the list had been acquitted by juries while others, such as *The Evil Dead* and Andy Warhol's *Frankenstein*, had received critical acclaim.[6] The 'list' had no legal force, although fear of prosecution deterred retailers from stocking any film title which appeared on it. The Video Recordings Act has replaced the list by requiring all videos containing sexual or violent scenes to be certified by the BBFC, and imposing heavy penalties on the sale of uncertified videos.

The Video Recordings Act

As we have seen, this Act was passed in 1984 with the ostensible object of suppressing trade in about sixty video titles regarded as dangerous if taken into the home by reason of their concentration on sex and violence. But the Act goes much further, and sets up a bureaucratic system of pre-censorship unprecedented since the demise of the Cromwellian 'licensers of the Press' in 1695. It establishes by statute an Authority (the BBFC) designated by the Home Secretary to classify video-cassettes as 'suitable for viewing in the home', and to censor them if they are not suitable. Fines of £20,000 are visited upon dealers and distributors who make cassettes available to the public without a BBFC classification. The BBFC has been enlarged to cope with its censorship role: it has quadrupled its staff, acquired additional premises, and now has two vice-presidents 'approved' by the Home Secretary – the first direct political link in its seventy-year history.

All video works must be submitted to the Board for censorship, unless they are educational or concerned with sport, religion or music. However, even videos which fall into these categories must also be submitted if, '*to any significant extent*' they deal with 'human sexual activity' or 'mutilation or torture or other acts of gross violence towards humans or animals'. Thus news and current affairs videos must be submitted if they cover battles or bombings or bullfights, and so must videos which offer counselling in the field of human sexual relations or films which deal with nuclear war or acts of terrorism. Although music is exempted, video-cassettes of operas like *Il Trovatore* and *The Tales of Hoffmann* require certification. A video series of *Great Fights of the Century* would require certification, because it deals to a significant extent with 'acts of gross violence'.

In practice, then, the Act requires the great majority of video titles to be submitted to the BBFC, both for classification as appropriate for sale to particular age groups and for censorship if deemed unsuitable for viewing in the home. The cost of submitting a full-length film on video-cassette will be about £500 (the BBFC currently charges £4.60 a minute for its viewing time). The fact that the work has been made by or shown on television is irrelevant: the Minister of State for Home Affairs took pleasure in announcing that BBC programmes like *The History Man*, *Tinker, Tailor, Soldier, Spy* and *The Borgias* would require classification before they could be sold to the public on video-cassettes.

Section 4 of the Act contains its main censorship implication: the BBFC is to have 'special regard to the likelihood of (certified) video works being viewed in the home'. This test applies to every video submitted for classification, even those which are to be restricted for sale only in licensed sex shops, and is designed to underline the greater potential for harm by the technological capacity to freeze-frame and replay scenes of sex or violence. The Act does not, as some critics mistakenly assume, lay down that videos must be 'suitable for viewing in the home' in the sense of being appropriate for family viewing: that would be to negate the whole system of age-classification and point-of-sale restriction. The video must be 'suitable for classification' in a particular category, having special regard to the impact it will have upon persons in that age group and below through the devices available for home viewing. Thus a video work which is suitable for the classification '18' or '18R', given that it will be viewed by adults at home, should not be refused classification because of the danger that children may obtain access to it when it is left in the home by careless parents. None the less, 'where horror material is concerned, we have exercised a restraining influence on the explicitness of gory imagery because of our awareness that children and younger teenagers may be particularly tempted to watch such material . . .' the BBFC states in its *Guidelines on Violence*. This is a consideration which goes to age-group classification rather than censorship: Section 4 does not justify the deletion of 'gory imagery' from '18' or '18R' films because of the danger that they will be seen by children. Parliament could (as some MPs wished) have insisted that *all* videos be suitable for children: it provided a classification system based on the notion of parental responsibility. This system is logically undermined by the BBFC whenever it makes cuts in '18' videos on the grounds that younger persons may watch.

The Video Recordings Act has necessitated a censorship system which goes far beyond the initial concern about 'video nasties'. It would have been possible to deal with this very limited mischief by legislation which permitted the BBFC, on a complaint by the police or a member of the public, to designate a specific video-cassette as prohibited from public sale. Any subsequent breach of a prohibition order could have constituted a criminal offence, pending a right of appeal by the distributor to a jury. Such a reform, which would effectively have banned the 'video nasty' without exposing much of the industry to a bureaucratic apparatus of censorship, went entirely overlooked. The worst feature of the new system is that it imposes double jeopardy on video distributors because it keeps alive the power of the police, the DPP and private prosecutors to proceed against the suppliers of certified videos for offences against the Obscene Publications Act. Distributors are in breach of one criminal law if they sell uncertified cassettes, and they may still be in breach of another criminal law if they sell certified ones. No censorship system which permits such double jeopardy holds out much hope of rational enforcement.

There have been other unsatisfactory consequences. At the end of the first two years of the Act's operation, it appeared that the high classification fees were forcing many distributors to delete less profitable videos from their catalogues, thereby reducing viewer choice, especially in relation to vintage movies and minor classics. This is the hidden cultural cost of the Video Recordings Act: its true casualties have not been the trashy films which are banned, but the significant cinematic works which do not have sufficient popular appeal to justify the costs of classification. The Act may have diminished the degree of explicitness of sex and violence, but not the numbers of cassettes dealing with these themes or the prominence given to them. Distributors are discovering the level of 'acceptable' sex and 'acceptable' violence, and their films are full of it. Meanwhile, some films of real worth are not being distributed because the profits from small audiences do not justify the classification fee.

The worst result of the Act has been to establish a State censorship apparatus in Britain. The BBFC expanded from a family-size firm of twelve in 1982 to a bureaucratic organization with a staff of fifty (including twenty-two full-time 'film examiners') by 1985. Its members at present are reasonable and liberal, although the powers of 'approval' given to the Home Secretary could at some future date turn into a force for suppressing 'unacceptable' political messages on film or video. As an official censorship body, it believes in its duty to censor, and encounters little opposition from a trade that is more interested in profits than in defending artistic integrity. 'Cuts' are negotiated between the BBFC and the film or video distributors – the voice of the film-maker is never heard, as the system permits no consultation with or complaint from the artist whose vision is being dimmed. For example, distributors who wish to obtain a '15' certificate to maximize audiences will sometimes agree to cuts which seriously undermine or distort the impact of the film.

This is made all the more unsatisfactory because the BBFC purports to adopt artistic judgements. It claims, in relation to violence, to take into account 'the moral position of the film-maker towards his own material' by applying the following tests:

(a) Is the sympathy of the film-maker on the side of the victim or the aggressor?

(b) Is the process of the violence indulged in for its own sake, rather than to tell us anything significant about the motives or state of mind of the persons involved?

(c) Does the camerawork or editing belie the ostensible moral stance of the film by seeking to enlist or encourage our vicarious enjoyment of the atrocities portrayed?[7]

Like Miss Prism's view of fiction, the BBFC's view of feature films is that the good should end happily and the bad unhappily. But these generalized statements are little more than window-dressing, giving some rational justification for cuts which are made because the violence is of a kind which turns the examiner's stomach. Films which glorify wars and mercenary operations have been passed without deletions: those which depict extremes of violence will be censored, however 'moral' the context. 'Moderation is a useful ideal, and the process of violence can often be toned down by judicious cutting' says the BBFC (ever so pleased at being able to improve on the cinematographer's art) in its *Guidelines on Violence*.

Some film-makers, of course, have no wish to have the impact of their images 'moderated' by paternalistic censors. *Christianne F*, a powerfully aversive film about the degradation of heroin-taking, lost some of its impact by four minutes of cuts. Even the comic cocaine-sniffing scene in *Crocodile Dundee* had to be excised before the Board would grant the film a '15' certificate for video release. The BBFC boasts that scenes which show oriental fighting methods are 'banned absolutely', and takes great care to delete scenes where 'everyday instruments', such as cigarette lighters and garden tools, are used to inflict violence, lest this give the audience ideas. It prides itself on being the strictest censorship board in the Western world in cutting scenes of violence (especially sexual violence) against women, 'even where the point of view of the film as a whole is a critical one'.[7] (The Alfred Hitchcock classic *Frenzy* had one of its scenes cut, despite the fact that it had twice been shown unexpurgated on television, while *Death Wish*, which had also been shown on television, was refused a certificate for video release.) Like the Lord Chamberlain's censorship of the theatre, and the prosecutors who applied the 'purple passages' test to books before the Obscene Publications Act of 1959, the BBFC believes itself to be justified in removing images which depict appalling actions, for fear that those actions might be imitated by suggestible viewers. The result is that a great many films and videos have become suggestive rather than explicit, and it may be doubted whether the supposed danger is any the less. Most viewers, of course, receive such scenes as fantasy, and enjoy them as such: the possibility of an appeal to a few unbalanced minds is the basis for curbing the rights of a majority to view as they please. There is an Appeals Tribunal, but it is open only to the distributor who has submitted the film and not to directors, who may object to the manner in which expurgation has altered or minimized their message. The public, needless to say, are not informed by any message on the video container that the film they are about to buy or hire has been censored.

Film and video censorship has become a comfortable institution in the United Kingdom. The BBFC even offers to advise on film scripts before shooting begins. The film-industry distributors, traditionally motivated by profit rather than principle, have willingly cooperated with the system, recognizing that it helps to protect them from the vagaries of prosecution. They have cooperated to such an extent that many submit videos of films which have been so heavily cut *before* submission that the BBFC has no role other than to approve self-censorship. Of the forty-two videos it ordered cut in 1985, not one distributor bothered to appeal. Yet some of these cuts were quite absurd: five seconds were solemnly chopped from the Douglas Fairbanks classic *The Thief of Baghdad* and six seconds from a trailer for Elia Kazan's *On the Waterfront*, while Walt Disney Productions suffered the loss of seventeen seconds from *The Littlest Outlaw*, sixteen seconds from *Old Yeller* and twenty-four seconds from *Nikki, Wild Dog of the North*. The BBFC justify such cuts on the grounds of 'unsuitability due to the emotional power of the scene, and particularly to its potential for producing nightmares . . .' On this basis, should the BBFC allow Bambi's cry of 'Mother' to haunt future video generations?

TELEVISION

The BBC

The British Broadcasting Corporation is a body incorporated by royal charter. It has nine governors (including the chairman and vice-chairman), who are appointed by the Crown on the advice of the Prime Minister. Three of the governors must be 'national' representatives of Scotland, Wales and Northern Ireland, but otherwise there are no requirements that Board members should be politically balanced or even have broadcasting experience. Appointments are unadventurous and conservative, and guided by the Home Office reluctance to see people of great distinction or originality in any position of power. (The BBC has itself submitted the names of Margaret Drabble, Iris Murdoch, John Mortimer QC and Moira Shearer as potential governors: all have been turned down.)[8] In general the Board tries to keep aloof from specific controversies and to allow these to be dealt with by the Director-General and his staff, although in recent years it has proved sadly vulnerable to political pressure. It intervened in 1985 to stop the transmission of one programme, *Real Lives*, about an IRA sympathizer in Belfast, after the Prime Minister had condemned it, unseen, as showing support for terrorism. The Home Secretary thanked the BBC governors for banning it, journalists both in the Corporation and in ITV companies held a one-day strike, and the BBC's reputation throughout the world for independence and reliability suffered enormous damage. *Real Lives* was subsequently screened with a few face-saving deletions, but the episode showed that the Board of Governors could not be trusted to uphold the BBC's freedom. The Board was silent when the police raided BBC premises to carry off the *Secret Society* series which included the Zircon film, and in 1987 it notably failed to appoint Jeremy Isaacs, the best-qualified candidate, as Director-General. Both Harold Wilson and Margaret Thatcher have appointed BBC chairmen for personal rather than publicly obvious reasons, and it is difficult to perceive the Corporation as being independent of Government so long as Prime Ministerial patronage is allowed to decide the membership of its governing body.

The BBC is established under a charter, and is licensed by the Home Secretary to provide radio and television broadcasts. Section 19 of its licensing agreement enables the Home Secretary, when in his opinion there is an emergency and it is 'expedient' so to act, to send troops in to 'take possession of the BBC in the name and on behalf of Her Majesty'. This clause was framed during the General Strike, when Winston Churchill and other members of Government wanted to commandeer the Corporation. It has never been used for that purpose, although Sir Anthony Eden contemplated invoking it for Government propaganda during the Suez crisis, and during the Falklands recapture it provided the legal basis for the Government's use of BBC transmitters on Ascension Island to beam propaganda broadcasts at Argentina.

A more worrying power is contained in Section 13(4) of the Licence Agreement, which gives the Home Secretary the right to prohibit the BBC from transmitting any item or programme, at any time. The power is not limited, like Section 19, to periods of emergency. The only safeguard against political censorship is that the BBC 'may' (not 'must') tell the public that it has received a Section 13(4) order from the Home Secretary. This safeguard was invoked in 1972 by the Director-General, Lord Hill, when Home Secretary Reginald Maudling threatened a Section 13(4) order to stop transmission of a debate about Government actions in Ulster. Lord Hill called his bluff by threatening to make public the reason why the programme could not be shown. Of course, a less courageous Director-General could simply cancel the programme without revealing the existence of a Government order. For all the public knows, there may be secret Section 13 directives in force at present. In 1981, Parliament unanimously renewed the BBC Licence Agreement until 1996, without debating these powers. Similar powers exist, in relation to commercial television, in Section 29 of the Broadcasting Act 1981.

The Home Secretary's power to ban broadcasts of specified 'matter or classes of matter' under Clause 13(4) of the Charter and Section 29(3) of the Broadcasting Act was invoked in 1988 for the purpose of direct political censorship when the BBC and the IBA were ordered not to transmit any interviews with representatives of Sinn Fein, the Ulster Defence Association, or the IRA, or any statement which incited support for such groups (see earlier, page 92). The broadcasting authorities did not challenge the directive, nor confine it to its narrowest possible interpretation: they made decisions erring on the safe side, and ran to the Home Office for help with its 'interpretation'. The ban is a serious infringement on the right to receive and impart information: it prevents representatives of lawful political parties (Sinn Fein has an MP and sixty local councillors) from stating their case on matters which have no connection with terrorism, and it denies to the public the opportunity to see and hear those who support violent action being questioned and exposed. The Government believes that terrorists survive by 'the oxygen of publicity', but television confrontations generally demonstrate the moral unattractiveness of those who believe that the end justifies the means. The ban prevents the re-screening of such excellent programmes as Robert Kee's *Ireland: a Television History* or Thames Television's *The Troubles*, which contain interviews with IRA veterans. The BBC and IBA meekly complied with the ban, which further underlines the lack of constitutional protection for freedom of speech in British law. In theory, the Home Secretary's unrestricted powers under Section 29(3) and Clause 13(4) could permit a directive against transmitting attacks on the Government made by members of the opposition party.

The BBC's Charter and Licence is silent on the subject of obscenity, although in 1964 the BBC gave an undertaking, which is now annexed to the Licence, to avoid programmes which would give widespread public offence. The undertaking states:

> The Board accept that, so far as possible, the programmes for which they are responsible should not offend against good taste or decency, or be likely to encourage crime or disorder, or be offensive to public feeling. In judging what is suitable for inclusion in programmes they will pay special regard to the need to ensure that broadcasts designed to stimulate thought do not so far depart from their intention as to give general offence.[9]

This undertaking is not legally enforceable, and Mrs Whitehouse and her ilk have spent the last two decades complaining about 'offensive' BBC programmes, from *Steptoe and Son* to *EastEnders*. This has created a climate in which Corporation executives regularly delete expletives and sexual imagery, even in the work of outstanding playwrights like Alan Bleasdale and David Hare, who have had plays performed to acclaim in the theatre either banned or cut by the BBC. BBC censorship operates by a process of 'reference up' the corporation hierarchy. Any producer who foresees possible offence must alert middle management, which may pass borderline cases to departmental heads, who may in turn consult the Managing Director or even the Director-General.[10] Internal directives are issued from time to time about programme content, especially in relation to sex, violence and drugs. The 'middle ground' is occupied by avoiding extreme political views and ensuring that controversial opinions are 'balanced' by dispensation of conventional wisdom either in the same programme, or over a series. 'Gratuitous' bad language or behaviour is 'eliminated' when not essential to plot or purpose, and four-letter words chanted by football crowds are solemnly edited out of *Match of the Day*, but the Corporation promises to strike the balance in favour of creative freedom where it is exercised for genuine or socially redeeming purposes. Such promises are not always honoured: in 1983 three crucial minutes were deleted from an important documentary on female circumcision, because they showed female circumcision.[11]

When Ian McEwan's play *Solid Geometry* was unaccountably banned in 1979 after being rehearsed for some weeks, the Regional Board of Drama explained the decision to David Hare by saying: 'How do you think it would look if in the very week Margaret Thatcher was elected we were stupid enough to record a play which featured a twelve-inch penis in a bottle?' Hare was later reminded that his contract allowed him to be sacked if he leaked the story to the Press.[12] This is a good example of the real motivation behind censorship decisions, which frequently belie the seemingly reasonable sound of the Corporation's 'guidelines' and 'policies'. When the BBC banned *The Naked Civil Servant*, the IBA screened it with one alteration: the caption 'Sexual intercourse is a poor substitute for masturbation' was replaced by 'Wasn't it fun in the bath tonight!'

Brimstone and Treacle, a morality play by Dennis Potter, the renowned television dramatist, about the dilemma of reconciling the existence of both God and evil, was vetoed at the highest level although it contained no single scene which was offensive or in poor taste, and it was subsequently made into a successful feature film. It was not blasphemous at common law, because it lacked any element of indecency or scurrility. But its anti-Christian overtones, and particularly its portrayal of the Devil doing good, upset the Director of Programmes, who 'found the play brilliantly written and made' (at a public expenditure of £70,000) 'but nauseating'.[13] The Chairman of the BBC maintained that 'the whole central theme of the play . . . would outrage viewers in a way that was unjustifiable'.[14] The play was finally screened in 1987, ten years after it was made, without any public complaint.

In 1978 the BBC banned *Scum*, a violent and disturbing play about conditions in Borstal, based on actual experiences of both inmates and prison officers. This time the BBC deferred to the opinion of Home Office 'experts' invited to view the film prior to transmission. It was conceded that every incident had real-life parallels, but the play distorted reality because they could not all have happened in the one Borstal at the one time.[15]

For twenty years the BBC refused to show *The War Game*, a film about the horrors of nuclear war made for it in 1965, and shown at many public screenings since. Director-General Sir Ian Trethowan said: 'I do not believe that any broadcasting authority could take the responsibility for what the effect might be on elderly people and people of limited mental intelligence, particularly among those three million licence payers whom we know live alone.' The effect might have been to make them enlist in CND – a prospect that many thought was the real reason behind the ban.

BBC censorship is frequently 'political', and its senior executives are vulnerable to pressure from politicians and policemen alike. One play, *Willie, The Legion Hall Bombing* actually had both its opening and closing scenes rewritten by corporation executives to modify criticism of the 'Diplock' non-jury courts in Northern Ireland. The author (Carol Churchill) and director (Roland Joffe) took legal action to have their names removed from the credits, and supplied the original script to the Press so that the BBC's action could be publicly criticized. In 1985 the BBC suppressed a *Brass Tacks* film which had been made about a notorious 'supergrass', after 'representations' from Scotland Yard. BBC executives claimed that the film had been canned because of libel difficulties – an excuse which was shown to be threadbare when their researcher took the material to *World in Action*, which remade the film and screened it.

These *causes célèbres* relate only to films which have been made and then withdrawn from screening. The real casualties of political censorship are the subjects which are not tackled in the first place, because of fear of political fall-out. There has been a certain reluctance within the Corporation to devote investigative resources to stories which might directly undermine Government policies, and which are tackled with more enthusiasm by quality newspapers and independent television. The Corporation's independence from Government, which is so vital to the reputation of its external services as the purveyor of unbiased news, suffered a further blow in 1985, at the same time as the *Real Lives* affair, when it was revealed that a Security Service official, Brigadier Ronnie Stonham, occupied room 105 in Broadcasting House and was employed to 'vet' staff appointments and promotions. Several distinguished journalists had been black-listed from Corporation jobs as the result of MI5 influence. It also emerged that for many years political journalists and other senior staff had been obliged to sign the Official Secrets Act, and that all staff at Bush House (Headquarters of the BBC's overseas broadcasting network) had been routinely required to sign the Act. This obligation, which has in any event no legal force (see earlier, page 137), has never been imposed on journalists working for the Press and Independent Television, and seems to have been a grave error of judgement on the part of BBC management. The Corporation has now promised to end Security Service vetting and to put room 105 to a use more consistent with its proclaimed independence. Ironically, the BBC's tarnished reputation for independence and integrity was partly restored a year later when its offices were raided by the police during the Zircon affair, and the Conservative Party Chairman made a much-publicized accusation of left-wing bias in its coverage of the US bombing of Libya. These accusations were baseless and promptly rebutted by the BBC, but the fact that they were made at least demonstrated to the outside world that the Corporation was not, like many national broadcasters, merely a tool of Government.

Independent broadcasting

Commercial radio and television is supervised by a Government-appointed licensing body called the Independent Broadcasting Authority, which has wide powers to interfere with programme content. These powers date from 1954, and reflect the exaggerated fears of that period about untried and untrusted commercial exploitation of the medium.

Lord Reith described the introduction of commercial television as 'a betrayal and a surrender . . . somebody introduced smallpox, bubonic plague and the Black Death. Somebody is minded now to introduce sponsored broadcasting in this country.'[16] One eminent Law Lord confessed to a 'sense of sacrilege' at the very prospect of an advertisement broadcast on the Sabbath. In this atmosphere, it was understandable that commercial television should be placed under the close scrutiny of a licensing body, empowered by what is now Section 4(1) of the Broadcasting Act 1981 to ensure:

(a) that nothing is included in the programmes which offends against good taste or decency or is likely to encourage or incite to crime or to lead to disorder or to be offensive to public feeling . . .

(b) that due impartiality is preserved on the part of persons providing the programmes as respects matters of political or industrial controversy or relating to current public policy.

There are fourteen commercial television companies, and a host of commercial radio stations. They owe their commercial existence to a contract with the IBA, which must be renewed every eight (or in the case of local radio, every ten) years.[17] The IBA comprises a board of eighteen Government appointees, with a staff of several hundred and one subsidiary company responsible for running Channel 4. Its all-important decisions to grant or renew contracts are cloaked in utter secrecy. This is wholly unacceptable. Licensing bodies in other countries have obligations to hold public hearings and to receive submissions from the public about the fitness and the track record of licence applicants – in the United States, for example, there are procedures of a judicial kind which are calculated to ensure that these decisions are arrived at fairly and impartially. There has been a good deal of criticism of particular IBA licence decisions, and it is regrettable that Parliament has not legislated to require public hearings, publication of memoranda by successful applicants, and publication by the IBA of its reasons for giving or withholding licences. Appointments to the IBA board are made by the Home Secretary, sometimes at the Prime Minister's insistence, and are as politically vulnerable as appointments to the BBC. There is no requirement for political balance or broadcasting experience, and in 1989 the Government was widely condemned for appointing Lord Chalfont, a notorious theorist about left-wing 'infiltration' of the media to the position of deputy chairman of the IBA.

Under its contracts with ITV companies, the IBA has the right – and indeed the duty – to vet programmes to ensure that they are neither offensive nor biased. Programme-makers often criticize IBA pre-censorship, which is, after all, a direct interference with freedom of expression by way of prior restraint, imposed by Government appointees. The IBA has been particularly concerned with programmes about Northern Ireland, and its interference has ranged from banning an entire programme (e.g. a *This Week* report about RUC brutality) to cutting provocative scenes lasting a few seconds (such as pictures of flowers on an IRA grave). It was, however, supportive of an important *This Week* investigation into the SAS shootings of three IRA members in Gibraltar, and defended the programme against exaggerated attacks from the Prime Minister and Foreign Secretary. These reached such a pitch that Thames Television set up an independent inquiry into the making of *Death on the Rock*, chaired by Lord Windlesham. It conclusively rejected allegations that the programme had been deliberately biased or had interfered with judicial processes in Gibraltar.

IBA vetting of programmes before transmission was approved in 1973 by the Court of Appeal in the case of *Attorney-General ex rel. McWhirter* v. *IBA*, which involved a documentary about the work of avant-garde artist Andy Warhol. Lurid newspaper pre-publicity provoked a clean-up campaigner to seek an injunction against the screening because it would allegedly be a breach of the IBA's duty to ensure that no offence was committed against the canons of good taste and decency. The Court of Appeal criticized the members of the IBA board for delegating responsibility for vetting the programme to its executive officers, and delayed transmission until the board members had seen it and decided for themselves. The board endorsed its officers' decision that the film could be shown without a breach of Section 4(1) of the Act. The judges, while personally disagreeing with the decision, declined to interfere with the IBA's performance of its duty unless its decision could be shown to be manifestly unreasonable.[18]

The Annan Committee, reporting on the future of television in 1977, was unimpressed by the IBA's censorship activities in the years after the *McWhirter* case.[19] Instead of a detached and supervisory role, the IBA had become deeply involved in the editorial and creative process, casting a blanket of pre-censorship over current affairs programmes like *This Week*. Annan deplored the fetters on initiative and imagination caused by IBA intermeddling with programmes prior to broadcast. It recommended that the Authority should intervene to preview programmes only when it had good reason to believe that its policy was being flouted. Post-censorship should replace pre-censorship: criticism of errors of taste should be made by privately communicating IBA views to the television company concerned *after* the broadcast, while major errors of judgement should be publicly condemned and draw an apology from the company responsible. The ultimate sanction – loss of licence – would be sufficient to ensure that television companies did not repeatedly outrage public feeling. In particular, Annan recommended that the canons of good taste and impartiality should not shackle the fourth channel. But by this time, the IBA had grown accustomed to its role as censor. Its then Director-General, Sir Brian Young, saw the Authority as a 'thoughtful editor', vetting scripts, pre-viewing programmes and occasionally banning 'unbalanced' programmes (like *This Week* on Ulster) in response to high-level pressure. 'We are given teeth for biting, not for gnashing' was his response to criticism. In Channel 4's first week, the IBA bit a large chunk out of *The Animals Film*, apparently worried that it would encourage crime by encouraging viewers to join animal-liberation groups.

When Channel 4 first scheduled the film of *Scum*, a powerful drama about violence begetting violence among young offenders in a Borstal, IBA officials refused to approve it. The play on which the film was based had been banned by the BBC (see above, page 233). But they were overruled by the IBA's Director-General, John Whitney, who had been a prison visitor and actually knew something about the subject-matter of the film. His experience enabled him to see its merits, and he ordered it to be screened at 11.30 p.m. Only three viewers complained – two to Channel 4 and one (Mrs Mary Whitehouse) to the High Court. At first instance, the Divisional Court ruled that John Whitney had committed a 'grave error of judgement' in approving the transmission of a controversial film without first showing it to members of the Authority for their approval.[20] Had this approach been confirmed by the Court of Appeal, the IBA board would have had to act as a major censorship body, with members required personally to approve any film or documentary which seemed likely to provoke protest from pressure groups or interested parties. Other unsatisfactory consequences of this original ruling were felt in the twelve months before it was upset on appeal. Programmes which would previously have been approved by IBA officers were delayed until debated by the full board at monthly meetings. One foreign country and several large companies, fearing condemnation in forthcoming current-affairs programmes, were able to delay transmission and to mute criticism by commencing legal action against the IBA. Board members feared that their 'duty' to approve controversial programmes in advance might make them personally liable to be joined in legal proceedings brought against television companies. The theoretical possibility, however remote in practice, of board members being arraigned in an Old Bailey dock charged with aiding and abetting Cathy Massiter's breach of the Official Secrets Act led to their extraordinary loss of nerve in delaying the Channel 4 programme on MI5.

The Court of Appeal decision on *Scum* removed these fears by acquitting the Director-General of any 'error of judgement', and paved the way for the IBA to adopt a less interventionist role in television programming. The Master of the Rolls, Lord Donaldson, pointed out that the statutory duties of ensuring 'good taste' and 'due impartiality' are imprecise, and require only that board members should do their best to establish and supervise a system which provides a reasonable prospect that these values will be preserved by the television companies.[21] They are not obliged personally to vet every controversial programme: a system which enables them to monitor standards and be kept informed of public reaction was satisfactory, with the Director-General retaining discretion to 'refer up' only those programmes which he regarded, exceptionally, as appropriate for board consideration. The *McWhirter* case turned on its own special facts: henceforth the courts should only intervene when convinced that the *system* adopted by the IBA was so bizarre that no reasonable person could believe it would assist in maintaining programme standards at the general level required by the Act.

The appeal decision in the *Scum* case shows that the IBA could legally make its regulatory procedures conform more closely to the Annan recommendations by placing greater reliance on *ex post facto* criticism and public reprimand rather than prior restraint. The line-by-line scrutiny of certain current-affairs programmes, so deplored by Annan, is not normally necessary: the IBA will be entitled to assume that the independent television and radio companies which it licenses will not deliberately infringe the criminal law or put themselves in jeopardy of losing their licence by causing serious offence. The IBA must maintain its monitoring functions, investigate minor complaints, and provide guidelines on standards of taste and decency, and there must always be provision for test cases to be 'referred up' for board decision. But routine previewing and pre-censorship of programmes on controversial subjects by IBA officials or board members can no longer be defended as legally necessary. The Court of Appeal's description of the statutory duties of the IBA may also have put paid to fears that its members could properly be joined in any prosecution of a television company or programme contractor for breaches of criminal law. A general supervisory duty cannot carry personal liability for aiding and abetting a programme transmitted in breach of the law, unless there is both knowledge of the illegal content of the programme and a positive encouragement to transmit it. In exceptional cases these elements may be present, but normally the Authority can safely leave such questions to the television companies and their legal advisers.

The IBA's efforts to be both a broadcaster and a regulator have led to frequent friction between its bureaucrats and programme-makers, especially those from Channel 4. Section 11 of the Act imposes a specific duty on the IBA to ensure that programmes on Channel 4 '*contain a suitable proportion of matter calculated to appeal to tastes and interests not generally catered for by ITV*' and '*to encourage innovation and experiment in the form and content of programmes*' on the fourth Channel. In balancing all its statutory duties, the Authority has considerable latitude in allowing programmes which may be unpalatable to some sections of the viewing public. In 1983, Mrs Mary Whitehouse demanded that it stop transmission of a Channel 4 documentary about 'video nasties' which in the course of calling for legislation showed clips from the offending films. Although such clips were undoubtedly in bad taste and offensive to public feeling – the very reason why they were included in the programme – the Authority was justified in permitting the transmission to proceed, in view of the context and purpose of the programme and its duties under Section 11. Rather cravenly, it did insist on transmission at a later time than would normally have been scheduled, although the publicity generated by the affair ensured a higher-than-average viewing audience.

The IBA has, in the opinion of Jeremy Isaacs, the distinguished ex-controller of Channel 4, sometimes used its powers against both the interests of programmes and the interests of the public. Many of its censorship requirements in relation to current-affairs programmes have not been made public. However, when the Channel was running a late-night movie season, the IBA banned *The Exorcist*, *The Life of Brian* and *Last Tango in Paris*. These films had been seen by millions throughout the nation on cinema release, but were deemed unsuitable for screening on television at 11 p.m. on Friday night. On the other hand, it must be conceded that the IBA regulation has in many respects served the purposes of public-service broadcasting by setting high programme standards, encouraging quality television (especially by insisting on prime-time slots for current-affairs programmes) and by resisting the trivial, advertising-oriented values of the American media market-place. Its fatal mistake has, as the Annan Committee pointed out, been to act as editor as well as regulator. It has alienated programme-makers by its editorial interference, and then alienated politicians by not interfering enough. Its valuable supervisory role has been jeopardized by its censorship initiatives, which have ironically sown the seeds of its own destruction. The Government is planning its abolition to pave the way for more competitive (and lower-quality) television, which will be more stringently controlled, at least in the interests of good taste and good politics, by *ad hoc* bodies like the Broadcasting Standards Commission and the Broadcasting Complaints Commission.

Programme standards

Both the BBC and the IBA impose censorship through the application of policy guidelines on sex and violence and coverage of terrorism. Bad language, nudity and racism are discouraged, criminal techniques are never demonstrated, and interviews with law-breakers (whether IRA terrorists or animal-liberation activists) are rarely shown. A 'family viewing policy' operates to increase restrictions until the 'watershed hour' of 9 p.m., when more 'adult' programmes can progressively be screened.

There are special provisions for 'news black-outs' on hijackings and kidnaps, at the request of the police. The codes on violence are regularly revised and have become increasingly complex, with rules which range from 'dead bodies should not be shown in close-up' to 'film should not dwell on close-up pictures of the grief-stricken in the wake of natural disasters and man-made violence'. Such rules are easy to agree in principle, but frequently ignored in practice. Thus dead bodies *are* shown in close-up, if they are black and lying in some foreign field, and weeping relatives were depicted in television coverage of the 1987 cross-Channel ferry disaster. However, television is notably more restrained in invading personal privacy than the Press (it would be inconceivable for any news programme to broadcast a picture of a rape victim on the steps of her church). The balance to be struck, in Hugh Carlton Greene's words, is 'between what is true and what is tolerable'.

Section 4 of the Broadcasting Act requires that '*all news given in the programmes (in whatever form) is presented with due accuracy and impartiality*' and that '*due impartiality is preserved on the part of the persons providing the programmes as respects matters of political or industrial controversy or relating to current public policy*'. An important addition to the latter duty is that a series of programmes may be considered as a whole. This addition allows the IBA to sanction a programme or series of programmes which is 'committed' to a politically controversial subject, so long as other programmes on the same channel at similar times present the other view. Thus a John Pilger documentary which presented the case for unilateral disarmament was only allowed to be screened after Central Television had undertaken to make and transmit a documentary presenting the opposing view.

The term 'due' is significant in the phrase 'due impartiality'. It gives the IBA the power to approve one-sided programmes if the side taken is generally acceptable. Thus the IBA is not required to secure impartiality on matters such as drug trafficking, cruelty, racial intolerance or other subjects on which 'right-thinking people' are largely unanimous. The BBC, too, claims that there can be no duty to balance the claims of 'basic moral values', defined by Sir Hugh Greene as 'truthfulness, justice, freedom, compassion and tolerance'.

Cable television is subject to the same restraints as commercial television, in that nothing may be shown which offends against good taste or decency or is likely to incite crime or be offensive to public feeling. One Government report had originally proposed that cable viewers should be entitled to receive 'adults only' films, screened on a channel which could be specially 'locked' and hence be rendered inaccessible to young children.[22] This prospect was derided in predictable quarters, and the Government hastened to reassure the public of its commitment to family viewing. The inclusion of the 'good taste' requirement will ensure that '18R' films are not offered by cable companies, and may necessitate some editing of movies classified as '18' for the cinema. The meaning of the phrase 'offensive to public feeling' may be more limited in the Cable bill than in the Broadcasting Act: it would be sensible to take account only of the paying public in the locality where the cable service operates, and to give broad scope to the coverage of issues which have aroused strong local feelings, however much the subject and its treatment might hypothetically offend national sensibilities.

Advertising

Fears of advertising excesses were responsible for the original injunction on bad taste and offensiveness in commercial broadcasting, and the IBA vets both advertising copy and visual material before transmission to remove 'potentially offensive sexual overtones'. Until 1987 the IBA repeatedly declared that condom advertisements would be offensive to a large section of the British public. This attitude reflected an irresponsible double standard: the media were prepared to promote promiscuity by snigger and insinuation, but refused to help minimize the casualties, and as recently as 1984 the IBA banned advertisements made by LWT for the Family Planning Association. It needs to be stressed that such IBA decisions are entirely ungoverned by rules of law: they reflect the moral prejudices of the IBA's officers and board members as to what constitutes 'good taste'. In 1987, the advent of AIDS made the IBA finally relent in its total ban on condom advertisements, although so far it has rejected most that have been submitted. Any trace of humour, any attempt to put information about condoms across in ways which might actually appeal to a youthful audience, is rejected as being 'in poor taste'.

The truly distasteful aspect of IBA policy is its discrimination against minority advertisers on Channel 4. A ten-second commercial for a homosexual newspaper was banned on the grounds that it would be offensive to public feeling: a wholly unreasonable decision, given that it was unexceptionally worded and photographed, and came at the end of an hour-long programme specifically for homosexuals. The IBA ruling could have been challenged on the grounds that it was perverse, and conflicted both with the IBA's Section 11 duty (to ensure that Channel 4 carried matter calculated to appeal to minority tastes and interests), and with paragraph 6 of its statutory Advertising Rules, which requires that 'in the acceptance of advertisements there must be no unreasonable discrimination either against or in favour of any particular advertiser'.

Other controversial IBA decisions have been to refuse advertisements for left-wing journals such as *Tribune*, *Morning Star* and *New Socialist*, while accepting them for committed Tory newspapers which make up the majority of the daily Press. This discrimination is purportedly justified by reference to Rule 8:

> No advertisement shall be permitted which is inserted by or on behalf of any body the objects whereof are wholly or mainly of a religious or political nature, and no advertisement shall be permitted which is directed towards any religious or political end or has any relation to any industrial dispute.

The purpose of this rule is clearly to avoid party propaganda, and the IBA would be justified in refusing to advertise journals, like the *Morning Star*, sponsored by a particular political party. *Tribune* and *New Socialist*, however, are independent left-wing weeklies, which are more concerned with probing the divisions within the left than they are with promoting the electoral triumph of the Labour Party. Once again, the interpretation of the rule is not dictated by law. The IBA has chosen one of several, equally admissible, approaches – the approach which happens to ensure maximum discrimination. In 1983 it refused to allow advertisements for a West Indian newspaper, on the ground that the front-page which featured for a few seconds in the trailer included headlines about a politically controversial inquest.

Political broadcasts

The BBC accepts a special duty to permit Ministerial broadcasts on matters of national importance, which may range from a declaration of war to emergency arrangements for coping with a drought. So long as there is general consensus on the subject-matter of the broadcast, no right of reply will be given to the Opposition. Where there is, however, an element of partisan controversy in a Ministerial broadcast, the Opposition must be given equal time to broadcast a reply.[23] When Mr Tony Benn sought to make a Ministerial broadcast in 1975 on the Petroleum and Submarine Protection Act, the BBC detected political controversy in his script and informed him that the Opposition would be entitled to put its point of view. He cancelled the broadcast rather than allow his opponents free air-time.

A limited number of party-political broadcasts are allowed each year on all channels, determined by a committee comprising representatives from the BBC and IBA together with the major parties, chaired by the Lord President of the Council. Air-time is parcelled out according to seats held in Parliament and performance at recent polls, although no definitive formula has been adopted. Party propaganda is not welcomed by viewers other than at election time, and after thirty years of complaint the BBC and IBA have finally abolished the rule that party broadcasts should be carried simultaneously on all channels. The SDP/Liberal Alliance felt that it was losing out, not merely in the number of permitted broadcasts but also in news coverage: an analysis of major television news programmes in 1984 showed that 70 per cent of political comment reflected Tory views, 25 per cent Labour and only 5 per cent Alliance. It is natural that Government policy should obtain substantial coverage, but the Alliance complained to the Broadcasting Complaints Commission that it was being denied, as a matter of policy, a coverage in which viewers might perceive it as an alternative Opposition. The courts upheld the Commission's refusal to adjudicate the question, on the ground that it raised issues of policy which were for the broadcasting authorities to determine.[24]

Party-political broadcasts during election periods have become an influential part of the democratic process. In 1987, Hugh (*Chariots of Fire*) Hudson produced a remarkable propaganda film which boosted

Neil Kinnock's personal rating by 16 per cent overnight, while the Tories counter-attacked with a theme tune specially composed by Andrew (*Evita*) Lloyd-Webber. These broadcasts, too, are allocated by the Party Political Broadcast Committee: by tradition, the Opposition has the penultimate broadcast and the Government the very last before the election. These arrangements have worked satisfactorily, although a decision in 1974 to give propaganda-time to every party fielding more than fifty candidates led to an inevitably controversial broadcast by the National Front. Much less satisfactory has been the broadcasting authorities' craven acceptance of the right of parties to dictate the choice of spokespeople. Election discussion programmes have become a cosy dialogue between chosen broadcasters and chosen politicians, with none of the fire traditionally associated with the hustings. Questions at carefully arranged Press conferences and studio discussions are predictable and deferential – professional broadcasters were put to shame in the 1983 elections, when the only person to subject the Prime Minister to searching questions about the sinking of the *Belgrano*, the Argentinian warship, was a housewife who took part in a 'phone in' programme. In the 1987 elections, the Labour Party was allowed to keep its left-wing candidates well away from the television screen: while much was heard about Ken Livingstone from other parties, he was never permitted to speak for himself to national audiences.

The least justifiable legal infringement on freedom of speech at election time is Section 93 of the Representation of the People Act, which prevents the broadcast of any radio or television programme featuring candidates for a particular constituency unless all of them take part or else consent to the broadcast. This 'candidate's veto' means, in practice, that sitting M Ps who decide they have nothing to gain by appearing will often refuse to appear or to consent to the programme going ahead without them. It means, in addition, that a single candidate can veto a programme in order to stop the public from hearing the views of a specific opponent (many Labour candidates for this reason veto programmes which would include a candidate from the National Front). These consequences are wholly unacceptable. The voting public in a democracy should be entitled to see the candidates for local and national elections ranged against each other, and local radio and television stations perform a public service by setting up such debates. The law which permits a single candidate to ban them, from motives of self-interest or political censorship, should be repealed.

British television effectively abdicates any pretence to investigative journalism at election time, and presents the major parties and their leaders as they want to be seen. In other respects, too, it is super-sensitive at this period, postponing any plays or current-affairs programmes which might be thought to carry a political message. In the run-up to the 1987 election (i.e. in 1986) the BBC turned down a play which depicted Mrs Thatcher heroically and compassionately during the Falklands War, and in 1974 it postponed *The Perils of Pendragon* because of its comic portrayal of a Communist. In 1964 it agreed to move *Steptoe and Son* from peak time on polling day at the request of Harold Wilson, who feared potential Labour voters would stay at home to watch it. The BBC did, at least, decline Wilson's further suggestion, to 'replace it with Greek drama, preferably in the original'.

The Broadcasting Complaints Commission

The BBC and the IBA operate a close control over the ethics of the programme-makers under their supervision, and serious demands for the equivalent of a Press Council for broadcasters did not come until 1971, when the Labour Party took offence at unfair treatment of its leaders in a programme entitled *Yesterday's Men*. The Annan Committee on the Future of Broadcasting, which reported in 1977, recommended the setting-up of a Broadcasting Complaints Commission (BCC) as part and parcel of its proposals for public accountability: it wanted an Inquiry Board to conduct public hearings which would gauge popular dissatisfaction, and an opportunity for individuals to complain about misrepresentation to a tribunal of persons 'skilled in the assessment of evidence and knowledgeable about broadcasting'.[25] The BCC was finally established in 1981. The terms of its mandate were vigorously opposed by programme-makers and enthusiastically championed by media critics: it has so far done little either to fulfil the fears or to justify the hopes which were expressed at its inception. It does have a potential, however, to restrict the freedom of broadcasters, and its operations should be carefully watched.

The BCC comprises at least three (currently, five) paid but part-time members, appointed by the Home Secretary. No member is allowed to have any current interest in broadcasting, so there is a danger that this tribunal of political appointees will make value judgements on the conduct of a profession they may not understand. The first members were a former Tory Minister, a magistrate, an academic, a retired trade-union general secretary and a former BBC programme executive.

The function of the Commission, defined by the statute, is to consider and adjudicate upon complaints of: (a) unjust or unfair treatment in broadcast programmes; (b) unwarranted infringement of privacy in, or in connection with the obtaining of material included in, broadcast programmes.[26]

'Unjust or unfair treatment' is defined to include 'treatment which is unjust or unfair because of the way in which material in the programme has been selected or arranged'. There is a sense in which the broadcast medium must be 'unfair' to those it interviews – in fading light or in harsh studio light, and with the inevitable pressure of editing for a short sharp slot. In its first decision, the BCC accepted that 'fairness' had to be considered in relation to the entire programme rather than its individual elements, and that a short programme could do no more than to highlight a few major issues surrounding a complicated controversy.[27] This is a helpful ruling for programme-makers constrained to edit for brevity. In another decision, the BCC has accepted the need for current-affairs programmes to be hard-hitting, and for interviewers to play the 'devil's advocate' when cross-examining representatives of controversial organizations.[28] However, by 1985 it was adopting principles more akin to the Queensberry rules than to the expedients to which it is necessary for *Checkpoint* journalists to resort occasionally in order to expose fraudsters and charlatans. For example, it has insisted that people against whom allegations are to be made should be given written details of these allegations well before the interview.[29] Such a rule would mean that fraudsters would simply decline to be interviewed, or would be ready with lawyers and a prepared story. There is, inevitably, a 'catch as catch can' quality about investigative journalism, which would be hopelessly inhibited if this rule were to be stringently applied. (Even the most dedicated libertarians have never suggested that the police should give written notice of questions they propose to ask their suspects.)

The BCC has, in its rulings to date, been over-tender to the wealthy and the powerful: in one palpably foolish adjudication, it upheld a complaint that the Newspaper Society (which represents the most powerful newspaper publishers in the land) had been unfairly treated because it was 'not made sufficiently aware of the distinctive format of *Diverse Reports*'.[30] The notion that a trade association for Press barons should be protected from the consequences of its own ignorance of a long-running 'personal view' programme (in order, presumably, so it could decline to participate) demonstrates the extent to which the BCC is capable of twisting the 'fairness' test to protect the powerful from criticism.

The BCC could become a valuable alternative to libel actions, by ordering factual mistakes to be speedily corrected. Unfortunately, it is a small and dilatory organization, which normally takes at least nine months before providing an adjudication. This is an outrageously long time to correct simple errors of fact, and means that the publication of the decision is of little use to complainants. There have been very few complaints of invasion of privacy, doubtless because victims have no desire to relive their distress, and others have no standing to complain on their behalf. If the BCC is to perform any useful function in this area, it will need to be given the power to monitor programmes or to investigate invasions of privacy as and when they occur.

The BCC's own procedures are remarkably unfair to programme-makers. They have no right to defend their programmes – any defence is made on their behalf by the IBA, and in some cases is notably lukewarm. It is obviously unjust for producers and presenters to be condemned unheard, but the BCC is happy to pontificate about 'unfairness' without noticing this mote in its own eye. It has not functioned, as the Annan Committee recommended, as an effective fact-finding tribunal: most of its cases are decided on paper submissions, and when it accords an oral hearing to the parties it meets each side secretly and separately, allowing no scope for cross-examination. As a tribunal, it is something of a travesty of justice, although it does have potentially wide powers to order its findings to be broadcast 'in any manner' it chooses to specify. This could include a direction that its adjudications be read as the first item on evening news bulletins. In fact, its adjudications are generally confined to small print in the back of the *Radio Times*, although where a complaint is upheld against a continuing programme it sometimes insists that a summary be carried after the next edition. As this will usually be about nine months after the offending broadcast, viewers will be hard put to remember what all the fuss has been about.

The Broadcasting Standards Council

Notwithstanding its rigid self-censorship rules, which run into hundreds of pages of 'programme guidelines', television has become the scapegoat for what is perceived by politicians and the popular Press as an upsurge in violence and immorality. The outcry has been fuelled by self-interest (newspaper proprietors are keen to destroy the IBA with its rules which prevent them adding television stations to their Press monopolies) and the most exhaustive surveys establish that only one in ten viewers have ever been personally offended by anything they have seen on television. There is, moreover, no credible evidence that appalling incidents like the Hungerford massacre are triggered by violence depicted (whether as factual news or fictional drama) on television. None the less, in 1988 the Government announced the establishment of a new 'watch-dog', the Broadcasting Standards Commission, to monitor television and adjudicate complaints from viewers. It will preview – and perhaps pre-censor – foreign programmes, it will draw up new codes on sex and violence, and it will try to devise ways of stopping satellites from transmitting European erotica into British homes. Its first Chairman is Lord Rees-Mogg, whose behaviour in stopping the screening of *Real Lives* when Deputy Chairman of the BBC indicates a penchant for political censorship. He immediately criticized the level of violence on news and current-affairs programmes, which may mean that under his regime what is tolerable will coincide less frequently with what is true.

The Broadcasting Standards Council will be given statutory powers in due course. By early 1989 it had acquired a Director-General and a staff of twelve, and was busy recruiting 2,000 'television monitors' throughout the country who would send reports on sex and violence and bad language to its headquarters at 'The Sanctuary', next door to

Westminster Abbey. Its 'codes' will merely duplicate those already in operation at the BBC and the IBA, and its deliberations as to whether these codes have been breached will duplicate the functions of television's governing bodies. It is not yet clear what sanctions it will have to enforce its judgements, or what will happen should the BSC disagree with the BBC Board of Governors over whether a particular programme is acceptable. The Broadcasting White Paper predicts that it will be amalgamated with the Broadcasting Complaints Commission, which has statutory powers to put broadcasters on trial for 'unfair treatment'. The likelihood is that the BSC will become a tribunal of Government appointees who can be trusted to judge and condemn programmes like *Death on the Rock* without the commitment to freedom of expression displayed by the Windlesham Report. There is a legitimate fear amongst programme-makers that the BSC will develop into a State censorship body supervising television output by way of subjective judgements on 'decency' and 'fairness', affecting the ability of the medium to provide viewers with the entertainment they relish but which Lord Rees-Mogg finds unseemly, and (more important) to tackle controversial issues which may appear, to the Government's own appointees, as unfair to the Government. Politicians supported the creation of a BSC because they expected it to censor television: there is no reason to doubt that their expectations will be fulfilled.

The political pressures at work behind the establishment of the BSC should be recognized. Britain is generally reckoned to have the least objectionable television in the world, thanks to professional programme-makers who decide what their craft requires and win the support of experienced executives (for the most part former programme-makers) within the constraints of strict rules about sex and violence and unfair treatment. The role of the IBA and the BBC Board of Governors has been to maintain these strict standards, and the evidence is that they have erred on the side of caution in doing so, while producing a television output which is acceptable to the vast majority of viewers. The demands for stricter controls did not come because of sex (there is little of that allowed on television) or even because of violence (feature films and American series are heavily edited to protect sensibilities on this score), but because of a series of current-affairs programmes which angered the Prime Minster, certain of her Cabinet ministers and many back-bench

Tory MPs. These included *Panorama*, Duncan Campbell's *Secret Society* series, the coverage of the American bombing of Libya, *Real Lives* and *Death on the Rock*. The Government has sought to change the climate in which such programmes can be made in several ways: by orchestrating public attacks on broadcasters, by a new Official Secrets Act, by appointing its supporters to the BBC and IBA, by extending the Obscene Publications Act to television, by formulating plans to turn the BBC into a subscription service and to reduce the capacity of ITV companies to make expensive current-affairs programmes, and by establishing the BSC. Under the deceptive banner of 'deregulation', more controls are being forged, most of which will work through behind-the-scenes political pressure rather than through law. The BSC will become part of a network of external pressures upon broadcasters to bring their professional judgements about what the public interest requires to be seen into line with official judgements about what the public does not need to be shown.

Future controls over television

The Government's plans for deregulation of television in the 1990s were announced in a White Paper published at the end of 1988. 'Deregulation' is a misleading description of the process it envisages, as one objective is to secure an even tighter, more centralized censorship of the media in the interests of 'good taste' (by which is meant the exclusion of sex and violence and political discomfiture, rather than any control on the quality of programmes). The IBA will be abolished and replaced by the Independent Television Commission (ITC) which will inherit the IBA's existing duties to ensure balance and to ban 'offensive' programmes, but will have a new range of tough sanctions (including financial penalties and the ultimate sanction of licence withdrawal) to punish television stations which make errors of taste or partiality. The ITC will be the first level of censorship control for television, cable and satellite transmissions uplinked from the United Kingdom. A second level of censorship will be provided by the Broadcasting Standards Council, which will be placed on a statutory footing and thus given direct powers to monitor sex and violence and to draw up binding programme standards. (The

BSC is likely to be combined with the BCC, so that the one body will be able to adjudicate complaints about both unfairness and too much sex in television programmes.) A third tier of control will be achieved by bringing all broadcasting within the ambit of the Obscene Publications Act.

This massive, three-tier statutory censorship apparatus belies the Government's claim that it is deregulating broadcasting and replacing the IBA with a body which will have 'a lighter touch'. Its plans, on the contrary, envisage three heavy hands: the ITC, with additional powers to punish any lapses in taste or impartiality; the BSC, with similar powers; and the police, able to launch obscenity prosecutions against programme-makers if all else fails. The one welcome measure of deregulation is to abolish the IBA's 'publishing' role of intervening prior to programme transmission: television companies will no longer have to submit controversial programmes for IBA 'vetting'. However, given the all-pervasive censorship apparatus which will by then be in place, it must be doubtful whether relief from this burden will effect any liberalization: some controversial programmes will simply not be made, for fear that they will incur reprisals in the form of ITC or BSC sanctions, or a possible criminal prosecution. The main reason why programmes of high quality, controversial or otherwise, will diminish, however, will be as a result of the other projected Government measures. The BBC will be turned into a subscription service, losing the revenue from the licence fee; ITV stations will be auctioned to the highest bidder, without guarantees of high-quality programmes; there will be two more channels, with 'freedom to match their programmes to market conditions'. The consequences of these changes are outside the scope of this book, other than to note that when the White Paper speaks of 'high standards' and 'maintaining quality' in programming it is referring to standards and qualities of inoffensiveness, decency, balance and mundanity which the new censorship codes and bodies will be designed to ensure, and not to standards and qualities which relate to merit. When it speaks of 'consumer protection' by the ITC and the BSC, it means protecting the consumer from being offended by, rather than from taking offence at, anodyne programmes. Although the panoply of new rules and enforcement bodies cannot readily apply to satellite programmes uplinked from foreign countries, in 1988 the British Government embarked upon diplomatic initiatives in an effort to secure European agreement (or at least bilateral treaties with some European countries) on uniform standards for satellite transmissions.

SEVEN

Freedom of Expression

Free speech does not mean free speech: it means speech hedged in by all
the laws against defamation, blasphemy, sedition and so forth. It means
freedom governed by law ...

Privy Council, 1936[1]

British law regards free speech as a very good thing so long as
it does not cause trouble, at which point it can become expensive
speech, visited with costly court actions, fines and damages, and occasionally imprisonment. It is curious that for all its rhetorical flourish
and historic associations – 'freedom of the Press' was chanted with
'Wilkes and Liberty' by the mobs celebrating jury acquittals of publishers who attacked George III – the law makes no presumption in
favour of freedom of expression when balancing it against rights of
property in information. The principle of freedom of expression does
find protection in Article 10 of the European Convention on Human
Rights, but as this is not directly applicable in English courts it means
a long trek to Strasbourg before media organizations can oblige the
Government to make any changes in the law.

Journalism is not just a profession. It is the exercise by occupation
of the right to free expression available to every citizen. That right, being
available to all, cannot in principle be withdrawn from a few by any
system of licensing or professional registration, but it can be restricted
and confined by rules of law which apply to all who take or are afforded
the opportunity to exercise the right by speaking or writing in public.
Defamation, breach of confidence and contempt of court are complex
laws which can involve heavy damages and legal costs. So newspapers

and broadcasting organizations employ teams of lawyers to advise on stories which might otherwise court reprisals. Press lawyers are inevitably more repressive than Press laws, because they will generally prefer to err on the safe side, where they cannot be proved wrong. Since most laws pertaining to the media are of vague or elastic definition, the lawyers' caution is understandable if they are instructed by proprietors or insurance companies who want to avoid the high legal costs of defending, even sucessfully, defamation and breach-of-confidence actions brought by the Government or by wealthy private plaintiffs.

PRIOR RESTRAINT

The Duke of Wellington's taunt 'publish and be damned', reflects an important principle. The media should be free to publish, and to take the risk of being damned in costs and damages afterwards. Journalists cannot claim to be above the law, but they can claim, in any legal system which takes free speech seriously, the right to have their conduct judged after they have chosen to put the information into the public domain. 'Prior restraint' – the use of injunctions obtained secretly to stop information being made public – is obviously an interference with freedom of expression, and it denies the public the right to judge whether the importance of the revelation justified the decision to risk legal reprisals by publishing it. The rule against prior restraint was given definitive shape by the venerated legal writer Blackstone:

> The liberty of the Press is indeed essential to the nature of a free State; but this consists in laying no *previous* restraints on publications, and not in freedom from censure for criminal matter when published. Every free man has an undoubted right to lay what sentiments he pleases before the public; to forbid this is to destroy the freedom of the Press; but if he publishes what is improper, mischievous or illegal, he must take the consequences of his own temerity.[2]

It was this message which went out in the eighteenth century, and became enshrined in the First Amendment to the American Constitution. But in Britain, which lacks a written constitution, the rule against prior restraint has been badly eroded. Almost every week, at secret hearings in the High Court, judges are asked to issue injunctions against the media.

An injunction imposes prior restraint, by stopping presses from rolling and film from running. Whether an injunction will be granted often depends on whether the alleged wrong is a libel or a breach of confidence. In libel cases, the rule against prior restraint is still powerful: no injunction will be granted against defendants who swear that they can prove the truth of the defamatory statement or intend to defend it as 'fair comment'. But in confidence cases, injunctions against the media are given on the same basis as in commercial disputes, that is, whenever the 'balance of convenience' warrants it. The judge must balance the commercial interests of the plaintiff against the value of the defendant's right of free speech. For some judges, brought up in a world which accords pre-eminent value to rights of property, this means balancing hard cash against hot air.

One example of 'prior restraint' was the injunction which stopped the scheduled screening of a Thames Television documentary on the pregnancy drug, Primodos. The programme referred to some material which the producer had seen while engaged for a few days as a consultant to the drug manufacturers. Lord Denning thought it should be shown, on the grounds that 'the *public* interest in receiving information about the drug Primodos and its effects far outweighs the *private* interest of the makers in preventing discussion of it'.[3] But he was outvoted by his brethren, who ruled that the producer was bound by an obligation of confidence which should be honoured, at least until the court had decided at a trial, several years into the future, whether the confidence was outweighed by the public interest. The *Primodos* case shows how judges are inclined to give property claims more weight than freedom of expression. The information in that case, as in most cases where breach of confidence is used by wealthy plaintiffs to stop their secrets getting out, was not of itself valuable, like a trade secret which must be kept from competitors. The fact that the producer had once been a consultant to the drug manufacturers was used as a device to stop a television programme which might have proved embarrassing to the manufacturers.

An 'interim injunction' is a device by which the plaintiff obtains an order suppressing publication until trial. In reality, neither side will be concerned about a trial several years in the future, by which time the information will be out of date or published in some other form. The purpose of the 'interim injunction' is usually to stop publication until embarrassing plans can be reconsidered, or become a *fait* sufficiently *accompli* that no public protest can have any effect. In defamation law, as we have seen, the courts will not injunct publication of the alleged libel if the media are prepared to defend the case. The greater willingness of the courts to give prior restraint in cases of confidence and copyright and contempt means that plaintiffs will, wherever possible, rely on these doctrines as a pretext for stopping articles and broadcasts which they fear because of the criticism contained in them, rather than because of secrets divulged as the basis for criticism. It is anomalous that Blackstone's rule against prior restraint, soundly embedded in libel law, should be so precarious when the case is brought within a different legal category.

The most deplorable development in use of the 'interim injunction' as a means of political interference with free speech has come about by the Government's exploiting the court's power to order discovery of documents to obtain copies of programmes and articles before they are published. In 1987 BBC Radio 4 made a somewhat academic series about the security services entitled *My Country Right or Wrong*, and advertised it in the *Radio Times*. On the strength of this advertisement, the Government persuaded a High Court judge to grant an 'interim injunction' against the broadcast, because it feared that ex-employees of the security services might have breached confidence in the course of their interviews.[4] It had no evidence of this: the BBC had on principle refused an invitation to submit the programme to the Government for 'vetting' in advance, and its lawyers were satisfied that no breach of confidence had taken place. The interim injunction stopped the broadcast until the matter could be tried, and in due course the court ordered the BBC to 'give discovery' to the plaintiff, i.e. to disclose the tapes of the programmes to the Attorney-General who brought the action on behalf of the Government. After hearing the tapes, and being satisfied that they contained no breach of confidence, the Government discontinued the action and the BBC was finally able to broadcast *My Country Right or Wrong*, six months after it had originally been scheduled, and after being forced in this fashion to submit it for State 'vetting'. The High Court had allowed its interlocutory procedures to be used as devices for enabling the Government to postpone and to pre-view an entirely innocuous public-interest programme, in the absence of any evidence that the broadcast would contravene the civil or criminal law.

Not only Governments benefit from censorship imposed by breach-of-confidence injunctions. In 1983 a High Court judge granted an injunction against the European edition of the *Wall Street Journal* preventing it from publishing a Lloyds Bank internal memorandum which had been sent to it anonymously. It related to foreign lending policy, a matter of clear public interest, but this, the court held, did not outweigh the claim of confidence.[5] This decision was otiose, given that the *Journal* had published details of the document in its American edition, and disseminated it via its world-wide electronic news services which in turn had been picked up by other British papers. As the *Wall Street Journal* commented after the case:

> The five or six million readers of our American edition and subscribers to our news services throughout the world knew something about the policies of a major international lender that folks in Britain weren't supposed to know. Aside from the more general importance of the news, that is an especially curious result because the Lloyds group itself has shares traded on the London stock exchange. It strikes us as odd that a nation's legal system should try to deny its own investors access to information already available to investors in New York and the rest of the world, unwittingly promoting an Outsiders Trading Law.

This power to restrain publication by an 'interim injunction' is in effect a power to censor – upon hearing claims which may never subsequently be justified. It has been used in recent times to suppress material as diverse as the background to Thalidomide manufacture, the financial manipulations of James Slater, the law-breaking of MI5 and the sex life of the Rolling Stones. Since 1986 the Government has abandoned prosecutions under the Official Secrets Act and used civil actions for breach of confidence as a substitute, claiming that any book written by a civil servant without permission could be embargoed. The courts obligingly granted 'interim injunctions', leaving the merits of 'public interest' defences to be decided at trials in years to come. In the case of *Spycatcher* and *One Girl's War*, these books had been published abroad and there was no conceivable public interest in banning them from Britain. This result, which made both the law and the courts which enforced it look asinine, could not have been achieved had the rule against prior restraint, rather than the 'balance of convenience' test, applied to actions for interim injunctions on grounds of breach of confidence.

The US Supreme Court ruled prior restraint impermissible in its historic *Pentagon Papers* decision. The Government got wind of *The New York Times* plan to publish a set of Army research papers on the history of US involvement in Vietnam. It sought to injunct the newspaper on the ground that the material contained military and diplomatic secrets, disclosure of which would substantially damage the national interest. The Supreme Court refused to allow any restraint on publication, on the principle that any system of prior restraint on expression comes to the court bearing a heavy presumption against its constitutional validity.

> The only effective restraint upon executive policy and power in the areas of national defence and international affairs may be in an enlightened citizenry – an informed and critical public opinion which alone can here protect the values of democratic Government. For this reason, it is perhaps here that a Press that is alert, aware and free most vitally serves the basic purpose of the First Amendment. For without an informed and free Press there cannot be an enlightened people.[6]

The importance of this principle was emphasized by those Justices who accepted that disclosure would substantially harm the national interest, and that publication might even render the newspaper liable to subsequent criminal action under the Espionage Act. None the less, they ruled that only when the Government could prove that disclosure would cause 'grave and irreparable injury to the public interest' (examples given were details of troop deployments in wartime, or information which might trigger a nuclear holocaust) was a court entitled to stop the presses. Because of the *Pentagon Papers* ruling, the British Government was powerless to sue in the USA to stop publication of *Spycatcher*. But when newspapers in Britain published a few extracts, the courts immediately slapped 'interim injunctions' on them.

BREACH OF CONFIDENCE

How has this particular doctrine of civil law acquired such an importance as a means of stopping media revelations of misbehaviour in high places? Until recently, nobody would have thought that it could affect information published by books and newspapers, because it had been developed to protect trade secrets and commercial formulae from being pirated by business rivals. It was an action which developed, in effect, to stop unfair competition by exploiting commercial information obtained by industrial espionage. But in 1967 the concept of 'confidential information' was extended by a judge to cover intimate communications made between husband and wife, in a case which injuncted a newspaper from publishing the Duke of Argyll's account of his stormy marriage to the Duchess.[7] Since then, the doctrine has grown like Topsy, and can now be made the basis for stopping any revelation of information which has been imparted under an obligation of confidence. Such an obligation is normally deduced from a contract of employment, a consultancy or merely a 'confidential relationship'. (Thus in the *Crossman Diaries* case, Cabinet discussions were held to be 'confidential',[8] and in 1981 the courts granted an interim injunction to stop alleged tape-recordings of Prince Charles's telephone discussions with his bride-to-be from being published.)

It follows that every business company can claim to stop employees from divulging information about what they have seen or heard in the course of their employment. In 1980 British Steel Corporation sued Granada Television for revealing documents, provided by an employee, which demonstrated waste and mismanagement. Although they did not have time to stop the programme, they exploited the discovery process to obtain an order to disclose the name of Granada's source. The House of Lords gave scant consideration to the importance of protecting the free flow of information, especially information about waste in a nationalized industry.[9] BSC had a proprietary right in its own documents, and that was that: the courts were prepared to send journalists to gaol if they did not cooperate to help make good the loss.

What defences are open to the media against a breach-of-confidence action? The main defences are:

1. *Staleness*. Information ceases to be confidential when it is out of date. Thus the 'Cabinet secrets' of the *Crossman Diaries* could be published because they were ten years old. On the other hand, the Government claims that security-service secrets remain confidential for ever: *One Girl's War* was injuncted because of its revelations of low-level MI5 operations during the Second World War.

2. *Public domain*. A confidence is no longer a confidence when it

has been published elsewhere. It if has been published at the behest of the person to whom the confidence is owed, then this is a complete defence. However, it is not clear how far the 'public domain' argument will protect those who wish to divulge authoritatively matters which have been placed in the public domain at second hand. Thus an 'insider' may be stopped from confirming what 'outsiders' have long and publicly suspected.

3. *The other side of the story.* Where the owner of the confidence has promoted one version of events or encouraged a favourable image, others are permitted to publish confidential material which shows the proprietor in a true, and less favourable, light. This defence is regularly employed against celebrities who try to stop their ex-employees from telling about the seedier side of their life beneath the glossy PR hand-outs. Thus when Tom Jones tried to stop his former public-relations consultant from exposing his jumbo-jet orgies, Lord Denning held:

> If the image which they fostered was not a true image, it is in the public interest that it should be corrected ... it is a question of balancing the public interest in maintaining the confidence against the public interest in knowing the truth – the public should not be misled.[10]

4. *Iniquity.* There is no confidence in iniquity, and ex-employees are entitled to reveal evidence of crime or fraud. This defence is absolute where the revelation is made to the police or to other appropriate authorities, but it may be more limited when it is made for profit to a newspaper which will use the revelation as a circulation-building scoop. It may also be unavailable as a defence where the media have obtained the information illegally. Thus the Court of Appeal granted an interim injunction to stop the *Daily Mirror* publishing the transcripts of illegal telephone taps which were alleged to show that a leading jockey might be involved in criminal offences.[11]

5. *The public interest.* The media will not be stopped from publishing confidential material if the court can be convinced that the publication is in the public interest. What is 'in the public interest' for this purpose will depend very much on the outlook of the judge. The courts have unhesitatingly refused to suppress stories about drug-taking and sex orgies involving pop stars, and details of courses offered by the 'Church' of Scientology. When the *Daily Express* obtained confidential information

about the vagaries of the Intoximeter, an injunction was refused. The Intoximeter case is important, because the Court of Appeal conceded that although the information had been obtained in blatant breach of confidence, the possibility that persons were being convicted of drink-driving offences as a result of instrument inaccuracies provided a serious defence of public interest which might be vindicated at an ultimate trial.[12]

The problem with the law of breach of confidence is that it has developed on a case-by-case basis, with interim injunctions being granted on the basis of convenience rather than principle. It is difficult to resist the conclusion that the courts are really deciding the issue on the basis of a subjective appreciation of the merits of the applicant rather than the application, with pop stars and Scientologists being denied the benefits of a legal rule which protects the privacy of royalty, drug manufacturers and nationalized industries. The courts are using the doctrine to provide a form of back-door protection against certain invasions of privacy, but are producing exceptions which justify the revelation of personal sexual peccadilloes while prohibiting serious stories about dubious behaviour in public or corporate office. The result is that 'popular' newspapers devote their energies to 'kiss and tell' stories about people in the public eye without any danger of legal restraint, while serious investigative journalism is hampered by the difficulty in using documentary evidence to expose malfeasance (official misconduct) in Government or in powerful corporations. Reform of the law of confidence is long overdue, and should begin by reasserting the rule against prior restraint on publication. Where the media can raise a real defence of public interest, there should be no legal embargo imposed. On the other hand, where the claim of public interest is merely a cloak for public prurience (as it was in the *Sun*'s claim that Myra Hindley's parole application should be published in order to whip up hostility to her before the Parole Board even considered it) there would be a reasonable claim to protect the privacy of the individual.

The Spycatcher *verdict*

The law against breach of confidence was marginally liberalized for the media by the long-awaited House of Lords decision in the *Spycatcher* case.[12(a)] It will be recalled that Wright, a long-serving MI5 officer now in retirement in Australia, had published in that country and in the USA a book detailing some of his unattractive exploits in the Secret Service (including the bugging of foreign embassies, trespassing into private homes and plotting against Harold Wilson). The British Government had failed in its action against the book in the Australian courts, on the ground that its claim was of a political nature which domestic courts were unable to adjudicate at the behest of a foreign power, and had been unable to bring any action in the USA because of the 'freedom of expression' guarantee in the First Amendment to the US Constitution. In Britain, however, the Government had taken action against any who published Wright's memoirs: it sued the *Observer* for running a news article about them and the *Sunday Times* for publishing an extract from the book, having paid Wright's publishers for the copyright. In 1987, a 3–2 majority of Law Lords, in this century's most publicly derided legal decision, had upheld an injunction banning any mention in Britain of Wright's allegations (whilst they were being read throughout the rest of the world) until the proceedings against the *Sunday Times* and the *Guardian* were completed.

It was a differently constituted court which considered the final appeal, and decided that the previous summer's majority decision to prevent publication of *Spycatcher* revelations in the British Press had been a mistake – 'a misuse of the injunctive remedy'. The courts, however much they might deplore treachery by people like Wright, cannot put genii back into bottles by stopping British citizens from reading reminiscences already published abroad. Making valuable use of Article 10 of the European Convention, the Law Lords declared that such bootless exercises do not correspond with that 'pressing social need' which alone can justify State censorship in a democracy. Once an MI5 secret is out, albeit in a foreign country, the British public cannot be stopped from reading about it. Short of an international treaty to control the publication of security-service information (an unlikely possibility) there can be no *cordon sanitaire* against the claims of embittered Secret Service men who have emigrated.

However, the Law Lords confirmed that persons who have been employed on secret Government work must, if they wish to be buried in the United Kingdom, take their secrets to the grave. They owe a lifelong duty of confidence to the State, which is defeasible only in three circumstances: where the information they wish to publish is utterly trivial; where it has already come into the public domain (either here or abroad); or where it takes the form of substantial allegations of serious wrongdoing. The overriding principle decided by *Spycatcher*, at the end of the day, is one which should never have been in doubt: a Government which wishes to suppress information by civil action must prove that its censorship is for the public interest. The Government will fail – as it failed, in the end, in its claim against the *Observer* – when the projected publication is manifestly in the public interest and will do little or no damage to national security.

None the less, the Law Lords made it clear that the Government would have succeeded in stopping Wright from publishing *Spycatcher* had he lived in this country. The genuine 'public interest' in his revelations (such as his allegations that those within the Secret Service plotted to have the Wilson Government defeated and, prior to Suez, to assassinate Nasser) extended to only a small proportion of the text. And the Lords applied a qualitative test to decide the point at which editors and publishers are entitled to reveal wrongdoing to the general public rather than to State authorities. There must at least be a prima facie case that the allegations have some substance. It follows that editors will need some corroborative evidence for 'revelations' that may be no more than the product of paranoia or disaffection. Lord Griffiths (who is also head of the Security Commission) thought that editors should loyally report such allegations to the responsible Government Minister, and publish them only if 'no effective action had been taken'. But he recognized that this advice was not legally binding. 'Ultimately, if we are to have an efficient Security Service, we have to trust its members and if we are to have a free Press we have to trust the editors.' The Government may have found this a counsel of despair, although others may see it as a motto for a free society.

At the end of the day, the Government's extensive and expensive litigation against *Spycatcher* was massively counter-productive, achieving little more than to elevate an otherwise undistinguished book to the top of the best-seller lists throughout the world, and ultimately in Britain as well. The Government took a few crumbs of comfort from a victory over the *Sunday Times* which was forced to disgorge the money it had paid to

Wright's publisher at a time prior to the book's publication in the United States. It kept the lid on his allegations being publicly analysed in this country for two years: ironically, when the lid was finally lifted by the House of Lords, some of these allegations were authoritatively refuted and Wright himself was revealed as a conspiracy theorist of McCarthyite proportions. That, after all, was the real public interest in *Spycatcher* – a public interest which had never been mentioned in any of the court proceedings. How came it that this paranoid electrician was ever allowed to rise to a position of power and influence in MI5? Although he caught few spies, he and his henchmen destroyed a number of careers: their secret inquisitions drove one Labour MP to suicide and another Minister (Niall Macdermott QC, who would in time have made a fine Labour Lord Chancellor) out of the Wilson Government. The judges contented themselves with reviling Wright for treachery, but the real question was about the control of an organization which allowed his mentality to flourish to the point of damaging both its own reputation and the reputations of innocent citizens. This is the true public interest in *Spycatcher*, which affects the civil liberties of all who may find their liberal instincts anathema to the likes of Wright and perhaps to the likes of his successors in office. The Government took steps in 1989 to ensure that 'public interest' would not be a defence to criminal charges brought under its new Official Secrets Act. Having lost *Spycatcher* in the civil courts, it will in future rely upon the threat of prosecution to deter leaks from the security services.

DEFAMATION

It was originally a crime to speak ill of the living. As early as the eleventh century we find the ecclesiastical courts penalizing slander, on the biblical principle in Leviticus that 'Thou shalt not go up and down as a tale bearer among the people.' But at common law, defamation was only actionable if accompanied by actual injury, such as assault or false imprisonment. However, in 1275, the offence of *scandalum magnatum* was created by statute expressly in order to protect 'the great men of the realm' against discomfiture from stories which arouse the people against them. Again, it was the threat to civil order which was the gravamen of the criminal offence, hence Lord Coke's famous maxim, 'The greater the truth the greater the libel' – the populace would react more vigorously to real, rather than imagined, grievances. The Star Chamber enforced the libel laws with monumental ferocity – William Prynne had his ears cut off for criticizing the immorality of courtiers; when he repeated his accusations in a polemic entitled *Women Actresses – Notorious Whores* they cut off the stumps of his ears, and branded his forehead with the letters 'SL' for 'seditious libeller'. But this penal jurisdiction was always exercised on the basis of an apprehended threat to the peace.

It was in fact the Star Chamber which paved the way for *civil* libel when it tried to provide an alternative to duelling, which was the traditional method of redressing damage to reputation. The courts became inundated with libel actions and the King's judges tried to discourage them by severely limiting the circumstances in which damages could be recovered. But these early restrictions on defamation were forgotten in the Victorian era, when libel actions became a fashionable and indeed necessary method of answering insults. The idea that large sums of money must be awarded to compensate people for words which 'tend to lower them in the estimation of right-thinking members of society' directly derives from this age, when social and political life was lived in gentlemen's clubs in Pall Mall, an age when escutcheons could be unblotted and society scandals resolved by writs for slander. Libel damages came in this period to call for a metaphysical evaluation of dignity, the notion being that they should show the world a gentleman's real value, rather than be used to punish the publisher for error. Libel was a method for deciding whether the plaintiff really was a gentleman, and leading cases involved allegations of cheating at cards and shooting foxes (it being a dreadful slur on a country gentleman's reputation to suggest he shot foxes rather than hunted them down with hounds).

Today, London has become the libel capital of the world. Foreign plaintiffs prefer to sue in this country, because the law favours them more than anywhere else. Tax-free damages awarded in cases which actually come to court are just the tip of a legal iceberg which deep-freezes large chunks of interesting news and comment, especially about wealthy people and companies which have a reputation for issuing writs. There is nothing objectionable in the principle that a person's reputation should be protected from falsehood. The libel law makes an entirely reasonable demand that the media should be restrained from lying or making reckless allegations with impunity. But the strictures of British law sometimes go too far in the opposite direction, restraining investigations into the behaviour of public figures who threaten to sue. The fault lies partly in the complexity of the law, but particularly in certain practices and procedures which work to prevent the exposure of wrongdoing. A rational law would ensure both the speedy correction of false statements and the protection of honest expressions of opinion, but the British libel law secures neither goal adequately. In the United States, the law is much more favourable to the media, which may cast any honest aspersion on a public figure without running the risk of a libel action. In most European countries, a rather better balance between the claims of free speech and personal reputation is achieved by 'right to reply' laws.

A libel is simply a statement, either of fact or opinion, which lowers plaintiffs in the estimation of right-thinking people, or exposes them to hatred, ridicule or contempt. Any statement which attributes blameworthy conduct, or any criticism which casts a shadow over a person's fitness for a job or profession is on the face of it defamatory. Judges and juries place themselves (without very much difficulty) in the position of 'right-thinking members of society', and ask themselves whether they think the statement would injure the plaintiff's reputation. The court must bear contempory social standards in mind in making what will in some cases necessarily be a value judgement. The values of judges in the Deep South in the United States of America, who have held it defamatory to suggest that a white person has 'coloured' blood, would not be shared in England. Not, one hopes, for the reason given in 1848 by the Chief Justice, who argued that being black was 'a great misfortune, but no crime'.[13] Ideas about immorality and what constitutes dishonourable conduct change over time, but the views of judges change more slowly than most. The question, always, is whether the words, in their published context, would be likely to lower the plaintiff in the minds of ordinary, decent readers. That depends, of course, on how the ordinary, decent reader interprets the words, 'reading between the lines in the light of his general knowledge and experience of worldly affairs'.[14]

All that a plaintiff has to prove is that the defendants published a defamatory accusation about him: the burden then shifts to the defence to prove, on the balance of probabilities, that it was true or was published as an honest comment on the basis of true facts, or was 'privileged' in law. The rules relating to these defences are extremely complex, and it is often difficult to disentangle a statement of fact (which must be proved accurate) and an expression of opinion (which need only be honest, if there are sufficient facts which can be proved to support it). Privilege may be absolute, as in the case of reporting evidence given in court, or qualified, in cases where the publication is made only to those who have a duty to investigate the allegation, and it is made in good faith. If the defence fails, the jury (or judge, if both sides agree to waive jury trial) may fix damages ranging from a halfpenny to a million pounds to compensate the plaintiff for the slur on his or her reputation. There is no doubt that libel is the chief legal headache for reporters and commentators. In many cases the prospect of heavy damages serves as a spur to accuracy and fairness, in others it prevents or waters down the publication of matters that ought in the public interest to be ventilated. Although British libel law is the most favourable for plaintiffs at the end of the day, it has a number of defects which sometimes prevent them from obtaining corrections for falsehoods published by lazy or incompetent journalists.

One defect in the law is that an action for libel does not rectify all, or even most, false statements. An assertion is not defamatory simply because it is untrue – it must lower its victim in the eyes of right-thinking citizens. To publish falsely, of an Irish priest, that he informed on members of the IRA is not defamatory. It may cause him to be executed by terrorists, but the law offers him no way of securing a correction.[15] In 1981, the Court of Appeal disallowed a libel action by Stephane Grappelli, the renowned jazz musician, who had falsely been described as 'very seriously ill and unlikely to recover', since illness was a misfortune rather than a defect in character.[16]

Another drawback is that defamation is the *only* branch of common law for which legal aid is unavailable. This stark inequity means that wealthy plaintiffs, and those backed by professional associations (like the Police Federation), enjoy privileged access to a powerful weapon of redress. And it means that newspapers may print the most deliberate or reckless lies about poor people, secure in the knowledge that the victim cannot afford the cost of financing preliminary legal skirmishings, let alone the potentially vast fees of a contested trial. An extension of legal aid for libel actions is, in principle, impossible to resist. But this would only mean a more equal application of a bad law. The unreformed law of defamation already restricts far too much public-interest reporting, because massive damages may be awarded for statements on matters of public interest which publishers believe to be true after taking every reasonable step to confirm their accuracy.

A libel is, in effect, a criticism of a person or corporation. The facts stated may well be true, but the newspaper carries, in law, the burden of proving they are true, by testimony which satisfies strict rules of evidence law. Where the source for a story dies, or is out of the country, or has been promised confidentiality, it will be difficult for the newspaper to satisfy that legal burden. In the United States and in most Western European countries, newspapers are provided with a specific public-interest defence which allows them to escape damages if they show that they had reasonable grounds for believing statements published about important persons and organizations. This defence has no equivalent in British law, and there are a number of recorded cases where damages have been awarded for libellous statements subsequently proved true. John Profumo collected libel damages for the suggestion that he was sharing a prostitute's bed with an officer of the KGB, and Richard Crossman later boasted of how he had perjured himself in the witness box to obtain damages against the *Spectator* for alleging that he was drunk at a conference in Venice. Liberace, who won large damages against the *Daily Mirror* in 1959 for implying that he was a homosexual – describing him as a 'winking, sniggering, chromium-plated, scent impregnated, luminous, quivering, giggling, fruit-flavoured, mincing, ice-covered heap of Mother Love' – finally died of Aids in 1987.

Of course, in an age of instantaneous communication, satellite television, international magazine distribution and simultaneous book launches, British libel law is not just an eccentric anachronism. US publications are constantly being edited to avoid the possibility that American public figures will descend upon our courts to vindicate reputations they cannot protect at home. There were twenty-two changes made to *Sideshow* – William Shawcross's indictment of US policy in Cambodia – before it was published in the UK. One book about the Sharon Tate murder traced the killer Manson's thinking to the doctrines of an obscure American religious cult. The cult could not sue under US law when the book was widely published in the United States, but it turned up in the Strand to put the British publishers through a long and expensive libel trial. Daniel Moynihan's famous jibe about Kissinger ('Henry doesn't lie because it's in his interests. He lies because it's in his nature') was solemnly edited out of U S books about contemporary politics before they were published in this country.

Such caution is understandable, given the cost and complication of defending a libel action.[17] Libel actions launched by wealthy and determined plaintiffs are frighteningly expensive to combat. Even if successful, the defendant is unlikely to recoup all the costs. When the *Daily Mail* was sued by the head of the Unification Church in Britain over allegations that the 'Moonies' brainwashed converts and broke up families, the editor was warned by his lawyers that an adverse verdict might, with legal costs and damages, cost him £1 million. The case lasted one hundred days, required the attendance of many witnesses from abroad, and the defendant's legal costs alone amounted to some £400,000.

How can judges and juries assess the 'value' of a person's reputation? Women who are raped receive £2,000 from the Criminal Injuries Board, and recently a middle-aged man whose brain was damaged through his employer's negligence was awarded £22,000 for his pain and suffering. Those who throw sticks and stones which break bones can be better off in law than those who project hurtful words which leave no permanent mark. In 1987, libel damages of £450,000 were awarded against a Greek newspaper, although only fifty copies of it were circulated in Britain. This was followed by a £500,000 award to Jeffrey Archer against a newspaper which wrongly suggested (albeit on circumstantial evidence) that he had sex with a prostitute, and by an award of £300,000 against a small trade journal. Koo Stark was awarded £300,000 by a jury the following year, and Elton John set a record with his £1-million settlement against the *Sun*. Such awards are unprincipled, unpredictable and excessive, but Appeal Courts have been reluctant to interfere with jury assessments. The prospect of a large libel award has a chilling effect on what is published about powerful people and organizations, especially by small magazines which could be sent into liquidation as a result. Another consequence has been that most publishers are driven to take out expensive libel insurance, which gives their insurance companies the right to insist on copy being 'vetted' by lawyers and the right to settle, often with fulsome or grovelling apologies and secret payments of damages, actions which could possibly (but not certainly) be successfully defended. Awards of libel damages have become so unpredictable and extravagant that it is time to implement the Faulks Committee recommendation that they should be fixed by the trial judge, on a reasoned basis, after the jury has indicated whether they should be substantial, moderate, nominal or contemptuous. When film star Telly Savalas was awarded £34,000 for a gossip columnist's unjustified remark about his drinking habits, the foreman of his jury complained to *The Times*:

> Where a jury has to decide, as men and women of the world, 'how much', the degree of uncertainty is so great that a random answer, consistent only with a total lack of any sort of yardstick, can be expected. Their Lordships would do as well to use an Electronic Random Number Indicating Machine.

The Temple of law should not be allowed to become a casino, with entry open only to the wealthy. At the same time, no civilized society can permit a privately owned Press to run vendettas against individuals powerless to arrest falsehoods and innuendoes. In the United States, the Supreme Court held in the great case of *The New York Times* v. *Sullivan* that no libel action could succeed if the plaintiff was a public figure and the allegation was honestly and diligently made.[18] This ruling has freed the American media to probe Watergate and Irangate in a depth and a detail which could not be attempted in equivalent circumstances in Britain, where the merest hint of impropriety in public life calls forth a libel writ. But the 'public figure' doctrine denies virtually any protection to persons who are prominent in public affairs, simply because of that fact. True, public figures voluntarily step into a fish-tank which entails close public scrutiny of their every move, and they ordinarily enjoy greater access to channels of communication which provide an opportunity to counter false statements. But that opportunity is circumscribed, none the less, and in a country where Rupert Murdoch, Robert Maxwell and Lord Rothermere, with their powerful and partisan views, control 80 per cent of national newspapers, there is an understandable reluctance to give their newspapers a blank cheque to attack political enemies.

Two essential freedoms – the right to communicate and the right to reputation – must in some way be reconciled by law. British libel law errs by inhibiting free speech and failing to provide a system for correcting factual errors which is speedy and available to all victims of Press distortion. US libel law gives no protection at all to the reputation of people in the public eye. Many European countries have opted for a more acceptable solution in the form of 'right to reply' legislation, which allows judges or 'ombudsmen' to direct newspapers to publish corrections and counter-statements from those who claim to have been misrepresented. It is not widely recognized that a legal right of reply has existed, in a limited form, in English law ever since 1881. This has been achieved by granting qualified privilege from libel suit to Press reports of defamatory statements made at certain public meetings, company AGMs, and in notices issued by police and Government departments; but this privilege can only be relied upon if the person defamed has been offered the opportunity to provide for publication 'a reasonable letter or statement of explanation or contradiction'.[19]

The Faulks Committee on Defamation, reporting in 1975, recommended that the privilege of reporting defamatory statements, subject to a right of reply by the person defamed, should be extended much further: to the proceedings of EEC committees, foreign courts, Press conferences, statements by foreign Governments, reports of the Take-over Panel, and to all reports and adjudications issued by the Press Council.[20] These reforms have not been implemented, and newspapers have in recent years often paid heavy damages for accurate reports of statements made on occasions which would, had the Faulks proposal passed into law, have been protected by the 'right of reply' privilege. A legal right of reply to persons who have been the subject of newspaper attack could most readily be encouraged simply by extending privilege from libel action for those attacks to newspapers prepared to publish 'a reasonable statement of explanation or contradiction'. This would be preferable to the scheme envisaged by a strongly supported Private Member's bill in 1989, which called for a statutory body of twenty-one 'Commissioners of the Press' to enforce corrections in newspapers.

THE PRESS COUNCIL

The Press Council is a portentously titled body which affects to supervise the standards and ethics of the British Press. It is a private organization, funded almost entirely by newspaper proprietors as a form of insurance against the advent of laws to protect privacy or to permit a right of reply. It has eighteen members of the public and eighteen representatives of the Press, who adjudicate complaints against newspapers. It was founded in 1953, after legislation had been threatened which would have set up a statutory body to deal with complaints, and its first ruling was that a *Daily Mirror* opinion poll on whether Princess Margaret should be allowed to marry Group Captain Townsend was 'contrary to the best traditions of British journalism'. It has never won any real respect or obedience from Fleet Street, and Press standards have dramatically declined during the years it has been in operation. The last Royal Commission on the Press, reporting in 1977, found that it had failed to combat 'flagrant breaches of acceptable standards' and 'inexcusable intrusions into privacy' (see earlier, page 99). The Commission concluded: 'It is unhappily certain that the Council has so far failed to persuade the knowledgeable public that it deals satisfactorily with complaints against newspapers.'[21] In 1980, the National Union of Journalists withdrew all support, declaring that the Press Council was 'wholly ineffective' and 'incapable of reform'. A study in 1983 showed that the great majority of those who complained successfully to the Press Council were thoroughly dissatisfied and disenchanted with the experience.[22] The Council is, in short, a confidence trick that has ceased to inspire confidence.

The Council's problem is that it raises more expectations than it can hope to satisfy. Quite simply, it has no power. Newspapers pay for it not because they believe in it, but because the pretence of self-regulation helps public relations. Its declarations on standards of conduct are ignored whenever a scoop is in the offing. Adverse adjudications are tucked away in small print on back pages, or occasionally made the subject of self-serving editorials ('The Paper They Can't Gag'). When the Council conducted an inquiry into chequebook journalism at the time of the 'Yorkshire Ripper' prosecution, several 'distinguished' newspaper editors and executives lied about their conduct of 'blood money' negotiations with the accused's relatives. For the most part, the Press Council's censure is ignored, although occasionally editors or commentators let their real contempt for it show. When a reader threatened to report *Daily Express* columnist John Gordon to the Council, he responded: 'You can report me to the Press Council, Madame Tussauds, The Society for the

Protection of Sputniks, NATO, UNESCO or the Dancing Dervishes Association as you wish. May you enjoy yourself.' His successor, Sir John Junor, shared the same contemptuous view. When admonished by the Council for publishing a racial slur, he repeated it in the next edition, with a snipe at the 'po-faced, pompous, pin-striped, humourless twits who sit on the Press Council'. In 1986, the *Daily Telegraph* announced that it would not obey the Press Council's rules on race reporting. Some popular newspapers breach Press Council guidelines on race reporting, chequebook journalism and invasion of privacy in almost every edition, and the Council is utterly powerless to stop them.

The existence of an impotent Press Council probably does more harm than good. By setting standards which the Press will not fulfil it encourages public contempt for the profession of journalism, while its complaints system deludes some people into thinking that it offers a speedy and effective redress for misstatements and misrepresentation. Its failures may, in time, lead to the very legal controls that it was created in order to forestall.

Why is the Press Council so ineffective? Some of its defects are procedural: complaints take over six months to adjudicate, and it places many obstacles in the way of those who approach it with a grievance. Unlike the Advertising Standards Association, a much more successful example of self-regulation, it has no resources to monitor compliance with the standards it sets. Citizens who are outraged by breaches of its rules must do all the investigation themselves, obtaining evidence and in effect appearing before the Council as a prosecutor. The whole process is designed to deter people from complaining about ethical lapses by making them appear as busy-bodies. But the principal defect in the Council is its lack of any effective sanction. The only force that a Press Council adjudication can have, either as a reparation for an original injury or to work as a deterrent against repetition, is if it is published prominently and in some detail in the offending publication. With the exception of certain provincial newspapers and the heavyweight dailies, this simply does not happen. Adverse adjudications are generally truncated, sometimes distorted, and usually relegated to small print in the back section of the paper, more than twenty pages in, after the news and the television pages. Thus in one month in 1985, the *Daily Express* carried its adverse adjudication in five column inches on page 30; the *Star* tucked away its three upheld complaints on pages 22, 24 and 25; the

Sun buried two criticisms of its conduct on pages 23 and 24; while the *News of the World* hid its censure in small print on page 36, intermingled with advertisements for G-strings and 'sexsational glamourware'.

If the Press Council is to work effectively, it must be able to respond immediately to allegations of factual error or denial of a right of reply, and have sufficient muscle to direct a prominent correction or publication of a reply. It must have the resources and the resolve to monitor newspapers for breaches of its codes, without relying upon complainants to 'prosecute', and it must ensure that its criticisms are brought home to persistent offenders in ways which will make them think twice before they buy up rapist's wives and door-step rapist's victims. It must find a means of satisfying the public that it can promote compliance with its codes by more persuasive means than the 'moral obligation' it claims at present to impose.

In 1962, a Royal Commission on the Press suggested that the Council could work, as a non-statutory body, with powers provided by legally enforceable contracts with newspaper proprietors, whereby the proprietors undertake to publish Council rulings in a form and with a prominence dictated by the Council itself.[23] The newspaper would remain free, of course, to disagree with the verdict in its editorial columns, but would at least be under a contractually enforceable obligation to carry the undistorted judgement with a prominence that draws it to the attention of readers and enables them to make up their own minds. The Swedish Press Council operates satisfactorily on a contractual basis, and there is little doubt that such a formula would produce much more serious attention to Press Council guidelines. If editors were obliged to publish condemnations of their journalistic standards on the front page of their newspapers, rather than hiding them in small type amid the racing results, there would be reason to hope that standards might improve.

There is also scope for some legislative action to curb chequebook journalism. A ban would be unjustified, because many major public-interest revelations (including the *Sunday Times* Thalidomide story) have involved payments to law-breakers. Perhaps the best working test of whether an exercise in chequebook journalism is justified is whether or not the newspaper is prepared to own up to it. Whenever a newspaper publishes a story bought for more than a nominal sum from a criminal or associate, there should be a legal obligation to carry alongside it, in heavy type, a full statement of the amount of the payment. Such a law would not infringe Press freedom: on the contrary, it would ensure the disclosure of information of genuine public interest. Readers would be alerted to the dangers of fabrication and exaggeration, by being put in a position to judge whether the sensations in the story might be related to the sensation its source felt when receiving a large cash sum for telling it. An obligation to disclose would positively deter editors from making payments which could not be openly justified.

While it may not be much loss if the likes of the editors of the *Sun*, the *Star* and the *Sport* were suspended from editing newspapers, the freedom of the Press is irreconcilable with any system of statutory licensing of journalists. The freedom to deceive is, however, another matter, and the absence of legal aid for libel means that the Press Council is the only recourse for persons of modest means who simply wish to set the record straight. There is much to be said for replacing both the Council's complaints machinery and the libel law with a 'Press Ombudsman' – a judge empowered by statute to consider complaints about factual inaccuracies in newspapers and to direct a prompt and prominent correction, and to order that newspapers give space to letters written by persons they have attacked. The Ombudsman would have no powers to censor or punish or award damages, merely to correct falsehoods and to ensure that readers have some opportunity to hear the other side of the story. The great advantage of the system for the Press would be to relieve it of much of the legal game of bluff and counterbluff which goes on at present in libel litigation, attended by heavy legal costs and the risk of heavy damages. Instead, victims of factual errors would have a speedy and certain remedy were the editor to refuse them a correction or reply, and the very existence of a Press Ombudsman would make unreasonable refusals by editors much less common. The victims of deliberate and malicious falsehoods would retain, as a last resort, the right to sue for damages, a right which should be extended, through legal aid, to all members of society.

Criminal libel

Criminal libel is an ancient offence which is unlikely to be invoked against the media by prosecuting authorities: the Law Commission has recommended its abolition,[24] and Lord Diplock has pointed out that its provisions conflict with the European Convention on Human Rights.[25] There have only been two modern instances in which it has been invoked by private individuals as part of a vendetta against their journalist-tormentors. In 1977 Sir James Goldsmith was granted leave to prosecute the editor of *Private Eye*.[26] The following year a London magistrate, struck by the notion that there should not be one law for the rich unavailable to the poor, permitted a man named Gleaves to bring proceedings against the authors and publishers of a book entitled *Johnny Go Home*, based on a Yorkshire Television documentary which had exposed his insalubrious hospitality to feckless youths. Neither case was an edifying example of law enforcement. Goldsmith was allowed to withdraw his prosecution after a settlement with *Private Eye*, and an Old Bailey jury took little time to acquit the authors of *Johnny Go Home* after a two-week trial. These precedents do not hold out great hope for private prosecutors determined to teach their critics a lesson in the criminal courts. Leave must be obtained from a High Court judge before any libel prosecution can be brought in relation to an article in a newspaper or periodical.[27] The judge must be satisfied that there is an exceptionally strong *prima facie* case, that the libel is extremely serious, and that the public interest requires the institution of criminal proceedings. In the most recent attempt to obtain leave, the High Court ruled that the public interest was insufficient to allow a man who had been described by the *Sunday People* as a violent and drunken bully to bring a prosecution for criminal libel.[28]

Fair Trial

Trial by jury is revered by radicals and reactionaries alike. It is seen as the bastion of liberty, 'the lamp which shows that freedom lives'.[1] Freedom, of course, is alive and well in most European countries, which have long abandoned the jury in favour of trial by professional judges, often sitting with lay or expert assessors. Yet for Britain and its traditional cultural allies – the USA, Canada, Australia and the West Indies – it remains the basic institution upon which we pin our faith for fairness of trial. Ironically, the jury has won its laurels in the rhetoric of liberty because of its ability to acquit the guilty – to nullify laws which are unpopular or prosecutions which are perceived as oppressive. The jury, it is said on high authority, may 'do justice', whereas a judge, obliged to follow the letter of the law, has no such discretion. In this chapter, the jury's constitutional role as a check on executive power to punish will be considered, together with some of the more recent Government efforts to avoid legal confrontations with the 'gang of twelve'.

One hallmark of British trials which has been almost universally accepted as a guarantee of fairness is the open-justice principle. The rule that justice must be seen to be done is not observed as often as it should be, and in recent years a good deal of litigation has been directed to opening court proceedings to public scrutiny. Ironically, the British media have had to look to the European Convention on Human Rights to secure a guarantee that originally won its place in international law as the result of admiration for the traditional British practice. There are some occasions, of course, where openness is at odds with fairness, and this delicate balance between two fundamental principles is maintained by the law of contempt of court. In the USA, the values of openness and freedom of speech are given absolute protection, and juries are sometimes 'sequestered' in hotels to prevent them seeing prejudicial media comment. In Britain, such expedients have not found favour, and contempt cases reflect a view that 'trials by media' are distasteful in themselves and illegal whenever there is a danger that they will prejudice trial by jury.

THE OPEN JUSTICE PRINCIPLE

The most fundamental principle of justice is that it must be seen to be done. Lord Halsbury, in the great constitutional case of *Scott* v. *Scott*, proclaimed that 'Every court in the land is open to every subject of the King.'[2] The rule became established almost by historical accident from the fact that courts in the Middle Ages were badly conducted public meetings in which neighbours gathered to pass judgement on their district's notorious felons. The Star Chamber followed the practice and heard all its cases in public, in order that its vicious punishments would have a general deterrent effect. In time, jurists like Blackstone and Bentham elevated the practice into a fundamental pre-condition of justice. They acclaimed it on a number of grounds, principally as a safeguard against judicial error or misbehaviour. In Bentham's words, 'Publicity is the very soul of justice. It is the keenest spur to exertion and the surest of all guards against improbity. It keeps the judge himself, while trying, under trial.' Moreover publicity deters perjury, in that witnesses are likely to come forward to confound lies when they learn that they are being told. Press reporting of court cases enhances public knowledge and appreciation of the workings of the law, it assists the deterrent function of criminal trials and it permits the revelation of matters of genuine public interest. Indeed, the very first newspapers were 'chapbooks' consisting entirely of reports of Old Bailey trials, hawked in the streets of seventeenth-century London for a penny a piece. The advantage of the open-justice principle to the Press, of course, is that contemporaneous reports of what is said in court are absolutely privileged from any action for defamation – the court-room is the only place outside Parliament where an Englishman may cry '*J'accuse*' and be utterly safe from a libel action.

The open-justice principle is now found in many constitutions and Bills of Rights, including the European Convention. In Britain, its somewhat insecure legal basis is the 1913 House of Lords decision in *Scott* v.

Scott, which confirmed the general rule that courts must be open to Press and public unless statute specially provided that they must or might be closed. To this 'general rule', alas, several of the Law Lords grafted an exception: the court could sit in secret if justice could not be done at all if it were done openly. They had in mind cases involving young children and litigation about secret processes, but like most exceptions to legal rules there has been much ingenuity expended upon extending them. Parties and witnesses – especially in criminal cases – will frequently be embarrassed by Press reports of their misconduct, and their lawyers sometimes convince judges (and, more often, lay Justices) that justice cannot be done unless names or addresses are withheld or portions of evidence suppressed. Thus reporting restrictions have been imposed to protect police informers from reprisals, to encourage witnesses to testify, to avoid publication of extravagant allegations, and even on occasions where a court has thought that publicity would be too harsh a penalty for a minor offence. These claims are usually spurious – all the Law Lords in *Scott* v. *Scott* made it clear that considerations of humiliation or embarrassment should never be a ground for suppressing reports or closing the court.

The Divisional Court has recently disapproved various attempts at secrecy, ranging from withholding the name of a witness from a celebrated family lest publicity interfere with her treatment for drug addiction,[3] to suppressing the address of a former Tory MP who feared that his ex-wife would read it and harass him.[4] Section 11 of the Contempt of Court Act allows courts to order that names or other matter may not be mentioned in open court or published in the Press, but only when such orders are justified by statute (such as the law which prevents the naming of rape victims) or by the *Scott* v. *Scott* exception for circumstances where justice could not otherwise be done. The Press could always appeal against gag orders imposed by magistrates, but until 1988 no remedy existed against gag orders imposed by Crown Court judges. In 1987 the European Commission of Human Rights ruled, after applications from Channel 4 Television and Old Bailey reporter Tim Crook, that this absence of legal remedy against court-ordered interference with freedom of expression was a breach of the Convention.[5] The United Kingdom Government settled these cases by legislating to allow the media to challenge Crown Court secrecy orders by making a special and urgent application to the Court of Appeal.

Temptations to secrecy are difficult to resist at a time when the popular Press is distrusted and the open-justice principle is not embedded in a written constitution. In the 1980s this gap emboldened a number of magistrates' courts to adopt a policy of anonymity, refusing to divulge to reporters the identity of JPs sitting on any particular case. The *Observer* newspaper and its chief reporter, David Leigh, successfully challenged this policy in the Divisional Court, which condemned it as inimical to the administration of justice and an unlawful obstruction to the right to know who sits in judgement.[6]

There are, however, a number of areas where secrecy is quite sensibly imposed by law in order to avoid prejudice to the outcome of a trial. Details of committal proceedings, for example, cannot normally be reported until the case is over, lest publicity be given to evidence which is subsequently ruled inadmissible. Nor can legal arguments heard in the absence of the jury, which frequently involve discussion of evidence which is deemed too irrelevant or prejudicial for them to hear in court, let alone read about in the Press. Parliament has decided that the peculiar problems of rape cases justify anonymity for victims, in order to mitigate their humiliation and encourage other victims to come forward, and the same consideration is frequently extended to victims of blackmail. Trials under the Official Secrets Act may also be partly heard in camera. There are special statutory protections for juveniles charged with crime: the Press may attend their trials and report the evidence, but without identifying the children involved. The sordid details of divorce proceedings, once the stock-in-trade of popular newspapers, are now published only rarely: undefended divorces, and maintenance and custody proceedings, are heard 'in chambers' – in a judge's room to which reporters are not permitted entry.

These exceptions may be reasonable, but there are many aspects of British justice which are unnecessarily hidden from public scrutiny by the 'in chambers' proceedings which form a large part of the work of the High Court. In 1987, two senior Family Division judges severely criticized the automatic exclusion of the Press from chambers hearings involving important issues of sorting out property and income in divorce proceedings. The absence of Press and law reporters was said to have led to 'lax and sloppy advocacy' and poor conduct of cases: Mrs Justice Booth admitted that 'Everything is in danger of becoming too cosy and too informal and we are forgetting that we are lawyers. We do not have the Press or the public or even members of our own profession there to keep us up to the mark'[7] – an echo of Bentham's point that publicity 'keeps the judge himself, while trying, under trial'. A more extraordinary anomaly is provided by the routine practice of the Queen's Bench Division of the High Court to hear applications for injunctions or eviction orders in chambers, whilst its Chancery Division hears such applications in open court. Since there is a good deal of overlap in jurisdiction, plaintiffs may opt for secrecy by bringing their actions in one Division rather than the other. In 1987, when the Government embarked upon its court-room crusade to stop the media from publishing interviews with former security-service personnel, its first actions against the Press were commenced in the Chancery Division and were fully reported. By the end of the year, when it sought an injunction against the BBC in relation to the programme *My Country Right or Wrong* it chose the Queen's Bench Division, where its arguments were heard in secret.

There is no sensible basis for this distinction, and no reason why the open-justice principle should not apply to applications, which may be of great public interest, made to Queen's Bench judges. (The anomaly is made more glaring by the fact that any appeal against a decision in chambers is heard in open court.) Nor is there any justification for recent regulations which require bail applications and similar matters at Crown Courts (but not in magistrates' courts) to be heard in chambers. If there is any danger that the Press will publish prejudicial matter, the court can invoke Section 4(2) of the Contempt of Court Act, which requires such reports to be postponed until after the conclusion of the trial.

In short, Britain does not live up to the open-justice principle which has been its most enduring contribution to the law of other nations. Secrecy in some divisions of the High Court, and in pre-trial proceedings in Crown Courts, has become routine. In criminal trials, advocates are allowed to make secrecy applications in secret, and so the public may never know whether bogus reasons are being advanced. At Reading Crown Court in 1986, a five-day trial on a drug-importing charge was heard entirely in secret, at the request of both prosecution and defence. The Press later discovered that it involved allegations by customs officers that an informer had exploited his relationship with the police to import cannabis – a matter of public interest which the case should have publicly ventilated.

Press reporting can, at times, be shallow, sensational or just plain incompetent. Courts have some corrective powers and can usually protect parties from any prejudice. A more persuasive objection to entrenching the right to report is the desire to protect witnesses against loss of face or loss of job, or even, where police informers are concerned, against possible loss of life. Does it really matter if a few cases go unreported so that prosecution witnesses are relieved from the anxiety of reading their names in newspapers? It does, for the reasons given by Blackstone and Bentham. Trials derive their legitimacy from being conducted in public; the judge presides as a surrogate for the people who are entitled to see and approve the power exercised on their behalf. Those who assist the prosecution can and should be protected by other means. No matter how fair, justice must still be seen before it can be said to have been done.

But how far should the open-justice principle stretch? If every court in the land is open to every subject of the King, does it not logically follow that subjects should be entitled, quite literally, to see justice done through the medium of television? That conclusion has been reached in many U S states, which permit radio and television broadcasts from their court-rooms. Bar associations, initially hostile, report some good results: the lawyers are better prepared, the judges better behaved, and the public better informed. In Britain, the Criminal Bar Association is in favour of some television coverage. The communications revolution can bring benefits to justice, and we are beginning to accept the advantages of videotaped testimony of child witnesses and the possibility of cross-examining overseas witnesses via satellite link-up. Appeal courts would be better able to evaluate the testimony of trial witnesses if they could see and hear it being delivered, and most barristers have had occasions to regret that they could not include in grounds of appeal against judges' summings-up some reference to prejudicial tones of voice or body language which are not apparent from a typed transcript.

The danger, of course, is that witnesses may prove camera-shy and that television's coverage of the day's play in a sensational Old Bailey trial will feature heavily edited 'highlights' chosen for entertainment value rather than as fair and accurate reporting. None the less, the public is genuinely interested in significant court cases, and the arguments in favour of open justice apply with even greater force to aural or visual coverage. Present television news reporting, in sixty-second 'slots' with breathless presenters pictured outside court quoting snatches of evidence, sometimes over inaccurate 'artists' impressions' of the court-room, is of minimal value. When Channel 4 launched a late-night *Court Report* programme, on which news-readers read large slabs of the day's transcript in the Ponting trial over half an hour on every evening of the three-week trial, over 500,000 viewers watched every edition. There would seem to be little objection to radio coverage of important appellate proceedings, but the BBC has been refused permission to go even this far.

In 1987 the Lord Chief Justice banned a 'dramatized reconstruction' on television of the Court of Appeal's rehearing of the 'Birmingham bombers' case, which was due to be transmitted at the close of the evidence but prior to judgement. Although the programme was an hour and a half long and scrupulously accurate, he feared that selective editing and the use of actors to impersonate witnesses would be liable to give false impressions and to undermine public confidence in the court, at least if its ultimate decision were contrary to the expectation fostered by the programme. This ban marks an extraordinary and unjustified extension of a court's power to suppress: there was no jury, and no danger of prejudice to the result. The latest studies show that more people in Britain obtain their news and information from television than from newspapers: the ban on the Birmingham appeal re-enactment (imposed by the judges without even seeing the programme) is an obstacle to further innovative use of this medium to make court proceedings 'come alive'. There are, of course, problems in presenting such a serious matter by way of drama, although it can hardly be doubted that those who stayed up to midnight to watch a ninety-minute re-enactment would have been better informed about the serious issues involved in the appeal than by reading the desultory and disjointed newspaper reports of 'highlights' of evidence and argument which were spread over six weeks.

CONTEMPT OF COURT

The power to punish for contempt is the mechanism by which the judiciary – unassisted by juries – decides where the line is to be drawn between fair trial and free Press. Media comment about matters which are subject to litigation may poison the minds of potential jurors or influence or intimidate potential witnesses. It may equally inform public debate and even warn of public danger – for example, when a remand prisoner is armed and on the run. Some publications are blatant contempts, arising from Press ignorance or error, and are dealt with by heavy fines after grovelling apologies. (The publication of a defendant's previous convictions before his trial is over is a frequent example.) In most cases there are public-interest arguments on both sides. Anything smacking of 'trial by media' is abhorred by judges, but it is easy to exaggerate the dangers of ephemeral publicity. Prejudicial comment at the time of a suspect's arrest is generally forgotten by the time the case comes to trial, and any residual impact on a jury is attenuated by weeks of live testimony, powerful advocacy and judicial admonition to judge according to the evidence heard in court. We know little about the psychological realities of the jury room, or the extent to which the trial process vacuums the jurors' minds of prejudices they may have picked up from their newspapers, so every contempt case involves guesswork: how great is the risk that the publication will have an impact which cannot be cured by judicial directions to forget about it?

In deciding whether a publication amounts to a contempt, the court must apply the test of whether it creates a *substantial risk* that justice, either in a particular case or as a continuing process, will be *seriously impeded or prejudiced*. This test was first formulated in the 1981 Contempt of Court Act, which the UK Government was obliged to pass after the European Court of Human Rights held that the old contempt law was so strict that it violated the Convention guarantee of freedom of expression. The courts had banned the *Sunday Times* from conducting a campaign against Distillers, the manufacturers of the deforming drug Thalidomide, and their reluctance properly to compensate victims. There were many legal actions outstanding against Distillers at the time, and the courts took the view that the newspaper campaign would prejudge issues arising in the litigation and put unfair pressure on the drug manufacturers to settle for more than might otherwise be awarded against them. The European Court rejected the British Government's argument that a strict law of contempt was necessary to uphold the authority of the judiciary: the Thalidomide disaster was a matter of national concern, and the mere fact that litigation was in progress did not alter the right and indeed the responsibility of the media to impart information and comment about a public tragedy.[8] The old law, by applying the test of *possibility* of prejudice, and by finding that test satisfied whenever media comment prejudged issues under litigation, led to a restraint which went much further than was necessary to protect the authority of the courts in a democratic society. It involved an interference with freedom of speech which was out of proportion to the social need to protect the impartiality of the courts and the rights of litigants.

The 1981 Act, then, originated as a liberalizing measure, and has in some respects had a liberalizing effect. It altered the odds: instead of requiring a *possibility* of some prejudice, it called for a finding of a *substantial* risk of *serious* prejudice. That the new test is more liberal can be seen from the Court of Appeal's decision in 1986 to refuse to injunct the *News of the World* from publishing allegations about Ian Botham's involvement with drug-taking during a cricket tour of New Zealand. These allegations were already the subject of a libel action brought by Botham against another newspaper which had published them some time before, and the case would be tried by a jury some ten months after the date of the proposed republication in the *News of the World*. The Court of Appeal accepted that there was a possibility that fresh publication in a national newspaper would influence a jury at a later date, but in view of the ten-month delay such a risk could not be assessed as 'substantial'.

This occasion marks an important judicial recognition of the psychological phenomenon that involvement in the immediate drama of a trial will help to eradicate dim memories of media comment. As Lord Donaldson put it,

> This trial will not take place for at least ten months, by which time many wickets will have fallen, not to mention much water having flowed under many bridges, all of which would blunt any impact of the publication ... the fact is that for one reason or another a trial, by its very nature, seems to cause all concerned to become progressively more inward-looking, studying the evidence given and submissions made to the exclusion of other sources of enlightenment.[9]

This phenomenon is amply evidenced by the jury which awarded Jeffrey Archer £500,000 for an allegation which had been the talk of every pub and party in the country after the Press exposure of his dealings with a prostitute, and the jury acquittal of Jeremy Thorpe after years of Press speculation about his involvement in a conspiracy to murder Norman Scott. But there are limits to the extent to which the media may be permitted to vilify individuals facing trial, either by publishing prejudicial facts which would be inadmissible as evidence against them or by whipping up hatred against them generally. The *Sun* newspaper clearly exceeded those limits when it publicly accused a doctor of sexually assaulting a small child, and then (after the DPP had refused to prosecute, on the basis of insufficient evidence) itself funded a private prosecution. The court held that the newspaper had published the attack with the specific intention of prejudicing the proceedings which it had already determined to bring.[10] This is a particularly odious form of 'trial by newspaper', and the newspaper was fortunate to escape with a fine of £75,000. When the *Daily Mirror* published sensationalized suggestions that a man arrested for one particularly foul murder was not only guilty, but guilty of other murders as well, its editor was gaoled for three months.[11]

A society's respect for the values of fair trial is judged by the protection it affords to those charged with the ugliest of crimes, and the liberalizing intentions of the 1981 Act were in some respects restrained by the unedifying media circus which accompanied the arrest of Peter Sutcliffe, the 'Yorkshire Ripper', while the law was passing through its parliamentary stages. The series of gruesome murders of young women for which Sutcliffe ultimately accepted responsibility had fanned fear and terror in Northern cities, but relief at the arrest of a suspect did not justify the police holding triumphant Press conferences or the media publishing every kind of prejudicial detail which its reporters, with blank cheque-books, could purchase from potential witnesses. Had Sutcliffe denied the charges, it would have been difficult to empanel a jury unaffected by the saturation publicity given to his arrest, and his trial in any event badly miscarried, when his plea of insanity was rejected by a majority verdict despite unanimous medical evidence that he was suffering from paranoid schizophrenia. (Subsequently his illness became so pronounced that he had to be removed from prison to a secure mental hospital.) Although no prosecutions were brought as a result of this episode – the Attorney-General lamely explained that he would have to put all of Fleet Street in the dock – it influenced Parliament to set a strict timetable within which 'strict liability contempt' may be committed.

'Intentional contempt', i.e. when a newspaper deliberately sets out to influence a trial (as in the case mentioned above of the *Sun* criticizing and privately prosecuting a doctor) is rare, but may be committed at any time, even before charges are brought. 'Strict liability contempt' – the normal case of publishing prejudicial material negligently or in ignorance of a forthcoming trial – can be committed only during the period when proceedings are deemed to be 'active'. In criminal cases, this is as soon as the first formal step in launching a prosecution is taken, either by arrest or the issue of a warrant for arrest or a summons to appear in court. Civil cases become 'active' as soon as the case is listed as being ready for trial. Publication of prejudicial material outside these time-frames will not be capable of amounting to contempt unless intended to prejudice some further trial, while publication within the 'active' period will be contemptuous if it constitutes a substantial risk of serious prejudice. A case ceases to be 'active' when it has concluded, although it 'reactivates' when an appeal is lodged. The reactivation period causes the media little concern, as appellate judges are reluctant to concede that they are influenced by anything they might read in newspapers. They are, however, only human, and advocates who strive to appeal deterrent sentences which have been stridently endorsed by popular newspapers can feel they have an uphill task.

Another liberalizing aspect of the 1981 Act was its introduction of a 'public interest' defence which ensures that public debate on matters of current controversy can continue even if it reflects upon issues before the courts. Section 5 exonerates publications which discuss in good faith matters of general public interest 'if the risk of impediment or prejudice is merely incidental to the discussion'. The first beneficiary of this defence was Malcolm Muggeridge, who had written critically of the 'common practice' of doctors who allowed deformed babies to die, in a newspaper article which appeared during the trial of a doctor who was alleged to have committed manslaughter in these very circumstances. Incidental prejudice to the trial was insufficient, the House of Lords held, to curtail robust criticism of medical euthanasia.[12] Sir John Junor, however, was heavily fined for a snide and misleading personal attack on the doctor while his trial was in progress, made without any attempt to discuss the wider issues. Section 5 will not protect publications which directly relate to imminent or ongoing jury trials and which criticize witnesses or vilify defendants or set out inadmissible evidence or encourage a particular outcome.

The basic thrust of the 1981 Act, with its test of substantial risk of serious prejudice and its public-interest defence, reasonably balances the conflicting values of fair trial and free Press. It allows courts to impose a stricter test where trial is by jury rather than by magistrate or judge, and the 'cut-off point' at the moment of arrest allows the media latitude to expose wrongdoing which may otherwise go unprosecuted. It does make it more difficult than in America or Europe to criticize the conduct of particular prosecutions or the behaviour of those engaged in court cases while they are 'active', but it serves to dampen the sensationalistic hue and cry against unpopular defendants which disfigures justice in other countries. Contempt prosecutions may only be brought by the Attorney-General, whose control prevents trivial prosecutions but has also served to immunize the police force, whose Press statements and public conferences and inspired 'leaks' are directly responsible for much avoidable prejudice. On occasions politicians – including Government Ministers – have been unable to resist grabbing headlines by denouncing prospective defendants or announcing police breakthroughs in proving their guilt: the Attorney-General has taken no action.

There are several respects in which the law of contempt presently overvalues the claim of due administration of justice. First, the absolute prohibition of any kind of post-trial interview with jurors precludes sensible and serious analysis of how that system works (see later, page 303). Second, the powers given to judges and magistrates to postpone reports of proceedings (Section 4(2)) or to ban the mention of names or other items of evidence (Section 11) are apt to be used in contravention of the open-justice principle (see earlier, page 279). The third unsatisfactory feature of contempt is the 1981 Act's failure to reform the law of 'intentional contempt', which survives with all its common-law features intact. It applies outside the statutory periods imposed on 'strict liability' contempt, and requires only a potential risk – not a substantial risk – of prejudice to litigation. The 'public interest' defence given by Section 5 of the Contempt Act does not apply.

Although there was good reason to punish the *Sun* for internationally prejudicing the trial of a doctor whom the newspaper itself had decided to prosecute privately, the Attorney-General's deployment of the same device to punish newspapers which published revelations by Peter Wright was altogether more controversial. These complicated contempt proceedings were commenced in 1987 against the *Independent* and two evening newspapers which reported detailed extracts from Wright's book just before it was published in America. The previous year, the Government had obtained injunctions against the *Guardian* and the *Observer* over brief reports of Wright's main allegations, on the ground that these amounted to breaches of a duty of confidentiality owed to it. The *Independent* was not a party to these proceedings, had not had the opportunity to contest the injunction and could not in natural justice be said to be bound by it. Its decision to publish Wright's allegations on the eve of their publication in America was, if anything, a further breach of confidence. Yet the Court of Appeal upheld the Attorney-General's contention that the *Independent*'s publication could amount to 'intentional contempt' because it 'destroyed the subject-matter' of the Government's action against the *Guardian* and the *Observer*. (It would not amount to 'strict liability' contempt, because that earlier action had not yet been set down for trial.)

This case – *Attorney-General* v. *Newspaper Publishing PLC* – shows just how far the law of contempt can be stretched when combined with another exceedingly supple common-law doctrine, namely breach of confidence.[13] The 'subject-matter' of the initial confidence action against the *Observer* was a report of Wright's allegations. This subject-matter was likened to an ice-cube: it would 'evaporate' if exposed to the light of day by the *Independent*. There would be no point in the Attorney-General continuing his action against the *Observer* if Wright's revelations were published elsewhere. Since contempt is a power deployed by the courts to prevent interference with the due administration of justice, the courts were entitled to punish the editor of the *Independent* by way of a criminal action for contempt of court on the grounds that by publishing Wright's allegations he had destroyed the confidential nature of information that another court had injuncted the *Observer* from publishing pending the trial of the Government's claim to exclusive possession of this information. It was, said the Court of Appeal, as if the Government and the *Observer* had commenced a legal action over the ownership of a racehorse, and the court had ordered the horse to be kept alive until the dispute over its possession could be resolved after a full trial. The editor of the *Independent* had shot the horse prior to that full trial, and thereby rendered the proceedings pointless. The Attorney-General, in his role as guardian of the administration of justice, was entitled to seek to commit the *Independent* editor to prison for intentionally aborting legal proceedings in which, quite coincidentally, the Attorney-General happened to be a party.

There can be no objection to the principle that courts should have power to protect judicial proceedings from third parties who deliberately set out to prejudice or subvert them. Where the argument in the *Newspaper Publishing PLC* case becomes metaphysical is in assimilating Wright's allegations (that MI5 plotted to assassinate Nasser, bug foreign embassies and destabilize the Wilson Government) to items of physical property like ice-cubes and racehorses. Information of this kind is not 'subject-matter' which can be possessed exclusively by a Department of State; any more than a conspiracy to murder is the exclusive property of the conspirators. The 'subject-matter' of an action for breach of confidence is not the information itself, but the confidential relationship in the course of which it was acquired. In fact, the *Independent*'s publication did not abort the proceedings in the case against the *Observer*: they continued to trial and appeal, irrespective of the fact that over a million copies of *Spycatcher* had been published throughout the world and many copies had been imported into Britain. The ice-cube had by this stage been transformed into a flood of dirty water, but what was at stake in the litigation was the question of whether the *Observer* had become party to Wright's breach of his duty owed to the Crown by publishing his allegations. The *Independent* did not frustrate the administration of justice in that case by further publishing Wright's allegations, although by so doing it may well have become a party to his breach of confidence. The *Independent* should have been sued for breach of confidence, and not prosecuted for the crime of contempt.

None the less, *Attorney-General* v. *Newspaper Publishing PLC* stands for the proposition that it can be a crime for one newspaper to breach the spirit of an injunction imposed upon another, despite the fact that it has had no opportunity to present a case against the imposition of any restraint. It must go cap in hand to the court and ask for permission to publish. This was the course taken by Derbyshire County Council to request permission for its local library to stock a copy of *Spycatcher*. Although numerous copies of the book had by this time been imported into the country, and were being sold by enthusiastic entrepreneurs at inflated prices, the High Court followed the *Newspaper Publishing PLC* case and held that the book's availability in a public library would 'constitute an interference with the due administration of justice' in the ongoing cases against the *Guardian* and the *Observer*.[14] This decision shows just how far the contempt/confidentiality doctrine has moved in the direction of prior restraint: had the Council simply ordered a copy of the book pursuant to its duty to provide a comprehensive and efficient library service, it is doubtful whether it would have been charged with intentional contempt. This crime is only committed by those who specifically intend to impede or prejudice the administration of justice, and even recklessness as to whether such prejudice may be caused is insufficient to ground a conviction. For this reason, individuals and bookshops who sold a handful of imported copies of *Spycatcher* were not prosecuted for contempt.

It must be remembered that the *Newspaper Publishing PLC* case was a decision on a theoretical point of law – whether an injunction would in principle be binding against third parties – and not an actual finding of guilt against the *Independent*. It will always be open for editors and journalists to exculpate themselves from contempt charges by claiming that their intentions were not to prejudice existing legal actions against others but rather to fulfil a public duty or to place important facts in the public domain. There is, however, no public-interest defence against 'intentional contempt', and it remains to be seen how judges will assess the 'intention' of a newspaper editor who may not desire to prejudice proceedings, but who none the less has knowledge of an injunction against another newspaper and might therefore be held to have foreseen the risk. Anomalously, all the prosecution will have to prove is foresight of some risk, not of 'substantial risk of serious prejudice'. The editor will not be permitted trial by jury, and will if convicted be liable to up to two years' imprisonment and unlimited fines. In these circumstances most will choose, like Derbyshire County Council, to apply to the court for guidance as to whether they can properly publish material which has been made the subject of an injunction in some other action – a procedure calculated to give High Court judges a good deal of experience in editing newspapers.

One form of contempt which should have been abolished by the 1981 reforms is the arcane crime of 'scandalizing the Court' by criticizing the judiciary (in Scotland, the offence goes by the delightful name of 'murmuring judges'). It was deployed in the eighteenth century against radicals like John Wilkes, and was revived in 1900 to punish the editor of the *Birmingham Daily Argus* for describing Mr Justice Darling, not in-accurately, as 'an impudent little man in horse-hair' who was 'a micro-cosm of conceit and empty-headedness'.[15] In 1930 the *Daily Worker* was fined for describing a conservative judge as 'a bewigged puppet exhibiting a strong class bias', but there have been no successful prosecu-tions in Britain since then. Some of the credit for this restraint must be accorded to Quintin Hogg MP (later Lord Chancellor Hailsham) who was privately prosecuted for contempt in 1968 over an article he had written in *Punch* which was severely and inaccurately critical of the Court of Appeal. That Court declined to regard itself as scandalized, ruling that no criticism of a judgement, however vigorous, could amount to contempt if it was made in good faith and with reasonable courtesy.[16]

The bounds of reasonable courtesy may well have been exceeded by the *Daily Mirror* in 1987, when it published upside-down photo-graphs of the Law Lords who had injuncted *Spycatcher* under the banner headline 'YOU FOOLS!' No prosecution was forthcoming. The danger, however, of leaving such a crime on the books is well illus-trated by recent contempt prosecutions in other countries which have inherited the common law, where robust condemnation of court de-cisions (Trinidad), suggestion that a decision was influenced by trade-union demonstrations (Australia) and minor inaccuracies in justifiable criticism of the conduct of proceedings against an opposition MP (Singapore) have all been treated as contempt. It may be that the Brit-ish Press has itself to blame for Parliament's refusal to abolish this head of contempt. During the 1981 reforms, an amendment to this effect was rejected, after Lord Hailsham recalled a recent incident which had arisen after the Court of Appeal denied a divorce to a woman who claimed that her husband was unreasonable in having sex with her only once a week. A journalist from the Fleet Street gutter telephoned the wives of the three appellate judges to ask how often a week they regarded as reasonable. The offence of scandalizing the court, said the Lord Chancellor, was still required to deal with such conduct.

TRIAL BY JURY

If Britain had a written constitution, its most predictable clause would provide that no citizen should be liable to lose his or her liberty for longer than a year without at least the opportunity of submitting to trial by jury. With the exception of the crime of contempt (which has a two-year maximum sentence, and is triable by judges alone) this reflects the actual position today, and as recently as 1987 a powerful lobby to have complicated fraud cases heard by a judge and expert assessors was rebuffed. The jury system is too deeply entrenched to be directly supplanted, however much senior police officers may despair of its propensity for acquitting one in four defendants who contest their charges in Crown Courts. Undermining the defendant's right to trial by jury can take more subtle forms than outright abolition, however: there has been a steady increase in offences which are triable only by magistrates; 'jury vetting' has been instituted for official secrets and terrorist cases; civil injunctions, backed by contempt powers, are preferred to politically controversial jury trials; and in 1988 the defendant's right to challenge up to three members of the jury panel was abolished. There is little doubt that further restrictions on the right to jury trial will be attempted in years to come, in order to reduce the public expense of criminal justice and in an attempt to boost conviction rates.

Jury trial is a unique British institution. It was hit upon by happy accident over 700 years ago, to replace trials by the ordeal of fire or water, in which guilt or innocence was decided by ritual tests overseen by parish priests. Divine providence was getting a bad name from priests who accepted bribes to rig the trials – by choosing shallow ponds, or making sure that water did not boil – so in 1215 the Pope refused to allow them to participate, and the system collapsed. It was replaced by the procedure which Henry II had instituted to resolve land disputes: a group of worthy citizens from the district, summoned by a judge to decide between rival claimants on the basis of their knowledge of local history and customs. In criminal cases their verdict, delivered after solemn conclave, was endowed with some of the ritual and sanctity which had attended 'the ordeal' before it fell into disrepute. Some centuries passed before juries won the right to stand out against the prejudices and partiality of the King's judges – they could be starved into submission by being locked up without food or fire until they returned a 'guilty' verdict, and the Star Chamber went so far as to punish jurymen who refused judicial invitations to convict by seizing their lands and goods. The turning-point came in 1670, when twelve courageous jurors at the Old Bailey refused to convict two Quakers, William Penn and William Mead, of holding a seditious assembly. They were locked up for two nights without food or water or even a chamber-pot. When they nevertheless insisted upon a verdict 'according to conscience' of 'not guilty', the Recorder of London sentenced them to prison. Four of them, led by Edward Bushell, challenged the legality of their punishment by a writ of *habeas corpus*. The Lord Chief Justice, Sir Robert Vaughan, decided that a jury was entitled to act according to its own conscience and appreciation of the evidence, irrespective of judicial direction or expectation.[17] *Bushell's Case* is the foundation of the constitutional independence of the jury: it can do justice, whatever the law may be.

This independence remains the most remarkable feature of the modern jury, and an important safeguard against oppressive prosecutions. It means that an ordinary, everyday sense of mercy is built into our criminal-justice arrangements, in a way which defies logic but has won popular acceptance. Throughout the brutal period of the late eighteenth and early nineteenth century, when the death penalty was visited on all who stole goods valued at more than forty shillings, juries consistently undervalued property so as to enable petty thieves to escape the gallows. Recent studies estimate that some fourteen per cent of acquittals are 'sympathy verdicts', where the jury strives to find a reasonable doubt because it believes, with good cause, that the defendant has been the victim of oppressive police behaviour or has in any event suffered enough.[18] The rule in *Bushell's Case*, by enabling the jury to temper the legal wind to the shorn lamb, has had important implications in politically motivated prosecutions brought under vague or unpopular laws. The jury most noticeably lit 'the lamp which shows that freedom lives' by ignoring judicial directions to convict radicals charged with publishing seditious attacks on George III and his Ministers. In 1985, the Old Bailey jury which refused to convict Clive Ponting, a civil servant who had clearly breached Section 2 of the Official Secrets Act by supplying classified information to an MP, was duly celebrated in many quarters for upholding the traditions of the 'gang of twelve'. In America, Penn and Mead had their counterpart in Peter Zenger, a New York printer whose colonial jury refused to convict him for publishing anti-British sedition just before the Revolution. In some states in the USA, judges even remind jurors of their constitutional right to nullify unpopular laws by acquitting defendants.[19] In Britain, this right is celebrated in theory but regarded as subversive in practice: it is not mentioned in court.

The other feature which contributes to the esteem in which the modern jury is held is that it is drawn at random from a representative cross-section of society. This is not a historical survival, but a very recent adaptation of the system to satisfy democratic ideals. Before 1972, juries were mainly 'male, middle-aged, middle-minded and middle class' – because only those who owned property could serve upon them. But in that year Parliament accepted the recommendation of the Morris Committee that almost all who were entitled to vote should be eligible for jury service.[20] Then the modern jury – the very modern jury – became, in Lord Simon's words, 'a microcosm of democratic society'. It was an important change of principle, from the idea that only sound citizens with a proprietary stake in society were fit and proper persons to pass upon questions of guilt or innocence, to the principle that every class – the dispossessed, young people, members of minority groups – should be available for selection. Since 1972 the jury has become, truly, the people's court.

Right to jury trial

There has been some erosion of the right to jury trial in recent years, by the simple expedient of making certain criminal offences triable only by magistrates. The State forgoes the prospect of a heavy prison sentence in return for a cheap and speedy trial and a better chance of conviction. The most commonly deployed public-order offences, such as obstruction of the highway and the use of threatening or abusive or insulting language and the new crimes of disorderly conduct and disobedience to police bans or restrictions on demonstrations, do not carry the right to jury trial. It is ironical that were the Quakers Penn and Mead to return today to hold their meeting in Gracechurch Street in the City of London, they would be brought before a stipendiary at Tower Bridge Magistrates' Court rather than Edward Bushell's 'gang of twelve' at the Old Bailey.

Cases of assaulting police carry no right of jury trial, although conviction is a serious matter which often occasions a prison sentence. Crimes which can severely affect personal reputation, such as kerb-crawling and homosexual soliciting, have carefully been made triable only by magistrates, and forfeiture proceedings against books and magazines and videos are regularly used to destroy 'obscene' material which might well be acquitted by juries. The notable thing about many of these offences is that they generally involve contests between the evidence of the police and the evidence of the defendant – contests which cry out for jury adjudication. Often, too, they raise questions of civil liberty or morality which are better decided by a tribunal which is in touch with ordinary and contemporary standards than by lay Justices drawn from an unrepresentative class base.

Another method of evading the right to jury trial is to give prosecuting authorities the discretion to decide whether to proceed against defendants in a way which permits them to elect trial before a jury in the Crown Court. In the case of an allegation of criminal damage, for example, this right of election is reserved to defendants charged with damage exceeding £2,000. Police now have High Court approval to select from amongst damaged property only items which total less than £2,000, and so remove the defendant's right to elect.[21] In public-order cases, they may pick and choose those charges which are triable only by magistrates – a common tactic at Greenham Common and in the wake of the miners' strike (when magistrates generally convicted, while juries usually rejected more serious allegations of riot and unlawful assembly). It would, in principle, be preferable that all cases carrying a substantial risk of imprisonment or involving a value-judgement about community standards should be capable of trial by jury, but the pressures of cost and convenience are hostile to such a reform. It is difficult enough to hold the line against powerful lobbies in favour of abolishing jury trial for simple theft charges where the goods are valued at less than £50 – a reform which a Labour Government attempted to institute in 1979. It would have covered precisely those shoplifting cases which have the capacity for destroying hitherto unblemished reputations. We are in grave danger of reserving the 'palladium of liberty' for occasions involving the liberty of persons charged with bank robberies and burglaries, rather than the occasions which are most likely to threaten the character and careers of ordinary citizens.

Jury challenges

A more direct attack on a traditional right associated with jury trial was made in 1989, when the defence right to challenge was abolished. It had been reduced from twenty (in serious cases of murder or treason) to seven in 1948, and further reduced to three per defendant in 1977. It was the only mechanism available to assist the defence in obtaining a representative jury: the first twelve 'called to the book to be sworn' may be wholly unbalanced in terms of sex or age or class or race, and the availability of challenges offered some prospect of readjustment. In the great majority of cases, no challenge was offered to the panel. But where a black defendant was arraigned before twelve white jurors, or a young woman before twelve middle-aged men, the exercise of the challenge could secure a 'peer' or two amongst the decision-takers.

There is, of course, no art to find the mind's construction in the face, but there are a number of cases where brief visual inspection will indicate a juror's unsuitability to participate in a particular trial. A juror who evinces fear or hatred of the defendant before taking the oath, who appears disruptive or uncomfortable, or mentally unbalanced or half-drunk, or who smiles encouragingly at the police or who seems to be wearing a badge or carrying a publication which indicates possible partisanship in relation to the facts of the case, or gives every indication of being likely to react over-emotionally to the nature of the evidence – all give grounds for genuine apprehension about ability to judge calmly and dispassionately. Such apprehensions on the part of defendants and their counsel may well be misplaced, but a system which boasts that justice must be seen to be done was right to provide some mechanism for dispelling them. At the very least, it could be said that no defendant was obliged to be tried by someone whose face he did not like.

The impetus for abolition came in a particularly unattractive way, from back-bench Tory MPs enraged at the acquittal of a number of young servicemen who had been accused of leaking secrets about a GCHQ base in Cyprus to enemy agents. A number of the original panel had been challenged and replaced by younger jurors, and the Government yielded to demands that the 'retirement age' for jury service be increased from sixty-five to seventy and that the defence right to challenge without cause be entirely abolished. This was an irrational response to the Cyprus case, in which any jury would have been influenced by the brutal methods of interrogation used by RAF police which were subsequently condemned by an official inquiry. The notion that a jury panel which has been subject to defence challenges is more likely to acquit had been exploded in 1986 by a study conducted by the Crown Prosecution Service, which demonstrated that conviction rates in court cases where jurors had been challenged were identical to those in trials where they had not. But Government MPs were not interested in facts, and the myth that the right to challenge was being 'abused' to obtain dim-witted jurors likely to be hoodwinked by clever advocacy carried the day. As it happens, jury studies show that intelligent jurors are much more likely to find 'reasonable doubts' about the logic of the prosecution case, and there is some reason to believe that older jurors are more resistant to judicial direction than persons under thirty.

It was otiose to make the right of challenge the scapegoat for inconvenient acquittals, which on closer examination will generally be shown to be justified by some reasonable doubt arising from the evidence or (in rare but important cases) from some justifiable doubts about the conduct of officials. If the Crown cannot convince ten out of twelve randomly selected citizens, only a handful of whom may have been random replacements at the insistence of the defence, that a defendant is guilty, any 'blame' attaching to the acquittal does not lie with the jury. At the Old Bailey in the first month after abolition of the right to challenge, defence counsel unavailingly protested that a black youth was to be judged by a panel of twelve white jurors and that the question of whether the display of ear-rings made from foetuses was 'an outrage to public decency' was to be decided by a panel ten of whose members were women. Judges ruled that they had no power to interfere, although it is precisely in such cases that racial or sexual balance is important in order that justice may be seen to be done. It is manifestly unfair that the prosecution retains its right to challenge, and although this is used only exceptionally, it is these exceptional cases – where information is obtained by secret 'vetting' of the panel – that cause most concern.

Jury vetting

The practice of 'vetting' goes back to the time of the French Revolution when Pitt, concerned to crush Republican stirrings, introduced 'special juries' of loyalists to try cases of sedition. They were 'guinea men', paid a guinea a day and made well aware that continued lucrative employment by the Crown was contingent upon their ability to reach verdicts congenial to the Crown. It was, said one defendant, 'like offering a man a basket of rotten oranges from which he was at liberty to take his choice', and it was a tribute both to the advocacy of Thomas Erskine and to the unpopularity of George III and his Ministers that on some occasions even 'special juries' acquitted. The best that can be said for the system is that it brought to prominence Jeremy Bentham, whose first book was entitled *Elements in the Art of Jury Packing*. He condemned a system of vetting 'which is become regular, quietly established and quietly suffered. Not only is the yoke already about our necks, but our neck is already fashioned for it.' In due course special juries were abolished, and replaced by juries comprising men (and a few women) of property.

In 1972, as a result of the report of the Morris Committee, the property qualification was abolished and all persons on the electoral role were made liable to jury service, subject to appropriate exclusions for lawyers, policemen, court staff, MPs, clergymen, and the mentally ill. All persons who have in the past ten years received any prison or suspended prison sentence or a community service order, or have been put on probation at any time in the previous five years, are disqualified. The Morris Committee made no reference to 'vetting' other than by court inquiries to check that disqualified persons did not serve. Both prosecution and defence were to be entitled to a list of the names and addresses and occupations of persons on the jury panel, although in 1973 the right to know a juror's occupation was abolished by the Lord Chancellor, as a result of allegations that defence counsel at trials arising from industrial picketing were using the information to deduce whether a juror might be a member of a trade union.

The 'jury vetting' controversy exploded in 1978, after it was revealed that the prosecution at Duncan Campbell's trial (the *A B C* official secrets case) had secretly obtained access to the jury panel six weeks before the trial started in order to run Special Branch checks on potential jurors. The Attorney-General, Sam Silkin, was forced to admit that he had personally sanctioned such vetting in twenty-six cases over the previous four years. In 1979 the Press got hold of a police vetting report about a jury empanelled to try a group of Anarchists: it revealed long-spent convictions, and the fact that one juror lived at an address 'believed to be a squat' and another had made a complaint against the police.[22] In that trial the defence had convinced a judge to extend £5,000 of legal aid to enable it to conduct its own 'vetting' of the panel by employing private detectives. The following year the issue of jury vetting split the Court of Appeal – or rather, two differently constituted Courts of Appeal reached diametrically opposed conclusions about the legitimacy of the practice. One set of judges thought that the practice was reasonable and even desirable when conducted to supply information about previous convictions,[23] while another thought the whole business was unconstitutional.[24]

These great issues of principle were, in familiar British fashion, ducked and defused by the issue of 'guidelines', both by the Attorney-General and the Association of Chief Police Officers (ACPO). 'Guidelines', as we have seen so often are not law, and there is neither any sanction against their breach nor any likelihood, given the secrecy in which vetting is conducted, that any breach will be made public.

The Attorney-General's guidelines approve Special Branch vetting of jurors in official-secrets and terrorist cases to ascertain whether any hold extreme political views which might colour their appreciation of the facts or, in security cases, lead them to divulge in-camera material to others. Presumably any potential juror discovered with Communist or Anarchist or Sinn Fein connections would be challenged, although it is unclear whether 'militant tendency' or National Front views would be regarded as extreme, or whether journalists would be regarded as a risk in official-secrets cases. The guidelines permit vetting to uncover whether any juror on the panel belongs to a 'pressure group' with views which might affect the 'fair assessment' of a case. Does this mean that jurors in official-secrets trials will be vetted to ensure that they are not supporters of the NCCL or the Freedom of Information campaign?

The ACPO guidelines permit police officers to undertake 'vetting' exercises whenever a juror is suspected of being disqualified or there is reason to suspect that 'jury nobbling' will be attempted – both perfectly reasonable grounds for checking on criminal records. But vetting is also approved 'in any other case in which in the opinion of the DPP or the Chief Constable it is particularly important to ensure that no disqualified person serves on the jury'. As to what cases these might be, the guidelines give no guidance. They permit a general trawl through police records (which, as the Anarchist case shows, may contain much information other than a record of previous convictions); they permit the use of information by the prosecution in order to challenge jurors (whether disqualified by law or not); and they do not require the fact that the vetting exercise has been undertaken, or the information it has disclosed, to be shared with defending counsel. These guidelines legitimize jury vetting without providing any equality to the defendant or any protection for the vetted jurors. It came as little surprise that in 1987 one police district admitted to making regular Criminal Records Office checks on all persons summonsed for jury service.

The principal objections to 'jury vetting' are that it is conducted in secret according to deliberately vague guidelines, that it has become the prerogative of the police and the prosecution, that it goes far beyond what is required to ensure that persons disqualified by law do not sit as jurors, and that it involves an invasion of the privacy of those summonsed to do a public service. Where checks are desirable, they should be made not by police officers involved in a particular case but by senior court staff, who could be given access to police computer records for the strictly limited purpose of ensuring that persons who attend in response to a jury summons do not have a conviction which disqualifies them. In a particular case where 'jury nobbling' is suspected, police checks may be legitimate as part of a general investigation. In view of the majority-verdict provisions, which permit one or two dissenters to be overridden, it should not (even in 'terrorist' cases) be necessary to check on the 'loyalty' or politics of potential jurors. As there is little prospect of this view being accepted by the present Government, the procedure for doing so should at least involve an application to the trial judge, after notice to the defence, so that the court can control both the obtaining of information and the use which is made of it.

The dangers of jury vetting are easy to exaggerate: there is no evidence that police or prosecutors regard membership of a left-wing branch of the Labour Party as indicative of political views so extreme as to disentitle a person to sit on a case involving security issues. However, so long as the situation remains unregulated other than by vague and unenforceable 'guidelines', that possibility can never be excluded. If it should ever happen, it is highly unlikely that it would come to be exposed.

Jury secrets

There is no aspect of the criminal law so bedevilled by myth and anecdote than the system of jury trial. Until 1981 it was possible to interview jurors and for them to write about their experiences: on the whole the results were reassuring, and confirmed the general experience of legal practitioners that juries approached their task in a serious and intelligent way and produced common-sense results. Most defendants who are committed to Crown Court for trial in fact plead guilty, and senior policemen who inveigh against high acquittal rates overlook the fact that almost half of those acquittals are directed by judges, on the basis of lack of sufficient evidence. A careful monitoring of jury verdicts in contested cases undertaken by the Oxford Penal Research Unit concluded that the great majority of acquittals were justified by the evidence, or the lack of it. After the much-publicized acquittal of Jeremy Thorpe on charges of conspiracy to murder, one juror gave an interview to the *New Statesman* explaining the decision, and the High Court refused to find that the journal had committed a contempt of court.[25] A new clause was speedily inserted in the Contempt of Court Act prohibiting any disclosure of jury deliberations, for whatever purpose. While some restriction was necessary to prevent newspapers purchasing juror memoirs, the clause is couched in blanket terms to ban even anonymous accounts of deliberations in unnamed trials. It effectively prohibits serious research into the ways in which juries arrive at their verdicts. It has not worked as its advocates predicted to protect the jury system from attack: on the contrary, it has imposed yet another layer of secrecy which handicaps those who would wish to defend the system with more than anecdotal evidence.

Recent attention to the composition of jury panels – the abolition of the right of defence challenge at the same time as the legitimization of methods of police vetting – may foreshadow further changes. In the United States, the search for unbiased jurors is taken so seriously that many weeks can be expended in questioning the panel so as to winnow out any hint of prejudice from beliefs or background or even 'body language' assessed by psychiatrists sitting in solemn attendance on trial counsel. This does not always assist the defence – it can enable the prosecution to exclude jurors who manifest that same independence of spirit which led to the acquittals of William Penn and Peter Zenger. We need to work towards a system which preserves the randomness of jury service, with built-in safeguards against jury panels that are unrepresentative in particular cases or that contain individuals whose occupations or commitments provide a clear reason to apprehend bias. To this end, the right to know occupations should be restored, any information available to the prosecution should be shared with the defence, and judges should be prepared to question jurors in general terms about any associations they might have which would make it difficult for them to keep an open mind. There are a number of precedents for ordering a fresh panel when the jurors initially summoned contain no members of the defendant's peer group: in cases where black youths alone are accused of riot or affray, for example, it is unseemly to have them tried by twelve white jurors. What must be preserved is the public acceptability of the jury verdict: justice must be seen to be done by representative and unbiased groups of citizens, and not by panels which are secretly manipulated behind the scenes or which appear to be wholly ignorant of the pressures and predicaments of the defendant's social environment. The jury system will never be fully appreciated until the secrecy provisions of the Contempt of Court Act are relaxed to allow jurors to speak more freely, at least to *bona fide* researchers.

TRIAL BY MAGISTRATES

The alternative to trial by jury is trial by stipendiary magistrate or lay Justices. Magistrates' courts dispose of over 95 per cent of criminal charges brought in England and Wales, and function additionally to decide whether there is sufficient evidence to commit cases for jury trial. Justices have important powers to decide whether to issue search and arrest warrants, make care orders in respect of children, and supervise payments of maintenance in family split-ups. These courts deal with half a million citizens each year, dispatching some 25,000 of them to prison and imposing fines in relation to upwards of two million offences. There are seventy full-time stipendiary magistrates – experienced lawyers who sit alone – and 24,000 unpaid amateur JPs who generally sit on twenty-six days a year in benches of two or three, advised by a legally qualified clerk. The lay Justice system goes back to the fourteenth century, when men were selected 'from amongst the most worthy of the locality' to punish blemishes of the parochial peace. Its reputation for common sense and guardianship of liberty is poor beside that of the jury, but it has weathered the ridicule of Shakespeare and Dickens, the fury of radicals and the contempt of historians to play what is currently an impregnable part in the administration of justice. It holds a monopoly over trials of routine public-order offences, and many cases of an intermediate category such as theft and possession of drugs may be tried by magistrates if the accused so elects. Lay justice has the undoubted virtues of cheapness and speed: its critics claim that it often lacks consistency and fairness.

Lay Justices certainly do not represent the class, race or age of those (other than motoring offenders) who beg for their mercy. They are overwhelmingly culled from the middle and upper classes – the most comprehensive study suggests that only 8 per cent can be described as 'working class'.[26] In 1984 a survey of the 150 Stockport Justices revealed an average age of fifty-three (the youngest was thirty-seven) dealing with offenders over half of whom were under twenty-one.[27] The reason for the imbalance lies partly in the voluntary nature of the service, which can attract Ladies Bountiful with time on their hands and deter workers whose employers are reluctant to give them time off for magisterial duties. Selection procedures have also been to blame. The names of members of local advisory committees are kept secret in order to protect them from lobbying, which simply means they are lobbied by those 'in the know'. (There are several examples of undue influence by organizations like the Freemasons or Rotary.) Too much attention has in the past been paid to recruitment from local political parties, business organizations and charities, and too little to the claims of welfare and minority groups. There is a gross underrepresentation of the black community: between 1962 and 1970 there were only fifteen black Justices, and as of 1 January 1988 there were 455 (1.9 per cent) out of a total of 23,730 active Justices. Outside large cities, the local bench 'must be seen as part of a series of overlapping networks of doing, belonging, leading people – who in any community must form a small though egregious minority'.[28]

But if the lay magistracy is unrepresentative, does this affect the quality of justice on offer in their courts? Not according to Sir Thomas Skyrme, former president of the Magistrates' Association:

If one may take account of comments made to me by wage earners who have become involved in court cases, it would seem that they prefer to be tried by someone who is not a member of their own class. The right of every Englishman to be tried by his peers is not of overriding importance on these occasions.[29]

The idea that the poor really prefer to be tried by posher people is novel, but is hardly borne out by the fact that they and their lawyers generally opt for trial by jury when the alternative is available, and the case involves a conflict between their evidence and that of police officers. After all, the essential legal task of fact-finding in such cases is to judge whether the defendant's story *might* be credible, and thereby raise a reasonable doubt. Correct assessment of that credibility depends upon some ability to stand in the defendant's shoes, to test the account as a matter of common sense, compassion and street wisdom. Twelve randomly selected jurors offer a better chance of correct judgement – or, at least, a lesser likelihood of wrongful conviction – than three local worthies. Advocates often notice that in cases where there exists, objectively, a reasonable doubt about guilt, lay Justices will convict (thereby 'supporting' the police) but reflect that doubt in handing down a lighter sentence than the tariff for the offence really requires.

In 1983 the Lord Chancellor's Department recognized that the social imbalance was serious enough to justify advertising in popular newspapers for 'ordinary people' to come forward as candidates. This was a welcome departure from the old-boy network, but the root problem remains of attracting wage-earners who fear that magisterial commitments will jeopardize their chances of promotion or of obtaining new jobs. Employers are bound by statute to give trade-union officials paid time off for union duties, but are under no similar obligation towards those of their workers who are JPs. They may take such time off as is 'reasonable in the circumstances' and are paid a small allowance for loss of earnings, but career and remuneration disincentives still make service on the Bench primarily a charitable service. Regrettably, local Labour parties do little to find and promote candidates, citing 'political disillusionment' with the system (this becomes, through their inaction, a self-fulfilling prophecy) while occasional instances of magistrates being dismissed for involvement in CND demonstrations do little to reassure them that appointment is even-handed. Less secrecy about the selection process, a more active search for candidates from minority groups, proper remuneration and statutory protection from discrimination in employment will all be necessary before the lay Bench is perceived as a people's court rather than a police court.

One factor which has led to concern over the even-handedness of lay justice is the emergence of disparate sentencing patterns in different parts of the country. The Bench in Blyth Valley gaols 1.6 per cent of its defendants, and in Bradford 6.1 per cent: in Newbury 22 per cent go inside and in Oxford 32 per cent. In 1987 the BBC's *Panorama* programme contrasted the penal policies of Benches in two neighbouring towns, where similar crimes were punished in the one place by invariable imprisonment and in the other by community service. The disparity reflected the attitude of the local court clerks – officers whose responsibility for selection and training of Justices and advising them on the law gives them an overweening influence on their local Bench. The influence of the court clerk is also seen in legal-aid refusal rates, which vary greatly from court to court, even within the same locality – in 1984 defendants were eight times more likely to receive legal aid at Hampstead than at neighbouring Highgate. Clerks are legally trained, and are called in to advise Justices on points of law when they retire to consider verdict or sentence – an unhappy practice which can give the impression that the clerk is playing a determinative part in the outcome. If Justices wish for legal advice, there is no reason why they should not return to court and obtain it in the presence of prosecution and defence lawyers.

Amateur justice has drawbacks other than the difficulty in obtaining representative Benches, the inevitable dominance of the clerk and the expenses of training. As criminal law becomes more complex, and as 'duty solicitor' schemes ensure that more defendants are represented, most contested cases generate legal arguments which lay Justices cannot be expected to resolve. Hearings are protracted, and rulings are increasingly appealed to the Divisional Court. Hence the preference, in major city areas, for stipendiary magistrates appointed from the ranks of experienced criminal practitioners. Their courts function more efficiently, and their rulings are less prone to error. The 'stipe' or 'beak' has had his detractors since the days of Dickens's Mr Fang (within whose court 'enough fantastic tricks are daily played to make the angels blind with weeping') but recent appointments have been of higher quality and hold out hope that the stipendiary magistracy will become a greater bulwark of the liberty of the subject than it has appeared in the past. This optimism is not shared by Lord Gifford, who describes stipendiaries as 'case-hardened individuals who can be relied on to favour the police against the defence. Their number should be kept to a minimum.'[30] What should be kept to a minimum are imprisonable offences which carry no right to jury trial: stipendiaries who have had experience of both prosecuting and defending criminal cases are on the whole more likely to detect disingenuousness and dishonesty in police evidence than local worthies summoned from desirable residences to judge those who live on the wrong side of the tracks.

MISCARRIAGES OF JUSTICE

No system of justice is infallible. No matter how careful the investigation, how capable the lawyers and how conscientious the jury, mistakes will sometimes be made. Errors by magistrates, confirmed on appeal by circuit judges, may rankle and dog a defendant, who will at least be at liberty to complain to the Home Office, which may grant a 'royal pardon' if he can furnish absolute proof of innocence. But for the long-term prisoner whose appeal on points of law has failed, the jury verdict is almost impossible to dislodge unless a book or television programme or retired Law Lords take up the case and persuade the Home Secretary to make a 'reference back' to the Court of Appeal. Over the ten years ending in 1981, twenty-one convictions were quashed on references back to the Court of Appeal, and nine free pardons were granted – an officially recognized average of one serious miscarriage of justice per year. Yet Justice, the organization with most experience of the matter, estimates that some 200 innocent people are annually sentenced to lengthy terms of imprisonment. One of the most serious criticisms of the British criminal-justice system is its failure to provide a satisfactory safety-net for cases which go wrong. Even on the rare occasions when such cases are identified and 'offenders' are pardoned, they have no right to sue for damages for the years of wrongful imprisonment they have suffered. The Home Office will offer an *ex gratia* payment' which rarely reflects reasonable compensation for lost years in prison.

There are a number of well-authenticated reasons why justice can miscarry. They include:

(1) The possibility that the strongest circumstantial evidence will convincingly point to an innocent person. Sir Henry Fisher, a former High Court judge who fully and fairly investigated the circumstances of the Confait murder, concluded that two of the three boys convicted were guilty. Shortly after his report was published, the real murderer was identified and both boys were cleared.

(2) Many innocent persons are convicted on the strength of apparently reliable confessions to police. Occasionally, these are fabricated 'verbals'. More often, they are falsely volunteered in custody through fear or mental breakdown or in a desire to curry favour with police custodians.

(3) Evidence of identification is notoriously unreliable, because identifying witnesses genuinely believe the evidence of their eyes and cannot be shaken by cross-examination.

(4) The conclusions of Home Office forensic scientists and pathologists can be invested with a scientific certainty which subsequent discoveries show to be unsound. 'Experts' can display gross professional incompetence – a finding made in respect of Home Office scientist Dr Alan Clift in 1977, and which led to the quashing of several convictions (including one of murder) obtained on the strength of his erroneous findings.

(5) Innocent defendants who are jointly tried with those who are palpably part of a conspiracy can suffer 'guilt by association'. It is not always easy for juries to disentangle the evidence and obey directions to put out of their mind implications in lying statements by co-defendants.

(6) Failure by police to make available all the evidence in their possession to the defence has been a cause of several notorious miscarriages: clues which point to innocence sometimes lurk in statements by witnesses whose existence is not known to the defence.

(7) The 'tit for tat' rule of cross-examination, whereby defendants who attack – sometimes truthfully – the credibility of police or other prosecution witnesses face the prospect of their own past criminal record (which would normally be excluded from evidence) being put before the jury if they step into the witness box. If they put their defence in full to the jury, they will suffer from the prejudice of having their past record

revealed. Thus tactics can become more important than truth for those with bad criminal records who are in fact innocent of the charges they are facing. As it is often a previous conviction for a similar crime which arouses police suspicion against an innocent person in the first place, the 'tit for tat' rule underlines the adage 'give a dog a bad name and hang him'.

(8) Some defences are not properly prepared by solicitors, who may be incompetent, straight-jacketed by legal-aid limitations or simply lacking in the imagination or resources to do the necessary detective work on behalf of clients locked in prison prior to trial. Occasionally, too, late delivery or return of briefs, inexperience, tactical blunders or failure to grasp some important aspect of the case may affect a barrister's performance.

In trials where several of those factors are at work, there is a risk of convicting the innocent. To that risk must be added the danger of a prosecution-minded judge or a prejudiced jury. For all the public veneration of jury trial, panels can be affected by passions and prejudices against unpopular defendants. One study analysed 300 contested Crown Court trials in London and Birmingham, and concluded that sixteen of the convictions – 5 per cent of the sample – were 'doubtful', in the sense that the trial judge, the prosecution solicitor and the police officers involved in the case thought that a 'reasonable doubt' had emerged by the end of the evidence.[31] Most of these defendants were sentenced to prison, and only two of them appealed, both unsuccessfully. This same study discovered a serious underrepresentation of black jurors in the Birmingham courts, and noted that half of those who had been 'doubtfully convicted' were black.

Given that the adversarial system of trial produces, each year, a significant number of wrongful convictions, it might be expected that the criminal justice system would provide some form of long-stop – an agency empowered to investigate all the evidence in doubtful cases and to recommend release when those doubts magnify alarmingly. The Court of Appeal, however, cannot act in this capacity. It has no investigative staff, and its function is limited to assessing the reliability of the trial record. Most appeals succeed, not on merit, but because the trial judge has misstated the law or permitted a technical irregularity. Jury verdicts are notoriously difficult to dislodge: rarely do appeals succeed on the grounds that the verdict is against the weight of the evidence. The court is reluctant to assess 'fresh evidence' not placed before the court of trial, unless it is clearly material which could not have been discovered at the time by diligent defence solicitors. In such cases, the defendant will be penalized for the inadequacies of his lawyers (or, more often, the inadequacies of the legal-aid system which may not have covered the cost of adducing the evidence at the trial). There are good reasons for limiting the Court of Appeal to a review of the written record, but these very reasons make it imperative that some other agency should exist to go behind the transcripts and to examine the whole case afresh, when serious doubts have been raised.

The only recourse after appeal for an innocent prisoner is to petition the Home Office, whose C 5 Division employs a dozen officials to sift the documentary evidence. It has no trained investigators, does not even interview the prisoner, and turns down the vast majority of petitions without giving reasons. It adopts a narrow, legalistic test for deciding whether to refer a case back to the Court of Appeal: the prisoner must advance 'convincing grounds for thinking he is innocent'. On this test, it has turned down the petitions of a number of prisoners who were subsequently proved to be innocent by the BBC's *Rough Justice* team.[32] Even when a reference back is made – generally on powerful evidence and after political pressure – the Court of Appeal must in the end ask itself a subjective question, 'whether we are content to let the matter stand as it is, or whether there is not some lurking doubt in our mind which makes us wonder whether an injustice has been done'.[33] In the words of Viscount Dilhorne in *R. v. Stafford & Luvaglio*, 'this is a reaction which may not be based strictly on the evidence as such; it is a reaction which can be produced by the general feel of the case as the court experiences it'.[34] It is the 'general feel' of three appellate judges as to whether they are content with the conviction, and not the question of whether the original jury might have been content to convict had it known the full story, which will decide the fate of cases referred back by the Home Secretary. Lord Devlin, the most stringent critic of this approach, argues that it undermines the principle of trial by jury. Whenever a conviction is reopened, the test must be related to the effect of fresh evidence on the minds of a jury, and not to some 'general feel' about the case entertained by appellate judges.[35]

The problem with the 'reference back' procedure is that it raises expectations that it cannot fulfil. The judges decline, reasonably enough, to turn themselves into a public inquiry: they have no investigatory powers. The evidence put before them is still confined by rules of admissibility, rather than the need to get at the truth. They are naturally predisposed towards believing that the system has worked: to shake their faith in a conviction requires some convincing proof. By adopting the test of whether fresh evidence and analysis shakes their faith, rather than the test of whether it might well have induced a reasonable doubt in the minds of a trial jury, they are led to uphold a number of convictions in relation to which reasonable doubts abound in the minds of intelligent observers. Such was the public disquiet over the failure of two references back to the Court of Appeal in the Luton Post Office murder case that the Home Secretary eventually took it upon himself to release two men, Cooper and McMahon, from the life sentences they were serving. Public clamour, of course, is confined to sensational cases, generally of murder, which are taken up by MPs or investigative journalists: it took representations from the Irish Government to obtain a 'reference back' for the men convicted of planting the Birmingham bombs. Those who may have been wrongly convicted of lesser offences have little chance of being afforded even the opportunity to have their protests judicially considered.

So what should be done to provide the safety net that is so clearly needed to identify, investigate and rectify miscarriages of justice? One obvious area for improvement lies in Home Office procedures. The Devlin Committee, which investigated cases in which innocent men were convicted on the strength of false identifications, recommended that the Home Office should commence an inquiry whenever fresh evidence raised genuine doubts about 'guilty' verdicts,[36] and in 1986 the House of Commons Home Affairs Committee issued a report in which it urged the Home Office to interview petitioners, give reasons for rejecting petitions and hasten its investigations. It pointed out that under the present system, 'decisions of vital importance to the liberty of the individual were carried out in private, sometimes after unexplained delays and that no reasons were given to support the rejection of the complainant's allegations'.[37] The Government's response even to these mild suggestions was lukewarm and there is no doubt that the situation will remain both secret and inadequate until responsibility is taken away from the Home Office and from the Court of Appeal. A new institution – a 'Court of last resort' – must be established.

The Devlin Committee proposed an Independent Review Tribunal, unfettered by the evidential rules restricting the Court of Appeal. The Home Affairs Committee endorsed and elaborated the proposal: the Tribunal should have an investigative staff and the power to hold public hearings. It would report to the Home Secretary, who would invoke the royal prerogative of a free pardon on the basis of Tribunal recommendations. The 'reference back' procedure would cease to operate, other than in cases turning on questions of law. Regrettably, the Government responded with a glib White Paper which rejected any need for an independent safety-net.[38] It argued that miscarriages of justice in the judicial system should be handled within that system, and offered no more than that the Home Secretary would show greater willingness to refer cases back to the Court of Appeal (which has no investigative powers) and to order further police investigations (generally undertaken by the same police force which is alleged to have made the original mistake). The promise that more cases would be 'referred back' has been proved false. In the four years since it was given, only four cases annually have been selected for Court of Appeal review, compared with an average of five cases a year in the decade prior to publication of the White Paper. Given this intransigence, a 'trial by media' is likely to remain the only remedy where a trial by jury has miscarried.

NINE

Freedom of Movement

As I went aboard the steamer I asked myself with anxiety under which flag would she sail – Norwegian, German, English? And then I saw floating above the stern the Union Jack, the flag under which so many refugees, Italian, French, Hungarian and of all nations have found an asylum. I greeted that flag as from the depths of my heart.

Prince Kropotkin (1899)[1]

Although British citizens have no legally enforceable right to move freely about the United Kingdom or to travel abroad, Government interference with their freedom to do so has been minimal. The Prevention of Terrorism Act is responsible for turning back or removing to Northern Ireland hundreds each year who are 'suspected' (without hard proof) of being sympathetic to terrorism and are somewhat irrationally viewed as being of greater danger on the mainland than at home in the province. Police peace-keeping powers may be used to stop people travelling to demonstrations (see earlier, page 77) and there have been occasions when the Foreign Office has declined to issue passports to citizens wishing to travel abroad for politically unattractive purposes. But it is the freedom to enter Britain for settlement which has been massively restricted in recent years, as the result of a wider political debate which has been racist in both rhetoric and result. The two principal statutes, the Immigration Act of 1971 and the British Nationality Act of 1981, together with the all-important Immigration Rules, effectively throw a *cordon sanitaire* around the country, which may be breached permanently only by those who prove close family affinity with British citizens or who have claims to political asylum or refugee status, or whose wealth or special skills give a privileged route to settlement. The weapons of deportation and removal are widely used to extirpate those who 'overstay' or have entered unlawfully, and sometimes to rid the country of aliens whose political activities are regarded by the Government as non-conducive to the public good. The power of extradition is also available, with dwindling legal safeguards, to remove persons resident in Britain for trial in foreign States on charges of serious crime. Although 'political' offences were long regarded as non-extraditable, the rise of international terrorism has led to domestic laws, implementing international conventions, which severely restrict this historic exemption.

Every nation has the right to limit entry and to decide, subject to international conventions, to whom it shall afford shelter or the protection of citizenship. Historically, the United Kingdom has a more liberal record than most: the blue plaques around London bear testimony to the home it once was to Marx, Mazzini, Garibaldi, Lenin, Engels, Kropotkin, Kossuth and Sun Yat-sen. Although some of their modern counterparts would today be deported as undesirable aliens, the liberal tradition survives in respect of those refugees who can persuade an increasingly unsympathetic Home Office that their fear of persecution is well founded. But it survives as a political rather than a legal judgement: the courts are unable to interfere with the Home Secretary's decision unless it is manifestly irrational. The twin features of modern immigration control are administrative discretion and administrative secrecy: the broadest of legal powers are bestowed upon officials, who exercise them according to secret guidelines approving procedures (such as the X-raying of children and 'virginity tests') which cannot be justified once they see the light of day. Officially approved immigration after the war brought the challenges and the benefits of a multiracial country: lack of compassion (especially towards the reuniting of families) in administering immigration rules has proved a potent factor in exacerbating racial tensions. Both Labour and Conservative Governments are responsible for the present set of controls, which allegedly provide a 'fair but firm' basis for administration. Of the firmness there can be no doubt: this chapter will consider the claim of 'fairness', and the limited extent to which the law is available to promote it.

THE HISTORY OF IMMIGRATION CONTROL

The main shifts in immigration control in this century have come about as the result of war, entry into the European Community and the end of the British Empire. Nineteenth-century Britain was a confident country which exuded sympathy for those struggling against despised European monarchs, but this long tradition of tolerance ended in 1905, as a result of Jewish migration after the pogroms in Russia and Eastern Europe. The Aliens Act of that year was passed by a Conservative Government which found political mileage in anti-Semitism and workers' fears about competition for jobs. Henceforth, alien immigrants 'likely to become a charge on the rates' could be excluded, although refugees were excepted and immigration officers were required to set out full reasons in writing for refusing leave to land and there was a right of appeal to a Tribunal. Forty per cent of appeals were successful, but this brief experiment in fairness was ended by the Aliens Restriction Act of 1914, an oppressive piece of war hysteria rushed through all stages in Parliament in one day. It gave the Home Secretary untrammelled power to exclude and expel aliens, without any rights of appeal or even the right to make representations, and without any protection for refugees. Although described as a 'temporary measure', it was re-enacted after the war and then extended each year until 1969, and deployed as the spirit of the time (and the need for skilled workers) appeared to the Home Secretary.

Commonwealth citizens, meanwhile, enjoyed at common law a virtually automatic right of entry. There was a shortage of labour after the Second World War, and immigrants from the Caribbean and Asian colonies were encouraged to do the 'dirty jobs' of the 1950s, and in due course became scapegoats for fears about jobs and housing. In 1962, the Government introduced the Commonwealth Immigrants Act, a measure to deal with the 'troublesome phenomenon' of recent racial disturbances (by whites) in Notting Hill and elsewhere. It instituted a system of work vouchers, but it did not affect those who carried British passports – a precaution taken out by many Asians in East Africa as their countries prepared for independence. In the following years, as their fears of discrimination became well founded, they applied to enter Britain. Some 200,000 Kenyan Asians were principally involved, and the prospect of their arrival unleashed the racist passions and predictions of Enoch

Powell's 'rivers of blood' speech. Secret reports in 1967 predicted further large-scale expulsions of Asians from East Africa, and caused the Government to make what Richard Crossman was subsequently to describe as 'plans for legislation which we realized would have been declared unconstitutional in any country with a written constitution and a Supreme Court'.[2]

This legislation took the form of the Commonwealth Immigrants Act of 1968, which was passed through both Houses of Parliament in thirty-six hours. It was a dishonest, unjust and racist measure, later condemned as degrading and discriminating by the European Commission of Human Rights. It was designed to dishonour promises of citizenship previously made to East African Asians, but in doing so it adopted a formula which is now applied across-the-board to would-be immigrants from outside the EEC. The formula is that of ancestral connection (termed 'patriality') made by reference to parental or grandparental birth or naturalization in the United Kingdom. For the purposes of 1968, this had the advantage of discriminating against Kenyan Asians in favour of white settlers, without actually using discriminatory language. The European Commission, in its *East African Asians* decision of 1973, found that the Kenyan and Ugandan Asians holding British passports who were refused entry under the Act had been the victims of degrading treatment by virtue of legislation which intentionally discriminated by dispossessing them of a right to enter which they had been led reasonably to expect.[3] By that time, however, the patriality formula had become the basis of the main immigration measure, the 1971 Immigration Act.

This measure (together with the Rules and the 1981 British Nationality Act) is inordinately complicated, and its detailed provisions are outside the scope of this book.[4] In general terms, it places Commonwealth citizens on the same footing as other foreigners, save for citizens of EEC countries who have special rights of entry under the Treaty of Rome. Ironically, given the extent to which the fear of immigrants taking jobs was exploited in order to close the door on Asians, accession to the Common Market with its philosophy of freedom of movement has meant that business people, workers and self-employed may enter from EEC countries without let or hindrance, with their families, and remain even after their work has ceased. Immigrants from the Commonwealth, and from countries outside the EEC, are subject to stringent immigration control unless they are British citizens either through birth in the UK or through having a UK-born parent (in some cases, grandparent) or through naturalization or through having been settled in the UK for substantial periods prior to the 1971 Act. This effectively removes the 'right of abode' in Britain from most Commonwealth citizens: it bears disproportionately on blacks, although it also affects the migration of many whites from the 'old' Commonwealth. The citizenship arrangements made by the 1981 British Nationality Act were designed with the hand-over of Hong Kong to the Chinese very much in mind: citizenship of 'British Dependent Territories' carries no right of abode in the United Kingdom for those without at least grandparental connections. This measure also precluded many Falklanders from settling in Britain, and was one of the 'signals' that made Argentinian generals think that Britain would not resist their invasion of the islands the following year. In 1983, the Government found that the logic of its 1981 Act was impaled on the Prime Minister's rhetoric that the islanders were British to their boot-straps: the British Nationality (Falkland Islands) Act of that year specially extended full-blooded British citizenship to all of them. There will be no such indulgence to the Chinese in Hong Kong, irrespective of any re-criminations they may in turn suffer after the lease of the territory is surrendered. The most drastic change made by the 1981 Act was removal of the centuries-old principle that birth in Britain was sufficient for citizenship. This simple and symbolic test has been replaced with a patriality requirement.

Those who do not qualify for citizenship may of course obtain it by naturalization (usually by marriage or by a period of at least five years' lawful residence) or in certain circumstances by registration – a slow process without the fair political wind which set an immigration record for South African sprinter Zola Budd in 1984. Would-be immigrants are at the mercy of the rules and the administrative 'guidelines' which implement them. A voucher system is operated to allow limited immigration (currently 5,000 heads of households a year) by those holding UK passports who live in the Indian subcontinent. Most have been forced out of East Africa, and must queue for many years before their turn to enter comes. Their treatment contrasts remarkably with the one remaining permissive immigration rule, which permits residence to 'persons of independent means' who have amassed (however dishonourably) capital of at least £150,000 which they bring into the country. In this respect, at least, the colour of an immigrant's money has replaced the colour of his skin as the test for welcome: crooked South American generals, Australian media moguls, Arab princes and Asian millionaires may purchase with little difficulty the right to settle in the UK.

FAMILY LIFE AND PRIVACY

Immigration policy must primarily be determined by political considerations, but its implementation should respect the fundamental rights of those who live or are permitted to settle in Britain. The worst features of the implementation of the Immigration Rules have stemmed from failures to respect the rights to family life and to privacy. On an administrative level, examples are provided by long delays in processing applications and the rigorous and intrusive questioning which often accompanied them. X-rays have been done on the bone structure of children to determine age, and 'virginity tests' carried out on the assumption that Asian women who failed the test were likely to be married already. Both practices were authorized by secret guidelines, and were discontinued after public outcry. One particularly insensitive provision in the Immigration Rules precludes entry to men who intend to marry women already settled here unless the entry clearance officer 'is satisfied that the parties to the proposed marriage have met' – an attitude to arranged marriages which, in Lord Scarman's words, implies 'an attack on the social habits and custom of people who have come to this country and who are living according to the customs in which they were brought up'.[5] A requirement which subverts European notions of family life is the rule which allows the exclusion of dependent relations if they would require some maintenance from public funds, e.g. by claiming supplementary benefits or housing benefits. In the absence of a written constitution or a Bill of Rights which entrenches entitlement to family life, British courts are powerless to strike down decisions by immigration officers which have the result of keeping families apart.

The rule which has caused most anguish is the 'primary purpose' test for the entry of a spouse. There is nothing wrong in principle with the requirement that the parties should intend to live together as man and wife, but the Rules now additionally place the burden on the applicants to prove 'that the marriage was not entered into primarily to obtain admission to the UK'. The 'primary purpose' rule and the burden of proving it allow hundreds of spouses and fiancées to be turned back each year on mere suspicion. It has been used to justify the most intimate and intrusive questioning of applicants, by customs officers who sometimes seem to hold a Mills & Boon view of personal relationships. One applicant was turned down in 1984 because his letters were not 'sufficiently affectionate', while those who honestly hesitate over the sixty-four-dollar question, 'If your fiancée did not live in England, would you still go to her home to live?', are turned away.

The 'primary purpose' test was originally applied only to men who wished to marry women settled in Britain, but in 1985 the European Court ruled that this amounted to sex discrimination.[6] The Government responded by applying the test to women seeking entry as well. Where entry is permitted the marriage is subject to a 'probation period' of twelve months, with deportation for those who do not display sufficient commitment by the end of that period. This limited respect for family life is extended only in the context of marriage: the Immigration Rules recognize no other relationships, however successful or permanent (although there is discretion to admit a woman whose unmarried permanent relationship with a man is established 'by a local custom or tradition'). Local British custom and tradition was vindicated by the 1988 Immigration Act which precluded a wife of a polygamous marriage from exercising her right of abode if another wife preceded her into the United Kingdom. Needless to say the Rules are entirely silent about the plight of homosexual couples: British citizens have no entitlement to be joined by foreign lovers of the same sex.

Rules relating to the entry of 'dependants' are even more strict. Children may not join their parents if they are aged over eighteen. Elderly parents and other close relatives are not permitted entry to settle with their children unless they have become 'wholly or mainly dependent' on these children, are over sixty-five and have no other relations to turn to in their present place of residence. 'Dependence' means financial dependence, and not 'the normal love and affection of a united family'.[7] Even temporary reunion of families may be prevented where immigration officers have any suspicion that a visitor may 'overstay'. The introduction of visa requirements for visitors from the Indian subcontinent and Nigeria in 1986 led to 11,575 visa refusals in the first six months of the system's operation. A similar number of visitors are refused entry each year, and the Government has recently taken powers to fine airlines which permit passengers to travel to Britain without the proper entry documents. A particularly agonizing problem arises when husbands settled in this country die or decide to leave it or to end their marriage before members of their families have been granted permanent-residence status. In these circumstances, the wife and children will generally have to leave, especially if they cannot maintain themselves without 'recourse to public funds'. In 1984 the European Parliament condemned as callous the decision to deport a wife and family whose husband was killed in a fire. The assumption in many of these 'family deportation' cases is that the wife is a mere appendage, and the links that she and her children forge with a local community count for little once their 'bread-winner' has been removed.[8]

Literal compliance with these Rules can appear heartless to severed families, and although discretion to decide compassionately exists at every level there is little doubt that indulgence is more readily extended to white immigrants than to blacks and Asians. This is a major cause of the bitterness and anger which exists within ethnic communities in Britain, and the limitations of the appeal system have done little to defuse it. The appeal system is in two stages: first to an adjudicator, and then to the Immigration Appeals Tribunal. The major deficiency is that most people refused entry clearance, either in their place of residence or by being turned away on arrival, will not be in Britain to prepare or present their appeal. Unless the claim is for patriality or the applicant has already obtained a work permit or entry clearance, the appeal will have to be mounted from abroad.[9] Communication with lawyers will be difficult, and as Lord Bridge recently noted 'the person removed, being unable to attend the hearing of his appeal, has no realistic prospect of presenting it with success'.[10]

To help immigration officials decide whether and on what terms entry will be granted, they possess wide powers to detain and examine passengers, take copies of their correspondence, and order airlines and shipping companies to remove immediately those they reject. Regrettably, there is no 'duty solicitor' scheme for those detained at British ports: the only protection is an ancient, traditional right of Members of Parliament to intervene and request a 'stop' on a removal until the MP has time to make representations to the Home Secretary. This power was valuable, in that it enabled detainees to obtain legal advice and allowed information to be produced which leads to an official rethink, but in 1988 this privilege (which rested only on convention) was severely restricted. MPs' intercessions are now limited to requesting a review (if they are quick enough) of decisions to send visitors back on the next plane. Such decisions will only be reversed in 'compelling circumstances'.

DEPORTATION

The extirpation from a country of persons settled within its borders is the most direct infringement of freedom of movement: it requires the clearest justification and unobstructed rights of appeal. In the United Kingdom expulsion may be accomplished:

(a) by administrative directions to expel illegal immigrants;

(b) by deportation of those who 'overstay' or fail to observe other conditions of entry;

(c) by deportation on the recommendation of a court after conviction for a criminal offence;

(d) by deportation deemed 'conducive to the public good' by the Home Secretary;

(e) by extradition at the request of foreign countries to stand trial for alleged crimes abroad.

Removal of allegedly illegal immigrants by administrative direction is drastic, in that rights of appeal cannot be exercised except after removal, when they are virtually valueless. An 'illegal immigrant' is one who has secretly entered the country without passing through immigration control, or has presented false documents or otherwise secured entry by fraud. In 1980 the House of Lords extended this category alarmingly by ruling that it included persons who had not made full disclosure of every relevant fact to immigration officers, but this decision (which meant that jet-lagged applicants had a legal duty to answer questions they were never asked) met with an avalanche of criticism and was reversed three years later by *Khawaja*.[11] In that case the Law Lords opted for 'a robust exercise of the judicial function in safeguarding citizens' rights' against detention and removal without proper rights of appeal. The Government has not shown similar robustness in extending a right of appeal to persons detained on the allegation of being an illegal entrant. Another unattractive incident of the power is the way it is sometimes exercised by 'rounding up' members of ethnic communities in raids on homes, factories and supermarkets, and detaining them in custody until the legality of their status has been established. Detention usually lasts for several months before removal: supervision is privately contracted to Securicor, whose employees are not subject to police-discipline codes. It amounts to imprisonment without trial and without a right of appeal.

Deportation for overstaying in breach of entry conditions is subject to a right of appeal to an adjudicator and then to the Immigration Appeals Tribunal (IAT). Although it is the normal result of remaining in the country without authorization, the Home Secretary none the less has a general discretion not to make a deportation order when the circumstances warrant compassion or recognition of good character or close connections with the UK. The courts have ruled that the Home Secretary should consider the effect of the deportation on third parties, and in some cases upon the local community. A deportation order made by a court as part of the sentence for a criminal offence may be appealed through the court system, and is in any event no more than a recommendation upon which the Home Secretary is not obliged to act – he is enjoined by the Rules to take 'all relevant circumstances' into account, including representations, before giving effect to it. Deportation recommendations, the Court of Appeal has recently stressed, are serious matters, requiring 'full and proper inquiry' to produce evidence that the offender's continuing presence would be a potential detriment to the country. Where EEC nationals stand convicted, a deportation order must not be made unless they constitute a real threat to public order and security,[12] and in the case of other aliens minor offences do not justify a recommendation unless there is a gang element or a likelihood of more serious repetition.[13]

Despite these self-denying ordinances, there have been occasions when magistrates' courts have succumbed to the temptation to rid the country of foreign students convicted of minor offences in the course of demonstrating support for unpopular causes. Particularly bad examples were set by London magistrates who made mass deportation recommendations against Iranian and Libyan students, many of whom had been convicted of no more than minor obstruction offences outside the United States Embassy. Immigrants should not have their right to protest chilled by the possibility of expulsion for an offence of highway obstruction committed by most trade-union picketers, and in these instances the magistrates were made to look foolish when the deportees delightedly accepted free trips back to Tehran and Tripoli to receive acclamation on their arrival. Most offenders, of course, will not relish their homecoming, and may in some cases be subjected to persecution on political grounds. The Court of Appeal has emphasized that such considerations are irrelevant to the judicial decision to recommend deportation: they are 'political' matters of which the Home Secretary must alone be judge. This is one of many points in immigration law where the courts shrink from impinging upon the Government's exclusive prerogative to decide 'political' questions, although it might be thought that a judge is a better tribunal to decide, on evidence, whether an individual is likely to be persecuted on return to a particular country than the Home Secretary, who may be swayed by considerations of diplomacy rather than justice. An immigrant offender who has successfully argued against a court recommendation stands in the double jeopardy of being deported in any event by the Home Secretary, on the ground that his presence is 'not conducive to the public good' – a catch-all category that can be used to punish conduct which is undesirable but not illegal, or persons suspected of crime which cannot be proved in court. There is a right of appeal to the I A T, except where this power is exercised on national security grounds.

POLITICAL EXPULSIONS

The Home Secretary's power to expel aliens where he deems this 'conducive to the public good' was used during the Cold War years to deport American Communists, and in 1965 the Labour Government deported an American pacifist who was a member of the 'Committee of 100'. There was no right of appeal, and the court's attitude to natural justice in security matters was exemplified in 1962 in the case of Dr Soblen, who had been convicted of espionage in the USA after a trial much criticized for its unfairness. Soblen fled to Israel prior to sentence, where pressure from the US Government soon had him put back on a plane bound for New York. Over British air space he slashed his wrists, and he was landed and hospitalized in London. Under extradition law Soblen was safe – he was a political offender. But Washington's wish for his return was the British Home Secretary's command, and a deportation order was made on the ground that his presence – thus far confined to a prison hospital – was 'not conducive to the public good'. His application for *habeas corpus* was rejected by the Court of Appeal, on the basis that deportation was purely an administrative action and he had no right to make representations or to any other of the other protections normally afforded by the rules of natural justice.[14] The order could only be challenged if it was made in bad faith, i.e. as a device to achieve an illegitimate extradition requested by the United States Government. US Embassy officials had admitted as much to *The Times*, but its articles were not evidence. The crucial documents were the exchange of correspondence between the two Governments, and this the court refused to order to be disclosed, on the grounds of national interest. Soblen committed suicide on the morning he was due to be escorted to the airport by a US police officer.

The denial of natural justice to Soblen was a factor in the Wilson Committee recommendation, a few years later, that 'security' cases should not be exempt from the fundamental principle that 'any administrative decision should be subject to scrutiny and appeal before execution'. It accepted that the Tribunal might have to hear evidence in camera, 'but there would be no question of withholding from the appellant particulars of what is alleged against him'.[15] But when the Labour Government came to implement the Wilson Report by setting up an immigration appeals machinery, it provided that appeals in security cases were to be heard by a specially vetted panel whose judgement would not be binding on the Home Secretary.

This short-lived attempt to do a little justice in national security cases was soon tested when the incoming Conservative Home Secretary, Reginald Maudling, desired to rid the country of Rudi Dutschke. Once a radical student leader in Germany, Dutschke had been allowed entry to convalesce from an assassination attempt, and had been offered a research post at Cambridge. At his appeal, it was alleged he had engaged in political activities in this country, and some of the evidence against him was inspected by the Tribunal in secret. None the less he was given a 2,500-word statement of the case against him, which he was able to challenge with a large measure of success. Indeed, the Tribunal found that he had the qualities to make a 'significant contribution to historical research' and that 'up to the present time his presence in this country has not constituted an appreciable danger to national security'. But then, blandly and illogically, it ventured the view that 'there must be a risk in his continued presence', and Maudling confirmed the deportation order, expressing the fear that Dutschke might become 'a focal point for student and political unrest'. The obvious unfairness of this decision caused justified outrage and demands for changes in the composition of the Tribunal, which included two retired diplomats and a Deputy Chief of the Defence Staff.

But this was not the lesson taken to heart by the Home Secretary. Acting on the principle that the less that is known the less there will be to complain about, he abolished the right of appeal altogether in security cases. The 1971 Immigration Rules now permit only 'representations' to a civil service panel of 'three wise men' which proffers 'advice' to the Home Secretary in secret. The Government had been criticized for not allowing Dutschke to see *all* the evidence against him, so its solution was to allow others no right to see *any* of the evidence. Maudling claimed that the 'three wise men' system had worked well in civil-service 'purge' cases, which it had not (see earlier, page 168) and that the convention of the Home Secretary's responsibility to Parliament would be a safeguard against abuse of power, which it is not, for the simple reason that there is another convention which entitles Ministers to refuse to answer questions about decisions taken on security grounds.

The Labour Party, to its discredit, supported the abolition of appeal rights, and made first use of the new system to deport Philip Agee and Mark Hosenball. Agee was an ex-CIA officer living in Cambridge and writing books exposing his former employers, whilst Hosenball was an experienced journalist working for the *Evening Standard*. Agee had no secrets relating to British intelligence, and was not infringing US law: the damage he was doing to a friendly intelligence agency was presumably thought sufficient to justify his expulsion. Hosenball was given no information at all as to the reason his presence was not conducive to the public good. Both men attended at secret hearings of the 'three advisers' to recite their life stories: they were given no opportunity to cross-examine witnesses or to learn, let alone to test, the evidence against them. The 'three wise men' comprised a solicitor who had served in the security service, a retired civil servant who had formerly been Permanent Secretary to the Admiralty, and a retired Post Office official. It is not known how they 'advised' the Home Secretary, but both deportation orders were confirmed.

Hosenball appealed on the grounds that he had been denied natural justice by the Home Secretary's refusal to give him any details of the case against him. The Court of Appeal conceded readily enough that he had been the victim of an unjust proceeding, but the rules of 'natural justice' were not to be applied to deportation decisions taken by the Home Secretary on 'national security' grounds. Lord Denning delivered the most regrettable judgement of his career, sacrificing legality, fairness and equality in favour of blind obedience to Government claims of 'national security' ('The rules of natural justice have to be modified in regard to foreigners who prove themselves unwelcome and ought to be deported').[16] His words are enthusiastically quoted by counsel for repressive regimes throughout the common-law world which deport their critics. Hosenball has for the past ten years been working as a Washington correspondent for the *Sunday Times*: he is still not permitted to re-enter the country.

There have been several deportations on grounds of national security since the Hosenball case.[17] The Home Secretary has attempted to boost the image of the 'three wise men' by including a senior judge, but the unsatisfactory nature of the procedure remains. The Tribunal's advice is not disclosed, and is in any event not binding on the Home Secretary.

The Home Secretary has an unappealable power to direct that foreigners should not be allowed to enter the UK on the grounds that their presence would not be conducive to the public good. In the late sixties and early seventies this power was used to stop North Vietnamese politicians, European student leaders, Marxist professors and American radicals from entering the country to speak at political gatherings, and until 1980 it was regularly invoked against Scientologists. In the case of EEC nationals the power must not be used unless the person poses a clear danger to public health or order, but otherwise the Home Secretary has an absolute discretion to exclude any individual whose life-style or beliefs might outrage the British public. The most recent, and most ridiculous, exercise of the power was to stop an Oxford University debate in 1986 between Professor Timothy Leary, jaded apostle of sixties radicalism, and Gordon Liddy, defender of executive secrecy who organized the 'Watergate' break-in. These two had performed double-act debates across American campuses, but the Home Office had no doubt about which side was most conducive to British public good: Liddy was allowed to enter and Leary was turned away.

POLITICAL ASYLUM

The United Kingdom is a signatory to the Convention and Protocol relating to the status of refugees, which the Immigration Rules reflect by providing that applications for asylum may be made by any person

> on the ground that, if he were required to leave, he would have to go to a country to which he is unwilling to go owing to a well-founded fear of being persecuted for reasons of race, religion, nationality, membership of a particular social group or political opinion.

Applications for asylum and for refugee status are no exception to the general principle of immigration law that decisions are to be made by the Home Office, subject to such rights of appeal as may exist to the adjudicator and to the IAT. The question for the Home Office is whether the applicant would suffer persecution, and if this is determined in his favour, he is entitled to remain. The courts will not second-guess the Home Secretary, and exercise only a supervisory jurisdiction to ensure that his decisions are made rationally, with procedural fairness, and take cognizance of all relevant factors. The courts have at least been able to stop the Home Office in some cases from returning applicants already here, before their cases are heard, although they are powerless to prevent asylum seekers from being turned away at points of entry and even put on board planes returning them to persecution. This behaviour, which is immoral given that the returnee's life could be at stake, is contrary to the fundamental principle endorsed by the UN High Commissioner for Refugees that applicants for asylum should be permitted to remain in the country while their application, and any appeal from a refusal, is being considered.

One disgraceful example of political expediency overriding international obligations was the case of *Amekrane*, a Moroccan air-force officer who in 1972 fled to Gibraltar and requested political asylum after a plot to overthrow King Hassan's Government collapsed. The request was immediately refused and although no extradition treaty existed with Morocco, Amekrane was immediately handed over to its Government for execution. An application to the European Commission on behalf of his wife and children, alleging that he had been subjected to inhumane treatment by the UK Government in returning him to certain death for a political offence, was declared admissible:[18] the Government bought off an adverse verdict by an *ex gratia* payment of £37,500. As in the case of Dr Soblen, the Home Secretary had used his discretionary powers under the immigration laws to effect an 'extradition' which would not otherwise have been lawful: the lack of any substantive right to appeal the refusal of political asylum sealed the applicant's fate.

If an applicant for political asylum is permitted temporary entry, the basis upon which a claim for asylum is rejected can be reviewed by the courts for any evidence of irrationality or bad faith. Indeed, in *Bugdaycay* v. *Secretary of State*, Lord Bridge endorsed the principle that:

> The most fundamental of all human rights is the individual's right to life and, when an administrative decision under challenge is said to be one which may put the applicant's life at risk, the basis of the decision must call for the most anxious scrutiny.[19]

In that case the applicant was a Ugandan refugee whose father and cousins had been killed by the secret police, and who had reason to believe that the same fate would befall him should he be return. He had lived for some years in Kenya, to which country the Home Secretary had decided to deport him, ignoring a good deal of evidence that Kenya had (in contravention of its own obligation under the UN Convention) returned such refugees to Uganda in similar circumstances. The House of Lords held that the Immigration Rules must not be interpreted so as to conflict with the Convention on the Status of Refugees, Article 33 of which requires that:

No State shall expel or return a refugee in any manner whatsoever to the frontiers of territories where his life or freedom would be threatened on account of his race, religion, nationality, membership of a particular social group or political opinion.

Although Kenya was not a territory where the applicant would be directly threatened, the risk that it would return him to Uganda made his removal to Kenya a contravention of the convention.

This aspect of *Bugdaycay* is a welcome 1987 decision which shows what courts can do when they try, even under the severe limitations of judicial review which confines them to inspection of procedures rather than consideration of merits. It is impossible to read the facts, as set out in the speech of Lord Bridge, without despairing at the Home Office's consistent failure to inform itself of the political realities in East Africa. Its conduct at various stages was described as 'strange' and 'even stranger', and 'doing little to inspire confidence in its procedure'; its affidavits were 'at worst self-contradictory, at best ambiguous'. How many of the 3,882 applications for political asylum in 1986 (only 450 of which were granted) were dealt with in such slipshod ways, by incompetent or ignorant officials whose decisions cannot be reviewed on their merits? This is the price we pay for our commitment to executive discretion which permeates immigration law more deeply than any other field of civil liberties, preventing the courts from getting to grips with the merits of decision-making. In asylum cases, more than any other, it is essential to create an effective right of appeal, if not to the courts then to a special tribunal which can deploy an expert knowledge of the conditions in applicants' countries of origin.

Although asylum applicants are described as 'refugees', the concept does not extend to those who flee from their birthplace because of famine or poverty or earthquake. Nor does it include those who are innocently caught up in riots or revolutionary strife between contending parties, no matter how painful or distressing the experience awaiting them on their return. Refugees must not only fear personal persecution, but their fear must be objectively well founded, in the sense that they must be able to demonstrate a reasonable degree of likelihood that they will be persecuted in their own country for one of the reasons listed in the international Convention. This ruling by the House of Lords in another 1987 case disposed of applications by a number of Tamils who genuinely feared they would suffer violence if they were returned to Sri Lanka, where civil war between Government forces and guerrillas had brought suffering to most Tamil families. The court held that it was not sufficient for the fears to be genuine or even understandable if on an objective basis there was no reasonable likelihood of them being realized.[20]

What amounts to 'persecution'? It does not mean prosecution for an ordinary criminal offence, unless the defendant has been made a scapegoat as a result of his political opinions or race. All that the refugee should have to show is that, given the opinions which he holds, his fear of future persecution is well founded. Many cases depend on the Government's political alliances and diplomatic relations with the foreign country in question: dissidents and defectors from Communist regimes will more readily establish a 'well founded' fear of persecution than people like Amekrane, who had plotted against a Government whose support Britain needed at a time of its dispute with Spain over Gibraltar. All sorts of spurious reasons have been given by British Ministers for denying asylum to dissident Americans, however well-founded their fears were of being persecuted for the political opinions which led them to dodge the Vietnam draft or to escape the McCarthyite purges. Just how far Home Secretaries are prepared to go by way of condoning the malpractices of allies is demonstrated by the strange case of Dr Joseph Cort, a brilliant US pharmacist lecturing at Birmingham University when the McCarthy hearings began. He suffered from polio and myopia, and his US military service had been indefinitely deferred, but when his name was mentioned by the Committee for Unamerican Activities as a 'Communist sympathizer' he was promptly recalled for active service. He was ordered to leave Britain after his application for asylum was refused, on the grounds that 'The Government of the supplicant's country does not employ methods of political persecution'. Cort was accepted by the Czech Academy of Science, where he developed drugs now in worldwide use for diabetes and kidney disease, and in 1977 he was welcomed back to New York as a professor at Mount Sinai Hospital and a vice-president of a major drug company.[21]

Britain's current record in considering claims to refugee status is the worst of any country in Western Europe. It accepts only a few hundred asylum-seekers each year, intimidating airlines and shipping companies from carrying them by heavy fines for delivering fugitives who do not have the correct entry documents, and then providing these asylum-seekers with no right of appeal against deportation. This can be monstrously unfair to refugees fleeing for their lives who have not had time to wait around for a visa. Decisions to reject claims for asylum can be made on the recommendation of immigration officers with no expert knowledge of the conditions from which the claimant is fleeing, after short interviews with jet-lagged claimants denied access to legal advice. In many cases fugitives with claims to refugee status that are worthy of investigation are unnecessarily kept in custody for months before the Home Secretary decides their fate. In 1987, they were locked up in a disused car ferry moored off Harwich – a scene reminiscent of the 'hulks' which held convicts awaiting transportation two centuries ago. What makes this treatment so unconscionable is that refugee status is a legal right, which all civilized nations have a duty to recognize. Instead, the United Kingdom treats them as if they were illegal immigrants. The position is made the more untenable by the fact that claims on our compassion are so minimal compared with the burden shouldered by other and poorer nations: Pakistan is home to 3 million refugees, Jordan has 800,000, and Somalia and Malawi give sanctuary to 600,000. The Government's hostility to refugees was publicly displayed in 1989 by its forcible removal of Viraj Mendis from his fragile sanctuary in a Manchester church, but more worrying were the encouragements it was giving at the same time to other EEC countries to adopt its hard-line approach.

There is no excuse for Britain denying refugees fundamental rights to fair treatment. No person who presents at our ports with a claim to refugee status should be turned away without the opportunity to take legal advice and, if so advised, the opportunity to make representations in support of the claim. There must be a proper independent appeal system established, in order, in the event of an adverse decision from the Home Secretary, to consider the claim on its merits rather than by the limited judicial review which is currently available. And only in exceptional circumstances should claimants be detained while their appeal is being heard. These important principles have been lost sight of in recent years, and the fact that Britain now manages to take, annually, fewer than 500 of the world's twelve million refugees is a signal comment on the withering of its humanitarian traditions.

EXTRADITION

There is no branch of civil-liberties law which has undergone such a sea-change in public attitudes as extradition, the process by which the Courts and the Home Secretary decide whether to surrender a resident (frequently, a British citizen) for trial in a foreign country. In 1988, the Criminal Justice Act removed the traditional safeguard of the *prima facie* case, extended the definition of extradition crimes, and made it much easier for foreign Governments to obtain the return of those they claim to be fugitives from justice.

Extradition is based on reciprocal treaties between States: the UK Government undertakes to hand over persons within its power accused of crime in another country in return for that country promising to return persons within its borders who are wanted in Britain. Unlike domestic laws relating to criminal offences, extradition treaties are given the broadest possible interpretation to effect their purpose of bringing to justice those who are guilty of grave crimes.[22] The procedure, broadly speaking, is that a foreign State requests the extradition of a fugitive and the Home Secretary decides whether to accede to the request: if yes, a warrant is issued empowering arrest, and the evidence is forwarded to a stipendiary magistrate who must decide (subject to appeal) whether the extradition conditions have been met. Prior to 1988, the magistrate could only commit for extradition if satisfied that the evidence was sufficient to justify sending a defendant for trial – i.e. that there was credible evidence upon which a reasonable jury, properly directed, could convict. This test remains for extradition to Commonwealth countries, which is governed by the Fugitive Offenders Act of 1967. However, it had long proved irksome to European nations, whose inquisitorial system requires the attendance of an accused during the course of investigation by a magistrate. The 1988 Criminal Justice Act permits the Government to sidestep the *prima facie* case requirement by entering into arrangements with foreign States which preclude its application: in such cases the magistrate need only be satisfied that the offence is an 'extradition crime' – i.e. that it relates to conduct punishable in Britain by a prison sentence of twelve months or more. The fugitive, if committed, may apply for *habeas corpus*, and the High Court is given a discretion to order his discharge if satisfied that extradition would be 'unjust or oppressive' because of the triviality or staleness of the offence or because the accusation 'is not made in good faith in the interests of justice'. At the end of the day, the Home Secretary retains a discretion to decline to implement an extradition order approved by the courts.

The 1988 reforms, by permitting 'extradition on demand', abolish an important civil liberty hitherto guaranteed to citizen and foreigner alike. Once an appropriate treaty is in place, the magistrate will become merely a rubber stamp, making no examination of the evidence other than to ensure that the crime alleged has an equivalent in British law carrying a sentence of twelve months or more. There will be no presentation of the facts of the case, and no prospect of challenge or review of the evidential sufficiency of the request. The High Court's power to discharge a fugitive if the extradition would be 'unjust and oppressive' is limited to three circumstances, and the broadest − that the accusation has been made in bad faith − will be virtually impossible to prove (as Dr Soblen's lawyers discovered). Moreover, the 1988 Act permits 'special arrangements' to be made for particular cases with States with which Britain has no extradition treaty, suggesting that retrospective political bargains may be struck over the return of individual suspects. The Government resisted amendments which would have prevented extradition to countries which impose the death penalty. At present, some extradition treaties (e.g. with the USA) provide that the Home Secretary *may* ask for an assurance that the death penalty will not be carried out, but in 1987 the Divisional Court refused to require him to seek such an assurance before a mentally abnormal person was returned to a US state which was likely to execute him for murder.[23] Under the 1988 Act, it will be possible for British citizens to be arrested and sent abroad for trial and execution on evidence upon which no jury could, under British law, convict.

There remains the safeguard that no person who is accused (or has been convicted) of an offence of a political character shall be sent to a foreign country for trial. The 1988 Act brings extradition law into line with political asylum by further providing that there shall be no surrender if the request is in reality made for the purpose of punishment on account of race, religion, nationality or political opinions. The courts have been reluctant to define the concept of a 'political offence' with any precision, other than by requiring the fugitive to be at odds with the

State applying for extradition over an issue relating to political control or government.[24] In 1954, when seamen on a Polish trawler mutinied, wounded their captain and sailed into Whitby, there was a *prima facie* case of piracy and unlawful wounding, but the Polish Government's request for extradition was rejected because the mutineers' purpose was to escape from political tyranny.[25] Today, however, the scope of the 'political offence' exemption has been severely restricted by international conventions on terrorism. Thus the Suppression of Terrorism Act (1978) lists a wide range of offences – murder, wounding, hostage-taking, possession of firearms and explosives, etc. – which are not to be regarded as being of a 'political character' when application for extradition is made by most European countries and the United States. The exception for fugitives who are in danger of political persecution did not originally apply to those sought by Commonwealth countries, but it was added to the Fugitive Offenders Act in 1967 after the Home Secretary had ordered the return of suspects to Nigeria and Cyprus to face blatantly political proceedings.[26] The provisions are reciprocal: if the British Government applied to extradite Mr Peter Wright to face charges under the Official Secrets Act, the Australian courts would have no hesitation in refusing the request on the grounds that such proceedings would be blatantly political.

FREEDOM OF TRAVEL

Magna Carta asserts the right of every free man to leave the realm at his pleasure in time of peace. In the eighteenth century, Blackstone held that this right was part of the common law, subject to the prerogative of the Crown to restrain departure by the writ of *ne exeat regno*, in cases where the traveller is required for military service or court appearances.[27] This writ has been superseded by the advent of the passport, surrender of which to the police is a common condition of bail. The passport has become a form of international currency, serving as an identity card at frontiers, a symbol of nationality and a certificate of immigration status. It is not a legal document, merely *prima facie* evidence of nationality and identification, yet its convenience has made it indispensable for the modern traveller. Despite a common belief to the contrary, immigration officials have no power to stop citizens from leaving the country without a passport.

They may request evidence to establish identity and nationality, but cannot detain or turn back persons who cannot produce such evidence in the form of a passport. Citizens re-entering Britain will be required to prove their right of abode, and production of a valid passport is the simplest and speediest means of so doing.

Although UK citizens are free in law to enter and leave Britain without a passport, they will encounter innumerable difficulties in practice if they try to do so. Airlines and shipping companies may be contractually entitled to insist on production of a passport prior to boarding. At the journey's end, foreign immigration control may well refuse to admit passengers without a passport, at least if they cannot produce a separate visa. Many countries have reciprocal treaties with the UK whereby they undertake to admit British citizens without visas but on condition that they produce a passport as proof of nationality. So for all practical purposes, a passport is crucial for overseas travel, and it is all the more remarkable that British citizens do not have an enforceable right to obtain one.

Passports are issued by the Foreign Office under the royal prerogative – the most discretionary form of power, and hence the most difficult to review in the courts. The Foreign Secretary may refuse to issue or review a passport, or may cancel it or even insist on it being handed back – the passport itself is so worded that it remains at all time the property of the Crown. A number of passports are withheld each year, in four classes of case:

(1) where it is suspected that the intention is to take children out of the jurisdiction illegally;

(2) where stranded tourists have been brought back to the UK at Government expense, and have not yet paid their fare;

(3) when the applicant is a person suspected of leaving the country to avoid imminent arrest; and

(4) in the case of persons whose activities 'are so notoriously undesirable or dangerous that Parliament would be expected to support the action of the Foreign Secretary in refusing them a passport'.[28]

It is the last category which gives rise to most concern. In the absence of any legal right, the Foreign Secretary can stop British citizens from travelling abroad for purposes which, although legal, are popularly or politically deplored. During the Cold War, British scientists who wished to attend conferences in Moscow were refused passports, and the same treatment was meted out to several British supporters of the Smith regime in Rhodesia. These actions of withholding passports on political grounds are outside the review powers of the Ombudsman, because they are said to relate to matters affecting relations between Governments. The situation is typical of the British attitude towards 'rights': what ought to be a constitutional entitlement is entrusted to Government, decided in secret and virtually unreviewable by any outside agency. The position is defended by recourse to the fiction of Ministerial responsibility to Parliament, which means, as one participant in a debate over passport withdrawal in 1968 pointed out, 'The only action open to one aggrieved would be in fact to defeat the Government.'

The royal prerogative was regarded by lawyers as untouchable until the GCHQ case in 1984, where the House of Lords held that in certain instances the exercise of a prerogative power (in that case, the banning of trade unions) was subject to the limited discipline of judicial review.[29] In 1988, the Court of Appeal applied this ruling to permit review of the Foreign Secretary's refusal to issue a new passport to a British citizen living in Spain.[30] Although the Foreign Secretary was entitled to refuse to issue a new passport to fugitives from justice, the decision in each case had to be a carefully considered one. Since the denial of a passport is an administrative act affecting the citizen's freedom to travel, the Court of Appeal was prepared to review it on the same principles as it reviews official decisions in immigration cases. This case at least opens up the prospect of overturning refusals and withdrawals of passports if they are made irrationally or unfairly, although judicial review, as we have seen, is a far cry from any right to appeal the merits of the decision. Prerogative powers only survive to the extent that Parliament has not intervened to place them on a proper statutory footing: the practical importance of passports to freedom of movement demands such legislation, in which the grounds for refusal should be both narrowly defined and appealable.[31]

The most controversial exercise of the freedom to travel is by British mercenary soldiers, who have played a wretched part in civil wars, especially in Africa. They are recruited, generally from the ranks of ex-servicemen, through newspaper and magazine advertisements in Britain, and have notoriously figured in 'war crime' trials when captured.

Several hundred left for Angola in 1976, when they killed innocent civilians and in some cases murdered each other. The Foreign Enlistment Act of 1870 makes it an offence to recruit for or enlist in the military service of a foreign State at war with any country which is 'at peace' with Britain. The Government declined to take action against the Angolan mercenaries or their recruiters because of legal doubts about whether the Act could apply to enlistment for another country's civil war, and a Committee chaired by Lord Diplock recommended additional legislation to provide the Government with power to ban recruitment in respect of particular conflicts in which it was not in the public interest for British citizens to participate.[32] This begs difficult questions, and no Government has yet attempted the task of distinguishing the right to leave the country to risk one's life for a cause from 'the right to be a hired killer in a foreign war'.[33] Overt and organized recruitment of mercenaries for foreign armies waging civil war may well require prohibition, but any Government power to stop citizens voluntarily choosing to serve in particular forces or movements invites political distinctions of the sort which would, in the thirties, have made it a crime to fight against Franco.

British citizens may be excluded from Great Britain (i.e. from England, Wales and Scotland) or alternatively from Northern Ireland, if they have been ordinarily resident there for less than three years and are suspected of involvement, actual or potential, in acts of terrorism. There is no right of appeal against an exclusion order, other than the right to make representations in writing to the Home Secretary and to put one's case in a 'personal interview' with a Home Office adjudicator. The 'national security' context makes any court challenge virtually impossible. These powers to make 'exclusion orders' were provided by the Prevention of Terrorism Act, passed in 1974 after the Birmingham bombings, which contains ancillary powers to detain for extended periods (see earlier, page 36). The contribution made by the Act to the containment of terrorism has been much debated, but it has not been shown how it helps to diminish terrorism to oblige a suspect to live in one part of the United Kingdom rather than another. A number of Irishmen active in Sinn Fein have been banished from England and obliged to live in Northern Ireland, in circumstances which suggest that their political activities in Irish communities on the mainland is the danger that is really feared. Terrorists are intolerable wherever they reside: does the notion that a suspect is less of a problem in Belfast than in London imply that English lives are more valuable than Northern Irish lives?

TEN

Freedom from Undue Control

This chapter is about various forms of State paternalism. The traditional justification for the exercise of power over individuals – to prevent them from harming themselves or harming others – justifies the withdrawal from prisoners and mental patients of certain rights enjoyed by free citizens. It does not, however, justify the infringements of basic rights which have gone on within British penal and mental institutions, such as denial of access to the courts and unfair trial of disciplinary offences. It is here that the European Convention has made its most marked contribution to the enhancement of civil liberties in Britain, in providing an external and objective standard by which to judge the fairness of prison rules and mental-health regulations.

There has been much controversy over the rights of children to make decisions about their own future without parental veto when they come of an age to appreciate the consequences. The House of Lords decision in *Gillick* makes clear that parent power begins to evaporate long before the age of eighteen, inversely to the growth of intelligence and understanding. It is also subject to the power of the State to intervene, through local authorities and social-work agencies, to rescue children from abuse. That this necessary control requires a greater measure of legal scrutiny was demonstrated by the Cleveland inquiry, which exposed how magistrates were permitting paediatricians and social workers to separate children from their parents on inadequate evidence and with insufficient accountability. When errors of judgement are made by social workers the consequences can be catastrophic, but public outrage at the deaths of children like Kimberley Carlile and Jasmine Beckford needs to be tempered by an appreciation that 'erring on the safe side' would deprive many children of a tolerable family environment, and deprive some innocent parents of their children. Further changes in the law are required to give parents greater legal rights to challenge the diktat of doctors and social workers, and to avoid the danger that child welfare powers will be used oppressively against parents who are poor rather rather perverse.

State paternalism is manifesting itself in attempts to control citizen access to advances in birth technology. The right to bear children, denied to many by physical impediment, can now be overcome by *in vitro* fertilization (IVF) and surrogacy techniques. The latter have to some extent been prohibited by criminal law, and access to IVF treatment is limited by resources, doctors' discretions and debatable ethical judgements. This field promises a great deal of legislation and litigation, in which the right to family life on terms convenient to individual couples will be balanced against moral standards assumed, perhaps optimistically, to reflect community values. Finally, this chapter looks at the prohibitions upon euthanasia. The law no longer embodies the Gilbertian paradox of suicide as a crime punishable by death, but it severely punishes those who help others to die with some measure of dignity.

PRISONERS' RIGHTS

The principle that 'men come to prison as a punishment, not for punishment' is difficult to credit at a time when 48,000 prisoners are crammed into accommodation originally built for 5,000. The Prison Inspectorate concedes that in many closed prisons one-person cells that now carry two or three prisoners are 'spartan, gloomy and stagnant', without access to sanitation; prisoners are locked up, sometimes for twenty-three hours a day; they are allowed to write one censored letter a week and receive one visit a month; and must defecate in each other's company at night and 'slop out' the next morning. The closest Britain comes to having a constitution is the Bill of Rights of 1688, which prohibits the infliction of 'cruell and unusuall punishment'. The degradation caused by overcrowding comes in some prisons well within that description, as does the practice of holding some convicted prisoners for months in police cells designed as overnight accommodation.

Reliance on the 1688 Act in court was once regarded as the last resort of a desperate advocate, but in the 1987 case of *Ex parte Herbage*

(*No. 2*) the Court of Appeal was prepared to make it the basis for a judicial review of a prison governor's decision to keep a sane prisoner in a psychiatric wing because of accommodation problems.

> If it were to be established that the applicant as a sane person was, for purely administrative purposes, being subjected in the psychiatric wing to the stress of being exposed to the disturbance caused by the behaviour of mentally ill and disturbed prisoners, this might well be considered as a 'cruell and unusuall punishment' and one which was not deserved.[1]

The decision is a welcome reminder of an often forgotten power in the courts to protect all those in detention against inhumane treatment, although in 1981 the High Court limited the effect of the Bill of Rights by requiring that the punishment (solitary confinement in a 'control unit') be 'unusual' as well as 'cruel'. The phrase is better understood as a compendious expression of a minimum standard of decency, rather than as a sanction for outrageous treatment which happens to be common within the prison system. At least it was acknowledged that the moral standard to be applied is contemporary, and not that which prevailed in 1688.[2] It follows that the Bill of Rights would certainly provide a basis for challenging, for example, the use of tranquillizers to control behaviour rather than to restore health or the deployment of brain-washing techniques to break the spirit of 'trouble-makers'.

The Prison Rules, made under the Prisons Act of 1952, have been the subject of many actions taken to Strasbourg in an effort to secure acceptable standards of treatment for prisoners. Until these European Court cases, the Rules imposed a blanket of censorship over prisoners' contact with the outside world, even in relation to correspondence seeking legal advice. The turning-point came with the 1975 decision in *Golder* that the rule which forbade a prisoner from seeking advice from a solicitor in relation to his rights against a prison officer was a breach both of his right to freedom of access to the court (Article 6) and of his right to respect for his correspondence under the privacy guarantee of Article 8.[3] The Rules were slowly liberalized, under the pressure of further European Court rulings against the United Kingdom and decisions by domestic courts prepared to scrutinize the Prison Rules for compliance with natural justice. In *Raymond* v. *Honey* in 1983 the House of Lords went so far as to hold a prison governor in contempt of court for refusing to forward to the High Court a prisoner's application for leave to apply for judicial review. The Prisons Act of 1952, it held, did not empower the making of any rule which would interfere with a prisoner's right of unimpeded access to the courts: 'Under English law, a convicted prisoner, in spite of his imprisonment, retains all civil rights which are not taken away expressly or by necessary implication.'[4] Attempts by the Home Office to make the right to legal advice about complaints against prison authorities subject to conditions – e.g. that the complaint should first have been taken up with prison authorities – have also been held to be impediments on access to the courts.[5]

Prisoners suffer many other deprivations of civil rights which are not justified by the need to maintain discipline or security. They are deprived for no logical reason of the right to vote in both national and local elections, and they only acquired in 1983 the right to marry while in prison, as the result of another application to Strasbourg. The Prison Rules allow them to send and to receive only one letter a week – a clear infringement of the right to freedom of communication, and many prison governors use their discretion to increase the allowance. All letters are in any event subject to censorship, and the authorities have discretion to stop those they view as 'objectionable' or as being of 'inordinate length'. The Rules permit only one personal visit a month (within the sight and often hearing of prison officers) which must not be by a 'journalist or author', and there is no right to make telephone calls. These Rules could all be relaxed without danger of disorder or escape: they have been framed to give entitlement to the very minimum of contact with the outside world, sometimes with the real objective of secrecy rather than security. Thus when Jimmy Boyle tried to write to a friend who happened to be a playwright, the letter was stopped on the grounds that the intended recipient was a 'media personality'. The Government was forced to concede before the European Court that this was a violation of the right to respect for private correspondence.[6] Another particular concern is the treatment of unconvicted prisoners who have been refused bail. Although presumed innocent, they can be made to suffer the same indignities as convicts. In 1988 the Home Office took the mean-minded and unnecessary step of abolishing their traditional 'right' to receive food parcels from friends and family.

The other battlefield in the struggle for prisoners' rights is the system of internal discipline. Over 80,000 charges are laid by warders against prisoners each year: the vast majority are dealt with by the governor (who may order temporary loss of privileges, or loss of remission of up to twenty-eight days) but the more serious offences are tried by a panel selected from the Board of Visitors – Justices of the Peace and other local citizens who meet each month to make recommendations about the state of the prison and the welfare of its inmates. In cases of assault or attempting to escape, they may order up to 180 days' loss of remission; in cases of mutiny or 'gross personal violence' to warders, their power to punish by forfeiting remission is open-ended. 'Remission' amounts to one third of the period of sentence, and is automatically deducted for good behaviour: on entry to prison, convicts are given their 'release date' calculated after the remission period has been subtracted. It follows that a 'loss of remission' is, for all practical purposes, an addition to the prison sentence: the loss of six months' remission is the equivalent of a nine-month custodial sentence by the courts. After the Hull Prison riot in 1976, some long-term prisoners were punished by losing 720 remission days – the equivalent of an additional three-year sentence, imposed in secret, non-jury proceedings. In other words, the consequence of conviction by the Board can be a substantial further loss of liberty. These internal 'trials', if they are to be held at all, must be properly conducted and procedurally fair.

At first, attempts to secure basic rights failed in the courts, where judges could see no difference between prison discipline and army discipline: speed was of the essence, and legal representations would produce delay. There was, however, a duty on the Board to act fairly, and some of the heavy punishments handed down to the Hull rioters were quashed because they had been given no opportunity to cross-examine the evidence against them.[7] It took the European Court, in *Campbell & Fell* v. *UK*, to give full effect to the principle that 'justice cannot stop at the prison gates': there had been a breach of the Article 6 right to a fair hearing by denial of legal advice and representation at a trial which imposed a 'sentence' of loss of fifteen months' remission.[8] As a result of this case, the Home Office has directed that prisoners charged with mutiny or 'gross personal violence' (i.e. where punishment may exceed 180 days' loss of remission) should be allowed to have legal representation if they wish. This is still a far cry from the recommendation of the Royal

Commission on Legal Services that no prisoner should lose remission for more than seven days without legal representation. This can only be achieved by a proper 'duty solicitor' scheme operating at all prisons – a much-needed and often-canvassed reform which has yet to gain the full support of the Home Office and Legal Aid authorities.

The prison disciplinary system is in need of further reform before the 'fair trial' guarantees are met. The prison governor is an appropriate authority to deal with minor complaints, but 'prison visitors' should have no role at all in convicting or sentencing prisoners. Their prime duty is to provide independent oversight of prison conditions, by visiting prisoners and listening to their grievances. Their independence, or at least any faith the inmates may have in them, is jeopardized by their disciplinary role, in which they are inevitably seen as part of the prison establishment. All serious disciplinary offences should be dealt with by circuit judges, publicly rather than privately, and with the prisoner being given a right to opt for jury trial where the allegation is of riot or serious wounding. The Government has consistently resisted such proposals, and it has declined to implement the Prior Commission recommendation that an independent Prison Disciplinary Tribunal be established to replace the punitive functions of Boards of Visitors.

MENTAL PATIENTS

It is wrong to punish the 'unblameworthy' – those who cannot be held morally responsible for actions arising from a disorder of the mind. They are 'not guilty', but having committed anti-social actions there is every justification for a court to order an appropriate treatment, which may include confinement in a secure mental hospital until, if at all, they are cured. The first objection to the way which English criminal law treats mentally disordered offenders is that it virtually obliges them to plead 'guilty' – to offences of which they are innocent because they committed them without criminal intent – in order to obtain appropriate treatment. The defence of 'insanity' is so limited that those who advance it run the risk of conviction and punishment (by being sent to prison) instead of treatment by confinement in a mental hospital.

The principle that it is wrong to punish mentally disordered persons was recognized far back in our legal history, by judges who, although they had no compunction in burning witches, drew the line at hanging village idiots. As one Chief Justice, Edward Coke, explained four centuries ago:

> The execution of an offender is for example, but so it is not when a madman is executed; that should be a miserable spectacle, both against law, and of extreme inhumanity and cruelty, and can be no example to others.

At first, the law demanded that the madness should be obvious and overwhelming: it had to be proved that the defendant 'doth not know what he is doing, any more than a brute or a wild beast'. This test remained until 1800, when Lord Erskine, the greatest advocate of that or perhaps any other age, was called upon to defend James Hadfield, a schizophrenic who had attempted to assassinate George III. Erskine opened the door to forensic psychiatry when he spoke to the jury of 'an insanity where imagination still holds the most uncontrollable domination over reality and fact; and there are cases which frequently mock the wisdom of the wisest in judicial trials; because such persons often reason with subtlety . . .'[9] Erskine established the broad principle that those who commit crimes under the influence of delusions are not responsible in law. Hadfield was acquitted, to the bewilderment of the Government. He was held in custody until a Criminal Lunatics Act could be rushed through Parliament, providing indefinite hospitalization for those found 'not guilty on grounds of insanity'. They were, in time, committed to the care of doctors in Bedlam (the Royal Bethlehem Hospital) rather than to the hangman.

This humane development of the law met with a serious reversal in 1843, when the judiciary succumbed to political pressures whipped up as a result of the acquittal, on grounds of insanity, of Daniel M'Naghten. He was a young Scot who killed Sir Robert Peel's private secretary (mistaking him for Peel) under the influence of schizophrenic delusions. The Press vilified the 'mad-doctors' who had given evidence for the defence, and some editorials, noting M'Naghten's Chartist sympathies, wondered whether socialism was a disease of the mind which might save other assassins from the gallows. The politicians were furious, and Queen Victoria was outraged. M'Naghten was 'not in the least mad', she declared. Twelve senior judges were ordered by Parliament, 'in consequence of the M'Naghten verdict', to restate the law of insanity, and they produced the 'M'Naghten rules' – a test of insanity which remains the law in Britain today. They abandoned Erskine's principle that a defendant is not criminally responsible for an act committed under the influence of delusions stemming from a disease of the mind. They decided that he was guilty, unless the disease was so severe that 'he did not know the nature and quality of the act he was doing, or if he did know it, that he did not know he was doing what was wrong'.[9]

Seen in historical context, the M'Naghten rules were in fact designed to hang future M'Naghtens. The assassin's ability to make careful preparations and penetrate the security around public figures requires an intelligence which, however disordered, must apprehend the illegality of the action. Judged in the light of our contemporary knowledge, the rules are based on the erroneous belief that if an ability to reason exists, it can control behaviour. The paranoid schizophrenic may retain an ability to reason within certain limits of his general alienation, without being able to exercise cerebral control. He cannot help his actions, even though he realizes they are against the law. An irresistible inner order, coupled with a delusion that it is morally right, provides no insanity defence. For lawyers, the definition of a madman is a person who cannot understand the law.

In 1953, the Royal Commission on Capital Punishment condemned the M'Naghten rules, and Parliament provided a special defence of 'diminished responsibility' to defendants charged with murder. It operates to reduce that crime (which carries a mandatory sentence of life imprisonment) to manslaughter (where the sentence is entirely at the option of the judge). To return a verdict of 'diminished responsibility' the jury should be satisfied that the mental disorder was a substantial causative factor in the killing. But how debilitating must a mental disease be before 'impairment of responsibility' is deemed 'substantial'? The test of causation is difficult for experts and juries to apply in the context of serious mental disorder. In cases of schizophrenia, where diagnosis must largely depend on what the defendant says about himself, there is no sure way of deciding whether he is ill, or feigning illness. (There is now no doubt that Peter Sutcliffe, whose plea of 'diminished responsibility' to the 'Yorkshire Ripper' murders was rejected as feigning by a jury, was in fact suffering from paranoid schizophrenia.)

The defence of insanity is hardly ever heard in English court-rooms, because if it succeeds the court (under legislation which began with Hadfield and the Criminal Lunatics Act in 1800) must order the defendant to be confined in a psychiatric hospital for as long as the authorities believe him a danger to the public – which may be for so long as he lives. But if the mentally ill offender pleads 'guilty' to any offence other than murder, the court has a whole range of humane treatments at its disposal, from which it can select the most appropriate. Thus schizo-phrenics who commit offences under the influence of delusions, which are then brought under control by treatment before trial, plead 'guilty' in order to receive a probation order, perhaps with a requirement that they continue out-patient treatment. Because of their illness, they were not responsible for their crime, but the M'Naghten rules afford them no defence. Even if the mental illness was severe enough to satisfy the M'Naghten test, what candidate for probation would plead 'not guilty' when the result would have to be indefinite confinement?

The Committee on Mentally Abnormal Offenders, chaired by the late Lord Butler, reported in 1975.[10] It recommended abolition of the M'Naghten rules and the installation of a new verdict: 'not guilty on evidence of mental disorder'. This verdict would be brought in if the jury were satisfied that at the time of the act charged as a crime, the defendant was suffering from severe mental illness or severe subnor-mality. Psychiatrists could testify to the question of fact – is he, the defendant, severely ill or is he not? The question of causality, so tortuous and speculative in relation to most forms of schizophrenia, would not need to be answered. After an acquittal 'on evidence of mental illness', the court would be empowered to make the most appropriate order, ranging from an absolute discharge for those demonstrably cured and harmless to indefinite detention in Broadmoor if there were any danger that violent episodes would be repeated. Now that the gallows no longer casts its shadow over the design of the criminal law it is time to adopt Butler's recommendation, which gives proper effect to the principle that persons in the grip of mental illness should not be branded as criminally responsible for their actions.

In other respects, British law relating to mentally disordered of-fenders has developed more rationally. Judges may make 'restriction orders' confining them in mental hospitals rather than prison, for fixed or unlimited periods, where the evidence shows that their disorder would make them a danger to the public if set free immediately. Mental Health Review Tribunals, comprising a lawyer, a psychiatrist and a lay person, advise the Home Secretary as to when an offender subject to an unlimited 'restriction order' can safely be released. Until 1983 release was always 'on licence', and the offender could be recalled at any time at the Home Secretary's discretion. The drawback in this system was that release and recall were decided entirely by the Home Secretary – a politician easily deterred by fear of adverse publicity. It took the European Court of Human Rights to produce a change in the law which made the restoration of liberty a matter of independent judgement rather than political discretion.

X v. *United Kingdom* involved a man who had been sent to Broadmoor for assaulting a workmate. After several years he was released into the community, to live for three years without problem until he was suddenly 'recalled' by the Home Secretary for reasons, it subsequently emerged, of unsubstantiated gossip by his wife during their divorce. The European Court held that the Home Secretary had been in breach of Article 5(4) of the Convention, which requires that all who are deprived of their liberty by detention should be entitled to have the lawfulness of their confinement decided speedily by a court. Although the Mental Health Review Tribunal was capable of being a 'court' it had no power to 'decide', but merely to make recommendations to the Home Secretary.[11] As a consequence of this ruling, the 1983 Mental Health Act abrogates the Home Secretary's discretionary power and leaves him to make representations to the Tribunal, which now has the final duty to decide questions of release and recall.

Tribunals have a delicate and sometimes agonizing task in predicting how offenders and patients will behave when set at large; on the occasions when mental illness reasserts itself and results in another act of violence or sexual assault, angry and sensational allegations of incompetence will follow in the Press. It is necessary for Tribunals to have the strength of mind to act on the evidence placed before them in cases of individuals who have recovered from a mental illness that caused them to commit serious offences, and failure to give cogent reasons for refusing a discharge in such cases will be reviewable in the High Court.[12] Judges in several recent cases of this sort have been prepared to quash Tribunal decisions where inadequate or irrational reasons have been given, and where the suspicion must be that the decision has been dictated by prejudice about the original offence rather than a fair appreciation of the offender's current mental state.[13] A 'restriction order', after all, may be imposed for a minor offence, and may last for life: it must not be viewed as 'punishment' for a 'crime' (for which it would be grossly disproportionate) but as confinement in order to treat a mental state – a confinement which must end as soon as that state is manageable enough for release. This point is reached when detention in hospital is no longer necessary for the patient's own health or the protection of others.

The 1983 Mental Health Act now sets out comprehensively the law relating to State power over those suffering from mental disorder. Compulsory admission to hospital must be upon the application of a relative or a social worker, supported by the recommendation of one doctor in any emergency (where the patient may be detained for up to three days – a 'Section 1' order) or by two doctors in cases requiring up to twenty-eight days' detention (a 'Section 2' order). There must be evidence of 'mental disorder', which is widely defined to encompass 'mental illness, arrested or incomplete development of the mind, psychopathic disorder and any other disorder or disability of the mind', although drug or alcohol dependence and promiscuity are excluded as sole grounds for admission. Admissions for emergency treatment and assessment are lawful if doctors think it necessary or appropriate for the health of the patient: only when longer-term detention is sought – under Section 3 of the Act – does the test of danger to self or others become the governing standard, and such confinements must be reviewed by the Mental Health Review Tribunal every six months. The other method of compulsory admission to hospital is by order of a court, on the evidence of two doctors that an offender is suffering from a form of mental disorder specified in the Act which can be ameliorated by hospital treatment. A court can make the more severe 'restriction order' only in cases where it is of the opinion that this 'is necessary for the protection of the public from serious harm'. Voluntary admission, of course, may be sought at any time, but patients in this category who seek to discharge themselves may be detained by a doctor under 'emergency treatment' powers.

These provisions are designed to balance the rights of mentally disordered individuals with the powers of professionals to put them out of circulation for a short period of assessment or a longer period if they are assessed as dangerous to themselves or others. Ultimately, there is judicial control through *habeas corpus* applications and the supervisory role of the Mental Health Review Tribunal, but in the short term there is still considerable potential for abuse.[14] A single, inexperienced GP may react to a patient in emotional crisis by making an emergency order; doctors are tempted to let 'assessment' run the full twenty-eight days: the catch-all phrase 'any other disorder or disability of the mind' is extraordinarily wide (one youth who laughed at police officers ended up in hospital allegedly suffering from 'euphoria').

Mental Health Review Tribunals are the only protection for 're-stricted' patients who have committed such serious offences that politi-cians – represented by the Home Secretary – are reluctant ever to release them. It frequently happens that killings are committed under the influ-ence of mental disorders that are either ended or brought under control by medication after a stay in a secure mental hospital. The offender, who is no longer a danger to himself or to members of the public, is entitled to be released under Section 72 of the Mental Health Act, after a Tribunal hearing at which the Home Secretary will be represented. But the Tri-bunal, although it is charged with making a decision of fundamental importance to the liberty of the subject, is not a 'court' for the purposes of the law of contempt, with the result that the Press is free to agitate sensationally against the release of the patient.[15] Although the prospect of the release of any person who has many years before committed serious offences is a matter of public interest upon which reasonable comment should be permitted, the absence of any legal restraint has encouraged hysterical Press campaigns of vilification against some 'restricted' patients and their expert witnesses in the weeks before the Tribunal sits. It is difficult for patients to accept that they will receive a fair hearing from a Tribunal whose members are placed under strident public pressure. It is anomalous that Tribunal proceedings are not pro-tected by the law of contempt – they are precisely the kind of hearings which most need to be insulated from passion and prejudice.

Some mental patients are unable to understand, let alone to give consent to, medical treatment which their own best interests may warrant. Routine operations occasion no difficulty, as doctors and relatives are entitled to make reasonable decisions as to what the health of the patient requires, just as they would in treating a young child. In the case of operations which raise serious ethical questions, such as sterilization or abortion or kidney donation, the approval of the High Court should be sought. In 1989 the Court of Appeal ruled in *Re F* that approval will normally be given if the operation is regarded by the general body of medical opinion as best calculated to promote the patient's true welfare and interests.[16] The court's decision that 'the right to reproduce is of value only if accompanied by the ability to make a choice' may be doubted as a general principle, although on the facts of the particular case the decision to approve sterilization was humane (a thirty-five-year-old woman with a mental age of five for whom pregnancy would be 'a disaster' was having a sexual relationship but could not be protected by normal methods of contraception). The ruling indicates both that the courts are prepared to oversee drastic medical decisions which affect the fundamental rights of mental patients, but that they will not override 'the general body of medical opinion'. Where there is a substantial conflict in that opinion, the judges will decide according to their perception of the public interest. It is of some comfort that such ethical conundrums will at least be resolved openly and by an independent body, rather than be left to the discretion of individual practitioners and health authorities.

The European Convention has influenced a number of reforms in the 1983 Act, such as giving mental patients the right to vote and removing certain restrictions on their correspondence. But there are still gaps in the protection which the Act affords to society's most vulnerable members. Although patients cannot resist routine treatment while they are detained, psycho-surgery must not be undertaken without consent or, where the patient is incapable of giving consent, without independent confirmation of that incapacity and approval of the treatment proposed. Treatment in the category of 'medication', however, which includes the controversial electro-convulsive therapy (ECT), may be given without consent where an 'independent doctor' has certified its benefits. This is a wholly inadequate protection against a form of treatment which some psychiatrists recommend but which has been shown to have dubious benefits and a potential for abuse.

Mental patients are particularly vulnerable to abuse, from both doctors and staff, yet they suffer discrimination in not being allowed to take legal proceedings unless the claim is based on allegations of negligence or bad faith, and even in such cases they must first obtain leave of the High Court, which is withheld unless there is 'substantial ground' for the allegation. High-security 'special hospitals' can easily become places of illegal brutality and malpractice, as the media investigations of Rampton Special Hospital and the criminal trials which followed demonstrated just after the 1983 Act was passed.

CHILDREN AND PARENTS

The legal right of parenthood is, at common law, 'a dwindling right . . . It starts with a right of control and ends with little more than advice.' Statute law provides certain rights on the basis of age gradations; at birth, still reflecting Victorian values, it permits inheritance and the possession of bank accounts and Premium Bonds; at seven it allows criminal conviction if the prosecution can prove knowledge of wrong-doing (full criminal responsibility comes at fourteen, together with the right to own a shot-gun and to enter pubs); at sixteen come the rights to buy lottery tickets and liqueur chocolates and cigarettes, pose naked for page 3 of the *Sun*, consent to medical treatment, leave school and work full time and have sex and join the army, while eighteen is the age for full civil rights except those of standing for Parliament or adopting a child or having homosexual relationships, which are not bestowed until the twenty-first birthday.

These age limits are inevitably arbitrary and those relating to sexual conduct in particular call for careful discretion in enforcement. Outside the framework of statutory rights, there lies a fertile area for conflict between the interests of parents, their children, and the State. The present Government has devised social legislation to reflect its faith in the family unit and parental responsibility, at a time of increasing divorce and dislocation and evidence of widespread child abuse. Somehow, the child-welfare system must be geared to social intervention at a point which will protect children from the possibility of abuse while at the same time preserving the rights of parents to have their child-raising capabilities judged carefully and fairly. The errors of assessment which led to the deaths of Maria Colwell and Jasmine Beckford and Kimberley Carlile received condemnation from a public which expects social workers to take children to places of safety whenever danger signals appear, but zeal for playing the Pied Piper without proper heed for parents' rights produced the crisis in Cleveland.

The general rights of a child vis-à-vis its parent were considered by the House of Lords in 1987 in a case brought by a moral crusader, Mrs Victoria Gillick, against her Area Health Authority because it refused to assure her that its doctors would never prescribe contraception to her daughters under sixteen without her consent. The decision – that parental consent was not required in cases where a doctor formed an honest view that contraception was necessary to the welfare of a girl who insisted upon confidentiality – was reached by reference to the capacity of individual children, below any arbitrarily set age, to make decisions for themselves. Parental rights to control a child exist for the benefit of the child and not of the parent, and they are justified only to the extent that is necessary to enable the parents to fulfil their duties of care and support. 'That parental right yields to the child's right to make his own decisions when he reaches a sufficient understanding and intelligence to be capable of making up his own mind on the matter requiring decision.'[17]

The effect of *Gillick* is to remove any right of parental veto over medical treatment, including abortion, which doctors believe to be necessary and which their patients are of sufficient mental development to comprehend and approve. It will also have important consequences for wardship proceedings, which local authorities or parents may commence to obtain Court Orders restraining persons under eighteen (and others who have dealings with them) from conduct regarded as dangerous to their welfare. Henceforth, the courts should be reluctant to exercise a paternal power over minors who are sufficiently intelligent to decide their own best interests, at least where the conduct concerned is lawful. When the young Jessica Mitford was made a ward of court by her family in an attempt to stop her marrying Churchill's nephew and fighting against Franco, the Government diverted a destroyer to collect the runaway from Spain. The decision in *Gillick* may signal the end of the use of wardship powers to impose such restraints upon headstrong youth.

The power to make a child a ward of court is sometimes used as a device for testing the legitimacy of actions which are open to question on grounds of morality. The yardstick applied by the court is not, however, moralistic: it decides strictly according to what it conceives to be the best interests of the child. A decision as to the fate of a surrogate child, for example, may call for a judgement of Solomon between competing claims of the natural mother and the couple who have procured the birth. In 1987, judges were criticized for permitting the sterilization of a mentally handicapped girl of seventeen who was made a ward of court by the local authority in order to obtain court approval for the operation, which had been unanimously recommended by doctors and was supported by the girl's mother.[18] Although the irreversible nature of such an operation should make it a last resort, the evidence established that the girl, who had a mental age of six and would not develop further, could not cope either with pregnancy (which would be an 'unmitigated disaster' for her) or with any other form of contraception. The courts – all the way up to the House of Lords – were called upon to sanction the decision which, while obviously humane in the particular circumstances, raised moral issues that made experts nervous. The case shows that doctors who fear accusations of 'playing God' can, at least where children are concerned, always obtain the approval of a higher authority.

Parents are entitled to chastise their children, within the bounds of reason and moderation. They are, equally, entitled to object to others inflicting corporal punishment. In *Tyrer*'s case, the European Court held that the birching of juvenile offenders, even those convicted of acts of violence, amounted to 'degrading punishment' contrary to Article 3 of the Convention. It was a form of 'institutionalized violence', constituting an assault on the individual's dignity and physical integrity. Although the British judge dissented (pointing out that he had come to no harm from being beaten at school) the UK Government was obliged to stop corporal punishment in the Isle of Man, and in 1982 the Court once again indicated that Britain was in breach of the Convention by allowing children to suffer canings in schools contrary to their parents' wishes and beliefs about how they should be educated. In 1986 Parliament formally passed – by one vote – a law prohibiting corporal punishment in State schools. Parents who want their children flogged must pay to send them to independent schools which remain, anomalously, free to administer corporal punishment.

Reverberations from the *Gillick* decision echo throughout the law relating to teenagers: this good lady's legal crusade to control children has ironically associated her name with a landmark in their liberty. The 'dwindling rights' doctrine would now permit doctors, for example, to provide abortions to stable and intelligent fifteen-year-olds without their parents' consent or even knowledge. It makes a substantial inroad on the traditional notion that parents are entitled to custody of their children until the age of sixteen. Youngsters who run away from home at fourteen or fifteen can be sheltered, and need not be returned home without a court order. Many thousands of young teenagers run away from home each year, and the *Gillick* ruling lends support to those hostels which (sometimes with police support) hide teenage refugees from angry parents until family problems can be resolved.

Undoubtedly the most common, and the most brutal, way in which teenagers have their rights infringed is by being subjected to severe corporal punishment within their homes. English law traditionally protects the authoritarian parent or guardian who 'reasonably chastises' children with cane or belt or gym-shoe. This is an urgent area for a reform in the law: now that canes are banned in schools, it is anomalous that they should be wielded in the privacy of the home. Some European countries forbid parents from beating teenage children, and it may be that *Gillick* will herald the demise of 'reasonable chastisement' as a defence to assault charges brought against parents: their 'right' to bruise their children should be the first to dwindle.

The abuse of young children by their custodians is such an appalling fact of life that inroads must be made on the right to have family life respected by agencies of the State. The law until 1989 allowed magistrates to grant 'Place of Safety Orders' if social workers had 'reasonable cause to believe' that a child was at risk of ill-treatment or neglect. These orders removed children for up to twenty-eight days, and were unchallengeable if the correct procedures were followed. In 1989 the Government moved to replace the twenty-eight day 'Place of Safety Order', which had proved so destructive of family relationships during the Cleveland crisis, with a new 'Emergency Protection Order' which would last only for eight days and would be challengeable by parents after seventy-two hours had elapsed. This reform, contained in the Children bill, was long overdue. It permits a court to remove a child from home if satisfied that social workers' belief 'that the child is likely to suffer significant harm' is reasonable. The court may further order that the child be examined by doctors or psychiatrists and that it should not have contact with any person who might harm it, although subject to such orders reasonable access must be permitted to parents or those who have been exercising parental authority. The 'Emergency Protection Order' will encourage social services to act immediately on strong suspicions that children are in danger (they were previously reluctant to take the serious step of removing a child for a whole month without having clear medical evidence) but at the same time it improves the opportunities for parents to assert their own rights in court. Regrettably, their rights will generally be asserted before lay Justices: the difficulty of assessing evidence about suspected child abuse makes these cases more apt to be decided by County or Crown Court judges. The Children bill additionally strengthens the powers of police officers to act in an emergency by taking children into protection for up to three days if it is believed they would otherwise be likely to suffer significant harm. This temporary power can be used to safeguard children in the period before a court can be convened to hear an application for an 'Emergency Protection Order', although whether parents will be allowed access will depend on the officer's judgements on whether this is in the child's best interests.

Local authorities have a duty to protect children within their area. Social services departments may apply to the court for 'care orders' (which can last until the age of eighteen) if the child is otherwise likely to suffer significant harm (whether by ill-treatment or by impairment of health or development), or is simply 'beyond parental control'. There are about 80,000 children 'in care' in Britain, yet the House of Lords has held that the courts have no power to review on their merits decisions which local authorities take in respect of these children.[19] Such decisions frequently deny or restrict parental access, and five parents who were thus deprived complained to the European Court. In 1987, the Court ruled that local-authority procedures had failed to respect the right to family life (Article 8) and had violated the guarantee of fair trial (Article 6), because social workers had not consulted parents about decisions to deny them access to their children, and these decisions were not appealable other than by way of judicial review. A judicial review did not amount to a 'fair trial' because the High Court could only examine the legitimacy of the procedures employed, and could not reassess the merits of the decision.[20] In an attempt to bring British law into conformity within the Convention, the Government legislated to provide a right of appeal for parents who are totally denied access to their children. The 1989 Children bill goes further by providing that a care order may be challenged by 'any person who has parental responsibility for the child' and by the child itself. The bill envisages that children with sufficient understanding to instruct solicitors will be represented, when appropriate, before courts which make or reconsider care orders.

Any system must strike a balance between the rights of parents to respect for family life and the right of the State to break up a family if there is evidence of children being ill-treated. The 1989 legislation has the welcome purpose of making allegations of child abuse both easier to investigate and easier to challenge. It draws upon the lessons of the Cleveland inquiry, and previous inquiries conducted by Louis Blom-Cooper QC into the deaths of two children – Jasmine Beckford [21] and Kimberley Carlile [22] – who were murdered despite being under the 'care' of social services departments. The Blom-Cooper reports argued strongly for a 'child assessment order' which would require parents to take children to a clinic for examination when child abuse was suspected – a much simpler and less coercive procedure than police protection followed by an eight-day 'Emergency Protection Order'. The most important result of the 1989 reforms will be to effect a shift of power from local authorities (which will no longer be able to take control of children by committee resolution) to the courts. Although the courts concerned will initially be magistrates' courts, they will be able to transfer more complex care proceedings to the County Court or to the High Court. Regrettably, the 1989 reforms do not create a structure for a Family Court, which alone could bring order and expertise to all disputes over the best interests of children.

Child sexual abuse poses intractable problems for the courts, especially in their preventive jurisdiction. Medical tests are rarely conclusive (in the absence of pregnancy or venereal disease or gross injury) and children abused by fathers or stepfathers have generally been emotionally blackmailed into secrecy. Obtaining disclosure from very young children by use of 'anatomically correct dolls' (one of the great euphemisms of our time) and other methods of interpreting children's play is open to ambiguity and allegations of 'coaching'. At what point does mere suspicion that a child is being sexually abused justify removing it from the family? This is one of the most agonizing dilemmas for a court, yet it is often entrusted to lay Justices, who have shown themselves incapable of resolving it fairly and responsibly. It was the incompetence of lay Justices, more than the doctrinaire beliefs of paediatricians and social workers, which produced the crisis in Cleveland in 1987, when so many children were suddenly removed from their families on inadequate and untested evidence. These removals were not ordered by the doctors (whom the media chose to blame) nor by the social-services department: neither had any power to make a 'Place of Safety Order'. These orders were made, often recklessly and without proper documentation, by lay Justices. The majority lasted for the full twenty-eight days and were made by a single Justice, at home rather than in court, and often at times when a full juvenile bench was sitting at Cleveland. As Louis Blom-Cooper QC concluded, reviewing the Cleveland inquiry report, 'The magistrates acted as rubber stamps to applications to remove and detain children on the say-so of social workers . . . (their) rush to *ex parte* judgement was inexcusable.'

The Cleveland crisis provides case-study support for the argument made in Chapter Eight that the lay Justice system is a major weakness in the protection of civil liberties. The most that lay Justices can be trusted with is an emergency power to remove children for assessment for a very short time with a right provided to parents to challenge their orders immediately by appeal to a Crown Court judge. The most painful aspect of the Cleveland crisis was the plight of parents who were powerless even to put the case for reclaiming their children until the system permitted it, and it was this frustration which did some of the permanent damage to family relationships. Doctors, social workers, police and council officials shared the public blame, but the real failure lay in a justice system which gave their victims – both parents and children – no choice and no voice.

BIRTHRIGHTS

The right to become a parent has been put in issue as a result of the development of *in vitro* fertilization (IVF) techniques. Science has relieved much of the anguish and frustration of human infertility, which dogs an estimated ten per cent of relationships in Britain. The first 'test-tube baby' was born in 1979, and many hundreds have followed. The creation in a test-tube of an embryo formed from a husband's sperm and a wife's egg, and its subsequent implantation so as to bypass an obstruction in the womb, is now scarcely controversial. But those who fear that the laboratory of Drs Steptoe and Edwards will lead to the hatcheries of *Brave New World* point to the way in which early human embryos are used for research and experimentation, and then tipped down a sink. They can be frozen, for implantation years or even centuries later, and they may soon be able to grow to babyhood in artificial wombs, or even in the male abdominal cavity. A committee chaired by Dame Mary Warnock comprehensively surveyed the ethical issues in human reproductive technology which had emerged by 1984, and the Government is still pondering its recommendation for legislation. In the meantime, questions are being dealt with by hospital 'ethics committees' overseen by the Voluntary Licensing Authority (VLA) set up in 1985 to regulate the work of IVF clinics. At present it operates on a persuasive rather than a legal basis, although it is likely that it will be given statutory powers to enforce its ethical rulings, with the criminal law as a back-stop to punish doctors who disobey. Parliament has so far narrowly resisted back-bench MPs' attempts to outlaw research on human embryos, which is conducted for the purpose of finding cures for infertility and unlocking the causes of genetic disease. The Warnock Report recommendation, which would permit experimentation with embryos for up to fourteen days after fertilization, has been endorsed by the VLA but will remain a precarious rule given the strength of MPs' feelings on the subject.

The difficulty of making people good by Act of Parliament is compounded where the objective deemed to be 'bad' is the creation of a child. Now that IVF techniques are available to married couples, what right has the State, or its hospital doctors, to withhold the benefits of treatment from unmarried couples, or from lesbian couples or single women? Article 12 of the European Convention guarantees to all citizens 'the right to found a family', and it is likely to be asserted against doctors who make value-judgements about applicants deemed 'unsuitable' for the opportunity of motherhood. The first such case was brought unsuccessfully by a prostitute who had been denied the opportunity of infertility treatment. The Hospital Ethics Committee's decision to turn her away was wrong in principle, although justified in terms of the practical need to give priority to married couples while waiting-lists are long. When *in vitro* treatment becomes more widely available, it will be difficult to deny access to single women. The Warnock Report was in some respects excessively paternalistic – by, for example, recommending that doctors should not be allowed to use the frozen sperm of recently deceased husbands to create embryos for implantation in their widows. The question of who owns pre-implantation embryos, and the consequences for the laws of inheritance of posthumous births from frozen embryos, will undoubtedly tax the courts in the future, but this is hardly a reason to ban the development of IVF as a means of assisting fertile women to beat the biological clock by having children after their menopause.

One matter upon which the British Parliament has hastened to legislate is surrogate motherhood. The whole idea of surrogacy is abhorrent to many, although from the perspective of individual rights this total hostility is difficult to understand. For women who cannot or should not bear children as a result of a medical condition (such as heart disease or a defective womb or a propensity to miscarry) the artificial insemination of a willing surrogate may produce a wanted child 'fathered' by the husband of the marriage. A woman with functioning ovaries but a damaged womb can achieve children who are genetically hers as well as her husband's by a combination of laparoscopy for ovum recovery and *in vitro* fertilization, followed by embryo transfer to a surrogate. Such cases may be rare, but they argue against the total legal prohibition on surrogacy recommended by Warnock. In the United States, surrogacy services operated by doctors and lawyers fulfil a powerful need, notwithstanding the legal problems which occasionally ensue when surrogates decide to renege on their contract and to keep the child. The rights of infertile couples to enter into surrogacy arrangements, with professional advice and subject to safeguards such as medical supervision, genetic screening of the surrogate and adequate counselling, would seem to follow from the right to found a family.

It was precisely this right which was ignored by Parliament in 1985 when it rushed through the Surrogacy Arrangements Act, which has the familiar defects associated with legislation inspired by moral panic. The much publicized saga of 'Baby Cotton', the offspring of a proselytizing US surrogacy agency, outraged MPs and convinced them that 'something ought to be done'. The Act imposes a fine or short prison sentence on any person who receives a fee for advising or assisting a surrogacy arrangement. It does not prohibit surrogacy as such, but by punishing professionals who would otherwise be involved, it forces the infertile couples and the surrogate to make amateurish 'do it yourself' contracts and to proceed without the benefit of medical, legal and other counselling services. It is a squalid piece of legislation, which places the burden of proof on defendants and denies them the right to jury trial, as well as effectively denying citizens who wish to make lawful arrangements their basic entitlement to legal advice and professional help.

There can be no objection to the State regulating surrogacy services or restricting the opportunities for profiteering from them. There is an obvious danger of exploitation, which calls for carefully drafted contracts which make provision for the surrogate to receive adequate counselling prior to signing, adequate remuneration and an effective right to change her mind and keep the child, at least if it is genetically hers. In 1986 one meddling Social Services Department seized a surrogate's baby after its birth and had it made a ward of court: the judge, sensibly, decided that since there was no dispute between the parties the child's best interests obviously lay with the infertile couple who had commissioned it. Although many find surrogacy arrangements unpalatable, they are a measure of the desperation of otherwise childless couples who are asserting their freedom as individuals to make private arrangements with another individual to bear their wanted child. Instead of providing a compassionate and supportive framework in which this aspiration may be realized, British law stigmatizes them and isolates them from professional help. Wealthy couples, of course, may (and do) find the liberty they seek in the United States.

THE RIGHT TO DIE

The bodies of suicides were once buried by night at crossroads, with a stake through their hearts and a stone on their heads. Until 1961, self-murder was a crime, and would-be suicides could be prosecuted for botching their own demise. The law took its cue from Blackstone, who condemned the suicide for the spiritual presumption of 'invading the prerogative of the Almighty, and rushing into His immediate presence uncalled for'. The Suicide Act of 1961 abolished the old crime, but perpetuated punishment for any person 'who aids, abets, counsels or procures the suicide of another or an attempt by another to commit suicide'. The compassionate doctor who, by request, shortens the life of a dying patient remains technically guilty of murder, while anyone else who dares to help or advise a sufferer commits an offence of 'aiding and abetting suicide', punishable by up to fourteen years' imprisonment.

The harshness of the law can be mitigated in practice by a certain turning of blind eyes by coroners and prosecuting authorities when terminally ill patients are put out of their misery by close family members unmotivated by greed for inheritance, and genuine 'mercy killers' who are prosecuted for aiding and abetting generally receive suspended sentences. Where the evidence is clear that life was taken with an intention to kill, however, there is no defence to a prosecution for murder no matter how compassionate the circumstances. Moreover, the penalty for murder is fixed at life imprisonment. At Manchester Crown Court in 1988, a man who admitted to smothering his crippled and dying wife with a pillow after she had repeatedly begged him to cut short her sufferings in precisely that way was ruled to have no defence to a murder charge. When he changed his plea to guilty and was sentenced to life imprisonment, his jury published a joint statement of outrage at the result. It was a barbaric outcome, but one dictated by the inflexibility of the law. At very least, the mandatory life sentence for murder should be repealed.

What other alternatives are open to those who urge legal recognition for the right to decide the time and place of one's own death? Two enthusiastic euthanasiasts who offered to dispatch elderly members of 'Exit' with plastic bags and sleeping pills were convicted and gaoled for aiding and abetting suicide, but the High Court refused to injunct *The Guide to Self-Deliverance*, a 'do-it-yourself' instruction manual for members of the organization which set out the arguments against committing suicide before proceeding to explain how it could be accomplished effectively, without resort to desperate and unreliable measures such as wrist-slitting and drug-overdosing.[23] The Voluntary Euthanasia Society has many supporters who believe that terminally ill and bedridden individuals have a right to choose death with dignity, and to receive the assistance of doctors and relatives in effectuating that choice. Several European countries have legislated to permit doctors to ease the passing of dying patients, but attempts to modify the law in Britain have been unsuccessful.

The subject of euthanasia calls for careful distinctions which the present law does not draw, and which are left, somewhat unsatisfactorily, to police and prosecuting authorities. There are cases (which are increasing with the ability of medical science to prolong the pain-racked life of the terminally ill) where assistance to a free and rational decision to end life requires neither condemnation nor punishment. In Sir Thomas More's *Utopia*, priests and magistrates were obliged to counsel the incurably ill towards an 'honourable death'. After proper inquiry, a citizen was entitled to 'either dispatch himself out of that painful life, as out of a prison or a rack of torment, or else suffer himself willingly to be rid out of it by other'. The danger is that total repeal of the 'aiding and abetting' offence in the Suicide Act would leave the elderly open to artful persuasion by greedy relatives, and even permit the kind of manipulated hysteria which produced the mass suicides at Jones Town. *The Guide to Self-Deliverance* might be acceptable in the hands of adult members of a Euthanasia society, but few would wish it to be on open paperback sale to any temporarily depressed teenager. Applications to the courts for the right to have an 'assisted death' would be prone to difficulty and delay, and would in any event be doomed to failure in Britain so long as Section 2 of the Suicide Act is unamended. The choice for reformers is between a new law carefully enumerating the circumstances in which assistance may be given, or an amendment providing a defence if assistance is given with legitimate reason. Those who choose to attempt suicide by drug overdose sometimes leave notes withdrawing their consent to any treatment designed to revive them, although it remains to be seen whether such an instruction would protect a doctor either from prosecution for manslaughter if he obeyed it, or from a civil action for assault if he disobeyed it and was sued by the patient whose unbearable life had been saved.

ELEVEN

Freedom from Discrimination

'We hold these truths to be self-evident, that all men are created equal . . .' begins the Declaration of Independence. Of course, all men and women are not created equal in physical or intellectual attributes, and their entitlement to equality is really a right to have the same respect accorded to them as is shown to others who share their characteristics as human beings. Discrimination on grounds of race or sex involves the application of criteria which are irrelevant to the intrinsic human quality of an individual. It is behaviour we have come to regard as immoral and to recognize as socially divisive. Law does not and cannot change the way people think about each other, but it can deter the translation of prejudice into actions which disadvantage and harm fellow citizens. In performing this deterrent function, it may further promote equality by educating others to recognize and despise racist and sexist actions, and encourage reconsideration of socially ingrained customs and prejudices which have hitherto justified discriminating behaviour. It may also – much more controversially – have a remedial role to play, by subordinating other freedoms to an overriding social objective of eliminating the root causes of inequality. British law has yet to endorse 'positive discrimination' – the policy of specially favouring minorities in order to redress existing imbalances.

The common law failed abjectly to counter inequality. Freedom of contract prevailed, and the providers of goods and services could discriminate against women and blacks to their heart's content. But in the USA, beginning with the great case of *Brown* v. *Board of Education* in 1954,[1] the Supreme Court was able to use constitutional guarantees of equality to strike down discriminatory rules, and in 1964 Congress passed the momentous Civil Rights Act. Under the influence of this American example, and shaken by the racial disturbances in Notting Hill and the racist hysteria whipped up during the Smethwick by-election, the British Parliament passed its first Race Relations Act in 1965.

This was a modest measure, much improved in 1968 and extended in 1976. In that year, and also associated with the commitment of Roy (now Lord) Jenkins as Home Secretary, came the Sex Discrimination Act and the implementation of the Equal Pay Act. This legislation gave victims of discrimination the right to sue for damages, and established Commissions with the powers to receive complaints and assist in bringing them before the courts. Judicial reception of the legislation was at first hostile to the exercise of these new powers, but there has been a growing respect for the objectives of the legislation and an increasing judicial awareness that seemingly inconsequential sexist or racist practices cannot be overlooked on the principle that *de minimis non curat lex* (the law does not concern itself with trifles). Petty apartheid is not petty at all to those who suffer it all the time.

Discrimination on grounds of religion is largely a thing of the past. What has emerged as the most virulent and obnoxious form of contemporary intolerance is denigration and discrimination aimed at homosexuals. There are probably, more homosexuals than there are black people in Britain, yet the law affords no special protection against discrimination on the basis of sexual orientation. Indeed the law itself still positively discriminates against homosexuality in a number of respects. Its total prohibition of homosexual acts between consenting adults was repealed as recently as 1967, and it will take many more years for society to come to terms with the rights of gay people to be treated with the respect due to them as law-abiding human beings. It is ironic that for all the progress made over the past decade in improving the legal lot of women and ethnic groups, prejudice against homosexuals has been allowed free reign, fanned by the advent of Aids. In 1988 MPs gave further expression to that prejudice by passing a special law – Section 28 of the Local Government Act – designed to prevent local authorities from taking positive action to counter hostility to homosexuality. Transsexuals, too, suffer special legal disabilities. There is no more urgent change required in the law securing civil liberties than the inclusion of 'sexual orientation' as a ground of wrongful discrimination.

RACIAL DISCRIMINATION

Britain has no laws which expressly impose disabilities on persons according to their race or colour. Subject to satisfying rules about nationality and residence, members of all races may vote or travel on public transport or apply for the benefits of education and social services. The Race Relations Act is necessary, however, to protect those who are liable to be treated less favourably, in a whole range of situations, simply because of their colour or race or ethnic or national origin. That is the basic test for unlawful discrimination, applied by the 1976 Race Relations Act. It protects 'racial groups', defined not by strict reference to biology but to cultural traditions and community perceptions. If a group of people regard themselves, and are regarded by the community, as a distinct racial group, as a result of common history or social actions or language or religion, their members will be able to invoke the Act to combat discrimination which is based on their membership of the group.

This broad interpretation of the Act was laid down by the House of Lords in *Mandla* v. *Dowell Lee*, where a private school was held to have discriminated on racial grounds by refusing to admit an orthodox Sikh because he would have been obliged to wear a turban in contravention of its rules about school uniform.[2] The Law Lords decided that Sikhs, although biologically no different from other Punjabis, were a 'racial group' as a result of their distinctive history, language and religious beliefs. The discrimination in this case would not be 'justified' under the Act because the rules had no purpose other than to prohibit a display of ethnic origin. (A rule discriminating against Sikhs on public-health grounds – e.g. preventing beards being worn in a chocolate factory lest hairs fall into the vats – has been held to be justifiable.) When the landlord of the Cat and Mutton pub in the East End displayed a sign saying 'Sorry, No Travellers' he was held to be indirectly discriminating against gypsies, who form a racial group on the test established in *Mandla*'s case.[3]

The Act entitles members of racial groups to bring proceedings if subjected to less favourable treatment than members of other racial groups in a wide range of situations where discrimination has proved a serious social problem. The first area specified is in the provision of any goods, facilities or services. These wide expressions cover places of public entertainment or refreshment like dance halls, public houses, theatres, cinemas, cafés and public libraries. The Act covers hotels, boarding houses, trains, buses and air services. Businesses and professions which provide services are included (doctors and estate agents, for instance) and so are public bodies which provide services. There must be no discrimination in educational facilities or in banking or insurance facilities. In decided cases, it has been held that a car-hire firm could not refuse a car to a Trinidadian on the ground that its insurance cover did not extend to those born outside the UK. Lloyd's had to rewrite its car insurance policies to replace the 'born abroad' test with merely a residence requirement and proof of driving experience. A life-assurance company was required to desist from asking applicants whether they were 'Caucasian, Negroid or Asian'. Mecca could not refuse black youths admission to its Locarno Ballroom, Streatham, merely on the ground that to admit any black person might result in disturbances, or because youths of the same race had caused trouble in the past. A Lancashire estate agent who offered mortgage facilities to house buyers could not refuse to put up to the building society for whom he acted as agent an application by a Pakistani.

The Act prohibits an employer from discrimination in recruiting schemes or by refusing a black applicant employment, or by giving him different terms of employment or opportunities for training or promotion or by dismissing him. Segregation will, almost inevitably, mean discrimination – separate toilets for white and Asian employees have been held to infringe the Act. A body like the Law Society which licenses people to practise in a particular profession is not allowed to discriminate in conferring authorization or qualification. It is unlawful for trade unions or employers' organizations to discriminate by denying membership or refusing benefits. The 1976 Act for the first time specifically makes it unlawful for clubs with twenty-five or more members to discriminate on racial grounds in the admission of or treatment accorded to members. There is a special exception for clubs whose main object is to promote the interests of a particular racial group, so long as colour is not a factor in membership rulings. The Australian Association would be entitled to exclude Frenchmen and Filipinos, but not Australian Aborigines.

The Act applies to discrimination in housing, either by refusing to dispose of it to the applicant (whether by sale or lease) or by treating him differently when he is in the accommodation. There is an exception where the landlord lives there, shares accommodation with others and has accommodation for fewer than seven persons other than those in his or her household. Municipal housing is covered, so that local authorities cannot have rules for allocating council houses which discriminate against blacks or coloured people or foreigners. A property owner could not refuse accommodation to a Kenyan on the ground that he did not mix white and coloured tenants; an Indian doctor was discriminated against when he was told on the telephone that a house on a new estate was available but when he promptly called at the agent's office in person was informed that all the houses were sold. In housing, employment and elsewhere discriminatory advertisements are also prohibited. The obsessive racist Mr Robert Relf was eventually gaoled for refusing to take down the sign outside his house which read 'For sale to an English family'. Most racist advertisements are less obtrusive, and classifieds seeking New Zealand nannies or Jewish flat-mates may well be overlooked by the CRE, which has the sole responsibility for enforcing this section of the Act, in order to avoid vexatious prosecutions. None the less, as the Government White Paper on the Act points out, 'the public display of racial prejudices and preferences is inherently offensive and likely to encourage the spread of discriminatory attitudes and practices'.[4]

The most important innovation in the 1976 Act was to outlaw 'indirect discrimination', which occurs where a condition applies in theory to persons of all racial groups, but is in practice such that a considerably smaller proportion from one social group can comply with it than the proportion from other groups. The concept was imported from American law, where it is founded on the US Supreme Court ruling in *Griggs* v. *Duke Power Co.* that a condition requiring applicants for manual work at a power station to have graduated from high school or to have passed an IQ test discriminated in practice against Negroes and could not be justified as a necessary qualification for the job.[5] British law permits the indirect discriminator to prove that the condition is 'justifiable' on non-racial grounds – a test that has caused a good deal of confusion in the courts. Some judges have permitted indirect discrimination to continue where the condition in question is justified merely in terms of sound and acceptable business practice, while others have required proof that the condition is necessary to the economic viability of the business.

A recent example of how the House of Lords approaches the question of indirect discrimination and whether it can be justified on non-racial grounds is provided by *Orphanos* v. *Queen Mary College*.[6] The College had sought to implement Government cost-cutting by charging overseas students at an increased rate, unless they could show that they had been ordinarily resident in Britain or the EEC for the preceding three years. It was held that this rule indirectly discriminated against students of non-British or non-EEC nationality who wished to be admitted to the College, a considerably smaller proportion of whom could comply with the residence condition than the proportion of British or EEC nationals who could take advantage of it. Moreover, the discriminatory condition itself was not capable of being justified without regard to race. Although the motive for introducing it was to cut expenditure in the interests of economy (a reasonable and non-racist consideration), none the less the method chosen for cost-cutting was directed against foreign students. An across-the-board fee increase, or restrictions by reference to academic qualifications, would have been acceptable: but the College could not implement its chosen policy without having regard to the nationality of the applicants at whose expense the policy was carried into effect. This approach is welcome in that it requires the justification for indirect discrimination to be scrupulously devoid of racial considerations and to be related to reasons for imposing the actual condition and not to background motives.

The prime responsibility for making the Race Relations Act work belongs to the Commission for Racial Equality. It has a chairman and not more than fourteen members appointed by the Home Secretary; the various racial minorities are substantially represented in its composition. It is the aggrieved individual, not the Commission, who instigates a complaint of discrimination. The Commission will, on application, be able to give assistance to a claimant or potential claimant where the case raises an issue of principle or where it is unreasonable, for instance by reason of the case's complexity or the respective positions of the parties to the dispute, to expect claimants to proceed on their own behalf. 'Assistance' includes advice, conciliation, arranging for legal advice and assistance, and representation.

If the alleged discrimination is in the field of employment, the individual complains to an industrial tribunal, which may award compensation up to £8,500, or recommend that the employer take action to obviate or reduce the adverse effect on the complainant of the act of discrimination. All complaints are made to the County Court, where complainants have the burden of proving discrimination. If they succeed the court has power to award damages (including damages for injured feelings) and to grant an injunction restraining the defendant from discriminating unlawfully against the plaintiff. Damages of up to £7,500 may be awarded, but most cases where discrimination is proved result in nominal awards for 'hurt feelings' of a few hundred pounds. Such amounts are derisory, and operate neither as a deterrent nor as an appropriate compensation for public embarrassment (compare the lavish awards in libel cases). In 1987 the Court of Appeal decided that £3,000 was appropriate to compensate a Sri Lankan scientist for injury to her feelings as a result of being discriminated against in employment by a local Health Authority: it is to be hoped that this precedent will encourage higher awards of damages. The CRE has strongly recommended a new head of damages, namely 'recompense for any public humiliation suffered'.

One of the Commission's main purposes is to conduct investigations into discriminatory practices. It has powers to require the furnishing of information and the production of documents and to issue 'non-discrimination notices' which last for five years. The CRE's power to conduct formal investigations has been the subject of much litigation and a good deal of judicial hostility. In 1984 the House of Lords confirmed that the Commission's procedures could be challenged by judicial review (which is reasonable enough) but that it could only conduct a 'named-person investigation' (which carries the power to subpoena evidence) where it has concrete reason to suspect that the targeted individual or organization is guilty of unlawful discrimination.[7] This ruling has severely restricted the work of the Commission, by depriving it of the power to investigate thoroughly organizations in which blacks are severely under-represented, although there is no evidence pointing towards any specific unlawful act of discrimination. The subpoena powers attaching to named-person investigations are frequently the only way that such evidence can be produced. The dangers inherent in 'fishing expeditions' by State agencies with powers of compulsion must be balanced against the social evil they combat, and such powers have greater justification when the fruits of their use are confined to civil action rather than criminal prosecutions. Court decisions have drastically curtailed the effectiveness of the CRE as an investigatory body.

Under Section 71 of the Race Relations Act local authorities have a duty to carry out their functions with due regard to the need to eliminate discrimination and to promote good race relations. The courts, however, have been reluctant to allow councils free reign to use this power other than against organizations involved in acts of unlawful discrimination. Labour-controlled Leicester City Council took the view that it was entitled, given its twenty-five per cent population of blacks and Asians, to refuse its sporting facilities to the local football club, because the club refused to criticize those of its members who had played in a politically controversial tour of South Africa. The House of Lords held that although a Council is entitled to exercise its discretions in a way which conduces to good race relations, it was an 'abuse of power' to punish a club which had 'done no wrong'.[8] It is difficult to see how local authorities can give much meaning to Section 71 if their policy decisions may only disadvantage 'wrongdoers': good race relations are frequently jeopardized by actions which are entirely lawful. What was unfair and objectionable on free-speech grounds was the Council's heavy-handed insistence that the club should make a public statement condemning the tour, irrespective of the real beliefs of its members.

The law cannot produce racial harmony, but it can remove some causes of tension and grievance. In 1988, the Home Secretary announced that the Government was satisfied that the Act had worked to make private acts of discrimination much less virulent. While it is true that such acts have become decreasingly overt, recent studies suggest that the real level of racial discrimination in employment has remained constant since 1975, with over one third of private employers favouring white applicants over blacks with equivalent qualifications. (Discrimination can rarely be proved in court against companies which secretly instruct employment agencies and consultants to exclude members of certain races before the final job interview.) Over the same period, only a small proportion of cases brought under the Act in County Courts and industrial tribunals were successful, despite CRE backing.

In other words, the Act has made racial discrimination more subtle and cautious: cases fail through lack of concrete evidence, and the courts have hamstrung the CRE in its attempts to uncover evidence through formal investigations. The option of redressing the balance by policies of positive discrimination are precluded by the very fact that the Act makes them unlawful (discrimination against whites on racial grounds is equally forbidden), and the exceptions – where it can be shown that a racial group has 'special needs' justifying more favourable treatment – have been infrequently used. Indirect discrimination is too readily 'justifiable', and the protection afforded against 'victimization' is absurdly limited to reprisals against those who complain under the Act, and does not help those who are subjected to persistent racial abuse or harassment. The Home Secretary's complacency at the way the 1976 Act has worked is misplaced: it requires a thorough overhaul.

DISCRIMINATION AGAINST WOMEN

Nineteenth-century judges stood firmly against the advancement of women, relegating them to the same legal status as dogs and lunatics when excluding them from statutes which entitled 'persons' to be admitted to universities and professions. It was not until 1922 that women were given equal voting rights with men. The courts could have brought about this result as early as 1868, by applying to the Representation of the People Act of that year a statute which required that legislative words importing the masculine gender should be interpreted to include the female gender. The Court of Common Pleas, however, rejected the suit, reasoning that the denial to women of the right to vote

> is referable to the fact that in this country, in modern times, chiefly out of respect to women, and a sense of decorum, and not from their want of intellect, or their being for any other reason unfit, they have been excused from taking any share in this department of public affairs.[9]

More than a century later, when the Sex Discrimination Act of 1975 came into force, the same male paternalism was immediately evident. 'I must say it would be very wrong to my mind', said Lord Denning in an early test case, 'if this Statute were thought ... to do away with the chivalry and courtesy which we expect mankind to give womankind.'[10] For eight years the notorious El Vino's Wine Bar in Fleet Street survived legal challenges to its obviously discriminatory practice of refusing to serve women journalists and lawyers who stood with male colleagues at its bar – it was a long-standing traditional practice born of courtesy and chivalry which reasonable people (in the view of a succession of male judges) would not find objectionable. In 1983, at last, the Court of Appeal applied the simple terms of the Act to hold that El Vino's had plainly discriminated against women by denying them goods and services on the sole basis of their sex.[11] Considerations of 'chivalry' and 'courtesy' can no longer excuse differential treatment in employment or education, or in the provision of goods, services, facilities or premises.

The 1975 Sex Discrimination Act contains most of the provisions of the Race Relations Act that have already been discussed, including the prohibitions upon unjustifiable indirect discrimination. It applies to all aspects of employment recruiting policy (for example, advertising only for male school leavers), arrangements for interviewing, training methods, selection for promotion or transfer, lay-offs, redundancy or dismissal. Trade unions and employment agencies are also within the net of the 1975 Act. A printing union operating where there is a closed shop cannot maintain a male preserve by barring women from the union.

The Act defines discrimination under four heads: treating a woman less favourably than a man on account of sex; conversely treating a man less favourably than a woman; treating a married person less favourably, on grounds of marriage, than a single person; and fourthly, victimization against a complainant who has invoked the Act. Indirect discrimination is also outlawed when tests are applied which appear neutral but which in practice place one sex (or married people) at a disadvantage – for example, a rule that all clerks must be at least 6 ft tall. Complaints about discrimination in employment and training are made to an industrial tribunal which may award compensation up to a present maximum of £8,500.

The 1975 Act also affects education. It is unlawful for those responsible for an educational establishment (including school governors and university governing bodies) to discriminate on grounds of sex in admissions policy. No institute can lawfully operate a quota system for females, or require higher A-levels from them, or discriminate in the benefits and facilities offered. A local education authority may not provide worse science laboratories in its girls' schools than its boys' schools and nor may it, by supporting a greater number of grammar schools that are only for boys, produce a situation in which girls require a higher examination mark than boys in order to obtain a grammar-school place.[12] Other areas where sex discrimination is outlawed include:

the provision to the public of goods, facilities or services, including facilities offered by building societies, insurance companies, banks, credit institutions and HP companies; restaurants, public houses and places of entertainment; and local authorities and transport authorities. These changes in the law banned many common business practices, such as making a husband sign an HP contract when his wife, who had a good job of her own, was buying the goods, and the building-society practice of looking askance at spinster borrowers. In 1980 a furniture store was held by the Court of Appeal to have acted illegally when it required a woman buying a suite on credit to have her husband enter into a guarantee.[13]

In all these cases, the female complainant must prove that she was less favourably treated than a man, in the same circumstances, would have been, and that the predominant reason for this unfavourable treatment pertained to her being a woman. The principal target of the Act has been stereotyped assumptions of the sort: 'I like women but I will not employ them because they are unreliable.' The indirect discrimination provisions bring more subtle, and sometimes unconscious, forms of prejudice within the net. Thus a civil-service rule that all applicants for executive-officer position must be under twenty-eight years of age was struck down because in practice a much lower proportion of women than men could comply with it, given the propensity of women to have children during their twenties and return to employment later in life.[14] (The age limit was subsequently amended to forty-five.)

One particularly difficult problem has been how the Sex Discrimination Act affects women who are treated less favourably not on account of their sex as such, but as a result of the prospect of pregnancy, which is an additional characteristic of their sex. The courts have yet to develop a coherent and intellectually satisfactory approach to such 'sex plus' discrimination, which does not admit of comparison because men are incapable (subject, perhaps, to IVF developments) of bearing children. To compare pregnant women with men who suddenly contract hepatitis is both to degrade childbirth and to misunderstand the prejudice behind, say, a decision not to promote a woman because she is likely to have children. Some interim relief is afforded by the Employment Protection (Consolidation) Act of 1978, which guarantees pregnant women the right to return to work, together with maternity pay and time off for antenatal care and treatment (although the two-year qualifying period deprives many women workers of these rights). In 1988 the House of Lords held that a pregnant woman had been unfairly dismissed when she was selected from amongst other employees for redundancy because she would need maternity leave. Lord Griffiths remarked that

> it is often an inconvenience to an employer to have to make the necessary arrangements to keep a woman's job open for her whilst she is absent from work in order to have a baby, but this is a price that has to be paid as a part of the social and legal recognition of the equal status of women in the workplace.[15]

There are, of course, exceptions, and these are set out in Section 7 of the 1975 Act. It is permissible to discriminate by imposing height or weight requirements for policemen and prison officers, and to discriminate in the employment of ministers by those religions which believe that the Deity declines to communicate through female intermediaries. The overriding test is whether 'being a man is a genuine occupational qualification for the job' in a set of carefully defined situations which are for the most part sensible (e.g. in dramatic roles, or attendance in male lavatories). One curious exemption, inserted after frantic lobbying from the CBI, permits sex discrimination in employment or promotion to jobs involving work in countries whose customs are such that the duties could not effectively be performed by a woman. The assumption that Arabs will not do business with British women other than Mrs Thatcher is highly dubious, but is unlikely to be invalidated so long as British firms appoint only salesmen. In any event, why should Britain kowtow to the sexist prejudices of foreign businessmen? This loophole, quite indefensible in terms of the Act's own logic, applies to work in any overseas country, so that firms might justify a 'men only' policy on the basis of male mateship rituals in Australia or the amount of business transacted in West German brothels.

The Act establishes an Equal Opportunities Commission, with similar (although not quite as extensive) powers as the CRE to monitor compliance with the legislation. It may conduct formal investigations, compel evidence and the production of documents, serve non-discrimination notices, seek injunctions against discriminatory practices and support action in the courts by aggrieved individuals. But most of these powers have proved ineffective, as a result of the complexity of the law and court rulings which have complicated and cut down the investigatory powers. In consequence, relatively few formal investigations have been completed, and any which are can be challenged by way of a complete rehearing in the courts. The remedies, like those for racial discrimination, are limited, and litigants will often receive no more than nominal damages. English law does not permit 'class actions' by groups of individuals who have been similarly disadvantaged by sexist policies, and those few who do bring cases can be 'bought off' by out-of-court settlements which do not result in any alteration of the discriminatory practice. Like the Race Relations Act, the Sex Discrimination Act has deterred overt discrimination, without making much difference to social patterns which provide statistical proof that women still suffer massive disadvantage in training and employment and promotion to positions of influence and responsibility.

Women in Britain have secured a measure of equality in pay and conditions of employment only as a result of European law and practice. 'Equal pay for equal work' has long been recognized by the European Court of Justice as a fundamental human right, and Article 119 of the EEC Treaty requires all member countries to secure not only equal pay for the same work, but equal pay for work to which 'equal value' can be attributed. The Treaty applies directly to the United Kingdom, and it was in preparation for membership of the EEC that the first Equal Pay Act was passed in 1970, although it did not come into operation until 1975. It writes an equality clause into every woman's employment contract. The Act applies not only to basic pay, but to other matters in the contract of employment. It may require equality in provisions for over-time pay, bonus payments, sick-pay schemes, health insurance, holiday pay and length of holidays, luncheon vouchers, and other fringe benefits.

A woman who proves that she is not getting equal pay for work similar to a male colleague's will succeed unless the employer can show that there is a 'material difference' in their situations which constitutes a genuine reason for the pay differential. However, a 'material difference' is not confined to a difference in personal qualities, such as skills, experience and training. In 1987 the House of Lords opened the door to pay discrimination where a 'material circumstance' could be found in economic factors affecting the efficient running of the employer's business. It is difficult to understand why external business considerations, rather than the personal qualities of employees, should justify a deviation from the rule of 'equal pay for equal work'.

The Equal Pay Act has not, as its detractors predicted, led to any significant shrinkage in the jobs offered to women. Its initial weakness stemmed from the high degree of job segregation between men and women, so that it was in many cases difficult for complainants to find male employees in order to make comparisons. Job-evaluation schemes, intended to provide for such contingencies, were blocked by many organizations. In 1982 the European Court of Justice held that in consequence Britain was in breach of its E E C duties, and the Equal Pay (Amendment) Regulations of 1983 were necessary to allow a woman to claim equal pay not only where there is 'like work' or 'work rated as equivalent' being done by men, but also where she is employed on work where the demands made upon her (e.g. in terms of effort, skill or decision-taking) are of equal value to those of a man in the same employment. It took further pressure from Europe to impose equality in retirement age, which was not implemented until 1987. The House of Lords has recently shown a more robust determination to construe British law according to the 'equal pay for work of equal value' philosophy of the Treaty of Rome. It has insisted that basic-pay terms in employment contracts should reflect that equivalence, thus preventing employers from arguing that non-wage benefits enjoyed by women could compensate for discriminatory pay terms.[16] It has also foreclosed the 'token male' defence, whereby employers could point to a few men who were treated just as badly as the women complainants. When a woman claims equal pay for work of equal value, she need only specify a man doing equivalent work who is paid at a significantly higher rate, irrespective of whether there also happens to be a male who is earning her lower salary.[17] In reaching these decisions, the courts have been concerned to harmonize United Kingdom law with the requirements of E E C law.

Much, however, still remains to be done before women will achieve full legal protection against unequal treatment. Remedies for victimization are very limited, compensation (especially for indirect discrimination) is often derisory, the two-year qualifying period for maternity rights is unjust and employers are given too many opportunities to 'justify' less favourable treatment. The ease with which the law may be side-stepped by employment consultants whose instructions to discriminate can rarely be proved has become notorious, and provides a strong argument for giving the EOC wider power to conduct formal investigations. The most glaring defect of all is the non-availability of legal aid to bring sex-discrimination cases before industrial tribunals: the costs (especially if the case goes to appeal) preclude most women from complaining unless they receive financial backing from a trade union or the EOC. This is a breach of the spirit of our obligation, under EEC law, to provide a procedure whereby all employees with an 'equal pay for work of equal value' complaint can ventilate it in court. There is particular need for reform so that 'equal value' claims may be brought by groups and classes of persons, as well as by individuals.

HOMOSEXUALS AND TRANSSEXUALS

Discrimination on grounds of sexual orientation finds no place in the legislation discussed in this chapter, although it is rife both in the law and in the community. Homosexuality was not 'legalized' in 1967: it was merely permitted in private between two consenting males aged over twenty-one. It remains a criminal offence if it involves more than two persons, or a consenting male under twenty-one. It is a crime, without heterosexual equivalent, for a man to procure an act of gross indecency with another man, or for homosexual acts to take place between adults in the armed forces or the merchant navy or in the locked cubicle of a public lavatory. Homosexual contact advertisements, facilitating meetings between men for sexual purposes, have been held by the House of Lords to amount to the common-law offence of 'outraging public decency' in circumstances where similar heterosexual advertisements would not offend.[18] This residual impact of the criminal law on homosexual men (lesbians, for arcane historical reasons, labour under no such restraints) provides an excuse for much discriminatory and degrading police action in and around public toilets, frequently involving the use of *agents provocateurs*. Men are sometimes arrested under local by-laws for displaying affection in public: massive raids are occasionally mounted on 'gay' parties in private homes; in 1987 police in London were issued with plastic gloves in order to raid public houses frequented by homosexuals. Customs officers, too, can display an obsessive homophobia: thirty-six of them were involved in a long operation to intercept books imported by Gay's the Word, at a time when the influx of cocaine and heroin might have seemed a higher priority in the allocation of resources.

It must be said that international human-rights law has been unconscionably slow to protect the human rights of homosexuals. Egalitarian principles fashioned to combat race and sex discrimination have not taken the next logical step, as a result both of religious taboos and secular prejudices (Catholic and Communist dogma on the subject has at times been equally cruel). However, a number of European countries have either abolished the age of consent or lowered it to sixteen or eighteen in the case of homosexuals, and in 1988 the European Court of Human Rights ruled that some particularly harsh laws against homosexuals in the Irish Republic violated their right to privacy. The Court has insisted upon uniformity within each nation, and in 1982 the United Kingdom was obliged to lift the total prohibition on homosexuality in Northern Ireland and to incorporate the 1967 reforms, notwithstanding the efforts of the Reverend Ian Paisley and his cohorts to 'save our sons from sodomy'.[19]

Discrimination against homosexuals has taken place in some areas of the civil law. In family disputes, the courts have been reluctant to award custody to a parent who has entered a homosexual relationship, and the notion that it is rarely 'in the best interests of the child' to be exposed to a homosexual environment can affect adoption and fostering decisions as well. The law, and the officials who apply it, will not equate a permanent homosexual relationship with either marriage or a permanent heterosexual relationship. In consequence, homosexual couples are discriminated against in housing, and in the operation of taxation and immigration rules. The Sex Discrimination Act is of no assistance, other than in the rare case where a male homosexual can prove that he has been treated less favourably than a lesbian in the same circumstances (or vice versa).

The worst examples of legally sanctioned discrimination have occurred in the context of employment, where some tribunals have pronounced it 'fair' to dismiss workers for no reason other than a sudden discovery of their homosexuality. Although it has been held in several cases that an entirely irrational prejudice on the part of fellow-workers does not justify dismissal, the courts have allowed 'strong feelings amongst the general public' to justify the sacking of law-abiding homosexuals from jobs entailing supervision of young persons. (In other words, blameless citizens are punished because of an assumed public ignorance of the distinction between homosexuality and paedophilia.)

The cases of civil discrimination mentioned above were decided in the seventies, and it may be that courts would today take a more fair and rational approach. One family court judge, Mrs Justice Booth, has urged that homosexual couples in a stable relationship should be accorded exactly the same property rights as an unmarried couple of opposite sexes. In the context of national security, however, the Divisional Court has refused to find unreasonable a decision by GCHQ to sack a homosexual employee (see earlier, page 167). There is a disinclination in Britain to follow the refreshingly value-free logic of the Supreme Court of California:

> [A] particular sexual orientation might be dangerous in one profession and irrelevant to another. Necrophilism and necrosadism might be objectionable to a funeral director or embalmer, urolagnia in a laboratory technician, zooerastism in a veterinarian or trainer of guide-dogs, prolagnia in a fireman, undinism in a sailor, or dendrophilia in an arborist, yet none of these unusual tastes would seem to warrant disciplinary action against a geologist or shorthand reporter.[20]

Combating any form of discrimination requires, in the first place, a firm resolve by Government. The laws relating to sex and race discrimination were introduced by a committed Home Secretary who had a considerable measure of cross-party support. The present British Parliament has no leader of any stature prepared to champion the cause of homosexual rights, while back-bench MPs vie for headlines in 'gay-bashing' popular newspapers. In 1988 the Government supported 'Clause 28', which purports to prohibit the promotion of homosexuality or 'the teaching in any maintained school of the acceptability of homosexuality as a pretended family relationship'. It is doubtful whether Clause 28 will have the consequence that its sponsors desire or its opponents fear. It is in fact Section 28 of the Local Government Act of 1988, and applies only to local authorities, i.e. bodies which have no direct responsibility for, or control over, what is taught in schools. As a result of the 1986 Education Act, the conduct of maintained schools is under the direction of the governing body and it is the ultimate responsibility of the head teacher to determine and organize the secular curriculum. Thus Section 28 does not permit teachers to be dismissed for discussing homosexuality sensibly and truthfully. Even where local authorities have an advisory role, Section 28 must be read subject to the Education Act, whereby the need 'to encourage pupils to have due regard to moral considerations' permits the teaching of tolerance in order to counter pupils' ignorance or hatred of homosexuals.

A local authority does not infringe Section 28 unless, at the time it decides to grant funds to a homosexual group, it either desires or is well aware of the fact that its action will 'promote homosexuality', i.e. result in an increase in the number of homosexuals. It follows that there is nothing to stop a local authority from funding gay youth groups or counselling services where the intention is not to 'promote' homosexuality but rather to assist homosexuals to cope with an existing sexual orientation. There is a crucial distinction between promoting homosexuality and promoting tolerance towards homosexuals. None the less, Section 28 will doubtless have a chilling effect on some local authorities, who will use it as an excuse for withdrawing from homosexuals services similar to those provided for other disadvantaged groups. A council which is panicked into misusing Section 28 as an excuse for prejudice and discrimination in the provision of services will be open to challenge in the courts. What the advent of Clause 28 does show, quite dramatically, is the depth of the prejudice which will have to be overcome before discrimination on the grounds of sexual orientation is made unlawful.

Transsexuals, whose psychological commitment to a gender at odds with their biology is reinforced by hormone implants and surgical acquisition of artificial vaginas and even serviceable penises (phalloplasty), invite reinterpretation of the words 'male' and 'female' in the statutes which determine sexual status. In *Corbett* v. *Corbett*, a 1971 case which decided that seaman-turned-model April Ashley had no right to marry a man, the High Court settled on a strict biological determination.[21] This rule – simple to apply at the end of the day, but productive of much misery for those who have to all intents and purposes shed their biological sex – has been vigorously applied, and transsexuals are denied any remedy against instant dismissal by employers who discover their former identities. The right to have a change in sexual status officially acknowledged (e.g. by alteration of or addition to one's birth certificate) is supported by several decisions of the European Commission of Human Rights, but the European Court has held that such arrangements are entirely within the discretion of member States.[22] While biology may be acceptable as a bar to marriage (an institution traditionally associated with reproduction), it is difficult to see why those who function on most meaningful levels as a man or as a woman should not be labelled as such for the purposes of other contractual relationships.

FREEDOM OF RELIGION

The last British heretic to be burnt at the stake by order of a Church court suffered his punishment in 1612. In the nineteenth century, Unitarians, Roman Catholics and Jews were relieved from legal disabilities, and Charles Bradlaugh won emancipation for atheists – the Oaths Act of 1888 permitted them for the first time to take seats in Parliament and to give evidence in court by way of a solemn affirmation. The only religious disability which remains today is the requirement that the Sovereign must be a member of the Church of England, and that his or her spouse must on no account be or become a Roman Catholic. The Acts of Settlement which define the monarchy are in blatant breach of the European Convention guarantees of religious freedom, although few seem concerned that the Prince of Wales would not succeed to the throne were he to be baptized a Pentecostalist, or if Princess Diana were to convert to Roman Catholicism. (If his entire family converted, Andrew rather than Anne would succeed, in breach of the Sex Discrimination Act, under the rule of primogeniture which favours male inheritance.) Like a number of ancient laws applicable to the Crown – the Treason Act, for example, still punishes with death any adulterous Royal Consort – these obnoxious rules seem to have acquired a historic immunity to rational reform.

The Church of England retains a few advantages as the 'established' religion – notably seats for its bishops in the House of Lords and a theoretical protection for its doctrines by the law of blasphemy (see page 210). In other respects mainstream religions compete on even terms: 'collective worship' in State schools must not favour a particular religious denomination. We have a fine tradition of moderation in religious education, avoiding the contradictory US extremes of outlawing all prayer in school yet permitting education authorities to sanction the teaching of 'creationism'. The head of religious education in a Hertfordshire comprehensive lost his claim before an industrial tribunal for unfair dismissal when he refused to comply with the agreed county syllabus by insisting on teaching the biblical account of creation as historical fact. The BBC and IBA ensure that 'religious broadcasting' generally takes the form of ecumenical discussion of moral issues, avoiding the hysterical propaganda associated with television evangelism in the United States.

The Sunday Observance Act of 1780 is one of the few operational relics of ecclesiastical influence: the Lord's Day Observance Society still prosecutes an occasional shopkeeper or entertainer for livening up the 'British Sunday'. It was trade-union opposition, however, that was primarily responsible for the Government's defeat in 1986 over its attempts to reform the Shops Act to allow more extensive Sunday trading. Foodstuffs, alcohol, motoring accessories and an illogical list of other commodities may be sold on the Sabbath, and in recent years exemptions have been made for cinemas, theatres, galleries and museums.

Although the law no longer imposes special disabilities on adherents to particular religions, to what extent should it require special allowance to be made for those whom conscience impels to behave in unusual ways? This question has assumed some importance in the quest for a multi-racial and multi-cultural society, where respect should be accorded to firmly based religious beliefs so far as is consonant with the public interest. Spiritual obligations cannot be prayed in aid by way of defence to criminal charges – Jehovah's Witnesses who physically prevented a doctor from giving their child a blood transfusion would be guilty of manslaughter if the child died as a result, and Rastafarians can claim no special religious defence when charged with possession of cannabis. Sikhs were routinely convicted of driving motor-cycles without crash helmets until Parliament amended the law to allow them to wear turbans – a religious duty to which it should have been sensitive when the law was first introduced. In civil law there is obviously scope for greater flexibility, although employers have been held to have acted fairly by dismissing workers whose religious devotions prove unreasonably disruptive and put them in breach of their contract of employment.[23] In 1978 employers in 'closed shop' industries were forbidden to dismiss workers for refusing to join the trade union where such refusal is based on 'conscience or other deeply held conviction', although regrettably the burden of proof is placed upon the employee and several industrial tribunals have failed to understand the religious requirements of certain Hindu sects. There is a special Advisory Committee which considers claims by members of the armed forces for discharge on grounds of conscientious objection, which may arise from religious convictions acquired in the course of service. In these instances, of course, the 'conscience' need not be affected by religious beliefs – a rationally developed, unshakeable conviction against trade-union membership or service in Northern Ireland would also be entitled to respect.

Article 9 of the European Convention guarantees freedom of 'thought, conscience and religion' and the right to manifest religion in worship, teaching, practice and observance, subject to considerations of public health and safety and the need to protect the rights and freedoms of others. Toleration of religion is most severely tested in relation to cults and cranks whose activities, while profitable spiritually to their adherents and financially to their leaders, are both socially offensive and objectively nonsensical. Scientologists have been the most notable victims of unfair treatment. Until 1980 foreign members of this church were denied entry to Britain, and the courts have refused to concede that it is a 'religion' for the purpose of rates and tax relief. These decisions conflict with a recent Australian High Court ruling that Scientology fulfils the only general criteria for religion: 'First, belief in a supernatural Being, Thing or Principle and second, acceptance of canons of conduct in order to give effect to that belief.'[24]

The real question is not whether 'E meters' and 'dianetics' have the same validity as the communion and the catechism, or whether brain-washing Moonies, sexually promiscuous Children of God, callous Exclusive Brethren and the zombie followers of fashionable Bhagwans are as socially acceptable as those who heed the words of the Pope or Jimmy Swaggert or the Reverend Ian Paisley. The issue should be whether *any* religion is entitled to special benefits which are withheld from other idealistic endeavours with equal or greater claim to social utility. Positive discrimination in favour of religion is most objectionable in charity law, which in large measure exempts trusts for the advancement of religion from the obligation of paying tax. This benefit it does not extend to ethical or humanist societies, nor to such worthwhile secular enterprises as Amnesty International. The antisocial activities of registered charities like the Moonies and the Children of God simply emphasize the irrationality of a law which exempts an organization from a civic duty for no better reason than its commitment to spreading belief in a supernatural Being. In 1981 the libel jury which sat for six months to hear evidence of how the Unification Church of Sun Myung Moon brainwashed young followers and destroyed families, added a rider to its verdict recommending that charitable status should be withdrawn. The Attorney-General promised to investigate, but his successor announced in 1988 that the Moonies were, so far as the law was concerned, unassailably engaged in tax-free charitable pursuits.

TWELVE

A Bill of Rights for Britain?

It can confidently be asserted that such improvements in civil liberties as have been achieved in the past decade have come about more as a result of Britain's obligations under the European Convention of Human Rights and the Treaty of Rome than from initiatives by its own Government or by its elected Members of Parliament. That this should be so is an emphatic refutation of the traditional theory elaborated by Dicey that liberty is best left to unwritten constitutional conventions, statutes passed by a sovereign Parliament and a common law developed by judges and applied by juries. Something is missing in our complacent constitutional arrangements if the only remedy for so many abuses of State power is an appeal to a European Court which may, years after the injustice has occurred, oblige the United Kingdom to legislate so as to ensure it does not happen again. What is missing is a set of fundamental principles, contained in a statute which would provide the courts of this country with a power to strike down official decisions that infringe the liberty of the subject, unless those decisions are directly sanctioned by laws approved in Parliament. Most of the objectionable decisions and practices described in this book have never received the stamp of parliamentary approval, but have been based upon Ministerial or bureaucratic discretions, Home Office circulars, exercises of the royal prerogative, 'guidelines' issued by Attorneys-General and police chiefs, or codes of practice and 'standards' issued by bodies of Government appointees and never debated in Parliament. They are largely outside the control of the courts other than by way of 'judicial review', which cannot consider their merits but only check that the decisions have been procedurally fair and have not been made wholly irrationally. Why not short-cut the long trek to Strasbourg by bringing the European Convention back home, making it a part of British law, to be interpreted and applied by British judges in deciding cases which raise issues of fundamental freedoms?

The present Government opposes this reform (although many of its senior members supported it when in Opposition) on the ground that a Bill of Rights would undermine the principle of parliamentary sovereignty, by which Ministers are accountable to Parliament rather than to the courts for the unfair actions of their officials. But this theory has little relevance to the real world of modern party politics, where Ministers preside over vast bureaucracies run by anonymous public servants for whose mistakes they are in no meaningful sense responsible. True accountability, in any event, presupposes the availability of information about the workings of Whitehall – which will not be forthcoming without a Freedom of Information Act. MPs may ask questions or refer individual cases of maladministration to the Ombudsman or investigate departmental functioning through Select Committees of the House: their powers in each case are limited and capable of deflection by a defensive civil service or a determined Government. Occasional back-bench revolts in the governing party may block a controversial clause in a particular Bill, but most MPs will cower under the three-line whip. Politicians, moreover, cannot be trusted to champion the liberties of all who elect them. Some of our most oppressive legislation – the original Official Secrets Act, the Commonwealth Immigration Act of 1968, the Prevention of Terrorism Act and Clause 28 of the Local Government Act of 1988 – have had all-party support at the time they were passed. Many attacks on specific freedoms, such as the right to challenge jurors or to give professional advice on surrogacy arrangements, have been initiated by back-bench MPs.

Democracy, of course, does make most of us safe most of the time, and there is little likelihood that any Government would risk electoral reprisals by passing laws which deprive the majority of any right which they value. But it is minorities who are at risk – immigrants, homosexuals, persons suspected of crime, demonstrators, parents of children taken into care, mental patients and other classes of persons insufficiently numerous to wield electoral power but large enough to attract obloquy or resentment. Their only remedy, once Parliament has legislated, is to appeal to the European Court in Strasbourg on the grounds that the legislation is contrary to the British Government's undertaking to abide by the European Convention on Human Rights.

The Convention was drawn up in 1951. Politically, it was the product of a desire for Western European unity: its ideals were shaped by the need to have some legal bulwark against a resurgence of Fascism, and by a wish to articulate those civil rights which seemed threatened by Communist regimes in Eastern Europe. Ironically, it was drafted by the senior legal adviser at the Home Office, and supported by the Attlee Government despite the dire predictions of the Lord Chancellor that it would 'jeopardize our whole system of law, which we have laboriously built up over the centuries, in favour of some half-baked scheme to be administered by some unknown court'. Britain ratified the Convention in 1951, but did not accept the right of individual citizens to petition until 1966, when a less paranoid Labour Chancellor, Lord Gardiner, came to office. Its impact on English law did not begin until the next decade, when the Court at Strasbourg began to hand down decisions holding the United Kingdom in breach of the Convention for failures to guarantee certain basic rights to its citizens. Any person who believes that his or her rights under the Convention have been infringed by a court ruling or an administrative act, and who has exhausted all the possibilities of redress in the British courts, may complain to Strasbourg. If the complaint is upheld, the British Government is required by the Convention to change the law which permitted the original infringement.

In recent years, 'going to Strasbourg' has become an increasingly important journey for those denied any remedy by domestic law in Britain. The path was blazed by Stanley Golder, a prisoner denied by prison rules the right to consult a lawyer. In 1975 his complaint was upheld and the Government was obliged to alter the rules so as to allow all prisoners access to legal advice. Subsequently, European Court rulings were responsible for: putting an end to 'in depth' interrogation of suspects in Northern Ireland, birching of juveniles in the Isle of Man, and caning in State schools; liberalizing the test for contempt of court, permitting journalists to see 'discovered' documents read in open court, and allowing the media a right of appeal against suppression orders; providing some safeguards against lawless telephone tapping; ending the prohibition on homosexuality in Northern Ireland; removing certain discriminatory clauses in the immigration rules; securing some citizenship rights for British passport holders in East Africa; and requiring changes in the law to enlarge the rights of prisoners, parents of children in care, and mental patients. Every chapter in this book records cases where the European Court has forced alterations in British laws which have proved deficient in protecting fundamental freedoms. At the last count over one hundred separate changes since 1975 – to laws or to regulations or to administrative practices – have been attributed to actions brought against the British Government under the European Convention. Other milestones in civil liberties, such as the Data Protection Act, the Equal Pay Act and the abandonment of customs powers to intercept 'indecent' books and films, have come about only because of the United Kingdom's obligations under the EEC Treaty, which is being interpreted by reference to the principles in the European Convention.

Why do so many British laws and procedures and administrative decisions fall foul of the bedrock standards embodied in international treaties? The absence of any written constitutional guarantees of liberty which would empower our courts to correct abuses of power by State agencies, an over-reliance on doctrines about the sovereignty of Parliament and the accountability of Ministers, and the reluctance to guarantee to citizens enforceable legal rights have produced a society in which civil liberties are regarded as privileges granted at the discretion of the powerful rather than as rights capable of direct assertion by members of the public. There are gaps in the pieces of common and statute law, precisely because the politicians and judges responsible for producing the jigsaw have no clear idea of the ultimate picture. Amongst the main characteristics of the 'rule of law' in Britain at the beginning of 1989 can be included the following.

DISCRETIONARY JUSTICE

We repose wide discretions in police and other officials in the hope that they will act fairly. These discretions are not controlled by the law, or by the courts, although they may be informed by 'guidelines' issued by the Home Office or the Attorney-General. 'Guidelines' cover such important matters as the use of informers and secret surveillance devices, the criteria for collection of information on law-abiding citizens, the operation of the security service, the handling of pickets and demonstrators, the censorship of films, the vetting of jurors, the use of CS gas and rubber bullets, and the treatment of immigrants. They do not have the force of law, and there is no sanction for disobedience. As one senior police officer said, when taxed with mounting secret operations in contravention of a Home Office circular, 'there is no reason to respect an obscure piece of paper'. There is no right of peaceful assembly guaranteed by British law – instead, we have a polite letter from the Home Office to Chief Constables, reminding them to bear such a 'right' in mind when exercising their powers under the 1986 Public Order Act to control meetings and processions. Even the Association of Chief Police Officers has taken to issuing its own secret guidelines, one of which advocates the striking of demonstrators 'in a controlled manner with batons about the arms and legs and torsos' in certain crowd-control situations. In this way, the rule of law is replaced by the rule of thumb, and occasionally the rule of fist.

NOMINAL MINISTERIAL CONTROL

Many basic decisions about civil liberties are made the responsibility of the Home Secretary rather than the courts. These include such important matters as the power to: issue warrants to tap telephones and burgle homes; detain suspects for up to seven days under the Prevention of Terrorism Act; refer doubtful convictions back to the Court of Appeal; exclude aliens on the ground that their presence is contrary to the national interest; grant asylum and carry out deportations. The notion that the Home Secretary makes all these decisions himself, after careful and judicious weighing of the evidence, is the sheerest nonsense. For the most part, he has little time to do more than rubber-stamp the decisions advised by his officials. His 'accountability' to Parliament is avoided, in individual cases, by invoking the rule that no explanation is required where issues of national security are concerned.

PERVASIVE SECRECY

Most decisions and many policies which affect civil liberties are made and even implemented in secret. The Official Secrets Act supplemented by the extended common law of confidentiality casts a blanket of secrecy over the operations of the public service. The Public Records Act ensures that work within Whitehall will not see the light of day for at least thirty years, and for much longer if there is any prospect of embarrassing civil servants who are still alive, or casting any light at all on security operations. Unjust practices develop for years unchecked by public outcry; jury vetting had been institutionalized for five years before it was accidentally uncovered, and 'virginity testing' of immigrant wives and X-raying of their children's bone structures went on for some time before these practices were publicized and prohibited. The Security Service Act shrouds every activity – lawful or otherwise – of the intelligence services. Freedom of information, now a routine characteristic of most comparable democracies, is firmly resisted.

VARIABLE LOCAL PRACTICES

The extent to which you are allowed to enjoy a particular freedom may depend on which part of the country you happen to be living in. Police discretion means that the forty-three different Chief Constables have different policies on such basic matters as the use of summonses instead of warrants for arrest and imposition of blanket bans on marches under the Public Order Act. While John Alderson, as Chief Constable of Devon and Cornwall, shredded Special Branch intelligence on CND activists, Phillip Knights, Chief Constable of Birmingham, defends surreptitious surveillance of those who write letters in their local newspaper critical of nuclear weapons. The citizens of Manchester, thanks to the moral outlook of its Chief Constable, are unable to purchase books and magazines freely sold in other parts of the country. The powers given to local councils over cinemas have led to marked inconsistencies, as controversial films are banned in some localities but not in others. Rates of conviction and sentencing patterns and legal-aid grants differ markedly from one magistrates' court to the next.

LIMITED POWERS OF JUDICIAL REVIEW

The courts have a narrow role in examining the exercise of discretion by agents of the State. They will seldom upset a decision unless it can be shown to be so irrational that no reasonable official or tribunal could come to the same conclusion, or unless it has been made in 'bad faith' (i.e. corruptly or from some ulterior motive). Courts hardly ever find a police chief's operational decisions to be unreasonable, and are usually reluctant to question the logic of Ministerial decisions in immigration cases. They can intervene if the Minister has applied the wrong legal test, or acted unfairly by refusing to receive representations, but their 'supervisory role' is limited to ensuring that due process is observed. And when proprieties are not observed, the victim of abuse of power has no claim for compensation or damages.

SHAM PROTECTIONS

Reliance is placed on certain institutions to protect citizens' rights or to check the oppressive use of power. Some of these are little more than confidence tricks. The Press Council, for example, merely pretends to combat invasions of privacy by the Press: its decisions are neither respected nor obeyed. The Police Complaints Authority has serious defects. Lay Justices are meant to scrutinize police applications for search warrants, but rarely do more than rubber-stamp applications, and the Cleveland affair exposed them as incapable of protecting the position of innocent parents accused of abusing their children. Coroners' courts are expected to resolve the most serious disputes over deaths caused or contributed to by police action: their personnel and procedures are inadequate for uncovering truth or placing blame. The Commission for Racial Equality and the Equal Opportunities Commission lack the powers necessary to uncover and eradicate pervasive but hidden forms of discrimination. The independence of the BBC and the IBA can be undermined by the Government's power of patronage, as it appoints its supporters both to the boards and to watchdog bodies like the BSC and BCC. The commissioners and tribunals appointed to monitor telephone tapping and MI5 lack the power to make proper investigations and to provide effective remedies.

PARLIAMENTARY SLOTH

The theory of Parliamentary sovereignty assumes that Governments and MPs will act to remedy defects in the laws affecting human rights. The Law Commission drafted a bill in 1979 to reform the law of breach of confidence: had it been enacted, much of the *Spycatcher* confusion would not have occurred. The Law Commission's reports on the need to reform the laws of treason, sedition, blasphemy and criminal libel have similarly been consigned either to the 'too hard' basket or to the waste basket. No action has been taken to implement the Younger Report on privacy, the Faulks Committee recommendations for reforming the law of libel, the Wilson Committee Report on the Public Records Act, the Prior Commission on Prisons, the Warnock Committee Report on reproductive technology, the Williams Committee Report on altering the law of obscenity or the Butler Committee's report urging changes in the law relating to mentally disordered offenders.

VULNERABILITY TO EMERGENCY LEGISLATION

Parliament's failure to implement carefully considered recommendations for improving the standards of civil liberties contrasts starkly with its capacity to rush into action to cut down freedoms when Government convenience dictates or where public emotions have been whipped up on the strength of an isolated case. Emergency legislation is generally bad legislation, which has a habit of remaining on the statute books long after the so-called emergency has passed. The Official Secrets Act, the Prevention of Terrorism Act, the Commonwealth Immigration Act and the ban on Sinn Fein broadcasts are leading examples. Back-bench MPs obsessed with getting their names in newspapers are a particular nuisance for civil liberties. In recent years they have erected a massive censorship apparatus to deal with a handful of 'video nasties', abolished the right to challenge jurors, passed the 'Surrogacy Arrangements Act' and inflicted 'Clause 28' after one local council was alleged to have stocked a Danish sex-education book in one of its libraries. In these repressive exercises they have been incited and supported by the popular Press, which frequently uses its own freedom to agitate against that of others, especially against its competitors in television.

LACK AND AWARENESS OF RIGHTS

There is a remarkable reluctance on the part of officialdom to acknowledge the existence of such rights as can be extracted from statutes and case law. This was epitomized in the Parliamentary debates over whether a person 'invited' to a police-station interview should be told of his clear statutory entitlement to leave at will unless or until he is arrested. The Government resisted, on the ground that explaining this fundamental liberty to suspects 'would impose an enormous administrative burden on the police'. The same reluctance was apparent throughout the debates on PACE – suspects should not be told of their qualified right to have a solicitor, or to have fingerprints destroyed after acquittal. 'Rights' are too much trouble, and there is always the danger that, if they are publicized, they might be exercised. (For this reason, juries are never told of their 'right' to bring back a verdict according to their consciences.) This is an attitude frequently displayed by officials towards complainants, who are perceived as 'trouble-makers' rather than citizens to be assisted in obtaining their due. It is partly explained, of course, by the lack of any formal constitutional guarantee of basic freedoms. It is difficult to be aware, let alone be proud, of 'rights' which derive from obscure sources – convoluted legal cases and complicated statutes – and which require the assistance of lawyers to extract and to explain.

VULNERABILITY TO COST-CUTTING

One consequence of the lack of public appreciation of civil liberties is that politicians are unable to detect many votes in enhancing them at times of financial stringency. Cut-backs in the health service arouse a public outcry far more vehement than cut-backs in legal aid. Lay Justices are cheaper than juries, so new penal statutes wherever possible exclude the right to elect for jury trial. Prisoners are treated inhumanely as a result of overcrowded prisons: the solution is to house them in squalid police cells rather than to devote resources to bail hostels. The opposition to enacting freedom-of-information legislation is based on the expense of answering requests for information. The Home Office resists demands for an independent tribunal to review doubtful convictions on the grounds that this would be too costly. The *value* of rights is rarely brought into account.

There is no single panacea which will cure all, or even most, of these unattractive features of British law relating to the liberty of the subject. Specific legislative reforms are required in almost every topic treated in this book, and may sooner or later receive piecemeal parliamentary attention. Changes in substantive law (such as the introduction of a Freedom of Information Act) are necessary, but not sufficient: attention must be paid to the procedures and remedies available to correct abuses of power. There is scope for considerable extension of administrative law, by providing the High Court with power to award compensation to victims of maladministration, to require that reasons be given for every decision – whether made by a Minister or by a civil-service mandarin – which infringes the liberty of the subject, and in some cases to scrutinize those reasons for justice as well as for due process. But the deepest defects lie in systems and in attitudes, with their pervasive secrecy and their preference for pragmatism over principle. The Government's refusal to make the European Convention of Human Rights part of British law represents both a symptom of the disease and a rejection of the best hope for a cure.

It frequently happens that judges who are constrained by existing law to turn down applications for relief against executive action remark that the action does, or may, conflict with the European Convention. This anomalous position is reached because the Convention, for all its influence, forms no part of British law. It cannot be applied by the High Court or used as a basis for suing the Home Office or raised by way of a defence against oppressive criminal prosecutions. There is no obligation on the Home Secretary or any of his officials to take it into account when exercising their discretion in deciding, for example, whether to allow an immigrant family to stay in the UK. It is only relevant in British courtrooms in two respects. Where a statute is ambiguous, the judge should not choose the interpretation which would breach the Convention (on the principle of construction that Parliament does not intend legislation to conflict with international treaties unless it uses the clearest language) and its terms may be taken into account when courts are considering questions of public policy. But judges are in no sense bound by it, or obliged to avoid decisions which conflict with it. When domestic law obliges them to reach such decisions, the losing party may, after exhausting all avenues of appeal in Britain, lodge a petition with the European Commission of Human Rights in Strasbourg. The Commission will investigate the application, and may hold a hearing about its admissibility or its merits. A decision by the Commission that Britain is in breach is not the end of the matter: its ruling is not definitive unless confirmed by the European Court. If the Court confirms that the United Kingdom is in breach, the Government is under an obligation (which is usually honoured, although not always speedily) to amend the law or regulation to bring it into line with the Convention.

'Going to Strasbourg', through all the procedures of the Commission and then of the Court, is a very slow process, rarely completed within four years and sometimes taking as long as seven. So why not short-circuit the procedure, by making the Convention directly enforceable in British courts? If an administrative practice is in stark conflict with a Convention guarantee, why permit it to continue for many years when it might be struck down in a matter of months by the High Court? Why the humiliation of Britain being condemned once again at the international bar by foreign judges, for abuses which British judges could have stopped years before, if only they had possessed the power?

The short answer is that the Government has blocked legislation, passed on several occasions in the Lords, which would incorporate the European Convention into British law. The most recent bill, drafted by Lord Scarman, simply provides that no Minister, bureaucrat or public body shall do any act which infringes the fundamental rights and freedoms set forth in the Convention. Any victim of such infringement may sue in a British Court – for an injunction to stop the practice, and for damages to compensate for any loss it has caused. The bill would not alter the balance of power between Parliament and the courts: it provides that legislation should not be interpreted as permitting any action which infringes fundamental rights, unless Parliament has specifically indicated in the legislation that human-rights considerations should not apply. In other words, Parliament remains sovereign, and may override the Bill of Rights (as far as UK courts are concerned) simply by indicating its intention so to do. It hardly seems an unreasonable imposition for a Government bent on infringing a basic freedom to declare its intentions openly.

The enactment of the European Convention as part of English law would measurably improve the protection for individual freedom. It would enable full-blooded challenges to be made to the way discretionary power is exercised by Ministers and officials, not merely by way of procedural review but from the first principles set forth in a Bill of Rights. There would, in addition, be the prospect of compensation for victims of abuses of power which is not available to them at present. There would be added protection against hasty legislation which impinges upon individual freedom, if only because its promoters would have the burden of justifying the clause which excludes the operation of the Convention. It would improve the quality and comprehensibility of judicial decision-making, since arguments from first principles are apt to be more logical, realistic and understandable than those artificially constructed from the rag-bag of case-law precedents. New generations of law students would be required to study human rights as a central part of constitutional law, and not merely as a diverting option or summer-term seminar. In criminal cases, it would provide a defence which could be raised against drag-net laws: juries could be reminded of their duty to uphold the rights of freedom of expression and peaceful assembly when considering their verdicts in cases brought under the Official Secrets Act or the Public Order Act.

Enactment of the European Convention would conduce to greater respect for the rights of minorities and provide the basis for challenging untrammelled discretions in Whitehall. It would not, however, provide a remedy for all, or even most, of the ills identified in this book, which require careful parliamentary amendment to specific pieces of legislation. In fact, its most beneficial force would be educative, as Harold Laski perceived in his pertinent comment on Bills of Rights:

> Granted that the people are educated to the appreciation of their purpose, they serve to draw attention . . . to the fact that vigilance is essential in the realm of what Cromwell called fundamentals. Bills of Rights are, quite undoubtedly, a check upon possible excess in the Government of the day. They warn us that certain popular powers have had to be fought for, and may have to be fought for again. The solemnity they embody serves to set the people on their guard. It acts as a rallying point in the State for all who care deeply for the ideals of freedom.

Incorporation of the European Convention into British law is opposed, for different reasons, by the Thatcher Cabinet, the Labour front bench and the heads of the Civil Service. It is not surprising Governments and their servants should oppose a reform which limits their opportunities to be judges in their own cause. Incorporation would bring administrative acts squarely within the supervision of the High Court – a prospect seen at best as inconvenient and at worst as meddlesome. The Thatcher Government claims that a directly enforceable Convention would undermine the traditions of parliamentary sovereignty and Ministerial accountability – traditions which notably serve to hide civil servants behind Ministers with parliamentary majorities. It also maintains that a Bill of Rights would somehow be alien to British jurisprudence, conveniently forgetting how the 1688 Bill of Rights secured freedom of speech in Parliament.

In the Labour Party, opposition to a Bill of Rights has a certain poignancy, when it is recalled how the last Labour Government persecuted pacifists for conspiracy, deported Philip Agee and Mark Hosenball, secretly approved jury-vetting, tried to suppress the Crossman diaries and made a very serious attempt to put Duncan Campbell behind bars on spying charges carrying up to thirty years' imprisonment (charges thrown out by a High Court judge on the grounds that they were 'unfair' and 'oppressive'). That era is conveniently captured in the story of James Malone, the antiques dealer who sued in the High Court when he discovered his telephone was tapped. The Labour Government sent its Solicitor-General hot-foot to the Strand to defend the lawless and unaccountable basis of State surveillance. The judge was unimpressed: he condemned the system as a blatant breach of the right to privacy guaranteed by the European Convention, but regretted that British law afforded no remedy. Malone took his case to Strasbourg: the Home Office spun it out for six years before their inevitable defeat. The moral, of course, is that all Governments, irrespective of their political philosophy, will put individual liberty at risk in the course of their exercise of the power of the State.

The left's suspicion of a Bill of Rights is fuelled by knee-jerk antipathy to judges, and to any measure which might increase the power of legal institutions that are perceived as hostile to socialist aspirations. This objection betrays a lack of understanding of both the nature of the European Convention and its potential for changing the very attitudes which are the subject of complaint. Fears about political conservatism of judges have been fuelled by their obeisance to Government claims of 'national security' and their hostility to collective action by trade unions. But judges have had no compunction in striking down decisions made by Tory Ministers and their civil servants on the grounds of procedural unfairness, as the many recent cases quoted in this book attest. (By 1987 the Cabinet Office had become so concerned about judicial scrutiny of executive decisions that it published a booklet – *The Judge over Your Shoulder* – instructing bureaucrats on how to make their actions less prone to challenge in the courts.) Judicial activism in the interests of fair play has been heavily influenced by the indirect effects of the European Convention: its incorporation would boost the power to do justice (to which the left should not be averse) and would assist in the process of predisposing the judiciary in favour of the liberties it guarantees.

The law, after all, is a discipline which trains and controls those who apply it. Should fundamental principles of liberty become part of that law, they will be reflected in the attitudes of the law's disciples. The great majority of judges may at present be white males from upper-middle-class backgrounds, but this will change as new generations with a more acceptable social, sexual and racial mix are appointed. In any event, the fear that incorporation of the European Convention would enable the courts to prohibit the policies of a future Labour Government is entirely misplaced: the rights set forth in the European Convention are not so much fundamental as elemental, and are no threat to socialist proposals for nationalization or redistribution of income.

The objection to judges having the necessary power to protect the liberty of the subject fails, at the end of the day, for want of any sensible alternative. The courts remain the only place where oppressive Government action against individuals may be checked. The parliamentary Opposition does not, by definition, have the numbers to intervene, short of a revolt by Government back-benchers. MPs may harass and embarrass Ministers over individual cases: they may call for explanations, but have no power to interfere further. The notion of Parliament as the sole guardian of liberty is risible: 3,000 pages of statutes and 2,000 separate statutory instruments receive Westminster's imprimatur each year, many of them without proper scrutiny or debate, their contents understood only by a handful of administrators and draftsmen. The media may take up particular cases of injustice, subject to their ability to obtain sufficient information and to the political allegiances of editors and proprietors. But trial by media – partial, simplistic and usually sensational – is no substitute for trials by judges, decided by fundamental principles of law.

A Bill of Rights is only a danger if it induces complacency about the state of civil liberties. Although the culture and history of England have produced a powerful public commitment to 'fair play', decisions taken by Orwell's 'striped trousered ones who rule' behind closed doors in Whitehall will always be liable to lack fairness, scruple or consistency. While Strasbourg is necessary as a court of last resort, it remains a serious reproach to British law that it lacks the internal dynamics to provide speedy and effective redress for many breaches of fundamental freedoms. The generalized promises of a Bill of Rights are no substitute for statutes which limit, precisely and clearly, the powers of officialdom, but they do provide a bedrock upon which such statutes may be built. A return to the first principles of a Bill of Rights would mark the recognition of the simple and demonstrable fact that individual freedom needs greater protection than Governments and their legislation, Parliaments and their elected representatives, or civil servants with their 'Home Office circulars' are capable of providing.

Recognition of the need for some checks on executive power has prompted thousands of people to sign 'Charter 88' – a demand for a new constitutional settlement which would enshrine in English law the fundamental freedoms guaranteed by the European Convention, provide effective domestic remedies for abuses of power, establish freedom of information and subject all executive prerogatives to the rule of law. The Charter was launched to mark the tricentenary of the 'glorious revolution' of 1688, which produced a Bill of Rights designed not to safeguard individual liberty but to effectuate a shift of power from the monarch to what was, by modern standards, an undemocratic Parliament. Today, the supremacy of Parliament means in practice the supremacy of the party with a majority in the House of Commons, and nothing in Charter 88 will change that. But a written constitution would make it more difficult for any ruling party to tamper with basic freedoms, and would provide a judicial system in which any victim of oppressive or discriminatory action by Government officials, unsanctioned by clear law, is entitled to a remedy. Charter 88 was drawn up in the month that the Home Secretary banned a political party from the air waves, proposed the abolition of the right to silence, and unveiled legislation which would empower him to order burglaries of private houses and which would make the revelation of scandals within the security services an offence punishable by two years' imprisonment. The shadow Home Secretary's response to Charter 88 was to condemn it, on the grounds that 'the only way to end the excess of a bad Government is to replace it with a better one'. Given the evidence in this book of excesses of power committed under both Labour and Conservative administrations, those genuinely concerned for individual liberty may find this response a counsel of despair.

NOTES

Introduction

1. Roger Bowles, *Law and the Economy* (Macmillan, 1982), pp. 90–91.

CHAPTER ONE: *Personal Liberty and Police Powers*

1. Report of an Inquiry by Sir Henry Fisher (HMSO, 1977).
2. *The Brixton Disorders*, Cmnd 8427 (1981).
3. Royal Commission on the Police (1962), Cmnd 1728, para. 30, approving the comment by the Royal Commission on Police Powers and Procedure, 1929 (Cmnd 3297).
4. *Rice* v. *Connolly*, [1966] 2 QB 414.
5. *R.* v. *Lemsatef* (1977), 1 WLR 812; *R.* v. *Houghton and Franciosy* (1979), Crim. LR 383.
6. Police and Criminal Evidence Act 1984, s. 29.
7. *R.* v. *Metropolitan Police Commissioner, ex parte Blackburn (No. 3)* (1973), QB 241 at p. 136.
8. ibid.
9. *R.* v. *Dytham* (1979), QB 722.
10. See *ex parte Blackburn* (1973), QB 241; *The Times*, 1 December 1979 and 7 March 1980.
11. *Arrowsmith* v. *Jenkins* (1962), 2 QB 561.
12. Police Act 1964, s. 4(1). And see generally, Laurence Lustgarten, *The Governance of Police* (Sweet & Maxwell, 1986).
13. PACE, s. 24.
14. (1914) 1 KB 595.
15. PACE, s.25 (5).
16. *Shaaban Bin Hussein* v. *Chong Fook Kam* (1970), AC 942, and see *Notham* v. *Police*, *The Times*, 28 November 1987.

17. *R.* v. *Gardner* (1979), 71 Cr. App. R 13, and see also *Chapman* v. *DPP, The Times*, 30 June 1988. But 'reasonable cause to believe' is decided objectively: the honesty of the appellant's belief is irrelevant (*Casterina* v. *Chief Constable of Surrey*, 10 June 1988 (Court of Appeal)).

18. *Baker* v. *Oxford* (1980), RTR 315.

19. *Christie* v. *Leachinsky* (1947), AC 573.

20. See PACE, s. 117, and *Swales* v. *Cox* (1981), QB 849.

21. See L. H. Leigh, *Police Powers in England and Wales*, 2nd edn (Butterworth, 1985), p. 62.

22. *R.* v. *Taylor* (1895), 59 JP 393.

23. Royal Commission on Criminal Procedure (1981), Cmnd 8092, paras. 3.69–3.70.

24. Police Complaints Board, *Triennial Review Report*, 1980 (London, HMSO, Cmnd 7966), para. 47.

25. Barry Irving, interviewed for *Tree of Liberty* (Granada Television, 1982), programme 3: *Arrest*.

26. *Sunday Times*, 18 March 1973.

27. *R.* v. *Hudson* (1980), 72 Cr. App. R 163.

28. See Cash Scorer and Pat Hewitt, *The Prevention of Terrorism Act: The Case for Repeal* (NCCL, 1981).

29. See Lord Shackleton's *Review of the Act* (Cmnd 7324, 1978) and Lord Jellicoe's *Review* (Cmnd 8803, 1983).

30. *Miranda* v. *Arizona*, 384 US 436 (1966).

31. Annex B, 'Delay in Notifying Arrest or Allowing Access to Legal Advice'.

32. *R.* v. *Yvonne Jones* (1978), 3 All ER 1098.

33. See *Lindley* v. *Rutter*, 1981 QB 128, and *R.* v. *Naylor*, 1979 Crim. LR 532.

34. See the Compton Report on *In Depth Interrogation* (HMSO, Cmnd 4823), and the Parker Committee on *Interrogation Procedures* (HMSO, Cmnd 4907).

35. *R.* v. *Mason* (1987), 3 All ER 481.

36. *R.* v. *Westlake*, 1979 Crim. LR 652.

37. *R.* v. *Isequilla* (1975), 1 WLR 716.

38. *R.* v. *Nottingham Justices, ex parte Davies* (1980), 2 All ER 775.

39. *Sommerset's Case* (1772), 20 State Tr. 1.

40. *R.* v. *Governor of Wormwood Scrubs Prison, ex parte Boydell* (1948), 2 KB 193.

41. *R.* v. *Governor of Brixton Prison, ex parte Kolczynski* (1955), 1 QB 540.

42. *R. v. Board of Control, ex parte Rutty* (1956), 2 QB 109.

43. *Ex parte Daisy Hopkins* (1891), 61 LJQB 240.

44. *White* v. *Metropolitan Police Commissioner, The Times,* 24 April 1984.

45. *Reynolds* v. *Metropolitan Police Commissioner* (1982), Crim. LR 600.

46. *Daly* v. *Metropolitan Police Commissioner, The Times,* 18 and 23 July 1980.

47. *Sturley* v. *Metropolitan Police Commissioner, The Times,* 27 June 1984.

48. *The Broadwater Farm Inquiry* (Karia Press, 1986), pp. 81–7.

49. *Lester Cooper* v. *Chief Constable of Merseyside, The Times,* 9 July 1985.

50. Pounder, *Police Computers and the Metropolitan Police* (GLC, 1985), p. 11.

51. Administration of Justice Act 1982, s. 62.

52. *R. v. Hammersmith Coroner, ex parte Peach* (1980), 2 All ER 7.

53. Paul Foot, *The Helen Smith Story* (Fontana, 1983), pp. 389–96.

54. HMSO, 1971, Cmnd 481.

55. Coroners' Rules 1953 (SI 1953, No. 205), p. 27 as amended by Coroners' (Amendment) Rules 1980 (SI 1980, No. 557), p. 8.

56. *Matto* v. *Wolverhampton Crown Court* Divisional Court, 20 May 1987. See also *Fox* v. *Chief Constable of Gwent,* 1985, 3 All ER 392, decided prior to PACE coming into force.

57. Compare *R. v. Delany, The Times,* 30 August 1988; *R. v. Allardice, The Times,* 11 May 1988; *R. v. Absolan* (Court of Appeal, 1 July 1988); and *R. v. Rarris, The Times,* 2 November 1988.

58. *R. v. Sang* (1980), AC 402.

59. See: *Bunning* v. *Gross* (1978), 19 ALR 641; *R. v. Ireland* (1970), 44 ALJR 263.

60. *Sorrells* v. *United States* (1932), 287 US 435; and *Shurman* v. *United States* (1958), 356 US 369.

61. *R. v. Ameer,* 1977 Crim. LR 104.

62. See G. Robertson, *Reluctant Judas* (Temple-Smith, 1976).

63. Report to the Home Secretary on the Actions of Police Officers Concerned with the Case of Kenneth Joseph Lennon (the Starritt Report), HC Paper 351.

64. *R. v. Macro,* 1969 Crim. LR 205.

CHAPTER TWO: *Public Protest*

1. *Hubbard* v. *Pitt* (1976), 1 QB 142.

2. *Hickman* v. *Maisey* (1900), 1 QB 752.

3. *Harrison* v. *Duke of Rutland* (1893), 1 QB 142.

4. *Arrowsmith* v. *Jenkins* (1963), 2 QB 561.

5. *Hague* v. *Committee for Industrial Organization*, 307 US 496 (Justice Roberts).

6. *Duncan* v. *Jones* (1936), 1 KB 249.

7. See 'Replies of Governments to the Secretary-General's Enquiry Relating to the Implementation of Articles 8–11 of the European Convention on Human Rights': Council of Europe, October 1976.

8. A local authority which cancels a firm booking of its hall by the National Front is liable for breach of contract: *Webster* v. *Newham Borough Council* (1980), *The Times*, 22 November.

9. House of Commons, 3rd reading, cols. 1069–70.

10. *R.* v. *Clarke* (No. 2) (1964), 2 QB 315.

11. Public Order Act 1986, s. 11.

12. See note 4 above.

13. Public Order Act 1986, s. 12.

14. ibid., s. 13.

15. See *Kent* v. *Metropolitan Police Commissioner*, *The Times*, 15 May 1981, and Application No. 8440/78, *Christians against Racism and Fascism* v. *UK* (1981, European Commission of Human Rights).

16. *News Group Newspapers Ltd* v. *Society of Graphical and Allied Trades*, 1982, *The Times*, 1 August 1986.

17. See, for example, *Kent* v. *Metropolitan Police Commissioner*, *The Times*, 15 May 1981; *R.* v. *Secretary of State for the Home Department, ex parte Northumbria Police Authority* (1987), 2 All ER 282.

18. *R.* v. *Howell* (1982), QB 416.

19. Templeman LJ in *R.* v. *Chief Constable of Devon and Cornwall, ex parte Central Electricity Generating Board* (1982), QB 458. This is a confused case, in which Lord Denning seemed to say that anyone who physically obstructs a worker would be guilty of breach of the peace. However, Lawton LJ makes clear that passive resistance cannot amount to a breach of the peace, and his view is consistent with *R.* v. *Howell* and later cases.

20. *Thomas* v. *Sawkins* (1935), 2 KB 249.

21. *Lavin* v. *Albert* (1982), AC 546.

22. *Parkin* v. *Norman* (1983), QB 92.

23. *Moss* v. *McLachlan* (1984), *The Times*, 29 November.

24. See *R.* v. *Mansfield JJ ex parte Sharkey* (1985), 1 All ER 193.

25. See 'The hounding of Valerie Waters', *Sunday Times*, 21 August 1977, and 'The Justice of Mrs Mercy', *Daily Mirror*, 20 March 1980.

26. *Lanham* v. *Bernard and Teye*, *The Times*, 23 June 1986.

27. *Nagy* v. *Weston* (1965), 1 All ER 78.

28. *Hirst* v. *Chief Constable of West Yorkshire*, *The Times*, 19 November 1986.

29. Once a section of the public is deprived of its *legal* right to use a road for travel, it ceases to be a 'highway' for the purpose of the Act. A physical obstruction does not affect a legal right, but exercise by police of these statutory powers to withdraw a lawful right (e.g. of vehicular access) by certain classes of persons may make a highway lose its character of a 'highway' in law: see *Bailey* v. *Jamieson*, 1978, 1 CPD 329; *Metcalf* v. *Australian Racing Club*, 78 WN (NSW) 1158.

30. *Hunt* v. *Brome* (1974), AC 587; *Kavanagh* v. *Hiscock* (1974), QB 600.

31. See Peter Thornton, *Public Order Law* (Financial Training, 1987), pp. 99–100, 119–20.

32. See *News Group* case, note 16 above.

33. See Thornton, note 31 above, at p. 16.

34. *R.* v. *Secretary of State for Home Department, ex parte Northumbria Police Authority* (1987), 2 All ER 282, *The Times*, 19 November 1987 (Court of Appeal).

35. *Platform 'Ärzte für das Leben'* v. *Austria*, European Court of Human Rights, 21 June 1988.

36. *Beatty* v. *Gillbanks* (1882), 2 QBD 308.

37. *Wise* v. *Dunning* (1902), 1 KB 167.

38. *Duncan* v. *Jones* (1936), 1 KB 218.

39. *Forbutt* v. *Blake* (1980), 51 FLR 465.

40. *Jordan* v. *Burgoyne* (1963), 2 QB 744.

41. *Brutus* v. *Cozens* (1973), AC 854.

42. Cmnd 6234 (1975).

43. *R.* v. *Malik* (1968), 1 All ER 582.

44. *Wiggins* v. *Field* (1968), 112 Sol. J 656; (1968), Crim. LR 503.

45. *Lees* v. *Parr* (1967), 3 All ER 181.

46. *Abrahams* v. *Cavey* (1967), 3 All ER 179.

47. See the Law Commission, *Offences against Religion and Public Worship*, Working Paper No. 79, 1981.

CHAPTER THREE: *Privacy*

1. *Baron Bernstein of Leigh* v. *Skyways* (1978), QB 479.
2. *Report of the Committee on Privacy* (1972), Cmnd 5012.
3. *Breach of Confidence*, Law Commission Report No. 110, Cmnd 8388, 1981.
4. *Duke of Argyll* v. *Duchess of Argyll* (1967), Ch. 302.
5. *Lennon* v. *News Group* (1978), FSR 573.
6. *Woodward* v. *Hutchins* (1977), 1 WLR 760.
7. *Kashoggi* v. *Smith* (1980), 130 NLJ 168.
8. Sir Robert Megarry VC in *Malone* v. *Metropolitan Police Commissioner* (1979), 2 WLR 700.
9. *Francome* v. *Mirror Group Newspapers* (1984), 2 All ER 408.
10. See *Janvier* v. *Sweeney* (1919), 2 KB 316.
11. *Sheen* v. *Clegg*, *Daily Telegraph*, 22 June 1961, and see *Daily Mail*, 15 May 1982, 'Love bug planted by the man next door'.
12. See G. Robertson, *People Against the Press* (Quartet, 1983).
13. *People under Pressure* (Press Council, 1980).
14. *Press Conduct in the Sutcliffe Case* (Press Council, 1983), Chap. 18, paras. 22 and 29.
15. 'Press Council: Ealing Vicarage rape case', *UK Press Gazette*, 9 March 1987.
16. See *Report of the Data Protection Committee* (the Lindop Committee), 1978, Cmnd 7341.
17. *Oxford* v. *Moss* (1978), 68 Cr. App. R 183; *DPP* v. *Withers* (1975), AC 852.
18. See Savage and Edwards, *A Guide to the Data Protection Act*, 2nd edn (Financial Training, 1985), p. 98.
19. Consumer Credit Act 1974, s. 158.
20. *New Statesman*, 5 March 1982.
21. *Semayne's Case* (1604), Eliz. 908.
22. *Entick* v. *Carrington*, 19 State J 1029 at 1066, per Lord Camden CJ.
23. *Wilkes* v. *Lord Halifax* (1763), 19 State Tr. 981.
24. *Robson* v. *Hallett* (1967), 2 QB 939; *Davis* v. *Lisle*, 1936 2 QB 434.
25. *McArdle* v. *Wallace* (1964), 108 Sol. J 483.
26. K. W. Lidstone, 'Magistrates, the police and search warrants' (1984) *Crim. LR* 449.
27. David Feldman, *The Law Relating to Entry, Search and Seizure* (Butterworth, 1987), p. 75.
28. *Application by Chief Constable of Avon and Somerset re Bristol United Press*,

Judgement of Stuart-Smith J, 23 October 1986. For the position of un-transmitted television film on subpoena, see *Senior* v. *Holdsworth, ex parte ITN*, 1976, 1 QB 23.

29. *The Brixton Disorders* (Lord Scarman), Cmnd 8427, 1981.

30. Code of Practice on Power of Stop and Search, Annex B: 'Reasonable Grounds for Suspicion'.

31. PACE (1984) s. 2(9)(a).

32. *R.* v. *IRC, ex parte Rossminster Ltd* (1980), AC 952.

33. *Boyd* v. *United States*, 116 US 616 at 625. And see Polyvios G. Polyviou, *Search and Seizure* (Duckworth, 1982), pp. 10–11.

34. *Columbia Picture Industries and Others* v. *Christopher Robinson and Others*, 19 December 1985, transcript p. 111.

35. L. H. Leigh, *Police Powers in England and Wales*, 2nd edn (Butterworth, 1985), p. 247.

36. *Report of the Committee of Privy Counsellors Appointed to Inquire into the Interception of Communications* (Chairman, Lord Birkett), Cmnd 283.

37. *Malone* v. *Metropolitan Police Commissioner* (No. 2) (1979), 2 All ER 620.

38. *Malone* v. *UK* (1985), 7 EHRR 14.

39. *Klass* v. *Federal Republic of Germany* (1978), 2 EHRR 214.

40. Royal Commission on Criminal Procedure (1981), Cmnd 8092, Chap. 3, paras. 53–60.

41. See 75 H. of C. Official Reports, pp. 159–60, 12 March 1985.

42. Interception of Communications Act 1985, s. 10.

43. See 75 H. of C. Official Reports, pp. 159–60, 12 March 1985.

44. *R.* v. *Secretary of State for the Home Department, ex parte Ruddock* (1987), 2 All ER 518. See also Ian Leigh, 'The security service, the Press and the courts', *Public Law*, Spring 1987, p. 15.

45. See C. Walker, 'Police surveillance by technical devices' (1980), *Public Law* 184.

46. *United States* v. *United States District Court*, 407 US 297, Mr Justice Powell.

CHAPTER FOUR: *Official Secrecy*

1. James Madison, cited by Mr Justice Michael Kirby, *The Right to Know* (Granada, 1984), p. 49.

2. Official Secrets bill (1989), Section 1(1).

3. See David Hooper, *Official Secrets – The Use and Abuse of the Act* (Secker & Warburg, 1987), Chap. 3.

4. *Report of the Select Committee on the Official Secrets Act* (HMSO, 1938).

5. See 22 November 1976, Hansard, House of Commons Debate, vol. 919, col. 1878 ff, and *Reform of Section 2 of the Official Secrets Act* (HMSO, 1978).

6. See Andrew Nicol, 'Official secrets and jury vetting', *Crim. LR* 284, 1979, and Crispin Aubrey, *Who's Watching You?* (Penguin Books, 1981).

7. See *Chandler* v. *DPP* (1964), AC 763, where four House of Lords judges considered the phrase 'interests of the State'. Lords Reid and Hodson said that 'State' meant the organized community, and implied that the phrase meant something akin to 'in the national interest'. Lords Devlin and Pearce adopted a narrower interpretation, indicating that the interests of the State were to be decided by having regard to the policies of the Government of today.

8. Geoffrey Cannon, *The Politics of Food* (Century, 1987), p. 32.

9. See Peter Thornton, *The Civil Liberties of the Zircon Affair* (NCCL, 1987).

10. See Police and Criminal Evidence Act, Schedule 1, paras. 12 (a)(11) and 14(c).

11. Hooper, op. cit., p. 201.

12. Departmental Committee on Section 2 of the Official Secrets Act 1911, Cmnd 5104, (1972) vol. 1.

13. *R.* v. *Boyer* (1949), 94 Can. Crim. Cases 195.

14. *The New York Times* v. *United States*, 403 US 713 (1971) at 729.

15. *Attorney-General* v. *Jonathan Cape Ltd* (1975), 3 All ER 484.

16. The *Spycatcher* saga is reported as *Attorney-General* v. *Guardian Newspapers (No 1)* (1987), 3 All ER 316, and (*No. 2*) (1988), 3 All ER 545.

17. *Attorney-General* v. *Brandon Book Publishers Ltd*, judgement of Ms Justice Carroll, 2 December 1986.

18. Lord Denning's *Report on the Profumo Affair* (1963), Cmnd 2152.

19. See the the House of Lords decision *in Re an Inquiry under the Company Security (Insider Dealing) Act 1985* (1988), 1 All ER 203.

20. Third Report from the Defence Committee 1979–80 HC 773 'The D Notice System'. See also *The D Notice System: Observations Presented by the Secretary of State for Defence* (1981), Cmnd 8129.

21. *Attorney-General* v. *Jonathan Cape* (see note 15 above).

22. *Committee of Privy Counsellors on Ministerial Memoirs* (Chairman Lord Radcliffe) (HMSO, 1976), Cmnd 6386.

23. See Lord Chancellor (Gardiner's) Parliamentary Statement: Hansard (1967), vol. 282, 5th series, col. 1657–8.

24. See David Rose, 'The secret world', *Guardian*, 7 January 1989.

25. *Modern Public Records* (1981), Cmnd 8024.

26. *Modern Public Records – White Paper Response* (1982), Cmnd 8531.

27. *R. v. Director of GCHQ, ex parte Hodges, The Times* law report, 26 July 1988.

28. *Statement on the Findings of the Conference of Privy Counsellors on Security* (1956), Cmnd 9715.

29. *Security Procedures in the Public Service* (1962), Cmnd 1681.

30. 197 House of Lords Debate, col. 1275, 21 June 1956.

31. *R. v. Home Secretary, ex parte Hosenball* (1977), 1 WLR 766.

32. *Council of Civil Service Unions v. Minister for the Civil Service* (1984), 3 All ER 935.

33. *Chandler v. DPP* (1964), AC 763.

34. See G. Robertson and A. Nicol, *Media Law* (Longman, 1984), p. 267.

35. *R. v. Joyce* (1946), AC 347.

36. Law Commission, *Treason, Sedition and Allied Offences*, Working Paper No. 72, (1977), pp. 31–2.

37. See *R. v. Miller* (1770), 20 State Tr. 870.

38. *R. v. Burns* (1886), 16 Cox's Crim. Cases 355.

39. And see the Canadian case of *Boucher v. R.* (1951), 2 Dominion LR 369, which is the best and most recent decision on the scope of sedition.

CHAPTER FIVE: *Censorship*

1. *R. v. Sedley* (1663), 1 Sid. 168.

2. *R. v. Curl* (1727), 2 Stra. 788; 93 ER 849.

3. *R. v. Hicklin* (1868), LR 3 QB 360 at p. 371.

4. *R. v. Thompson* (1900), 64 JP 456.

5. See Barry Cox, John Shirley and Martin Short, *The Fall of Scotland Yard* (Penguin Books, 1977), p. 160.

6. *Committee on Obscenity and Film Censorship (The Williams Committee)* (HMSO, 1979), Cmnd 7772, Chap. 4, para. 2.

7. See C. H. Rolph, *The Trial of Lady Chatterley* (Penguin Books, 1961), pp. 228–9.

8. *R. v. Martin Secker & Warburg* (1954), 2 All ER 683.

9. *R.* v. *Anderson* (1971), 3 All ER 1152 at p. 1160.

10. *Knuller* v. *DPP* (1973), AC 435 at 491.

11. *DPP* v. *Whyte* (1972), 3 All ER 12.

12. *R.* v. *Calder & Boyars Ltd* (1969), 1 QB 151 at p. 168.

13. ibid., p. 171.

14. *Calder* v. *Powell* (1965), 1 QB 509.

15. *R.* v. *Skirving* (1985), 2 All ER 705.

16. *DPP* v. *A & BC Chewing Gum* (1968), 1 QB 159.

17. *Olympia Press* v. *Hollis and Others* (1974), 1 All ER 108.

18. See Hansard, 7 July 1964, Cols. 296, 302 and 358. The undertaking was reaffirmed in 1975 (letter from Solicitor-General, Mr Peter Archer, to Sir Geoffrey Home, 22 May 1975).

19. *Committee on Distribution of Criminal Business between Crown Courts and Magistrates' Courts* (HMSO, 1975), Cmnd 6323, p. 73.

20. *Pornography and Prostitution in Canada* (Canadian Government Publishing Centre), 1985.

21. *Lambeth Borough Council* v. *Grewel, The Times*, 26 November 1985.

22. *Report of Joint Committee on Censorship of the Theatre* (HMSO, 1967), HC 255 and 503.

23. *Conegate Ltd* v. *Customs and Excise Commissioners* (1986), 2 All ER 688.

24. *Shaw* v. *DPP* (1962), AC 220 at p. 268.

25. *Knuller* v. *DPP* (1973), AC 435.

26. *R.* v. *Atwood* (1617), Cro. Jac. 421.

27. *R.* v. *Hetherington* (1840), 4 St. Tr. (NS) 563.

28. *R.* v. *Moxon* (1841), 4 St. Tr. (NS) 693.

29. *R.* v. *Lemon and Gay News Ltd* (1978), 68 Cr. App. R 381.

30. Law Commission, *Offences Against Religion and Public Worship*, Working Paper No. 79, 1981.

CHAPTER SIX: *Regulation: Film, Video, and Television*

1. *Mills* v. *London County Council* (1927), 1 KB 213.

2. (1942) 385 HC Deb 504.

3. See John Trevelyan, *What the Censor Saw* (Michael Joseph, 1973), p. 141.

4. Attorney-General's Reference, No. 5 of 1980 [1980] 3 All ER 816.

5. See Martin Barker (ed.), *The Video Nasties* (Pluto Press, 1984), and Michael

Tracey, 'Casting cold water on the ketchup', *The Times*, 25 February 1984.

6. See Statement of Attorney-General, House of Commons, 23 June 1984.

7. British Board of Film Classification, *Annual Report* (1986).

8. Nicholas Shakespeare, 'The independent front-line troops', *The Times*, 5 April 1985.

9. Letter from Lord Normanbrook (Chairman, BBC) to Postmaster-General, 19 June 1964. The contents of this letter are noted in the prescribing memorandum under Clause 13(4) of the BBC Licence.

10. *Report of Joint Committee on Censorship of the Theatre*, Appendix 3, 'Control over the Subject Matter of Programmes in BBC Television', p. 113.

11. See Nancy Banks-Smith, 'The sad scandal of the BBC infibulation', *Guardian*, 4 March 1983.

12. David Hare, 'Ah mischief: the role of public broadcasting', *Guardian*, 15 August 1981.

13. Letter from Alastair Milne (Director of Programmes, BBC) to Dennis Potter, 19 March 1976.

14. Letter from Sir Michael Swann (Chairman, BBC) to Ben Whittaker (Chairman, Defence of Literature and the Arts Society), 25 March 1976.

15. Peter Fiddick, 'Brutal truth barred from the screens', *Guardian*, 23 January 1978, p. 8.

16. Hansard, House of Lords, 22 May 1952, col. 1297.

17. Broadcasting Act 1981, s. 19.

18. *Attorney-General ex rel. McWhirter* v. *IBA* (1973), 1 QB 629 per Lord Denning at p. 652.

19. *Report of the Committee on the Future of Broadcasting*, chaired by Lord Annan (HMSO, 1977), Cmnd 6753.

20. *R.* v. *IBA, ex parte Whitehouse* (1984), *The Times*, 14 April.

21. *R.* v. *IBA, ex parte Whitehouse* (1985), Court of Appeal.

22. *The Development of Cable Systems and Services* (April 1983), Cmnd 8866 (the Hunt Report).

23. See 'Aide-Mémoire' of 3 April 1969 (between the BBC and the Conservative and Labour Parties).

24. *R.* v. *Broadcasting Complaints Commissions, ex parte Owen* (1985), 2 All ER 522.

25. *Report of the Committee on the Future of Broadcasting* (see note 19 above), Chap. 6, para. 11.

26. Broadcasting Act (1981) s. 54(1).

27. *National Anti-Fluoridation Campaign* v. *Medical Express*, Report of BCC (1982), p. 7.

28. *'Life'* v. *'Nationwide'*, adjudication dated 28 August 1982.

29. *Report of the Broadcasting Complaints Commission*, 1985, para. 2.

30. *Newspaper Society* v. *'Diverse Reports'*, 1985, Report of BCC, p. 22.

CHAPTER SEVEN: *Freedom of Expression*

1. *James* v. *Commonwealth of Australia* (1936) AC 578.

2. William Blackstone, *Commentaries* (1765) Book IV, pp. 151–2.

3. *Schering Chemicals* v. *Falkman Ltd* (1981) 2 All ER 321 at p. 334.

4. *Attorney-General* v. *BBC*, *The Times*, 5 and 18 December 1987.

5. *Lloyds Bank International* v. *Dow Jones (Publishing) Europe Ltd* (1983) 27 May, unreported.

6. *The New York Times* v. *United States* 403 US 713.

7. *Duke of Argyll* v. *Duchess of Argyll* (1967) Ch. 302.

8. *Attorney-General* v. *Jonathan Cape Ltd* (1975) 3 All ER 484.

9. *BSC* v. *Granada Television Ltd* (1981) 1 All ER 484.

10. *Woodward* v. *Hutchins* (1977) 2 All ER 751.

11. *Francome* v. *Mirror Group Newspapers* (1984) 2 All ER 408.

12. *Lion Laboratories Ltd* v. *Evans and Express Newspapers* (1984) 2 All ER 417.

12(a). *Attorney-General* v. *Guardian Newspapers Ltd* (*No. 2*) (1988), 3 All ER 545.

13. *Hoare* v. *Silverlock* (1848) 12 QB 630.

14. *Lewis* v. *Daily Telegraph* (1964) AC 234 at p. 258, per Lord Reid.

15. *Mawe* v. *Pigott* (1869) IR 4 CL 54.

16. *Grappelli* v. *Derek Block* (1981) 2 All ER 272.

17. *Boston* v. *Bagshaw & Sons* (1966) 1 WLR 1126.

18. *The New York Times Co.* v. *Sullivan* 401 US 265.

19. See Section 7 of the 1952 Defamation Act, Part II.

20. Committee on Defamation (HMSO 1975) Cmnd 5909.

21. *Royal Commission on the Press*, Chairman: Lord MacGregor, Cmnd 6810 (1977).

22. See G. Robertson, *People against the Press* (Quartet, 1983).

23. *Royal Commission on the Press*, Chairman: Lord Shawcross (HMSO, 1962), Cmnd 1811, para. 325.

24. The Law Commission, Working Paper No. 84 (HMSO, 1982).

25. *Gleaves* v. *Deakin* (1980), A C 477 at p. 483, per Lord Diplock.

26. *Goldsmith* v. *Pressdram Ltd* (1976), 3 WLR 191.

27. Law of Libel Amendment Act 1888, s. 8.

28. *Desmond* v. *Thorne* (1982), 3 All ER 268.

CHAPTER EIGHT: *Fair Trial*

1. Lord Devlin, *Trial by Jury* (Stevens, 1956), Chap. 6.

2. *Scott* v. *Scott* (1913), A C 417.

3. *R.* v. *Central Criminal Court, ex parte Crook* (1984), *The Times*, 8 November, Divisional Court.

4. *R.* v. *Evesham JJ ex parte McDonagh* (1988), 1 All ER 371.

5. *Godfrey Hodgson, Dennis Woolf and Channel 4 Television* v. *United Kingdom*.

6. *R.* v. *Felixstowe JJ, ex parte Leigh* (1987), 1 All ER 551.

7. Speech at Annual Conference, Family Law Bar Association, 1987.

8. *Sunday Times* v. *United Kingdom* (1979), 2 EHRR 245.

9. *Attorney-General* v. *News Group Newspapers* (1986), 2 All ER 833 at p. 842.

10. *Attorney-General* v. *News Group Ltd* (1988) 2 All ER 906.

11. *R.* v. *Bolam, ex parte Haig* (1949), 93 SJ 220.

12. *Attorney-General* v. *English* (1982), 2 All ER 903.

13. *Attorney-General* v. *Newspaper Publishing PLC* (1987) 3 All ER 276.

14. *Attorney-General* v. *Observer and Others, in re Application by Derbyshire County Council* (1988) 1 All ER 385.

15. *R.* v. *Grey* (1900), 2 QB 36.

16. *R.* v. *Metropolitan Police Commissioner, ex parte Blackburn* (No. 2) (1968), 2 QB 150.

17. *Bushell's Case* (1670), 6 St. Tr. 999; Vaughan 135.

18. See *The Shadow Jury at Work*, Oxford University Penal Research Unit (1974).

19. See *United States* v. *Dougherty* 473 Fed. Rep. (2nd series), p. 1113.

20. Morris Report (Cmnd 2627).

21. *R.* v. *Canterbury Justices, ex parte Klisiak* (1981), 2 All ER 129.

22. See David Leigh, *The Frontiers of Secrecy* (Booklist, 1980), p. 168ff.

23. *R.* v. *Mason* (1980), 71 Cr. App. R 157.

24. *R.* v. *Sheffield Crown Court, ex parte Brownlow* (1980), 2 All ER 444.

25. *A G.* v. *New Statesman & National Publishing Co. Ltd* (1981), QB 1.

26. See M. King and C. May, *Black Magistrates* (London Trust, 1985).

27. *Brass Tacks* (BBC Manchester), April 1984.

28. Elizabeth Burney, *Justices of the Peace: Magistrate, Court and Community* (Hutchinson, 1979).

29. Sir Thomas Skyrme, *The Changing Image of the Magistracy* (Macmillan, 1979).

30. Tony Gifford, *Where's the Justice?* (Penguin Books, 1986), p. 37.

31. John Baldwin and Michael McConville, *Jury Trials* (Clarendon, 1979).

32. See Martin Young and Peter Hill, *Rough Justice* (April 1983).

33. Lord Widgery CJ, *R.* v. *Murphy* (1975), 61 Cr. App. R 215.

34. *Stafford* v. *DPP* (1974), AC 878.

35. Patrick Devlin, *The Judge* (Oxford, 1979) Chap. 5.

36. Departmental Committee on Evidence of Identification in Criminal Cases (Chairman, Lord Devlin), 1976.

37. House of Commons Select Committee on Home Affairs, *Sixth Report 1981/2*, HC 421.

38. Cmnd 8856.

CHAPTER NINE: *Freedom of Movement*

1. Peter Kropotkin, *Memoirs of a Revolutionist* (London, 1899) p. 377.

2. Richard Crossman, *The Times*, 6 October 1972, quoted in Vaughan Bevan. *The Development of British Immigration Law* (Croom Helm, 1986), p. 81.

3. *The East African Asians* v. *UK* (*No. 2*) (1981), 3 EHRR 76.

4. The most detailed account is Ian Macdonald, *Immigration Law and Practice* (Butterworth, 1983).

5. Home Affairs Committee on the Immigration Rules and the European Convention, Evidence para. 110 HC 434.

6. *Abdulazis, Cabales and Balkandali*, case no. 15/1983/71.

7. *R.* v. *Immigration Appeal Tribunal, ex parte Bastiampillai* (1983), 2 All ER 844.

8. See *Worlds Apart: Women Under Immigration and Nationality Law* (Pluto Press, 1985).

9. *Swati* v. *Secretary of State* (1986), Immigration Appeal Reports 88.

10. *R.* v. *Secretary of State, ex parte Khawaja*, 1984 AC 74.

11. *R.* v. *Secretary of State, ex parte Khera, ex parte Khawaja* (1984), AC 74, reversing *Zamir's Case* (1980), AC 930.

12. *R.* v. *Bouchereau* (1977), ECR 1999.

13. *R.* v. *Nazari* (1980), 3 All ER 880.

14. *Ex parte Soblen* (1963), 2 QB 243.

15. Report of the Committee on Immigration Appeals, Cmnd 3387, 1967, para. 144.

16. *Ex parte Hosenball* (1977) 3 All ER 452.

17. See *Re H*, *The Times*, 24 March 1988.

18. *Amekrane Case*, 16 Year Book ECHR 356 (1973).

19. *Bugdaycay* v. *Secretary of State* (1987), 1 All ER 940.

20. *Ex parte Sivakumaran*, *The Times*, 17 December 1987.

21. Compare Sir David Maxwell-Fife, Written Parliamentary Answer, 24 June 1954 (529 HC Deb 50) with 'Noted scientist ends his exile after 25 years', *The New York Times*, 1 April 1977.

22. *Government of Belgium* v. *Postlethwaite* (1987), 2 All ER 985.

23. *R.* v. *Governor of Brixton Prison, ex parte Soering* (Divisional Court, 11 December 1987).

24. See *Cheng* v. *Governor of Pentonville Prison* (1973), AC 931; *Schtraks* v. *Government of Israel* (1964), AC 556.

25. *R.* v. *Governor of Brixton Prison, ex parte Kolczynski* (1955) 1 QB 540.

26. *R.* v. *Governor of Brixton Prison, ex parte Enaharo* (1963), 2 QB 455; *Zacharias* v. *Cyprus* (1963), AC 634.

27. The writ of *ne exeat regno* was revived in an unsuccessful attempt to stop a New Zealand rugby team from travelling to South Africa: *Parsons* v. *Burk* (1971), NZLR 244.

28. 209 HL Deb. 860 (16 June 1958) and see HC Deb. 265 (Written Answers), 15 November 1974.

29. *Council of Civil Service Unions* v. *Minister for the Civil Service* (1985), AC 374.

30. *R.* v. *Secretary of State for Foreign and Commonwealth Affairs ex parte Everett*, *The Times*, 1 November 1978.

31. There is an arguable right to a passport under EEC law. See directive 68/360, art. 2.

32. *Report of the Committee of Privy Councillors Appointed to Inquire into the Recruitment of Mercenaries* (1976), Cmnd 6569.

33. See Wilfred Burchett and Derek Roebuck. *The Whores of War – Mercenaries Today* (Penguin Books, 1977).

CHAPTER TEN: *Freedom from Undue Control*

1. *R.* v. *Secretary of State for the Home Department, ex parte Herbage (No. 2)* (1987), 1 All ER 324.

2. *Williams* v. *Home Office (No. 2)* (1981), 1 All ER 1211.

3. *Golder* v. *UK*, ECHR series A, vol. 18 (1975).

4. *Raymond* v. *Honey* (1983), AC 1.

5. *Ex parte Anderson* (1984), 2 WLR 725.

6. *Hamer* v. *UK* (1982), 4 EHRR 139.

7. *R.* v. *Hull Prison Board of Visitors, ex parte St Germain (No. 2)* (1979), 2 WLR 47.

8. *Campbell & Fell* v. *UK* (1983), 5 EHRR 207, (1984) 7 EHRR 165, and see now *ex parte Leech*, *The Times*, 5 February 1988, and *ex parte Hove/McCartan* (1988), 2 WLR 177.

9. See Richard Moran, *Knowing Right from Wrong* (Macmillan, 1981).

10. *Report of the Committee on Mentally Abnormal Offenders* (1975), Cmnd 6244.

11. *X* v. *United Kingdom* (1981), 4 EHRR 188.

12. *Home Secretary* v. *Oxford Regional Mental Health Review Tribunal* (1987), 3 All ER 8.

13. e.g. *ex parte Pickering* (1986), 1 All ER 99; *ex parte Clatworthy* (1985), 3 All ER 699.

14. See, for example, *R.* v. *Hallstrom (no. 2)* (1986), 2 All ER 306.

15. *Attorney-General* v. *Associated Newspapers*, Divisional Court, 20 October 1988.

16. *Re F*, Court of Appeal, 3 February 1989.

17. *Gillick* v. *West Norfolk and Wisbech Area Health Authority* (1985), 3 All ER 402.

18. *R.* v. *B.* (1987), 2 All ER 206.

19. *A.* v. *Liverpool City Council* (1981), 2 All ER 385; *in re M and H (Minors)*, *The Times*, 29 July 1988.

20. *O* v. *United Kingdom*, European Court, 8 July 1987.

21. *A Child in Trust – Report of Inquiry into the Death of Jasmine Beckford* (London Borough of Brent, 1985).

22. *A Child in Mind – Report of Inquiry into the Death of Kimberley Carlile* (London Borough of Greenwich, 1987).

23. *Attorney-General* v. *Able* (1983), 3 WLR 845.

CHAPTER ELEVEN: *Freedom from Discrimination*

1. *Brown* v. *Board of Education*, 347 US 483 [1954].
2. *Mandla* v. *Dowell Lee* [1983] 2 AC 548.
3. *CRE* v. *Dutton* (1989), 1 All ER 306.
4. Cmnd 6234, p. 19.
5. *Griggs* v. *Duke Power Co.*, 401 US 424 (1971).
6. *Orphanos* v. *Queen Mary College*, [1985] 2 All ER 233.
7. *Commission for Racial Equality* v. *Prestige Group PLC*, [1984] 1 WLR 335.
8. *Wheeler* v. *Leicester City Council*, [1985] 2 All ER 1106.
9. Willes J in *Chorlton* v. *Lings*, LR 4 CP 374 [1868].
10. *Peake* v. *Automotive Products*, [1977] 1 CR 968.
11. *Gill* v. *El Vino Co. Ltd*, [1983] QB 425.
12. *Birmingham City Council* v. *EOC*, *The Times*, 24 February 1989.
13. *Quinn* v. *William Furniture Ltd*, [1980] *The Times*, 18 November.
14. *Price* v. *Civil Service Commission*, [1978] 1 CR 27.
15. *Brown* v. *Stockton-on-Tees Borough Council*, House of Lords, 21 April 1988.
16. *Hayward* v. *Cammell Laird* (1988), 2 All ER 257.
17. *Pickstone and Others* v. *Freemans PLC*, *The Times*, 1 July 1988.
18. *Knuller* v. *DPP*, [1973] AC 435.
19. *Dudgeon* v. *United Kingdom* (1981), 4 EHRR 188, and see *Norris* v. *Ireland*, 26 October 1988, Series A, No. 142.
20. *Morrison* v. *State Board of Education*, 461 2d 375.
21. *Corbett* v. *Corbett*, [1971] p. 83.
22. *Rees* v. *United Kingdom*, [Judgement, 17 October 1986].
23. See *Ahmad* v. *Inner London Education Authority*, [1978] QB 36; *Essen* v. *United Transport Executive*, [1975] 1 RLR 48.
24. *Church of the New Faith* v. *Commissioner for Payroll Tax*, [1983] 57 ACJR 785.

Table of Statutes

Table of Cases

Index

FOR THE BEST IN PAPERBACKS, LOOK FOR THE

In every corner of the world, on every subject under the sun, Penguin represents quality and variety – the very best in publishing today.

For complete information about books available from Penguin – including Pelicans, Puffins, Peregrines and Penguin Classics – and how to order them, write to us at the appropriate address below. Please note that for copyright reasons the selection of books varies from country to country.

In the United Kingdom: Please write to *Dept E.P., Penguin Books Ltd, Harmondsworth, Middlesex, UB7 0DA*

If you have any difficulty in obtaining a title, please send your order with the correct money, plus ten per cent for postage and packaging, to *PO Box No 11, West Drayton, Middlesex*

In the United States: Please write to *Dept BA, Penguin, 299 Murray Hill Parkway, East Rutherford, New Jersey 07073*

In Canada: Please write to *Penguin Books Canada Ltd, 2801 John Street, Markham, Ontario L3R 1B4*

In Australia: Please write to the *Marketing Department, Penguin Books Australia Ltd, P.O. Box 257, Ringwood, Victoria 3134*

In New Zealand: Please write to the *Marketing Department, Penguin Books (NZ) Ltd, Private Bag, Takapuna, Auckland 9*

In India: Please write to *Penguin Overseas Ltd, 706 Eros Apartments, 56 Nehru Place, New Delhi, 110019*

In Holland: Please write to *Penguin Books Nederland B.V., Postbus 195, NL–1380AD Weesp, Netherlands*

In Germany: Please write to *Penguin Books Ltd, Friedrichstrasse 10–12, D–6000 Frankfurt Main 1, Federal Republic of Germany*

In Spain: Please write to *Longman Penguin España, Calle San Nicolas 15, E–28013 Madrid, Spain*

In France: Please write to *Penguin Books Ltd, 39 Rue de Montmorency, F-75003, Paris, France*

In Japan: Please write to *Longman Penguin Japan Co Ltd, Yamaguchi Building, 2–12–9 Kanda Jimbocho, Chiyoda-Ku, Tokyo 101, Japan*

FOR THE BEST IN PAPERBACKS, LOOK FOR THE

A CHOICE OF PENGUINS

Fantastic Invasion Patrick Marnham

Explored and exploited, Africa has carried a different meaning for each wave of foreign invaders – from ivory traders to aid workers. Now, in the crisis that has followed Independence, which way should Africa turn? 'A courageous and brilliant effort' – Paul Theroux

Jean Rhys: Letters 1931–66
Edited by Francis Wyndham and Diana Melly

'Eloquent and invaluable . . . her life emerges, and with it a portrait of an unexpectedly indomitable figure' – Marina Warner in the *Sunday Times*

Among the Russians Colin Thubron

One man's solitary journey by car across Russia provides an enthralling and revealing account of the habits and idiosyncrasies of a fascinating people. 'He sees things with the freshness of an innocent and the erudition of a scholar' – *Daily Telegraph*

The Amateur Naturalist Gerald Durrell with Lee Durrell

'Delight . . . on every page . . . packed with authoritative writing, learning without pomposity . . . it represents a real bargain' – *The Times Educational Supplement*. 'What treats are in store for the average British household' – *Books and Bookmen*

The Democratic Economy Geoff Hodgson

Today, the political arena is divided as seldom before. In this exciting and original study, Geoff Hodgson carefully examines the claims of the rival doctrines and exposes some crucial flaws.

They Went to Portugal Rose Macaulay

An exotic and entertaining account of travellers to Portugal from the pirate-crusaders, through poets, aesthetes and ambassadors, to the new wave of romantic travellers. A wonderful mixture of literature, history and adventure, by one of our most stylish and seductive writers.

A CHOICE OF PENGUINS

Beyond the Blue Horizon   Alexander Frater

The romance and excitement of the legendary Imperial Airways East-bound Empire service – the world's longest and most adventurous scheduled air route – relived fifty years later in one of the most original travel books of the decade. 'The find of the year' – *Today*

Voyage through the Antarctic   Richard Adams and Ronald Lockley

Here is the true, authentic Antarctic of today, brought vividly to life by Richard Adams, author of *Watership Down*, and Ronald Lockley, the world-famous naturalist. 'A good adventure story, with a lot of information and a deal of enthusiasm for Antarctica and its animals' – *Nature*

Getting to Know the General   Graham Greene

'In August 1981 my bag was packed for my fifth visit to Panama when the news came to me over the telephone of the death of General Omar Torrijos Herrera, my friend and host . . .' 'Vigorous, deeply felt, at times funny, and for Greene surprisingly frank' – *Sunday Times*

The Search for the Virus   Steve Connor and Sharon Kingman

In this gripping book, two leading *New Scientist* journalists tell the remarkable story of how researchers discovered the AIDS virus and examine the links between AIDS and lifestyles. They also look at the progress being made in isolating the virus and finding a cure.

Arabian Sands   Wilfred Thesiger

'In the tradition of Burton, Doughty, Lawrence, Philby and Thomas, it is, very likely, the book about Arabia to end all books about Arabia' – *Daily Telegraph*

When the Wind Blows   Raymond Briggs

'A visual parable against nuclear war: all the more chilling for being in the form of a strip cartoon' – *Sunday Times* 'The most eloquent anti-Bomb statement you are likely to read' – *Daily Mail*

The Diary of Virginia Woolf
Five volumes edited by Quentin Bell and Anne Olivier Bell

'As an account of intellectual and cultural life of our century, Virginia Woolf's diaries are invaluable; as the record of one bruised and unquiet mind, they are unique' – Peter Ackroyd in the *Sunday Times*

Voices of the Old Sea   Norman Lewis

'I will wager that *Voices of the Old Sea* will be a classic in the literature about Spain' – *Mail on Sunday* 'Limpidly and lovingly Norman Lewis has caught the helpless, unwitting, often foolish, but always hopeful village in its dying summers, and saved the tragedy with sublime comedy' – *Observer*

The First World War   A J P Taylor

In this superb illustrated history, A J P Taylor 'manages to say almost everything that is important for an understanding and, indeed, intellectual digestion of that vast event . . . A special text . . . a remarkable collection of photographs' – *Observer*

Ninety-Two Days   Evelyn Waugh

With characteristic honesty Evelyn Waugh here debunks the romantic notions attached to rough travelling; his journey in Guiana and Brazil is difficult, dangerous and extremely uncomfortable, and his account of it is witty and unquestionably compelling.

When the Mind Hears   Harlan Lane
A History of the Deaf

'Reads like a suspense novel . . . what emerges is evidence of a great wrong done to a minority group, the deaf' – *The New York Times Book Review* 'Impassioned, polemical, at times even virulent . . . (he shows) immense scholarship, powers of historical reconstruction, and deep empathy for the world of the deaf' – Oliver Sacks in *The New York Review of Books*

A CHOICE OF PENGUINS

Trail of Havoc   Patrick Marnham

In this brilliant piece of detective work, Patrick Marnham has traced the steps of Lord Lucan from the fateful night of 7th November 1974 when he murdered his children's nanny and attempted to kill his ex-wife. As well as being a fascinating investigation, the book is also a brilliant portrayal of a privileged section of society living under great stress.

Light Years   Gary Kinder

Eduard Meier, an uneducated Swiss farmer, claims since 1975 to have had over 100 UFO sightings and encounters with 'beamships' from the Pleiades. His evidence is such that even the most die-hard sceptics have been unable to explain away the phenomenon.

And the Band Played On   Randy Shilts
Politics, people and the AIDS epidemic

Written after years of extensive research by the only American journalist to cover the epidemic full-time, the book is a masterpiece of reportage and a tragic record of mismanaged institutions and scientific vendettas, of sexual politics and personal suffering.

The Return of a Native Reporter   Robert Chesshyre

Robert Chesshyre returned to Britain from the United States in 1985 where he had spent four years as the *Observer*'s correspondent. This is his devastating account of the country he came home to: intolerant, brutal, grasping and politically and economically divided. It is a nation, he asserts, struggling to find a role.

Women and Love   Shere Hite

In this culmination of *The Hite Report* trilogy, 4,500 women provide an eloquent testimony of the disturbingly unsatisfying nature of their emotional relationships and point to what they see as the causes. *Women and Love* reveals a new cultural perspective in formation: as women change the emotional structure of their lives, they are defining a fundamental debate over the future of our society.